LOVE ATLANTA

The Official Guide to Atlanta and Georgia

UXOR PRESS
541 Tenth St. NW #161
Atlanta, GA 30318
404-989-2595

Uxor Press
All rights reserved including
the right of reproduction
in whole or in part in any form

Published by Uxor Press
Atlanta, Georgia

Library of Congress Cataloging in Publication Data

Zimmerman, Robert Lee
Vanderburg-Tichelaar, Karin
  Love Atlanta

  Includes Index

ISBN 0-932555-01-2

Printed in the United States of America

1 2 3 4 5 6 7 8 9 10

First Edition

Acknowledgments

Very special thanks to the Atlanta Convention and Visitors Bureau: Uxor Press is a proud member; and the Georgia Department of Industry, Trade and Tourism for their tremendous efforts and successes in building and promoting Atlanta and Georgia as a premier visitor destination.

The publication of Love Atlanta was greatly aided by the intellectual and editorial input of Dr. Deborah Zimmerman, the graphic designs and maps provided by the Graphic Zone, 770-495-8616, (Mr. Eric Yaskot, proprietor), the editorial review of The Red Pen, 320-0162, (Mrs. Shelia Benoit, proprietor), the typesetting provided by Dianne's Desktop, 770-879-9490, (Dianne Schread, proprietor) and illustrations by Caricature Entertainment, 770-483-6913, (Susan Moreno, proprietor).

Dedication

Love Atlanta is dedicated to every person, native, newcomer and visitor who loves the City of Atlanta and the whole of Georgia as we do.

Outside of a book, a dawg is a person's best friend. Inside a dawg, it's too dark to read.

-Adapted from Groucho Marx

TABLE OF CONTENTS

Section I: **Introducing Love Atlanta-1**
                     Emergency Numbers-1
                     Useful Numbers-1
                     The Weather-2
                     Milestone Dates-3
                     Favorite Sons and Daughters-4
                     Attractions In Brief-5
                     Metro Atlanta Churches-6
                     What Others Say-8
                     Atlanta Statistics -9
                     State Stuff-9
                     Atlanta's Media-10
                     Additional Reading-12

Section II: **Getting Around and Getting Situated-19**
                     Native Terms-19
                     Mileages-20
                     Interstate Highway System-22
                     Automobile Repairs-23
                     Driving Tips-24
                     Licensing-24
                     Auto Insurance-24
                     Emissions Check and Registration-24
                     MARTA and Hartsfield Airport-24
                     Taxi's, Limo's and Rentals-26
                     Trains and Buses-26
                     Horse and Carriage-26
                     Banking-26
                     Insurance-26
                     Metro Atlanta Counties-26
                     Metro Atlanta Neighborhoods-29
                     Metro Atlanta Parks-32
                     Apartment Renting-33
                     Accommodations-33

Section III: **The 1996 Centennial Summer Olympic Games-37**
                     Olympic Sports and Venues-37
                     Paralympics-38
                     Centennial Olympic Park-38
                     Coca-Cola Olympic City-39
                     Ticketing and Merchandise-39
                     Housing and Transportation-39

Section IV: **Corporate Atlanta-41**
Headquarter Organizations-41
Corporate Profiles-41
Georgia's Top 100 Corporations-44
Employment Opportunities-45

Section V: **Metro Atlanta Cultural Attractions and Organizations-59**
Major Family Attractions-59
Kidstuff-66
Festivals and Events-66
Art Centers and Galleries-80
Libraries and Bookstores-83
Colleges and Universities-87
Private Schools-91
Vocational Schools-92
Summer Camps-93
Consulates-94
Ethnic Cultural Organizations-95
Cinemas and Film Societies-98
Music at the Clubs-98

Section VI: **The Metro Atlanta Health Care System-101**
Ancient and Nouveau Home Remedies-101
Summer Weather Cautions-102
Clinics and Hospitals-103
Plastic Surgery-106
Health Insurance and HMO's-107
Georgia State Motto and Song-109

Section VII: **The Sporting Life-111**
Sports Facilities and Organizations-111
Pro Sports Teams-116
Collegiate Sports-116
Nature and Wildlife Trails-117
Game and Fish Offices-119
State Parks-120
Historic Sites-123

Section VIII: **The Cuisines of Atlanta and Beyond-125**
Southern Food and Hospitality-125
The Atlanta Diet-125
Georgia's Seafood-125
A Wine Sampler-127
Atlanta's Nifty Fifty Restaurants-128
Nifty Eateries Beyond The Metro Atlanta-156
Other Metro Atlanta Restaurants-159

Section IX: **Top Value Golf Courses-167**

Section X: **Shopping Atlanta-**185
                     Ancient Prices-185
                     Shopping Malls-185
                     Special Shopping Areas-186
                     Special Stores-189
                     Antique and Flea Markets-206
                     Farmers Markets-207

Section XI: **Georgia's Green Harvest and Trails-209**
                     Harvest Seasons-209
                     Roadside Markets-209
                     Peach Orchards and Berry Farms-217
                     Gardening Guide-220

Section XII: **Traveling Historic Georgia-225**
                     Georgia's Small Towns-225
                     Visitors and Welcome Centers-226
                     Historic Covered Bridges-229

Section XIII: **Coastal Georgia and the Golden Isles-231**
                     Savannah Festivals-234
                     Golden Isle Festivals-241

Section XIV: **The Northeast Mountains-245**

Section XV: **The Northwest Mountains-265**

Section XVI: **Georgia's Historic Heartland-277**

Section XVII: **The Classic South-293**

Section XVIII: **The Presidential Pathways-301**

Section XIX: **Georgia's Plantation Trace-313**

Section XX: **The Magnolia Midlands-323**

                     Index-327

SECTION I
Introducing Atlanta

The center of Georgia and of the "New South." Emergency Numbers, Useful Numbers, Talk About the Weather, Beat the Heat, Welcome to Atlanta the Beautiful, Milestone Dates, Favorite Sons and Daughters, Metro Atlanta Notables, Attractions in Brief, What Others Say About Atlanta, Metro Atlanta Statistics, State Stuff, Atlanta's Media, Suggested Reading

Introducing Love Atlanta

Uxor Press is pleased to present *Love Atlanta*, a book made possible and thus hereby dedicated to the wonderful people of Georgia.

The book's content has been developed to benefit residents and visitors (whether domestic or international). Certain sections of the book deal with Atlanta proper, while other sections are devoted to the entirety of Georgia from the Northern mountains to the coastal beaches).

You will find a wealth of up-to-date information about businesses (large and small), employment opportunities (under Corporate Atlanta), shops and markets, festivals and attractions, transportation and tours, accommodations and nightlife, neighborhoods and architecture, restaurants and Southern recipes, spiritual, educational, recreational and cultural offerings, medical insurance and services (including home remedies), parks and nature trails, native terms and historical tidbits, folklore and folkways, stuff for kids, sporting facilities and associations.

Our writers and editors have endeavored to present you the very best of metro Atlanta as well as a feeling for the breadth and diversity of the entire state (see Section XII-Traveling Historic Georgia). But please keep in mind that things are ever-changing. Always call ahead to check on the availability of any good or service or the date and time of an event, festival or attraction.

Please write to us. Send us your suggestions. Help us correct our unintended inexactitudes and inadvertencies.

We wish you the very best of times. But, please, remember not to leave home without this book.

Emergency Numbers

Ambulance. 911
Fire. 911
Police 911
24-Hour Pharmacy 876-0381
Child Abuse. 870-6555
Pediatric Referrals 881-1714
Poison Control Center 616-9000
Toy Safety 800-638-2772
Traveler's Aid 527-7400
Visiting Nurse
 Health System. 770-454-0900

Useful Numbers

Airport 530-6600
Auto Repairs 989-2552
Atlanta Central Library 730-1700
Georgia Info 730-4636
Language Assistance 873-6170
MARTA. 848-5000
Time. 455-7141
Touring Info 255-9472
Travel Info. 231-1790
Weather 486-8535

Talk About the Weather

For folks who enjoy the seasons along with summer sun and humidity, Atlanta has near perfect weather. Below, by month, is a compilation of Atlanta's weather listing the average normal temperature for each month, the average high and low temperatures, average rainfall and average humidity.

Mo.	Avg Norm	Avg High	Avg Low	Avg Rain
Jan.	42	51	33	5"
Feb.	45	55	35	4"
Mar.	53	63	42	6"
Apr.	62	73	50	4"
May.	69	80	59	4"
Jun.	76	86	66	3"
Jul.	79	88	68	5"
Aug.	78	88	68	3"
Sep.	73	83	64	3"
Oct.	62	73	52	3"
Nov.	52	63	42	3"
Dec.	45	54	35	4"

Historical High: 105
July, 1980
Historical Low: 8
January 1985

A Heat-Beating Primer: How to Stay Healthy in July and August

- Slow down; strenuous activities should be rescheduled to a cooler time of the day.

- Dress cool; with light-weight, light-colored clothing. It reflects heat and sunlight.

- Drink plenty of water; your body needs water to keep cool.

- Spend more time in air-conditioned places-each day for a certain amount of time.

- Don't forget your pet; make sure pets have plenty of water and shady shelter. Don't walk your pet in the heat of the day. Never leave your pet in a closed car.

- Cool snacks for kids; frozen low-fat yogurt, fresh fruits and juices, frozen orange wedge or banana slices, low-fat milkshake, peanut-butter stuffed celery sticks.

- Air pollution; can cause scratchy, dry eyes and breathing difficulties. A 24-hour air quality number is 362-4909.

Welcome to Atlanta the Beautiful

Vigorously establishing herself as America's finest city, Atlanta was founded as Terminus in 1843 and renamed Marthasville in 1845. She became Atlanta (the feminine version of Atlantic) in 1864. After Sherman's devastation, and the end of the Civil War, Atlanta sought to rebuild. Like a phoenix, she rose from the ashes to become the South's gateway city.

Over the years Atlanta has steadily matured into a mecca for people of all nationalities, races, religions and cultures. Then, like a bolt from the blue, came 1990, truly a banner year. Atlantans rejoiced upon learning that their city was twice honored, selected as host city for both the 1994 Super Bowl and the 1996 Summer Olympic Games.

Atlanta from on high is a spectacular ocean of greenery, seemingly guarded by an occasional skyscraper peeping through the tree line. Yet, as beautiful as Atlanta is when viewed from above, it is at ground level where you will encounter the diverse richness of her wondrous cultures and communities.

Your choices are many, but wherever your adventures lead you, you will find parts of an ancient, yet evolving, tapestry of friendly neighborhoods, markets, parks, restaurants, gardens, boutiques and, of course, Georgia's famous Southern hospitality. You will also find Coca-Cola: Atlanta is Coca-Cola country. The two co-exist in perfect harmony. Headquartered here since its founding by Asa Candler in 1886.

Atlanta is a big city with enormous energy and lots happening, but it is also home to many quiet places. There's great shopping, mouth-watering cuisine and an abundance of attractions, festivals and nearly every recreational and professional sporting activity you can think of. Employment, cultural and educational opportunities are outstanding and, if you are so inclined, the nightlife is endless.

Beauty, diversity and friendliness are Atlanta trademarks, making Atlanta America's leading place to live and work.

Only the most profoundly diverse of cultures could have produced within but a few generations such leaders and visionaries as Dr. Martin Luther King, Jr. (Nobel Peace Prize 1964), Jimmy Carter (the 39th President of the United States) and Newt Gingrich, (presently Speaker of the U.S. House of Representatives).

Metro Atlanta is approximately 3,200,000 people with a median age of 31.8 years occupying 6,150 sq. miles, 20 counties, 111 incorporated cities and towns. Average household after-tax income is $43,000 with more than 1/4 of the people over 25 years of age having completed four or more years of college.

Please enjoy and cherish Atlanta as we do while strolling gently on her fine red soil.

Milestone Dates in the History of Atlanta

1782 Along the banks of the Chattahoochee River, Spanish explorers discover the Cherokee village, Standing Peachtree.

1812/13 Standing Peachtree becomes Fort Peachtree which is connected to Fort Daniel in Gwinnett County via Peachtree Road.

1820s The Cherokee and Creek Indian nations grant millions of acres to settlers as a means to peace.

1833 Hardy Ivy, Atlanta's first settler, builds a log cabin on what is now the intersection of Courtland and Ellis.

1837 Atlanta, then Terminus, is selected by the Western and Atlantic Railroad as the end of the line for the railroad connecting Georgia with the Tennessee River. (See the historic marker "Zero Milepost" in Underground Atlanta.)

1842 Dr. Crawford Long introduces the use of ether as an anesthetic.

1843 Terminus is renamed Marthasville and then Atlanta. What was originally "the end of the line" will become, in later years, the beginning of the "New South."

1865 The Civil War ends; love and time will heal the wounds.

1868 Atlanta becomes Georgia's capital and the Atlanta Constitution publishes its first paper.

1886 Henry Grady, editor of the *Atlanta Constitution*, enunciates a "New South" doctrine and John Pemberton's Coca-Cola, then a headache remedy, is first sold at Jacob's Pharmacy.

1892 Asa Candler founds the Coca-Cola Company.

1916 Coca-Cola introduces its now world-famous 6 1/2 oz. contour bottle.

1922 Georgia's first commercial radio station is introduced as "Voice of the South."

1928 Robert Woodruff is named President of The Coca-Cola Company.

1929 Dr. Martin Luther King, Jr. is born.

1929 The Fabulous Fox Theater opens.

1930 Bobby Jones wins golf's grand slam.

1931 The Atlanta Gas Light Company brings natural gas to Atlanta.

1936 Martha Mitchell's "Gone With the Wind" is published.

1936 Ty Cobb, the "Georgia Peach," is elected to baseball's Hall of Fame.

1939 "Gone With the Wind" premiers at the Loew's Grand Theater, where Georgia-Pacific Center now stands.

1939 James M. Cox, former Governor of Ohio, buys The Atlanta Journal and WSB.

1941 Delta Air Lines moves its headquarters to Atlanta.

1948 WSB-TV becomes Atlanta's first television station and Rich's Department Store hoists its first Christmas tree.

1955 Retail sales in Atlanta top $1 billion.

1959 Lenox Square Shopping Center opens as an open-air mall.

1961 Ivan Allen, Jr. defeats segregationist Lester Maddox and Atlanta's public schools begin to desegregate.

1964 The world's love and admiration are officially bestowed on Dr. Martin Luther King, Jr. in the form of the Nobel Peace Prize.

1965 The world loves them, but they are Atlanta Braves now.

1968 The Woodruff Arts Center and the Governor's Mansion are dedicated.

1970 A celebration of freedom and democracy, the 6.2 mile annual Peachtree Road Race is inaugurated on July 4th and will grow over the years to an amazing 50,000 runners and 250,000 spectators.

1971 The municipal airport is named William B. Hartsfield International in honor of the late visionary mayor.

1971 Willie B., the world's most loved gorilla, takes up residence at Zoo Atlanta.

1973 Maynard Jackson is elected Atlanta's first black mayor.

1974 Indefatigable Atlanta Brave Hank Aaron breaks Babe Ruth's home run record.

1976 Georgia's Governor Jimmy Carter is elected the 39th President of the United States.

1979 MARTA is inaugurated, with trains running from Avondale to Georgia State.

1981 Andrew Young is elected Mayor of Atlanta.

1983 The new High Museum of Art building is dedicated and one year later wins the coveted International Pritzker Architecture Prize.

1984 BellSouth is spun off from AT&T.

1988 Atlanta hosts the Democratic National Convention.

1990 Atlanta hosts the Super Bowl.

1996 Atlanta hosts the Summer Olympic Games.

Georgia's Favorite Sons and Daughters

Dr. Martin Luther King, Jr., minister, civil rights leader, Nobel peace Prize recipient, honored with a national holiday in his name, admired throughout the world as a great visionary leader.

Coretta Scott King, who rose from the deepest of tragedies to continue the work of her beloved husband.

Jimmy and Rosalynn Carter, America's first family, Governor of Georgia, then 39th President of the United States.

Robert W. Woodruff, the man who made Coca-Cola legendary and then gave over $400 million to help build Emory University, the Woodruff Arts Center and the High Museum.

Billy Payne, the man who brought the 1996 Summer Olympic Games to Atlanta.

Henry Woodlin Grady, the managing editor of the *Atlanta Constitution* who coined the term "The New South" and worked to see it implemented.

Joel Chandler Harris, founder of the *Atlanta Constitution*, consistently one of America's finest newspapers.

Margaret Mitchell, creator of *Gone With the Wind*.

Robert Edward "Ted" Turner, founder of CNN, Turner Broadcasting and TNT. He is owner of the Atlanta Hawks and Braves.

Charlene Hunter-Gault, world-famous broadcaster and humanitarian.

Cynthia Tucker, courageous editorial writer for the *Atlanta Constitution*.

Alonzo Herndon, a former slave from Social Circle who founded the Atlanta Life Insurance Company and became Atlanta's first black millionaire and a leading philanthropist.

Ray Charles, the man who merged blues, gospel and country and thus invented soul.

Otis Redding, soul singer from Macon who died in a plane crash at age 26.

Henry Louis "Hank" Aaron, a sports hero par excellance, the former Atlanta Brave Hall-of-Famer who shattered Babe Ruth's career home run record, raising it from 714 to 755. Currently serves on the National Board of the NAACP, the Atlanta Braves and Turner Broadcasting.

Jackie Robinson, a great hitter and third baseman for the Brooklyn Dodgers, he will always be remembered for enduring numerous threats, attacks and humiliations as he courageously became the first black to play major league baseball.

Tyrus Raymond "Ty" Cobb, the "Georgia Peach" was without a doubt baseball's greatest hitter and one of the most colorful people to ever play the game.

Mickey Mantle, honorary citizen of Georgia and the most exciting baseball player to ever grace the ballfield, and, yes Mickey, "It turned out all right."

Robert Tyre "Bobby" Jones, the world's greatest golfer,the only winner of golf's "Grand Slam" and the founder of the Masters Golf Tournament.

John Heisman, Georgia Tech football coach for whom the Heisman Trophy is named.

Jim Brown, the greatest running back in NFL history; he was born on St. Simons Island.

Evander Holyfield, twice, boxing's heavyweight champion of the world.

Metro Atlanta Notables

- The tallest building in the Southeast, the NationsBank Plaza.

- The second largest convention center in the world, the Georgia World Congress Center.

- Over 100 golf courses and 140 retail shopping centers.

- Tallest hotel in the Western Hemisphere. The Westin Peachtree Plaza.

- The largest hotel and shopping center in the Southeast, the Atlanta Marriott Marquis and Lenox Sq. respectively.

- Largest toll-free dialing area in the world.

- Over one zillion streets with Peachtree somewhere in the name.

- Largest 10K road race, the Annual Peachtree Road Race with over 50,000 participants.

- The world's tallest bas-relief sculpture at Stone Mountain Park.

- The largest suburban office center in the world, Perimeter Center.

Attractions In Brief

(See also sections on Attractions and Olympics for detailed information)

1996 Summer Olympics 224-1996
America Whitewater
    Adventures 770-424-9283
Art and Archaeology Museum . . . 727-4282
Atlanta Ballet. 873-5811
Atlanta Botanical Gardens 876-5859
Atlanta Cyclorama. 658-7625
Atlanta History Ctr. and Museum . 814-4000
Atlanta Opera 355-3311
Atlanta Symphony Orchestra 733-4848

Big Shanty Museum 770-427-2117
Bulloch Hall 770-992-1731
Bus Tours 767-0594
Carter Center and Library 331-3932
Centennial Olympic Park 224-1996
Center for Puppetry Arts 873-3391
Chastain Summer Concerts 231-5888
Chattahoochee Nature
   Center 770-992-2055
CNN Studio Tour 827-2300
Fernbank Natural History Museum,
Forest, Science Center and
Planetarium. 378-4311
Fox Theater. 881-2000
Georgia Dome 223-TOUR
Georgia State Capitol 656-2844
Governor's Mansion. 261-1776
Guided Walking Tours 876-2040
High Museum of Art 577-6940
Johnny Mercer Museum. 651-2477
Kennesaw Mtn. Battlefield. . . 770-427-4686
Lake Lanier Islands 770-932-7200
M. L. King, Jr. Historic Sites 524-1956
Rhodes Hall 881-9980
Road to Tara Museum 897-1939
SciTrek Science Museum. 522-5500
Six Flags Over Georgia 770-948-9290
Stone Mtn. Park 770-498-5600
Telephone Museum 223-3661
Welcome South Visitors Center. . 224-2000
Woodruff Arts Center. 733-4400
World of Coca-Cola 656-5151
ZooAtlanta 624-5678

Metro Atlanta Churches

— Baptist —

First Baptist Atlanta
Midtown, between North Ave., and 10th St.
754 Peachtree St.
347-8300

Briarcliff Baptist
NE AtlantaOff I-85, Clairmont Rd. exit
3039 Briarcliff Rd.
633-6103

Wieuca Road Baptist
Buckhead one mile north
of Lenox Square Mall
3626 Peachtree Rd.
814-4460

First Baptist Church
East Point
2813 East Point St.
766-3601

— Catholic —

Sacred Heart
Downtown
353 Peachtree St.
522-6800

Cathedral of Christ the King
Buckhead, corner of east Wesley & Peachtree
2699 Peachtree Rd.
233-2145

Immaculate Conception
Downtown
48 Martin Luther King Jr. Dr.
521-1866

St. Jude's
North Atlanta
two blocks east of Roswell Rd. at Spalding Dr.
7171 Glenridge Dr.
394-3896

St. John the Evangelist
Hapeville
3370 Sunset St.
768-5647

— Christian —

First Christian of College Park
294 Jenkins Rd.
Tyrone
770-969-7346

North Druid Hills Christian
Northeast Atlanta,
exit off I-85 Expressway Access Rd.
2490 north Druid Hills Rd.
325-3298

Peachtree Christian
Midtown,
corner of Spring & Peachtree Sts.
1580 Peachtree St.
876-5535

Christian Science
First Church of Christ Scientist Atlanta
1235 Peachtree St.
892-7838

— *Episcopal* —

Cathedral of Saint Phillip
Buckhead
2744 Peachtree Rd.
365-1000

Saint Anne's
Northwest Atlanta
3098 Northside Pkwy.
237-5589

All Saints
Midtown
634 West Peachtree St.
881-0835

St. Mary's
East Point,
one block off Sylvan Rd.
845 Glenway Dr.
768-9197

— *Jewish* —

Congregation Beth Jacob
1855 LaVista Rd.
633-0551

The Temple
Midtown
1589 Peachtree St.
873-1731

— *Lutheran* —

Lutheran Church of the Redeemer
Peachtree & 4th
731 Peachtree St.
874-8664

Peachtree Road Lutheran
Buckhead
3686 Peachtree Rd.
233-7031

Saint Matthew
I-85 N., to North Druid Hills Rd. exit.
566 Briarcliff Rd.
634-7505

— *Methodist* —

First Methodist
Downtown
360 Peachtree St.
524-6614

Peachtree Road Methodist
Buckhead
3180 Peachtree Rd.
266-2373

Sandy Springs Methodist
86 Mount Vernon Hwy.
255-1181

Forest Park Methodist
4473 College St.
366-2121

— *Greek Orthodox* —

Greek Orthodox
I-85 N. to Clairmont Rd.
2500 Clairmont Rd.
633-5870

— *Presbyterian* —

First Presbyterian
Midtown
16th & Peachtree St.
892-8461

Clairmont Presbyterian
I-85 N. to Clairmont Rd. exit.
1994 Clairmont Rd.
634-3355

East Point
2810 Church St.
767-4242

What Others Say About Atlanta

"America's Healthiest Metropolitan Area"

Atlanta is the healthiest metropolitan area in the country and Atlantans have the lowest mortality rate.

— American Demographics and the National Center for Health Statistics

"Atlanta is Centrally Located"

Atlanta lies within two truckload delivery days of 77% of U.S. metro buying power, 79% of America's consumer markets and 82% of the nation's industrial markets.

— Oglethorpe Power Corp.

"Top Real Estate Markets in U.S."

Atlanta
Washington-Baltimore
Dallas-Ft. Worth

— Ernst and Young (1993)

"Average Monthly Apartment Rental Rate"

Atlanta	**$550**
New York	$900
Tokyo	$6100
Hong Kong	$6500

— PHH Home Equity

"Top U.S. Cities for International Companies"

Atlanta
Baltimore
Columbus

— World Trade Magazine (1992)

"Best Environment for Competing in a Global Economy"

Atlanta
Seattle
New York

— Fortune Magazine (1992)

"Best Cities to Locate a New Facility"

Atlanta
New York
Los Angeles

— Lou Harris (1993)

"Best Places to Start and Grow a Company"

Charlotte
Atlanta
Indianapolis

— Entrepreneurial Hot Spots (1993)

"Growth Cities (U.S.) of the Future"

Atlanta
Houston

— Corporate Location Magazine (1993)

Annual Cost of Office Space-sq.ft.

Atlanta	**$ 23**
Bangkok	$ 23
Frankfort	$ 58
Hong Kong	$140
Houston	$ 16
London	$115
New York	$ 45
Paris	$ 75
Shanghai	$ 99
Singapore	$ 51
Sydney	$ 33
Tokyo	$134

Average Cost of Dining Out

Atlanta	$18
Milwaukee	$25
New York	$30
San Fran.	$27
Wash. D.C.	$26

— Atlanta Convention and Visitors Bureau

Metro Atlanta Statistics

Population: Approximately 3,500,000
Counties: 20
Highways: 110,000 roadway miles.
Sq. Miles: 6,150 and growing
Elevation: Varies
Pro Teams: 8
Peachtree Sts: 68 and growing
Hotel Rooms: About 60,000
Malls: 50 million sq. ft.
Restaurants: 8000+
Average Family Income: About average.
Unemployment Rate: Very low.
Crime Rate: Substantial downward trend.
Housing Starts: Too many to count.

State Stuff

State Motto: Wisdom, Justice, Moderation
State Song: Georgia on my Mind
State Capital: Atlanta
Statehood: January 2, 1788
Governor: Zell Miller
State Bird: Brown Thrasher
State Butterfly: Tiger Swallowtail
State Fish: Largemouth Bass
State Flower: Cherokee Rose
State Fossil: Shark Tooth
State Game Bird: Bobwhite Quail
State Gem: Quartz
State Insect: Honeybee
State Mammal: Right Whale
State Mineral: Staurolite
State Reptile: Gopher Tortoise
State Seashell: Knobbed Whelk
State Tree: Live Oak
State Wildflower: Azalea

Fact:

- Nobel Peace Prize Laureate, Dr. Martin Luther King, Jr. was born in Atlanta on January 15, 1929, now a national holiday in most states.

The Atlanta Convention and Visitors Bureau

President: Spurgeon Richardson
Since 1913 the Atlanta Convention and Visitors Bureau (ACVB) has, with enormous success, marketed Atlanta and Georgia as ideal convention and meeting centers. ACVB's intense skills and efforts have produced substantial benefits for our local economies by vastly boosting visitor revenue and local employment. Thanks to ACVB Atlanta is consistently one of the top five convention destinations in the U.S., a fact that helped produce the physical infrastructure necessary to host the Super Bowl and the 1996 Centennial Summer Olympic Games.

In the summer of 1995, ACVB and Georgia Department of Industry, Trade and Tourism created the nation's first regional visitors center, Welcome South Visitors Center at the Atlanta Market Center complex in the heart of downtown. The center presents state-of-the-art displays for six Southeastern states (Alabama, Kentucky, Louisiana, North and South Carolina and Tennessee), a feature film entitled *"One Day in Search of the South,"* and a national parks display. The center's visual displays combined with the extensive visitor information section and the services of the AAA Travel Agency, NationsBank ATM, and The Thomas Cook Currency Exchange provide invaluable assistance to travelers and business throughout the Southeast.

Atlanta's Media

Daily Newspapers

Atlanta Journal/Constitution. Downtown. 72 Marietta St. 526-5151. Founded in 1868 by Col. Cary Styles, the Atlanta Constitution and Journal has evolved into one of the nation's leading dailies with much of the credit acccruing to Henry W. Grady who joined the Constitution in 1875 and within 4 years rose to become its managing editor. Grady's courageous policies included promoting "the New South," a politically and economically progressive philosophy that encouraged looking forward rather than living in the past.

In 1950 the Constitution merged with the Journal. The Constitution publishing mornings and the Journal, evenings. Separate editorial policies continue. The papers combine for the Saturday, Sunday and holiday editions.

Marietta Daily Journal. 580 Fairgrounds St. Marietta 770-428-9411. Founded in 1867 the paper covers Cobb County, regional and national news.

Fulton County Daily Report. 190 Pryor St. 521-1227. Founded in 1890, this paper is primarily writ for the legal community and carries the court calendar.

Weekly-Monthly Newspapers

Atlanta Business Chronicle. 1801 Peachtree St. 249-1000. Published each Friday, this paper covers Atlanta's business community.

Atlanta Daily World. 145 Auburn Ave. Atlanta 659-1110. Founded in 1928 the Daily World is Atlanta's oldest African-American publication.

Atlanta Tribune. Roswell. 875 Old Roswell Rd. 587-0501. Founded in 1987, this bi-weekly newsmagazine covers seven metro Atlanta counties, with focus on the black

business community and reports on cultural and entertainment events. Subscriptions are available, but the paper is widely distributed free of charge at bookstores and many retail establishments.

Creative Loafing. 750 Willoughby Way. 688-5623. An alternative weekly that contains restaurant criticism, theater and movie reviews, music/club scene reports and a calendar of interesting events.

Two additional regional editions are published. *Topside Loaf*, reports on the towns just north of Atlanta:Roswell, Alpharetta, Marietta and Dunwoody, while *Gwinnett Loaf*, covers Gwinnett County. 770-368-1880.

Georgia Byways is a quarterly magazine which features attractions and events throughout Georgia that are off the beaten path. The publication is available in bookstores.

Hudspeth Report. 5180 Roswell Rd. 255-3220. A monthly restaurant guide.

Neighbor Newspapers, Inc. 580 Fairground St. S.E. Marietta. 770-428-9411. The company publishes 25 neighborhood newspapers.

Ethnic Newspapers

World Journal. A daily which covers local and national news in Chinese. 5151 Buford Hwy., Doraville. 770-451-4509.

El Nuevo Dia. A biweekly, bilingual Hispanic paper. 80% of the editorial is in Spanish, with twin front pages in Spanish and English. El Nuevo Dia's coverage of local and national news represents all 26 countries that comprise Latin America. 3745 Buford Hwy. Ste.A-4. 320-7766.

Mundo Hispanico. A monthly publication covering local Hispanic news. 881-0441.

Atlanta Jewish Times. Established in 1925. It covers local, national and international news of interest to the Jewish community. 352-2400.

Jewish Civic Press. A monthly publication. 231-2194.

Southeast Journal. Established in 1989, the paper published in both Korean and English. 770-454-9655.

Joong Ang Daily News. Covers local news for the Korean community. 770-458-7001.

Korean Journal. Local and southeastern news for the Korean community. 770-451-6946.

Korea Times. A weekly newspaper with local and Korean community news. 770-458-5060,

Sae Kye Times. Daily national news. 770-478-5497.

Magazines and Guidebooks

Atlanta Homes and Lifestyles. Decorating and style. 252-6670

Atlanta Magazine. A monthly lifestyle magazine with articles dealing with Southern history, a calendar of cultural and restaurant guide. 872-3100.

Atlanta Now. Published by the Atlanta Convention and Visitors Bureau. The bimonthly guide presents hotels, restaurants, nightlife, festivals and theatre. 249-1750.

Atlanta Parent is filled with items of interest to families. The free publication is available at libraries, schools and supermarkets. 770-454-7599.

Atlanta Apartment Book. An apartment rental guide. 237-7213.

Atlanta Happenings. An entertainment guide. 303-8608.

Atlanta Singles. Singles activities. 256-9411.

Atlanta Small Business Monthly. Info for entrepreneurs. 770-446-5434.

Communities Magazine. Housing for sale. 770-438-3030.

Etcetera Magazine. A free alternative lifestyle weekly. 525-3821.

For Rent Magazine. A guide to rental property. 770-988-0870.

Georgia Trend Magazine. Statewide business and politics. 770-931-9410.

Guide to Georgia. A monthly calendar of attractions, events and day trips. 892-0961.

KEY Atlanta. A weekly visitors guide to events and happenings of all kinds. 233-2299.

KNOW Atlanta. A quarterly magazine presentation of community information. 770-512-0016.

Metro Atlanta Apartment Guide. Apartment life. 770-457-1301.

North Georgia Journal. A quarterly magazine featuring articles the history, happenings and attractions in North Georgia. It is available in bookstores.

Our Kids. Helpful info for parents. 770-438-1400.

Peachtree Magazine. Southern lifestyles with the focus on Atlanta's leaders and celebraties. 770-956-1207.

Tafrija Magazine. An entertainment guide. 817-3570.

WHERE Atlanta. A monthly visitors guide. 843-9800.

Winsome Way. Published in an entertainment format to help children of color conquer real-life problems and challenges such as gang violence and drugs. 377-4541.

Young Horizons Indigo. An information and resource guide for the parents and teachers of black children. 241-5003.

News, TV, and Radio

News

ABC	770-431-7777
AP	522-8971
Cable News Network	827-1500
CBS	261-2227
Cox Enterprises	843-5000

The Georgia Network. 231-1888
GPTV-Georgia Public TV 756-2400
CNN Headline News 827-2600
Morris News Service 589-8424
NBC 881-0154
PR Newswire 523-2323
Reuters News Service. 870-7340
Turner Broadcasting. 827-1700
USA Today. 800-872-0001
The Wall Street Journal 865-0170

Television Stations

WSB/2-ABC. 897-7000
WAGA/5-FOX. 875-5555
WXIA/11-NBC 892-1611
WTLK/14 770-528-1400
WTBS/17 827-1717
WPBA/30 827-8900
WATL/36 881-3600
WGNX/46-CBS 325-4646
WVEU/69. 325-6929

Radio Stations

WABE 90.1 FM 827-8900
WAEC 860 AM 355-8600
WAFS 920 AM 888-0920
WALR 104.7 FM 688-0068
WAOK 1380 AM. 898-8900
WCLK 91.9 FM 880-8273
WCNN 680 AM 688-0068
WFOX 97.1 FM 770-953-9369
WGKA 1190 AM. 231-1190
WGST 640 AM 233-0640
WGUN 1010 AM. 770-491-1010
WKHX 590 AM & 101.5 FM 770-955-0101
WKLS 96.1 FM 325-0960
WLKQ 102.3 FM 770-932-1102
WNIV 970 AM. 365-0970
WNNX 99.7 FM. 266-0997
WPCH 95 FM. 261-9500
WPLO 610 AM 770-962-4848
WQXI 790 AM. 261-2970
WRAS 88.5 FM 651-2240
WREK 91.1 FM 894-2468
WRFG 89.3 FM 523-3471
WSB 750 AM & 98.5 FM 897-7500
WSTR 94.1 FM 261-2970

Additional Reading

Around Atlanta With Children. By Denise Black and Janet Schwartz is a very readable and very valuable guide to children's and family activities.

The Atlanta Journal and Constitution's Saturday Leisure Guide. Provides a comprehensive summary of weekly events. The daily and Sunday papers also provide a wealth of timely information about restaurant openings, festivals, travel in and about Georgia and entertainment.

Atlanta Walks. A very readable book by Ren and Helen Davis, describes about thirty different walks throughout the metro Atlanta area.

Georgia B & Bs. Produced in cooperation with the Georgia Bed and Breakfast Council, Carol and Dan Thalimer have surveyed over 150 B and B's throughout Georgia.

The Bed & Breakfast Directory. Published by The Georgia Department of Industry, Trade and Tourism is a free annual guide to bed and breakfast inns in Georgia. Call 651-9461 to obtain the directory.

Country Towns of Georgia. By William Schemmel is a book that takes you on a visit to 16 of his favorite Georgia country towns.

AIA Guide to the Architecture of Atlanta. Produced by the American Institute of Architects, with text by Isabelle Gournay and photos by Paul Beswick it surveys 400 buildings within the Atlanta metro area-from the old landmark buildings to the transformative skyscrapers.

How to Love Yankees with a Clear Conscience. Bo Whaley is "convinced that Yankees ain't all bad, just a little peculiar perhaps. And they talk funny." Tons of Southern humor from the, former FBI man, who is now an award-winning columnist at the Georgia Courier Herald.

The Complete Guide to Atlanta's Ethnic Communities. Janet Schwartz and Denise Black have scoured the town to produce this comprehensive guide to Atlanta's ethnic communities.

Contemporary Georgia. A scholarly book produced by the Carl Vinson Institute of Government, the University of Georgia. Edited by Lawrence Hepburn, the complexity that comprises Georgia's character emerges as you learn how contemporary Georgia has emerged from its early history, complete with triumphs, harshness, strengths and failings.

Fun Fact

- Jimmy and Rosalynn Carter were married on July 7, 1946.

Fun Fact

- Rumor has it that Georgia is considering the adoption of an Alabama law making it illegal to dig for fishworms under major highways.

LOVE ATLANTA

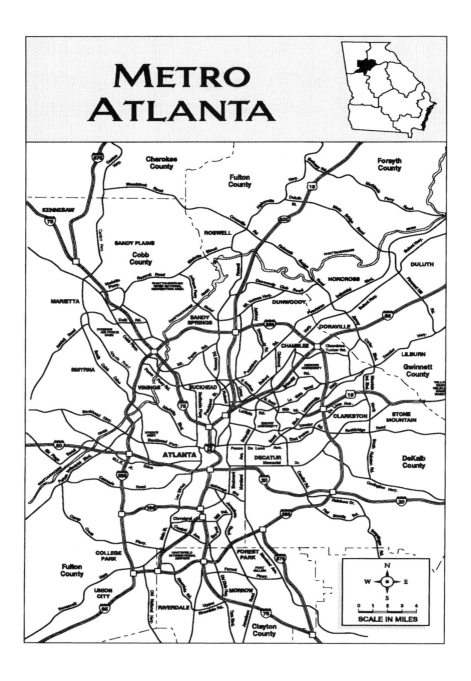

METRO ATLANTA

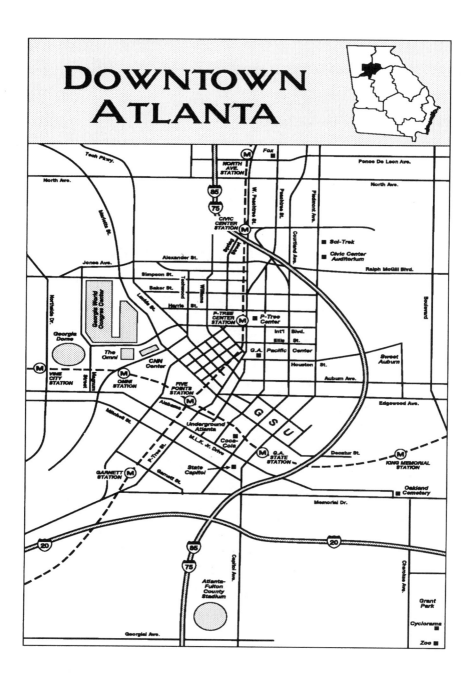

LOVE ATLANTA

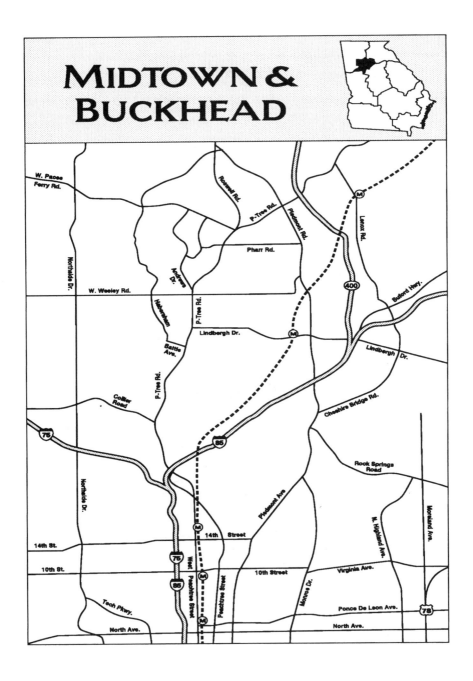

SECTION II
Getting Around and Getting Situated

Native Terms, Mileages, the Interstate Highway System, Transportation, Auto Repairs and Insurance, Driving Tips, Metro Atlanta Counties and Neighborhoods, Apartment Locator Services, Banking, Insurance and Accommodations

Native Terms

Commentary

Get one or two up on the native Atlantans, many of whom will not have heard of all of the terms listed below.

ACOG
Atlanta Committee for the Olympic Games.

Awften
Frequently.

Batries
The things you put in flashlights.

Barbecue
A cookout or hole-in-the-wall featuring ribs and sliced or chopped pork sandwiches drenched in a yummy tomato-based sauce.

Brookwood Station
Amtrak's downtown terminal.

Brunswick Stew
Another barbecue favorite, usually thick, hot and spicy with pork, chicken, beef and some local vegetables.

Buckhead
Just a smidge north of downtown and midtown, this multi-dimensional community features zillions of shops, restaurants and night spots.

Bulldogs or the Dawgs
The University of Georgia's football team.

Dinner
The Northern equivalent of lunch.

Downtown
Denoted by that set of skyscrapers that does not denote midtown.

The Downtown Connector
From the north and the south I-75 and I-85 merge as they approach downtown. But please remember, if you don't get lost at least a few times each day, you're probably not in Atlanta.

Drouthy
Very, very thirsty.

Five Points
Simply the center of downtown, where Peachtree, Decatur, and Marietta Streets meet up with Edgewood Avenue.

Fur Piece
More than a mile in distance.

Git
Acquire.

Goobers
Peanuts and/or nerds.

Good Ol' Boy
Any Southern man who evidences a genial personality and strong appetites for drinkin', huntin' and fishin'.

Good Ol' Gal
Any woman who is of sound mind and body who can put up with a good ol' boy.

The Highlands
An eclectic neighborhood community with a smattering of international restaurants, taverns and shops.

Hole-In-the-Wall
Tiny places with sawdust floors and gravel out front serving barbecue, cajun and creole.

Hooch
Whiskey, or a small cabin.

Lectricity
Stuff that runs through and powers your PC.

Likker
Homemade or store bought.

Little Five Points
An artsy neighborhood, 2.5 miles east of downtown, a 1990's version of Haight-Ashbury.

Low-Country Cuisine
Coastal seafood and veggies such as pan-fried soft shelled crab and shrimp, okra and she-crab soups.

MARTA
Metro Atlanta's mass transportation system, a combination of rail and bus, clean, safe and reliable. The $1.50 fare is well worth it.

Midtown
Denoted by that set of skyscrapers that does not denote downtown.

Nekked Dog Running
Plain hot dog.

Pot Likker
The liquid left after cooking turnip greens.

The Perimeter
63 miles of I-285 that encircles metro Atlanta.

PO-leece
Men of authority who wear blue suits and carry guns and badges.

Shoot the Hootch
Tubing and rafting on the Chatta- hoochee River.

Spaghetti Junction
That portion of I-85 that converges on I-285 N. (an amazing network of con- crete highway, access routes and bridges).

Sweet Tea
Table wine of the south.

Syllabub
A frothy topped holiday dessert treat.

Tacky
A Southern women's term for all inap- propriate clothing.

Tags
License plates.

Take two and butter them while they're hot.
Help yourself to the biscuits and hot breads.

Tawkin' Funny
The pronunciation of all peoples not born and raised in the South.

Tech
Georgia Tech University.

The Varsity
Perhaps the world's largest drive-in restaurant.

Willies
The shakes.

Wine of the South
Tea, almost always served sweet.

Y'all
Pronounced as one word.

Yankee
Anyone who tawks funny.

Mileages
from Downtown Atlanta

(Approximate)

Acworth	30
Adairsville	55
Airport, Hartsfield Int	10
Albany	180
Americus	135
Amicalola Falls St. Pk	100
Alpharetta	20
American Adventures	20
Americus	160
Amicola Falls	85
Andersonville	150
Anna Ruby Falls	85
Ansley Park	1
Athens	65
Auburn	65
Augusta	155
Austell	30
Bainbridge	230
Baldwin	80
Ball Ground	40
Barnesville	55
Barrow County	65
Bartow County	55
Berry College	65
Blairsville	105
Bowden	55
Braselton	40
Brasstown Bald	106
Brookhaven	10
Brunswick	275
Buena Vista	137
Buckhead	5
Buckhead Beach Club	35
Byron	65
Cairo	270
Calhoun	75

Callaway Gardens.	75	Grantville.	40
Canton.	40	Greensboro	60
Carl	65	Grovetown	150
Carroll County	55	Griffin	45
Carrollton	55	Gwinnett County	25
Cartersville	55	Hapeville	10
Cave Spring	80	Haranson	35
Chamblee	25	Hard Labor Creek St. Pk	40
Chastain Park	10	Hart St. Pk	100
Chatsworth	90	Hartwell	100
Cherokee County	40	Helen	105
Clarkesville.	10	Hiawassee	125
Clayton County	15	Holly Springs.	40
Cleveland	100	Jackson	45
Cloudland Canyon St. Pk	110	Jeckyl Island	278
Cobb County	25	Jesup	245
College Park	15	Jonesboro.	20
Columbus	90	Juliette	45
Commerce	60	Kennesaw Mountain	30
Conyers.	25	Kingsland.	270
Cordele	145	Lake Allatoona	30
Corinth	35	Lake Hartwell	100
Covington.	35	Lake Lanier Islands	45
Coweta County.	35	Lake Oconee	60
Cumberland Island	278	Lake City	30
Dahlonega.	75	LaGrange	70
Dalton	90	Lavonia	100
Darien	320	Lawrenceville	35
Dawsonville	100	Lithia Springs	25
Decatur	10	Little St. Simons Island	285
DeKalb County.	10	Lovejoy	30
Dillard.	125	Lumpkin	140
Doraville.	25	Mableton	10
Druid Hills	4	Macon	85
Dublin.	135	Madison.	65
Duluth.	20	Marietta	25
Dunwoody	15	McDonough.	25
East Point	10	Midtown	1
Eatonton	90	Milledgeville	105
Elberton	100	Moreland	35
Ellijay	90	Morrow	30
Etowah Indian Mounds	48	Moultrie.	200
Fairburn	20	Mount Berry	70
Fitzgerald	17	Mount Zion	55
Forest Park	20	Nelson	40
Forsyth	50	Newnan	35
Fort Valley	65	Norcross.	20
Gainesville	55	North Druid Hills	10
Golden Isles	278	Oglethorpe.	115

Okefenokee. 240
Old Clinton 95
Palmetto 35
Peachtree City. 30
Perry 105
Piedmont Park 2
Pine Mountain 85
Plains 170
Powder Springs 30
Providence Canyon St. Pk 153
Red Top Mountain St. Pk. 30
Riverdale. 35
Rome. 70
Roopville 55
Roswell. 20
Russell 65
Rutledge 60
Sandy Springs. 15
Sapelo Island 280
Sargent 35
Sautee 105
Savannah 255
Senoia. 35
Six Flags Over Georgia 9
Smyrna 25
St. Simons. 278
St. Mary's 278
Social Circle 35
Statesboro 210
Statham. 65
Stone Mountain Park 16
Summerville 81
Suwanee Canal 240
Tallapoosa. 60
Temple 55
Thomaston 70
Thomasville 230
Tifton 190
Toccoa Falls 100
Turin. 35
Tybee Island 268
Unicoi St. Pk. 85
Valdosta 235
Vidalia 194
Villa Rica 55
Vinings 15
Waleska 40
Warm Springs. 90
Warner Robins 105

Watkinsville. 85
Waycross 240
Westville 140
Whitewater Adventures. 20
Whitesburg 55
Winder. 65
Woodstock. 40
Young Harris. 125

Trying to Make Getting Around Atlanta A Tad Easier

The Interstate Highway System

When driving in the greater Atlanta area in particular, and in Georgia generally, good maps are essential and a good navigator and compass are advisable. But, fear not, getting lost in Georgia is a joy in itself. Most of the natives get lost at least once a day.

I-75 runs north to south from Canada to Florida. From Atlanta take it north to Marietta, Smyrna, Cartersville, Rome and Dalton; or south to Griffin, Macon, Perry, Columbus, Albany, Tifton, Thomasville and Valdosta.

I-85 runs from the southwest of Atlanta through and to the northeast of Atlanta. Heading southwest from Atlanta use it to reach East Point, College Park, Hartsfield International Airport, Fairburn, Peachtree City, Newnan, Warm Springs, Callaway Gardens, LaGrange and Columbus. Heading northeast from Atlanta you'll encounter Buckhead, North Druid Hills, Duluth, Norcross, Gainesville, Lake Lanier and Braselton.

I-20 runs west to east. To the west from Atlanta are Mableton, Lithia Springs, Douglasville, Villa Rica, and Bremen. To the east are Lithonia, Conyers, Covington Rutledge, Madison, Social Circle, Greensboro, Lake Oconee, Thomson and Augusta.

I-285 or "the Perimeter," is a 63 mile ring around Atlanta that connects up at various points with I-75, I-85, I-20, I-675 and GA 400.

I-675 is a 10-mile stretch that runs south from Moreland Avenue (downtown) to I-285. Even native Atlantans have trouble finding it.

I-575 is a short north/south stretch out of Marietta that sets you on the way to Dawsonville, Ellijay and the Blue Ridge Mountains.

Georgia 400-Really a great north-south road, if you can find it. From downtown, heading north, take exit 29. Once past Buckhead, there's a $.50 toll. Then head on to Chamblee, Doraville, Roswell, Alpharetta, Cumming, Lake Lanier, Cleveland, Helen, and Dahlonega.

Automobile Repairs

Whether you are a resident or a visitor, the prospect of repairing an automobile has been known to give the willies to even the sturdiest of people. Below, we have listed some numbers to call for info about honest, efficient and skilled auto repairs. 989-2552

Driving Tips

Georgia state and local police are very serious about enforcing traffic ordinances. Here are a few observations that will hopefully reduce their workload, increase roadway safety and reduce your driving costs.

1. Speed Limits-In town, 30 mph unless otherwise posted. Do not under any circumstances exceed in-town speed limits. This applies equally to Atlanta and every other Georgia city and town. Carefully observe all school speed postings and reduce your speed to a crawl. Officers are not as strict on highways but you should not exceed the rule of ten.

2. School Buses and School Zones-Unless you are on a divided highway, never pass a stopped school bus that has its lights flashing. Always slow to a crawl in school zones when school is in session.

3. In the Rain-Windshield wipers on, headlights must be on.

4. Disabled Cars-You must move it to the side of road and open the hood.

5. Re-licensing-After moving to Georgia you have 30 days to relicense yourself and to retag your auto. They mean it. Also, make sure your auto insurance is current. Bring cash or a money order ($15.00) and be prepared to take written and vision tests.

6. Rude Drivers-Unfortunately, there are some rather rude drivers in and around Atlanta. They will honk at you, tailgate and never yield a lane. Stay calm and do your best to safely ignore them. They are probably transients from other states anyway.

7. Insurance-Do not let your insurance lapse. A lapsed policy may lead to higher rates. See How To Obtain Automobile Insurance below.

8. Alcohol-Do not drink and drive. If stopped by a police officer, Georgia law requires you to submit to a sobriety test. Failure to do so will result in a one year suspension of your license. Open alcoholic containers are illegal.

9. Seat Belts-Required for all front seat occupants and for children over four years old in front and rear seats. Children under two must be restrained in a child safety seat. Children 3-4 years old must use either a seat belt of a child safety seat.

10. Bicycles-Operators and passengers under 16 must wear protective helmets.

11. Blind Persons-Always yield the right of way to a blind person.

12. Following Distance-Never tailgate and always allow emergency vehicles at least 200 feet.

13. Right and Left Turns-Right turns at red

lights are permitted, unless otherwise posted, after a complete stop. Left turns only from the left lane of a one-way street onto another one-way street.

14. Emergency Vehicles-Always yield to all emergency vehicles.

15. Documents-Always carry your drivers license, registration and proof of insurance.

How To
Get Your
Driver's License

Call 657-9300 for information relative to your situation. But remember that you must reli- cense yourself within 30 days of establishing residency in Georgia. Go to the licensing cen- ter in your area. There, you should obtain a driving instruction manual that will detail the do's and don'ts of driving in Georgia.

How To
Obtain
Automobile Insurance

No-fault auto insurance is required in Georgia and you cannot register your car without it. Call 989-2595 for broker recommendations or consult the *Yellow Pages*.

How To
Get Your
Emissions Checked

This is the easiest part of the process. Drive into any station with a state approved emission test sign in front (they're pretty numerous). It's fast and only a sawbuck.

How To
Register Your Car

Georgia license plates are called tags. With a hefty balance in your checking account go to the tag office in your county of residence. You can locate them by consulting the "Atlanta Blue Pages" at the rear of Southern Bell's "Greater Atlanta" business telephone book (Fulton County call 730-6100, DeKalb County call 371- 8247). Bring (1) your current registration; (2) the title and address of lienholder or copy of lease agreement; (3) proof of insurance; (4) proof your car passed the Georgia emissions test (not re- quired in all counties or for all cars); (5) your checkbook, and consider yourself lucky if you pay less than $200.00.

MARTA

MARTA Schedule Information . . 848-4711
MARTA General Information . .   848-5000

Other important MARTA numbers:
Airport Service 848-3454
Handicapped Services 848-5440
Lost and Found 848-5354
Public Information. 848-5156
Sports Event Service 848-3456
Rail Service 848-3450

Operating since 1979, MARTA is Atlanta's advanced mass transportation system. Reach most of Atlanta's major attractions riding the MARTA system.

Still growing, MARTA operates 240 electric rail cars on 40 miles of track with regular service to 33 rapid rail stations. In addition, 678 buses traverse 150 routes covering 1,545 miles. On an average weekday, the system records 450,000 passenger boardings with the frequency of trains about every 8-15 minutes, depending on the time of day. Connecting buses have a greater frequency variation.

MARTA fares are $1.50 which includes two free transfers (under age three rides free). You can save by purchasing a MARTA TransCard ($12 for the Monday through Sunday weekly card or $45 for the monthly card), which entitles riders to unlimited use of the entire system. Transcards and token value packs (20 for $25) are sold at Five Points, Airport, Lindbergh and Lenox stations, as well as at MARTA headquarters, and supermarkets and convenience stores.

Riding MARTA's Rail Service

The rail system is easy and fun to use. Two lines run the length and width of Atlanta. The 22-mile north/south "orange" line goes from the Airport to Five Points, Midtown, Lenox Square and ends at the northeast Perimeter. The 15-mile east/west "blue" line goes from Hightower station in the west to Indian Creek station in the east.

Riding MARTA's Buses

To board a MARTA bus, wait at a bus stop (indicated by either a white concrete obelisk or a tricolor pole-mounted MARTA sign).

The front of each bus is marked with the route number and the route name. Different bus routes use the same bus stops make sure to board the right bus. (Express bus routes include stretches along which passengers are neither picked up nor discharged. Before boarding a bus marked "express," ask the driver whether you'll be able to disembark at your desired stop).

When you see your bus approaching, raise your hand to signal to the driver that you wish to board.

If you're unsure about directions, tell the driver your destination as you board; sit up front and you'll be let off at the closest stop. Pressing the yellow "stop request" strip or pulling the cord will signal the driver that you want off at the next scheduled stop. Use the rear door when exiting.

Hartsfield Airport

10 miles south of Downtown (I-85).

Airport Administration	530-6600
International Info.	530-2081
Weather Info.	486-8834
Lost and Found	530-2100
Parking.	530-6725

Airlines

AeroMexico.	800-237-6639
Air Jamaica	800-523-5585
Alitalia.	800-223-5730
ALM Antilliean	800-327-7230
America West	800-247-5692
American	800-433-7300
Atlantic SE	404-765-2000
British Airways	800-247-9297
Cayman Airways.	800-422-9626
Continental	800-525-0280
Delta	404-765-5000
GP Express	404-984-9266
Japan Air Lines	800-525-3663
Kiwi.	800-538-5494
KLM Royal Dutch.	800-374-7747
Korean Air.	770-955-2800
Lufthansa.	800-645-3880
Midwest Express	800-452-2022
Northwest	800-225-2525
SABENA.	800-873-3900
Singapore.	800-742-3333
Southwest	800-435-9792
Swissair	800-221-4750
TWA	404-522-5738
United	800-241-6522
USAir.	800-428-4322
Valujet.	800-825-8538
Var/Brazil	800-468-2744

Taxi's

Waiting time costs $12 an hour. The minimum fare is $1.50 for the first 1/5 mile and 20 cents for each additional 1/5 mile.

American	874-3595
Ashby Street	586-0728
Atlanta Royal	584-6655
Buckhead Safety	233-1152
Checker	351-1111
Citywide	875-1223
London	222-9888
Quicker	522-5894
Rapid	688-9295
Star	758-6616
United	658-1638
Yellow	522-0200

Limo's

Rental fees range from $45-$65 per hour.

A Atlanta Inc.	351-5466
A-National	581-9731
Atlanta Livery	872-8282
Avanti Inc.	233-6100
Carey	681-3366
Clark Inc.	624-4492
Davis	524-3413
Dynasty	325-5466
Peach State	948-2520
Phoenix	876-3041
Simon's Stretch	691-2101
Tracy's	634-8557
Unique	237-1330

Rental Cars

Agency	991-1274
Alamo	768-4161
Atlanta	763-1160
Avis	530-2700
Budget	530-3000
Dollar	766-0244
Enterprise	763-0643
Hertz	530-2906
National	530-2800

Trains and Buses

Southern Railways/Amtrak	800-872-7245
Greyhound/Trailways	800-231-2222

Horse and Carriage

The average cost of a carriage ride is $12.50 per person.

Capitol City	221-1976
Inshirah Stables	523-3993

Banking

BankSouth	529-4111
Citizens Trust Bank	659-5959
Commercial Bank of Georgia	770-992-1800
Etowah Bank	770-479-8761
Fidelity National Bank	371-5500
First Alliance Bank	770-421-7604
First Union Bank	770-460-2410
NationsBank	581-2121
Summit National Bank	770-432-1000
Trust Company Bank	588-7711
Wachovia Bank	332-5000

Insurance

For recommendations regarding auto, health, homeowner, property, life, business liability and group benefits. 989-2595.

Metro Atlanta Counties, Neighborhoods and Parks

The 20 County Metro Atlanta Area

Barrow County-About one hour from Atlanta via I-85 N.; this is rolling hill country, primarily agricultural with a population of about 30,000. Comprised of Auburn, Bethlehem, Carl,

Russell, Statam and Winder. Home to the fabulous Fort Yargo State Park and the Chateau Elan Resort, Golf Course and Winery.

Bartow County-About an hour from Atlanta via I-75 N., with a population of 56,000. Comprised of rural Adairsville and Cartersville, it is home to fine public schools and colleges (Berry College Campus, the world's largest, is a don't miss) and recreational areas such as Lake Allatoona, Red Top Mountain State Park, Etowah Indian Mounds State Park and the Barnsley Gardens at Woodlands.

Carroll County-About 55 minutes from Atlanta via I-20 W., with a population of 72,000. It sits at the foothills of the Appalachian Mountains and it is both rurally and manufacturing oriented. Comprised of Bowdon, Carrollton, Mt. Zion, Roopville, Temple, Villa Rica and Whitesburg, it is home to John Tanner State Park, Lake Carroll, the Southwire Company, Gold Kist, SONY, Lamar, Bremen Bowden Investment, the Tanner Medical Center, West Georgia College and Douglas and Lomason.

Cherokee County-About 35 minutes from downtown Atlanta via I-75 N. to I-575 N.; with a population of 95,000. Essentially rural/suburban in character, it is comprised of Ball Ground, Canton (the county seat), Holly Springs, Nelson, Waleska and Woodstock; recreational facilities abound along the shores of Lake Allatoona and the Etowah River. Many fine colleges are within a mere stone's throw.

Clayton County-About a half an hour from downtown Atlanta (I-75 S.); with a population of 183,000. A blending of city and suburban life comprised of College Park, Forest Park, Jonesboro, Lake City, Lovejoy, Morrow and Riverdale. Here is the home of "Gone With the Wind's" Twelve Oaks and Tara, Clayton State College, Lake Spivey and Hartsfield International Airport.

Cobb County-About 10 minutes from downtown Atlanta via I-75 N. With a population of 450,000, Cobb is giving the City of Atlanta a run for its money as it becomes the nation's leading area for the locating of corporate headquarter offices. Booming with everything from major attractions to business, housing and historic charm. Comprised of Acworth, Austell, Kennesaw, Marietta, Powder Springs and Smyrna, it is home to Dobbins Air Force Base and over 600 multinational businesses including Lockheed (Georgia's largest employer), General Dynamics, British Telecom and Syncordia. Its major attractions include Kennesaw Mountain National Battlefield Park, Six Flags Over Georgia, Whitewater park, the Malibu Grand Prix, Sun Valley Beach and the Chattahoochee Outdoor Center.

Coweta County-About 35 minutes from downtown Atlanta (I-85 South), with a population of 55,000. An exemplary example of small town rural charm within spittin' distance of Atlanta, it is comprised of Corinth, Grantville, Haralson, Madras, Moreland, Newnan, Palmetto, Sargent, Senoia, Sharpsburg and Turin.

DeKalb County-About 25 minutes from downtown Atlanta (I-75 S. to I-20 E.). Comprised of Avondale Estates, Chamblee, Doraville, Clarkston, Decatur, Lithonia, Pine Lake and Stone Mountain, with a population of 550,000, DeKalb is the essence of ethnic diversity. World-famous Stone Mountain Park will host several 1996 Olympic events including canoeing and rowing, tennis, cycling, archery and the pentathlon. You can find just about everything in DeKalb, from the finest universities and hospitals to the Callanwolde and Fernbank Centers.

Douglas County-Only 20 minutes from downtown Atlanta via I-20 W.; with a population of about 75,000. Delightful parks and recreational facilities abound in this rapidly growing bedroom community comprised of Douglasville, Fairplay, Lithia Springs and Winston. Home to Sweetwater State Park, one of Georgia's finest, with many fine schools and medical facilities.

Forsyth County-About an hour from Atlanta via GA 400 N., bordering on the western edge of Lake Lanier Islands with a population of 55,000. Comprised of suburban Cumming, it is a gateway to the lake and the mountain areas to the north.

Fulton County North-Just 30 minutes from downtown Atlanta via Ga. 400 N. Growing rapidly, it is still rich in natural beauty as characterized by rolling hills, giant pines, historic antebellum homes and horse farms. It is comprised of Alpharetta, Mountain Park and Roswell. Within a stone's throw of its historic villages lie the Chattahoochee Nature Center, Lake Lanier, national parks and the Chattahoochee River. Within its tranquil setting you can find such major multinational corporations as Digital Equipment, American Honda, Equifax, Herman Miller, Kimberly Clark, CIBA Vision, Siemens and State Farm. Fine schools, recreational and health care facilities abound.

Fulton County South-Only 10 minutes from downtown Atlanta and just minutes from Hartsfield International Airport (I-75/I-85 South). With a population of 155,000 it is comprised of College Park, East Point, Fairburn, Hapeville, Palmetto and Union City, South Fulton County is home to the corporate headquarters of Delta Airlines and Chick-fil-A. Also located there are Ford Motor Company's top national plant, Ralston-Purina, U. S. Homes, Porex Technologies, Southern Mills, Owens-Corning Fibreglas and a multi-use cultural arts center. The Wolf Creek Trap and Skeet Range will host the 1996 Olympic shooting events and Cochran Mill Park and others provide over 2000 acres of equestrian, nature and hiking trails, tennis facilities and golf courses.

Gwinnett County-Less than an hour from Atlanta via I-85 N. Primarily suburban with a population of 350,000. Comprised of Buford, Dacula, Duluth, Grayson, Lawrenceville, Liburn, Norcross, Suwanee and Snellville. Characterized by thriving communities and a heavy emphasis on education and cultural activities.

Henry County-Less than 1/2 hour from downtown Atlanta (I-75 S.). Comprised of Hampton, Locust Grove, Stockbridge and McDonough with a population of about 62,000, the 585-acre Panola Mountain State Conservation Park and the Indian Springs State Park. Henry is a fully booming residential area with one of the finest public school systems in the state and home to the Henry Arts Alliance and an ever increasing number of corporations such as Ford, NEC Technologies, Pep Boys, Toppan Interamerica, BellSouth Ecolab and BK International.

Newton County-About 40 minutes east of Atlanta (I-20 E.), with a population of 45,000. Comprised of Covington, Mansfield, Newbern, Oxford, Porterdale and Social Circle, it is home to both corporations (Bridgestone Tire, Mobil Oil, Stanley Toolworks) and the charming main street community of Social Circle.

Paulding County-About 40 minutes from downtown Atlanta via I-75 N. to 120 W. Comprised of Dallas and Hiram with a population of 42,000, Paulding is in the early phase of its development. Young families and industry are finding its wide open spaces very attractive. Shaw Industries and Metromont have already opened facilities in Paulding.

Pickens County-About an hour from downtown Atlanta (I-75 to I-575). Comprised of Jasper, Nelson and Talking Rock, with a population of 15,000, Pickens, small town and mountainous in character, is home to the Georgia Marble Company and two highly rated mountain resorts, **Big Canoe** and **Bent Tree.**

Rockdale County-About 35 minutes from Atlanta (I-20 E.), with a population of 57,000. It is comprised of Conyers and Milstead and home to the wonderfully peaceful Monastery of the Holy Ghost and such corporations as AT&T, John Deere, and Maxell. Georgia International Horse Park in Conyers will host the 1996 Olympic equestrian events.

Spalding County-About 40 minutes from downtown Atlanta (I-75 S.). Comprised of Experiment, Griffin, Orchard Hill, Pomona, Rover, Sunny Side, Vaughn and Zetella, with a population of 55,000, Spalding is a great quiet place for a starter home and the site of the world-famous Cherokee Rose Shooting Resort.

Walton County-About 45 minutes east of Atlanta on I-20 E.), primarily suburban/rural in character with a population of 40,000. Comprised of Good Hope, Jersey, Loganville, Monroe, Social Circle and Walnut Grove. Home to the fabulous **Blue Willow Inn** (made famous by an editorial review by Lewis Grizzard acknowledging its fine Southern cuisine).

Talk About Those Metro Atlanta Neighborhoods

Downtown's Downtown and Sweet Auburn

Here, spreading out from historic Five Points (1830s), you'll find the origins of Atlanta mixed with the future of Atlanta. Numerous historic markers and examples of the grand architecture of the late 19th and early 20th centuries co-exist with an ever-increasing number of modern skyscrapers (don't miss the modern grandeur of 303 Peachtree St.). Amongst much, much more, there is the Martin Luther King, Jr. National Historic District (Sweet Auburn, including the MLK Center for Non-Violent Social Change (1981), the Big Bethel AME Church (1891), the Ebenezer Baptist Church (1914), the APEX Museum (1910), the MLK Birth Home (1894), the

Shrine of the Immaculate Conception (1873). Also, Atlanta City Hall (1930), the World of Coca-Cola Museum (1990), Rich's Building (1923), the Gold Dome (1889), the Candler Building (1906), the Odd Fellows Building (1912), the Federal Reserve Bank (1918), the Flatiron Building (1897), the Wheat Street Baptist Church (1920), the Rhodes-Haverty Building (1929), the Georgia-Pacific Building (1982), the Central Presbyterian Church (1884), the Broad St. Commercial District (1880s), Margaret Mitchell Square (1940s), the Henry Grady Statue (1891), the Atlanta Journal and Constitution Building (1960s), the Georgia World Congress Center, CNN Center and the Omni Hotel and Coliseum, the Peachtree Center Complex, SciTrek Museum, the downtown branches of the High Museum of Art, and the Atlanta Historical Society and Underground Atlanta (1870s).

Downtown's Grant and Inman Parks

About two miles southeast of downtown, I-20 exits 26 and 28 respectively. With the exodus to Atlanta's suburban neighborhoods, each of these areas suffered decline, but, fortunately, both have been rediscovered and are subjects of long-term and continuing restoration. In and around Grant Park are ZooAtlanta, the Atlanta Cyclorama, Julius Fischer House (1886), St. Paul Methodist Church (1906) and the William B. Hartsfield House (1902). Inman Park developed in the 1880s as Atlanta's first planned suburb. Here, in and around the Little Five Points shopping area (Euclid and Moreland Avenues), are many historic buildings, including the Old Police Lock-Up (1880), the Ernest and Emily Winship Woodruff House (1904), the Inman Park United Methodist Church (1898) and Joel Hurt's Cotage (1882).

Virginia-Highlands/ Little Five Points

Just about one mile northeast of downtown and oozing with old world charm. Home to the Carter Presidential Center and Library, Virginia-Highlands/Little Five Points is a wonderful blend of charming Victorian architecture, newer homes and a swatch of bookstores, neighborhood pubs, ethnic restaurants, coffee houses, art galleries, taverns and interesting shops.

Midtown's Midtown and Ansley Park

The magnificent NationsBank Building (1992) marks the corners of North Avenue and Peachtree St. From here Peachtree and West Peachtree Sts. proceed northward (to Buckhead) to form Midtown Atlanta. Here amongst gleaming corporate skyscrapers you will find the Georgian Terrace Hotel (1911), the Fox Theater (1929), the All Saints Episcopal Church (1906), the Robert W. Woodruff Arts Center (1968), the High Museum of Art (1983), the Piedmont Driving Club (1895), Piedmont Park, the Atlanta Botanical Garden. Also, Peachtree Christian Church (1925), the Varsity, Georgia Tech, the Temple (1920), Atlantic Center (1987), Rhodes Memorial Hall (1903), the North Avenue and First Presbyterian Churches, the First Church of Christ Scientist (1914), the Atlanta Women's Club, St. Mark's United Methodist Church, numerous hotels and residences dating from the early 1900s, and an array of fine restaurants.

Midtown's Georgia Tech and Olympic Village

One mile northwest of downtown, Georgia Tech University. Founded in 1888 on four acres, Tech now consists of four major colleges (Engineering, Architecture, Sciences and Liberal Studies, and Management) on a landscaped 300+ acres. See the magnificent older architecture, the Administration Building (1888), the A. French Building (1899), Lyman Hall (1905) and the Carnegie Building (1907), which blend with the newer additions such as Olympic Village (1995), the Fuller E. Callaway Manufacturing Research Center (1990), the Advanced Technology Development Center (1983) and the Centennial Research Building (1985). The area abutting the Tech campus, demarcated by Marietta St. and Northside Parkway has been primarily industrial/savage in nature. But it is rapidly being inhabited by a variety of artists, photographers, small businesses, antique and other shops. The old standbys like the vast scrap metal yard and the many salvage companies co-exist amongst their new neighbors which include the Nexus Art Center, The Carriage Works, The Block Candy Co., The Hotel Roxy and The King Plow Art Center.

Buckhead's Bucking Buckhead

Blessed with some of the best bookstores you'll find anywhere and home to three of Atlanta's premier hotels (Ritz-Carlton, Swissotel and Nikko), about six miles north of downtown lies Buckhead. Taken from a 19th century tavern Buck Head, this diverse neighborhood, once a stagecoach stop on the wagon route between Atlanta and Gainesville, is Atlanta's major entertainment and shopping center (Lenox Sq. and Phipps Plaza Malls lie side-by-side). Nearly every street off the main Peachtree drag offers a splendid array of magnificent homes and gardens, while Bennett St. and Miami Circle offer an unbelievable array of antiques, furniture and art. Among the numerous historic buildings and mansions that line historic West Paces Ferry Road you will find the unique complex that houses the Atlanta Historical Society, and the sprawling Governor's Mansion.

Ashford-Dunwoody/ Brookhaven

Ten miles north of downtown, bordering on Buckhead, these neighborhoods are classic examples of early 20th-century planned residential development at its finest. Nearby is Oglethorpe University.

Druid Hills/ Emory University

Three miles NE of downtown, Druid Hills is a stately residential area with many fine examples of early 20th century architecture, including Walter Rich House (1913), Oscar Strauss House (1917), Neil Reed House (1914), T. Guy Woolford House (1931), Lloyd Preacher House (1928), Cator Woolford House and Gardens (1920), Jessee Draper House (1915), William R. Prescott House (1915), and many more. Located within or nearby are the Carter Presidential Center, Emory University, Little Five Points, the Fernbank Science Museum and Nature Center and the Callanwolde Fine Arts Center.

Cobb County's Marietta

Take I-75 16 miles to exit 112. A city in its own right with a rich history, distinguished old and new architecture and many quiet suburban residential area. Here you will find houses and other structures dating from the 1850s including Kennesaw House (1855), the Hardware Store (1857), the First Baptist Church (1897), Montgomery House (1870), Marietta Sq. and Glover Park

(1852), the First Presbyterian Church (1852), and many more. Nearby attractions include Kennesaw Mountain National Battlefield, Dobbins Air Force Base and the Marietta-Cobb Museum of Art. Also, fine regional theater in Marietta's Theater in the Square.

DeKalb County's Decatur

Home of the huge DeKalb Farmer's Market and just 15 minutes east of downtown off I-20, festive Decatur is the essence of old village charm. Centered on Courthouse Square, historic Decatur hosts numerous festivals and other cultural events. Decatur's fascinating history predates Atlanta's. Here you will find the Old Decatur Cemetery (1830), the DeKalb Historical Society's Historic Building Complex (homes from the 1820s and 1830s), the John Pearce House (1876), High House (1830), the First Methodist Church Chapel (1897), the Old Courthouse (1898), the Charles F. Dana Fine Arts Building (1960), the Decatur Freight Depot (1891), the Charles Murphy and Milton A. Candler Houses (1885 and 1889) and much, much more.

Fulton North's Roswell

About 20 miles north of downtown, Roswell is steeped in Southern history dating back to the 1830s, Roswell today is a bustling suburb that has retained many of its historic traditions. The Roswell business district dates back to the 1830s and you'll find the Canton St. Antique Shops, Founder's Cemetery (1830), Roswell Presbyterian Church and Cemetery (1840), Bulloch Hall (1842), Roswell Sq. (1840), Primrose Cottage (1839), Barrington Hall 1842), Great Oaks (1842), the Roswell Visitors Center (1839) and plenty more.

Vinings

Founded around 1830 by Hardy Pace, all but destroyed by fire in the Civil War, Vinings today, located just west of bustling Buckhead, is a thriving community that oozes with with charm. The beautiful homes, local shops and antique stores serve as a role model for small urban communities throughout Georgia.

Atlanta's Parks

Chastain Park

Buckhead. W. Wieuca Rd. A most remarkable park. Beyond the traditional quiet places one usually finds in a park, Chastain is the home of a 6,000 seat amphitheater (venue for numerous cultural events), a riding stable (featuring horse boarding and equestrian events), tennis facilities, a gym, baseball, softball, football and soccer fields, a swimming pool, a 3.5 mile jogging trail and an arts and crafts center/gallery. 817-6785.

Grant Park

Downtown (2 miles SE). Cherokee and Georgia Aves. Here you will find the Atlanta Zoo and the Cyclorama as well as the many athletic fields that serve as home for numerous amateur leagues. The Oakland Cemetery and Sweet Auburn Historic District are nearby. 658-6374.

Piedmont Park

Midtown. Piedmont Ave. and 14th St. At once home of the Atlanta Botanical Garden and the Annual Arts Festival, its 185 acres make Piedmont Atlanta's largest park. Piedmont serves as venue for a relentless stream of festivals, concerts, fairs and exhibitions while sustaining an excellent environment for walking, bicycling, roller skating and jogging. Piedmont's athletic facilities include two soccer fields, two softball fields, 13 tennis courts and an outdoor swim-

ming pool. 876-2040. Adm: Free.

The Piedmont Park Conservancy has been established to help restore Piedmont to its former glory. Levels of membership are available ranging from $25.00 for an individual to $500.00 for a Hardwood Hero. For info call Gail Timmis, managing director of the conservancy. 875-PARK.

A Brief Guide to Apartment and Home Rentals

Helpful Tips

Begin by making a list of what is most important to you: price, location, number of bedrooms, amenities, pet policies, access to covered parking and the like.

Then call an apartment locating service. Most of these organizations provide extensive **free information and service**. Be sure to meet the apartment manager. This will give you good insights as to safety and building maintenance.

But don't make your final decision from seeing the model apartment only. Walk through the actual unit you will occupy.

As for the lease, don't sign it until you understand every clause. Seek legal counsel if you are unsure of anything in it or of your negotiating skills.

Apartment Locating Services

A&A Apartment Locators... 770-394-2088
Apartment Finding &
  Rental Service 633-3336
Apartment Hunting
  Specialist 770-934-0322
Apartment-Home Locator
  & Services 770-551-9797
Apartment Relocation

Council 800-232-RENT
Apartment Renters Aide 518-7717
Apartment Selector
   Central/Eastside 636-1788
   West/Northwest 770-956-0177
   North/Northeast 770-552-9255
   Airport/Southside 636-0873
Apartments Today 770-664-4957
Automated Apartment
   Locator Service 874-RENT
Corporate Suites 770-671-8777
Fred Lemon & Associates . . . 770-664-6319
Free Home Finder 770-455-1781
HomeRenters 633-8008
Leasing Atlanta 770-455-3897
National Interim
   Housing Network 1-800-742-6446
Oakwood Corporate
   Housing 770-452-8130
Post Corporate Apartments/
   Relocation Services 770-952-1022
Promove 842-0042, 800-950-MOVE
Rent Source 633-3331
Selina's Apartment
   Locator Service 875-0177

Atlanta's Accommodations

With about 60,000 visitor rooms at its disposal, each year Atlanta is home to over 200 conventions ranging in size from 1,000 at the small end to a 675,000 lollapalooza. Accommodations run the full spectrum from super-luxury hotels and inns to moderately priced bed and breakfasts. Below, we've listed many of Atlanta's accommodations by the price they chrarge per day for an average room followed by a smattering of bed and breakfasts.

$150-200
Atlanta Hilton
Hotel Nikko
Hyatt Regency Peachtree Center
Hyatt Regency Suites
Occidental Grand
Ritz Carleton Atlanta Downtown

Ritz Carleton Buckhead
Sheraton Colony Square
Stouffer Renaissance Waverly

$120-150
Atlanta Airport Hilton
Atlanta Marriott Northwest
Atlanta Marriott Perimeter Center
Atlanta Renaissance
Atlanta Renaissance Airport
Best Western Granada Suites
Doubletree Hotel at Concourse
Embassy Suites Airport
Embassy Suites Buckhead
Embassy Suites Galleria
Embassy Suites Perimeter Center
Holiday Crowne Plaza Ravinia
J.W. Marriott at Lenox
Marque of Atlanta
Marriott Airport
Marriott Atlanta Marquis
Marriott Suites Midtown
Omni Hotel at CNN Center
Residence Inn Buckhead
Residence Inn Midtown
Sheraton
   Airport
   Colony Square Downtown
   Century Square
   Gateway Airport
   Suites Cumberland
Stouffer Concourse
Swissotel Atlanta
Suite Hotel Underground
Summerfield Suites Buckhead
Terrace Garden Inn Buckhead
Westin Peachtree Plaza
Wyndham Midtown

$90-120
Ansley InnAtlanta Marriott Gwinnett Place
Best Western American
Biltmore SuitesCourtyard
   Cumberland Center
   Executive Park
   Gwinnett Mall
   Perimeter Center
   Windy Hill
Emory Inn
Evergreen Conference Center and Resort

French Quarter Suites
Guest Quarters Suites
Hawthorne Suites Northwest
Holiday Inn
   Airport South
   Buckhead
Homewood Suites Cumberland
La Quinta Atlanta West
Quality Inn Habersham
Radisson Hotel Atlanta
Ramada Airport North
   Downtown
Residence Inn
   Cumberland
Travelodge Downtown
The Apartment Inn
Wyndham Garden

$60-90

Atlanta Hilton Northwest
Atlanta West
Best Western
   Norcross
   Northlake
   Windy Hill
Beverly Hills Inn
Budgetel Inn
   Airport
   Lenox
Castlegate
Comfort Inn
   Airport
   Buckhead
   Downtown
   North Avenue
Courtyard
   Airport South
   Medical Center
   Midtown
   Norcross
   Northlake
Days Inn
   Airport
   Clairmont Road
   Peachtree
   Gwinnett Place
   Lenox
   Northlake Mall
   Northwest
   Stone Mountain

   Windy Hill
Econo Lodge Airport
Hampton Inns
   Airport
   Buckhead
   Druid Hills
   Northlake
   Stone Mountain
Holiday Inn
   Airport North
   Midtown North
   Northlake
Howard Johnson
   Airport
   Cumberland
   Midtown
Inn At Peachtrees
La Quinta
   Airport
   Norcross
   Stone Mountain
Lenox Inn
Quality Inn Midtown
Ramada Six Flags
Red Roof Inn
   Druid Hills
   Six Flags
   Regency Suites
Shellmont Lodge Midtown
Super 8 Motel Six Flags
Travelodge Midtown
University Inn at Emory
Vantage Northlake
Woodruff Inn

$30-60

Best Western Airport
Cheshire Motor Inn
Executive Inn Six Flags
Fairfield Inn
   Airport
   Gwinnett Mall
   Northlake
Ho Jo Inn Airport West
Masters Economy Inn Six Flags
Red Roof Inn Airport
Scottish Inn Six Flags
Shoney's Inn
Stone Mountain Park Inn

Bed and Breakfast

Beverly Hills Inn, 65 Sheridan Dr., Atlanta. A charming and intimate 1929 European-style Inn located close to first-class dining, shopping and entertainment. This pied-a-terre offers 18 individually decorated rooms with hardwood floors, balconies, kitchens, love seats and private bathrooms. Suitable for the business traveler and corporate meetings, amenities include library, fax, computers and breakfast in the garden room. Enjoy a warm reception from Mit and Hima Amin. 233-8520.

Sixty Polk Street B & B., 60 Polk St., Marietta. This French-Regency Victorian, circa 1872, was completely renovated in 1991, and is but a five-minute walk from historic Marietta Square. Relax, feel at home, and enjoy elegant pampering. Visit the Kennesaw Mountain Battle site just down the road, or shop for antiques on the Square. Two-miles away get drenched on the water slides at White Water Park or scare yourself silly at Six Flags Amusement Park. The home is furnished with antiques and Oriental carpets. Enjoy a large, delicious breakfast served in the red dining room; owners Mary and Chet Ladd always have the coffee on and a bottomless cookie jar. 770-419-0101, 800-497-2075.

Fun Facts:

- Fortune Magazine lists the Coca-Cola Company, the Home Depot Company and the United Parcel Service, all headquatered in Atlanta, in the top ten most admired companies in America.

- Dense though it is, there is no forest at Underground Atlanta, yet it attracts upwards of 13 million visitors a year.

- The annual Miss Georgia Pageant is held in Columbus.

Fun Fact:

- 70% of Georgia is forest and its state parks attract about 15 million visitors each year.

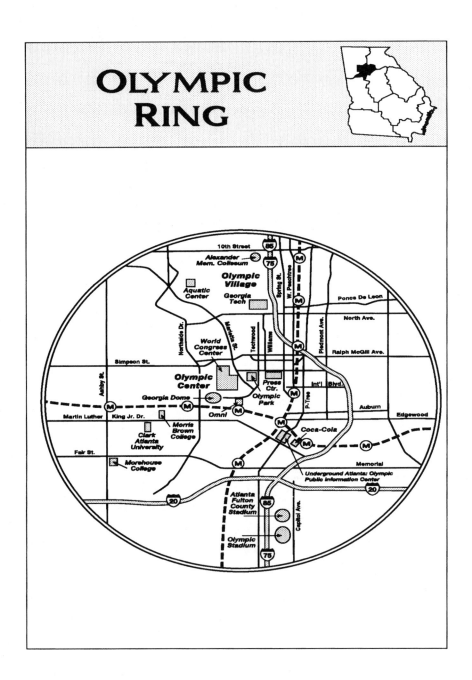

SECTION III
The 1996 Centennial
Summer Olympic Games

Olympic Sports Venues

Event	Venue	Location	Miles from Olympic Ring
Ceremonies-Opening/Closing	Olympic Stadium	Olympic Ring	0
Archery	Stone Mountain Park	Metro Atlanta	16
Athletics	Olympic Stadium	Olympic Ring	0
Badminton	Georgia State University	Olympic Ring	0
Baseball	Fulton County Stadium	Olympic Ring	0
Basketball	Georgia Dome / Morehouse College	Olympic Ring	0
Boxing	Alexander Mem. Coliseum	Olympic Ring	0
Canoe/Kayak-Sprint	Lake Lanier	Gainesville, GA	57
Canoe/Kayak-Slalom	Ocoee River	Cleveland, TN	121
Cycling-Mtn. Bike	International Horse Park	Metro Atlanta	33
Cycling-Road	Throughout Atlanta	Metro Atlanta	-
Cycling-Track	Stone Mountain Park	Metro Atlanta	16
Diving	GA Tech Aquatic Center	Olympic Ring	0
Equestrian	International Horse Park	Metro Atlanta	33
Fencing	World Congress Center	Olympic Ring	0
Gymnastics	Georgia Dome	Olympic Ring	0
Handball	Georgia Dome / World Congress Center	Olympic Ring	0
Hockey	Clark University / Morris Brown College	Olympic Ring	0
Judo	World Congress Center	Olympic Ring	0
Modern Pentathlon	Multiple Sites	Metro Atlanta	-
Rowing	Lake Lanier	Orlando, FL	57
Shooting	Wolf Creek Complex	Washington, DC	20
Soccer-1st Round	Florida Citrus Bowl	Birmingham, AL	450
Soccer-1st Round	RFK Stadium	Miami, FL	693
Soccer-1 - 2nd Round	Legion Field	Athens, GA	153
Soccer-1-2nd Round	Orange Bowl	Columbus, GA	785
Soccer-Semi & Finals	Sanford Stadium	Olympic Ring	66
Softball	Golden Park	Olympic Ring	108
Swimming	GA Tech Aquatic Center	Metro Atlanta	0
Table Tennis	World Congress Center	Olympic Ring	0
Tennis	Stone Mountain	Metro Atlanta	16
Track & Field	Olympic Stadium	Olympic Ring	0
Volleyball-Beach	Atlanta Beach	Metro Atlanta	25
Volleyball-Indoor	University of Georgia	Athens, GA	66
Volleyball-Indoor	Omni Coliseum	Olympic Ring	0
Water Polo	GA Tech Aquatic Center	Olympic Ring	0
Weightlifting	World Congress Center	Olympic Ring	0
Wrestling	World Congress Center	Olympic Ring	0
Yachting	Wassaw Sound	Savannah, GA	256

Commentary

The Olympic Ring, a 1.5 mile radius extending outward from downtown Atlanta, may be an imaginary line but the fact that Atlantans from every walk of life, including that playful Olympic mascot "IZZY," have joined hands to prepare for our city for this great honor is not imaginary; Atlanta's Olympic preparations are truly Olympian.

With the **Atlanta Committee for the Olympic Games (ACOG)** serving as host, for 16 exciting days, from July 19 to August 4, 1996, 10,700 men and women from 197 countries will compete in 26 Olympic sporting events ranging from archery to yachting. Most events will be held in the metro Atlanta area but other cities in Georgia will also serve as venues, including Athens, Columbus and Savannah. More than 11 million tickets to over 560 ticketed events will be sold to the two million plus visitors and residents who will attend these historic Centennial Olympic Games. And 3.5 billion people worldwide are expected to see various parts of the 3,000 hours of live TV coverage.

The **1996 Olympic Torch Relay** will begin in April 1996 when the Olympic Flame is lit in Olympia, Greece. After ceremonies and the traditional Flame Relay across Greece, the Torch Relay will begin in the United States on April 27, 1996 when the flame arrives in Los Angeles, California. Some 10,000 torchbearers will carry the Flame through the United States The 1996 Olympic Game's worldwide sponsor, is none other than **The Coca-Cola Company, the Presenter of the Olympic Torch Relay in the United States**.

Cultural Olympiad and Paralympic Games

Complementing the Olympic Games are the **Cultural Olympiad** and the **Paralympic Games**. The Cultural Olympiad is a multi-year, multi-disciplinary program featuring culture and the arts in a series of performances and exhibitions leading up to the 1996 Games, culminating in a spectacular eight-week **Olympic Arts Festival** in the summer of 1996. Following the Olympic Games, from August 17 through August 26, 1996, the 1996 Paralympic Games, featuring 4,000 physically challenged athletes in 17 sports from 105 countries, will use the very same venues.

Centennial Olympic Park Coca-Cola Olympic City

Downtown. Centennial Olympic Park is designated "the gathering place" for the Olympic experience. A 21-acre park built specifically to serve as a welcome and rest area for Olympic visitors. The park will house a temporary 8,000 seat amphitheater that will feature outstanding entertainers and the **Olympic Park Superstore** where one and all can purchase Olympic memorabilia. Additionally, the Park will host the Festival of the American South, a multi-cultural, multi-media presentation of life in the South.

Coca-Cola Olympic City is designed to complement **Olympic Park** and lies adjacent to it on 12 acres bounded by Simpson and Baker Sts,. on the north and south and Techwood and Hull Sts., on the east and west. The sharing of the glory of the Olympic experience is the guiding design concept for this unprecedented attraction. Visitors will compete, one-on-one, with Olympic athletes, be coached by Olympic coaches, score Olympic performances and meet and receive autographs and photos from Olympic athletes.

Tickets

Call 404-744-1996 for info on tickets to sporting and cultural events.

Olympic Games Merchandise.

Call 404-658-1996 for mail order items. Or visit the Olympic Experience at Underground Atlanta, Centennial Olympic Park, Coca-Cola Olympic City, and malls and retail outlets nationwide.

Transportation

The use of mass transportation during the Games is highly encouraged. Most Olympic venues are located at or near MARTA and newly designed and lighted pedestrian walkways will facilitate walking to and from events within the Olympic Ring.

What You Can Do Help Reduce the Olympics' Traffic Crunch

From July 19, 1996 to August 4, 1996 it is a substantial understatement to suggest that traffic will be heavy in the downtown area. If you can, avoid traveling to downtown. If you cannot avoid downtown, ACOG planners suggest the following:

1. Avoid driving to downtown at peak hours, 7:30 a.m. to 9:00 a.m., and 4:30 to 6:30 p.m.

2. Schedule pick-ups and deliveries to downtown for non-peak hours.
3. If you're not planning to attend the 1996 Summer Olympics, its a great time to take a vacation.
4. If vacation is out of the question, try to arrange for telecommuting, staggered work hours, a compressed work week and ride sharing.
5. Most parking lots in the downtown area will be overflowing. Try to arrange to have someone drop you at work and then pick you up.

Fun Fact

- Since 1868 Atlanta has served as Georgia's capitol city. Earlier it was Savannah (1733), Augusta (1786), Louisville (1795) and Milledgeville (1807).

Fun Facts:

- Georgia was colonized on February 12, 1733, the last of the 13 original colonies.

- The most well-known commercial peaches grown in Georgia are the Elberta, the Georgian Bell and the Hale.

- On July 4th of each year Atlantans celebrate democracy with a uniquely fervent enthusiasm. Freedom, freedom and more freedom is the theme that empowers Georgia's state motto-Wisdom, Justice, Moderation.

Fun Facts:

- Hartsfield International Airport, named after former Mayor William B. Hartsfield, is the second busiest in America and the sixth busiest in the world.

- The Piedmont Province (piedmont means foothills), home to Atlanta, sits south of the Blue Ridge Mountains and is covered by red clay soil. Once the center of Georgia's cotton trade, Piedmont is now Georgia's major urban/industrial area as well as its major agricultural producer.

- Georgia's largest fresh water turtle, the alligator snapper, has weighed in at over 150 lbs.

SECTION IV
Corporate Atlanta

Commentary

Tucked in and around metro Atlanta are an ever-increasing number of the world's finest U.S. and international corporations, large, medium and small. Corporate Atlanta has contributed much to Georgia's growth and diversity and has committed to even more in the future. Not only do the corporations bring jobs, training, skills, and technology but they have also heavily participated in civic, community and charitable functions.

Some of Metro Atlanta's Headquarter Organizations

AGCO
American Cancer Society
C.A.R.E.
Carter Presidential Center
Coca-Cola
Colonial Pipeline
Delta Air Lines
Equifax
Georgia Pacific
Hayes Microcomputer
Holiday Inn Worldwide
Home Depot
Medaphis
National Center for Disease Control
Ritz-Carleton Hotels
Turner Broadcasting
SunTrust
United Parcel Service
The Winter Group of Companies

Corporate Profiles

The Coca-Cola Company
CEO: Roberto C. Goizueta

While most businesses in the U.S. slept, the Coca-Cola Company went global, and that has produced substantial benefits for the company, for its zillions of stockholders, for Atlanta and for Georgia. When asked why Coca-Cola went global long before global enterprise was popular in the U.S., Coke Chairman Roberto Goizueta, in his understated way, explained, *"There are a lot more people outside the United States than there are here. This is not rocket science, just good common business sense."*

The implementation of Coke's global market strategy, together with its savvy financial reformation, have led to extremely impressive results. Now the fourth most valuable company in the U.S., and marketing its products in over 195 countries, Coke's market base of 2.2 billion consumers in 1984 has expanded to more than 5.2 billion consumers by the end of 1994, and its average annual compounded rate of return since 1984 is an amazing 17 percent, beating the Dow Jones Industrial Average and the S&P 500 by roughly 3-to-1.

Discipline and focus on volume growth within a framework of geographic expansion and creative consumer marketing will continue to guide Coke's fortunes as it heads strongly into the 21st-century. Or in the words of Chairman Goizueta, *"In effect we have been systematically building a global business machine, capable of sustaining strong profitable growth well into the 21st-century."*

Kroger Supermarkets

Atlanta Division President: Paul Smith

Though the product mix is ever-changing, Kroger, the largest supermarket chain in the nation and Georgia, has supplied the major Atlanta and Savannah markets since 1937 with everything from acidophilus milk and azaleas to Yoo Hoo and zinc vitamin supplements. Its combined revenue from supermarket and drugstore operations wins Kroger a striking 33 % market share, this even in the face of fierce competition from numerous other supermarket chains.

In facing its competitors, Kroger's strategy seeks the high road, a combination of learning and responding to neighborhood needs, improving service, maintaining competitively low prices, building product diversity, and building new stores while remodeling the older ones. A few examples of service improvements are the introduction of 24-hour pharmacy service, jewelry and perfume counters, placing frozen foods closer to the cashier so products won't melt and its freshness guarantee or free policy. Examples of it neighborhood friendly policy are the Belvedere location Senior Citizens Day on Wednesday, combined with five percent discounts, bingo and Glen Miller piped through the store. Howell Mill is ready for the onslaught of Georgia Tech students with great take-out foods and extra cashiers; and the Piedmont store catering to a large population of seniors provides coffee, healthy snacks and TV in a sitting area and a shuttle service.

Kroger has also acquired the reputation as a concerned corporate citizen promoting children's education and health by opening 57 mini-stores in schools complete with cash register, money, fresh produce and groceries to give pupils hands-on experience. "Earning for Learning," collecting Kroger receipts in exchange for computers and software, and raised and donated more than $5 million for children's hospitals.

Kroger is an excellent example of large chain responding to and participating in community needs and affairs. Paul Smith, Kroeger's Atlanta Division President, sums up neatly saying, *"We're not the Red Cross. You have to make money to be able to do these things. At the same time, if you don't fortify where your home base, then you shouldn't be in business."*

Kroger may not be the Red Cross but the list of charitable organizations supported by them includes the Scottish Rite Children's Medical Center, Egleston Children's Hospital, Hughs Spalding Children's Hospital, the Muscular Dystrophy Association, the Special Olympics, Toys for Tots, the Empty Stocking Fund, Must Ministries, the Leukemia Foundation, the United Negro College Fund, Children's Miracle Network, Sickle Cell Foundation of Georgia and the Sudden Infant Death Syndrome Foundation.

Turner Broadcasting System

CEO: R.E. "Ted" Turner

Turner Broadcasting System (TBS) marks its 25th anniversary focusing on the future. Turner is a company committed to innovation, excellence and achievement. In its 25th anniversary year it celebrates a history of dramatic global growth and works to position itself for future successes.

In 1970, TBS purchased an independent UHF television station (Channel 17) in Atlanta. By leveraging that initial acquisition into the creation of a leading global media company with a legacy of unprecedented achievement, TBS today is one the world's top producers of original entertainment, news and sport programming.

Chairman Ted Turner says, *"It's gratifying to reflect on the company's growth, but it is more important to remain focused on the future and on our commitment to informing, educating and entertaining audiences worldwide. Because of the support of viewers, employees, shareholders, advertisers, cable operators and distributors over the past 25 years, TBS is making a difference in the world."*

The 1976 decision to make a local Atlanta UHF television station available to viewers across the nation via satellite laid the foundation for a series of bold moves.In 1980, TBS launched CNN and changed the way the world gets its news. "CNN has turned viewers around the world into instant eyewitnesses of history," wrote *Time Magazine,* in naming Turner its 1991 "Man of the Year." In 1982, Headline News came on-line, followed by CNN International in 1985, TNT in 1988, SportsSouth in 1990, the Cartoon Network in 1992, CNN Airport Network in 1992, Turner Classic Movies in 1994 and the international expansion of TNT and the Cartoon Network in Latin America, Europe and Asia.

TBS made major acquisitions during this time period, including the Turner Entertainment Co. film library (1986), Hanna-Barbera Cartoons (1991), Castle Rock Entertainment (1993) and New Line Cinema (1994).

Upcoming projects for TBS include an even greater commitment to original programming, with new original productions, documentaries, theatrical releases and original animation. CNN continues to expand its commitment to global news with the opening of a Hong Kong production center as well as increased worldwide distribution and news gathering operations.

TBS is the leading supplier of programming for the basic cable industry and a major distributor of news and entertainment product around the world.

The Winter Group of Companies

Chairman: Robert L. Silverman
Far smaller than the Coke, Kroger and TBS, the Winter Group of Companies is also making significant contributions to metro Atlanta and beyond. The group includes The Winter Construction Company, Winter Properties, Inc., Winter Environmental Services, Inc. and

Winter Services; all are involved in new construction for corporate and institutional clients. However, they have a special commitment to the adaptive re-use of older buildings, especially in urban markets, and the redevelopment of meaningful communities in the inner city. Recent examples of such redevelopment include:

The Carriage Works and The Block Candy Company Building. These industrial buildings, (circa 1900), which housed the original White Star automobile factory (the first automobile manufactured in Atlanta) and one of Atlanta's first candy companies were renovated into magnificent multi-tenant office buildings.

This involved extensive structural repairs to the brick and wood timber; the roofs and 80% of the interior wood structure had to be replaced. A few additions which were made during the restoration including corridors, fire exits, restrooms, a roof deck and art galleries in the lobbies. The buildings are located at 512 and 530 Means Street near Georgia Tech. The redevelopment costs were approximately $6 million.

The Hotel Roxy Loft Apartments. The Roxy, circa 1921, is a former hotel where businessmen traveling through Atlanta could obtain a room for the night for $1.00. This is indicated by the original sign advertising the hotel which remains painted on the side of the building. The Roxy, a 30,000 sq. ft. brick and wood timber building located at 768 Marietta Street, is just a few steps away from Georgia Tech, and was redeveloped into loft apartments and two restaurants. Redevelopment costs were approximately $3 million.

The Roosevelt. Originally constructed in 1924 to house the Girls High School in Atlanta, the property was renovated in 1989 and presently contains 90 apartment units. Located in Grant Park at 745 Rosalia St., Winter Properties has renovated the gymnasium into 28 loft apartments.

Brumby Chair Factory. A 150,000 sq. ft. brick and heavy wood timber building located in Marietta, Georgia at 111 North Marietta Parkway. ThebBuilding formerly housed the factory which manufactured the oversized Brumby Rocking Chairs.

Winter Properties is renovating the property into 166 loft apartments. The renovation was completed in November, 1995.

The Fulton Cotton Mill. A complex of nine historic buildings located 1.1 miles east of the center of downtown Atlanta. The complex has a total gross floor area of 550,000 sq. ft. on a 12.5 acre site. The buildings were built over a forty year period beginning in 1881 and the mill operated continuously until 1977. The primary product was cotton bags used to package agricultural and industrial products. At its peak, the Mill employed 2,600 workers, housing many of them in an adjacent company-owned village. The mill and village (previously sold to the residents) have been added to the National Register of Historic Places.

Winter Properties plans to redevelop the mill into a community of loft apartments, offices, retail and cultural facilities.

Bass High School. A 166,000 sq. ft. building. It was originally built in 1921 as the Boys High School in Atlanta. The property is located in the heart of Little Five Points. Once renovated, the property will contain 125 loft apartments and 8,000 sq. ft. of office space.

The Winter Group undertakes projects small and large, ranging from $2,500 to $60,000,000. Examples of projects currently under construction are the Olympic Tennis Venue at Stone Mountain, the Cobb County State Courts Building, the Athens-Clarke County Classic Civic Center and numerous sites at Georgia Tech.

Winter contributes five percent of its pretax profits to support the arts in Georgia and has been honored by awards from the Georgia Business Community for the Arts. Such contributions include support for the Atlanta Botanical Gardens, the National Black Arts Festival, the Metropolitan Atlanta Arts Fund and many more.

Bob Silverman, Winter's Chairman, sums up succinctly, *"Our product is buildings. The quality and integrity of our work are apparent and obvious. Because our buildings will reflect our standard of quality for a lifetime and more, the quality of our work must be a source of pride."*

Georgia's Top 100 Corporations by Market Value

Market Value

Rank	Company	(millions)
1	Coca-Cola	$74,164
2	BellSouth	$30,581
3	Home Depot	$20,636
4	Southern Company	$13,623
5	Georgia-Pacific	$7,294
6	SunTrust Banks	$6,348
7	Genuine Parts	$4,890
8	First Financial	$4,549
9	AFLAC	$3,967
10	Turner Broadcasting	$3,549
11	Delta Air Lines	$3,264
12	Coca-Cola Enterprises	$2,907
13	Equifax	$2,494
14	Shaw Industries	$1,814
15	Scientific-Atlanta	$1,797
16	Synovus Financial	$1,388
17	National Service Ind.	$1,380
18	Riverwood International	$1,349
19	HBO & Co.	$1,291
20	Georgia Gulf	$1,271
21	Alumax	$1,232
22	Medaphis	$1,208
23	Bank South	$1,186
24	New World Communications	$1,149
25	Total System Services	$1,066
26	Rollins	$981
27	Atlanta Gas Light	$906

28	AGCO	$752
29	John H. Harland Co.	$697
30	Flowers Industries	$661
31	Atlantic SE Airlines	$611
33	Crawford & Co.	$550
34	WestPoint Stevens	$549
35	Charter Medical	$510
36	Post Properties	$505
37	Cousins Properties	$477
38	Greenfield Industries	$461
39	Caraustar Industries	$456
40	Roper Industries	$413
41	Apple South	$408
42	Mohawk Industries	$381
43	National Data	$359
44	First National Bancorp	$356
45	American Business Products	$289
46	Savannah Foods	$279
47	Scientific Games	$278
48	Interface	$273
49	I.R.T. Property	$238
50	Carmike Cinemas	$201
51	Intermet	$197
52	Friedman's	$182
53	Actava Group	$177
54	Oxford Industries	$172
55	Healthdyne	$155
56	Crown Crafts	$147
57	Healthdyne Technologies	$146
58	Haverty Furniture	$142
59	Aaron Rents	$142
60	Bankers First	$119
61	National Vision Associates	$118
62	Johnston Industries	$111
63	RPC Energy Services	$110
64	Allied Bankshares	$107
65	Rhodes	$107
66	Graphic Industries	$103
67	Cagle's	$100
68	Communications Central	$96
69	Inbrand	$94
70	Roadmaster Industries	$93
71	Republic Waste Industries	$92
72	Maxim Group	$91
73	Golden Poultry	$90
74	LXE	$88
75	Vista Resources	$83
76	Allied Holdings	$80
77	Electromagnetic Sciences	$79

78	Thomaston Mills	$74
79	Anacomp	$74
80	Gray Communications Systems	$74
81	Kuhlman	$74
82	Retirement Care Associates	$74
83	Longhorn Steaks	$73
84	Image Industries	$71
85	American Software	$69
86	Century South Banks	$64
87	Int'l. Murex Technologies	$60
88	Mountasia Entertainment	$59
89	Health Images	$58
90	Harry's Farmers Market	$57
91	IQ Software	$55
92	Immucor	$54
93	CytRx	$48
94	Checkmate Electronics	$46
95	Omni Insurance Group	$46
96	Theragenics	$46
97	First Liberty Financial	$45
98	VSI Enterprises	$43
99	Atlantic American	$42
100	Southern Electronics	$38

Corporate, University and Health Care Employment Opportunities

Before forwarding a resume, call the listed number to check on current openings. Also, Atlanta is chock full of prospective employers. The full-service bookstores generally carry job guides such as *Atlanta Jobs 1995* and *The Atlanta Job Bank*.

AGCO

CEO: Robert Ratliff

770-813-9200. With virtually no capital but a strong management vision, Robert J. Ratliff founded AGCO in 1990. In four years AGCO (NYSE symbol AG) has grown to be the most profitable company in its industry, and is now poised to dominate the global agriculture market. Including AGCO's 1994 acquisition of Massey Ferguson, AGCO is now the biggest name in tractors worldwide with projected sales for 1995 of over $2 billion. Send resume to: AGCO Personnel, 4830 River Green Pkwy., Duluth, GA 30136.

American Cancer Society
VP: Dr. John Seffrin
320-3333. National home office of the nationwide, community-based, voluntary health organization; also has state and local offices in Atlanta. Employs approximately 300 people here. Primarily interested in experienced personnel in, health education, fund raising, information systems and public relations. Send resume to: ACS Human Resources, 1599 Clifton Rd., Atlanta, GA 30329.

American Red Cross
CEO: Roger Svaboda
881-9800. Employs approximately 700 people in the Southern Region. Seeks accountants, nurses, medical technologists and lab technicians. Send resume to: Director of Human Resources, 1955 Monroe Dr., Atlanta, GA 30324.

American Security Group
CEO: Edward O'Hare
261-9000. Dutch-owned credit insurance company, U.S. headquarters in Atlanta employs 775 people. Hires recent college graduates and experienced personnel in all areas. Send resume to: Human Resources, POB 50355, Atlanta, GA 30302.

American Software USA, Inc.
CEO: James Edenfield
264-5599. Atlanta-based corporation that develops, manufactures and markets software for business applications. Employs approximately 600 people. Send resume to: American Software Corporate Recruiting, 470 East Paces Ferry Rd., Atlanta, GA 30305.

Arthur Andersen & Co.
CEO: Robert McCullough
658-1776. Largest CPA firm in Atlanta, providing auditing, computing, accounting, tax

and consulting services. Employs 1,300 people in Atlanta. Hires recent college graduates and experienced personnel. Send resume to: Anderson's Director of Recruiting, 133 Peachtree St., Atlanta, GA 30303.

AT&T
CEO: Bob Allen
800-505-2162. Southern Area Headquarters for long distance services, covering a 18-state territory. Employs approximately 20,000 people in Atlanta. Hires recent college graduates and experienced personnel in all areas and provides a variety of student employment programs, including INROADS, interns, and interns, in engineering, marketing, and computer science. Send resume to: AT&T Management Employment, 1200 Peachtree St., Atlanta, GA 30309.

AT&T Global Information Solutions
VP: Jay Reidenbach
770-623-7000. Designs, develops, and manufactures integrated software and hardware computer systems for retailers. Employs approximately 700 people. Hires recent college graduates mostly engineers and computer science majors. Offers interns and internships in engineering, computer science, and other business-related majors. Send resume to: AT&T Human Resources, 2651 Satellite Blvd, Duluth, GA 30136.

AT&T Network Cable Systems
CEO: J. D. Carboy
770-798-2600. Manufacturing facility producing wire and fiber optics communications cable. Employs approximately 2,700 people. Hires recent college graduates, especially engineers and computer science majors. Seeks experienced personnel for its sales staff. Offers internships in engineering. Send resume to: AT&T Technical and Professional Department, 2000 Northeast Expressway, Norcross, GA 30071.

AT&T Network Systems
CEO: Joe Mauriello

573-4000. Southern Region Headquarters location, with more than 3000 employees here.. Hires recent engineering graduates. Send resume to: AT&T Engineering Technical Associate Staffing, or to Management Staffing, 6701 Roswell Rd., Atlanta, GA 30328.

Atlanta Coca-Cola Bottling Company
CEO: Henry A. Schimberg
770-989-3500. Also functions as Atlanta Region of Coca-Cola Enterprises. Bottles and distributes Coca-Cola brands. Employs approximately 1,800 people here. Hires experienced personnel and recent college graduates for sales, computing, accounting and manufacturing positions. Send resume to: Coca-Cola Human Resources Manager, POB 723040, Atlanta, GA 31139-0040.

Atlanta Gas Light Company
CEO: David Jones
584-4705. Public gas utility headquartered in Atlanta. Employs approximately 2,000 people here. Hires recent college graduates in engineering, computing and accounting. Employs interns in engineering and computer science. Send resume to: AGL Personnel Manager, POB 4569, Atlanta, GA 30302.

Atlanta Journal-Constitution
CEO: Melody Darch
526-5092. Largest newspaper in the Southeast. Employs 7,300 people. Hires recent college graduates in computing and accounting, customer service, and advertising. Journalism experience is a prerequisite for journalism positions. Hires experienced personnel in all areas and interns in journalism. Reportorial personnel should direct their resume to: AJC Managing Editor, Non-reportorial personnel to AJC: Human Resources Department, 72 Marietta St., Atlanta, GA 30303.

Atlantic Steel
CEO: Jeff Webb
897-4500. Steel producer employing 750 people. Hires some recent college graduates, and seeks experienced personnel in all areas. Send resume to: Atlantic Steel's Human Resources Administrator, POB 1714, Atlanta, GA 30301.

BankSouth
CEO: Pat Flinn
529-4111. Corporate headquarters for one of Atlanta's largest banks with 140 branches and employing 3130 people in Atlanta. Hires recent college graduates and experienced personnel. Send resume to: BankSouth Human Resources Department Mail Code 8, POB 5092, Atlanta, GA 30302.

C.R. Bard
CEO: Phillip Ehret
770-784-6100. Urological division headquarters facility that manufactures and markets urological equipment. Employs approximately 500 people. Seeks both recent college graduates and experienced personnel. Send resume to: Division Personnel Manager, 8195 Industrial Blvd., Covington, GA 30209. Send resume to: C.R. Bard Staffing Department, Department 1175, POB 13010, Research Triangle Park, NC 27709.

BellSouth Publishing
CEO: Don Perozzi
770-491-1747. Employs approximately 1,100 people. Hires recent college graduates and experienced personnel. Send resume to: BellSouth Employment Manager, 2295 Park Lake Dr. Suite 490, Atlanta, GA 30345.

BellSouth Cellular
CEO: Stan Hamm
249-5000. Corporate headquarters. Employs approximately 500 people in Atlanta. Hires recent college graduates and experienced personnel. Send resume to: BellSouth Cellular Director of Personnel, 1100 Peachtree St., Atlanta, GA 30309.

BellSouth-Southern Bell
CEO: John Clendenin
770-391-3294. Employs 12,000 people. Seeks marketing graduates for customer serv-

ice positions and communications technicians. Send resume to: BSSB Human Resources, 183 Perimeter Center Pl. Atlanta, GA 30346.

Blue Cross/Blue Shield
CEO: Richard Shirk
842-8060. The nation's largest health care insurer employs approximately 900 people in Atlanta. Hires recent college graduates and experienced personnel. Send resume to: BC/BS Employment Representative, 3350 Peachtree Rd., Atlanta, GA 30326.

Byers Engineering Co.
CEO: Kenneth G. Byers
843-1000. Atlanta-based consulting firm that provides engineering and computer graphics services for major utilities; employs 900 people here. Hires only experienced personnel. Send resume to: Byers Human Resources Manager, 6285 Barfield Rd., Atlanta, GA 30328.

CARE
CEO: Philip Johnston
681-2552. World's largest private international relief and development organization. Employs approximately 225 people. Hires recent college graduates and experienced personnel. Send resume to: CARE Human Resources, 151 Ellis Street, Atlanta, GA 30303.

Centers for Disease Control and Prevention
CEO: Dr. David Satcher
332-4577. Employs approximately 3,500 people in Atlanta. Hires hundreds of scientific and medical research specialists annually, both recent college graduates and experienced personnel. Send resumes to: CDC Employment Services, 1600 Clifton Rd., Atlanta, GA 30333.

Chick-fil-A
CEO: Truett Cathay
765-8127. Corporate headquarters for 620-unit fast food chain. Headquarters staff numbers 200 people. Most openings will be for entry-level personnel. Send resume to: Chick-fil-A Personnel, 5200 Buffington Rd., Atlanta, GA 30349.

CIBA Vision Corporation
CEO: Glen Bradley
770-448-1200. Division headquarters for Ciba-Geigy unit that manufactures, distributes and conducts research/development of soft contact lens and eye care products. Total employment in Atlanta is 2600 people. Hires few recent college graduates. Seeks experienced personnel in numerous specialties, including manufacturing managers, product managers, accountants, sales representatives and research and development scientists. Send resume to: CIBA Staffing, 11460 Johns Creek Pkwy., Duluth, GA 30136-1518.

Coca-Cola Company
CEO: Roberto Goizeuta
676-2662 for a recorded employment message. 676-2665 for information and resume status. Second largest Fortune 500 corporation headquartered in Atlanta, employing 3,500 people here. Hires experienced personnel in such areas as finance, computing and accounting, marketing, and research chemists and engineers. Coke also has an in-house temporary agency, Talent Tree, which staffs more than 500 employees for Coke. Talent Tree's may be reached at 676-4026.

Coca-Cola Enterprises
CEO: Henry A. Schimberg
676-2100. The third largest Fortune 500 company headquartered in Atlanta, and is the world's largest bottler of Coca-Cola brands of soft drinks. Employs 375 people here. Hires experienced personnel in finance, computing and accounting; also in legal, sales, marketing, and purchasing. Send resume to: Coca-Cola Human Resources, POB 723040, Atlanta, GA 31139-0040.

Colonial Pipeline

261-1470. Atlanta-based, nation's largest petroleum pipeline company. Employs approximately 225 people in Atlanta. Hires recent engineering graduate and experienced engineers. Send resume to: Colonial Human Resources, POB 18855, 945 E. Paces Ferry Rd., Atlanta, GA 30326.

Compass Management and Leasing

CEO: Gary Sligar

240-2121. Subsidiary of Equitable Real Estate Investment Management, headquartered in Atlanta. Employs approximately 900 people here. Hires experienced personnel in finance, computing and accounting, property management and commercial real estate. Send resume to: Compass Human Resources Director, 3414 Peachtree Rd. NE, Suite 850, Atlanta, GA 30326.

Coopers & Lybrand

CEO: Bob Bird

870-1100. CPA firm employing 400 people in Atlanta. Hires recent college graduates for its audit staff. Send resume to: Coopers & Lybrand Personnel, 1155 Peachtree St., Atlanta, GA 30309.

Cox Enterprises

CEO: Jim Kennedy

843-5000. Atlanta parent of The Atlanta Journal-Constitution and Cox Cable Communications, it is the third largest U.S. television cable provider. Hires experienced personnel in telephone and cable TV operations. Send resume to: Cox Human Resources, 1400 Lake Hearn Drive, Atlanta, GA 30319.

Crawford and Company

CEO: Forest Minix

847-4080. Provides the insurance and risk management industries with a full-spectrum of claims-related services. The Atlanta headquarters employs 900 people and offers a summer intern program in risk management. Seeks experienced personnel in computing and accounting, finance and risk control. Send resume

to: Crawford Personnel, 5780 Peachtree Dunwoody Rd., Atlanta, GA 30342.

D & B Software

CEO: Douglas MacIntyre

239-2000. Designs and manufactures business software systems. Employs approximately 800 people here. Send resume to: D & B Recruiting, 3445 Peachtree Rd., Atlanta, GA 30326.

Data General Corporation

GM: Ron Edlin

705-2500. This Fortune 500 company manufactures and sells computers and provides systems integration services. Employs approximately 300 people in Atlanta. Hires only experienced sales and systems integration professionals. Send resume to: Data General Human Resources, 4170 Ashford-Dunwoody Rd. Suite 300, Atlanta, Ga 30319.

Deloitte & Touche

CEO: David Passman

220-1500. Third largest CPA firm in Atlanta. Employs approximately 450 people here. Has four divisions: computing and accounting, audit, tax services, and management consulting services. Hires recent computing and accounting graduates. Send resume to: Deloitte & Touche Human Resources, 100 Peachtree St., Atlanta, GA 30303-1943.

Delta Airlines

CEO: Ronald Allen

765-5000. Headquartered in Atlanta and its largest corporate employer. Only experienced personnel are hired as pilots, flight attendants, and reservation agents. Hires many entry level hourly clerical positions as well as trainees in baggage handling and airplane maintenance. Obtain an employment application by calling the number above or visiting any of Delta's numerous ticket offices. Send employment application and resume to: Delta Airlines Personnel, POB 20530, Hartsfield International Airport, Atlanta, GA 30320.

Digital Communications Associates
CEO: James Lindner
770-442-4010. Corporate headquarters for designer, manufacturer, and marketer of software products. Employs approximately 550 people in Atlanta. Send resume to: DCA Employment, 1000 Alderman Dr., Alpharetta, GA 30202.

Digital Equipment Corporation
CEO: Robert Palmer
770-343-0000. World's second largest manufacturer of computers, with 1,100 employees in Atlanta. Hires liberal arts and recent technical graduates and experienced personnel. Send resume to: DEC Employment, 5555 Windward Pkwy. West, Alpharetta, GA 30201-7407. Send resume to: DEC Personnel, POB 45485, Atlanta, GA 30320.

Eckerd Drugs
VP: Bruce Barkus
770-254-4400. Operates 120 retail stores in Atlanta, employing 1,500 people here. This office hires almost entirely for store management. Send resume to: Eckerd Human Resources, 36 Herring Rd., Newnan, GA 30265.

Electromagnetic Sciences
CEO: Dr. Tom Sharon
770-448-5770. Designs, manufactures and sells microwave components and sub-systems. Employs 750 people in Atlanta and hires recent college graduates in engineering and experienced personnel in sales and engineering. Also six co-ops in engineering. Send resume to: ES Human Resources, POB 7700, Norcross, GA 30091.

Emory University/
Emory University Hospital
CEO: William M. Chace
727-7611. Employs approximately 3,775 non-faculty university personnel and 2,800 hospital personnel. Job board postings are available for viewing outside the personnel office. For hospital and university positions, apply in person Monday-Thursday 9:00-4:00.

Send resume to: Emory University Human Resources Department, 1762 Clifton Rd., Atlanta, GA 30322.

Equifax, Inc.
CEO: Charles B. Rogers Jr.
885-8550. Headquartered in Atlanta, Equifax is the nation's largest computer-based information gathering company and employs approximately 3,000 people here. Seeks recent college graduates and experienced personnel in all areas. Send resume to: Equifax Human Resources, POB 4081, Atlanta, GA 30302.

Ernst & Young
CEO: Steven A. Harols
817-5269. A leading professional services firm with global resources of 64,000 people in more than 100 countries, including more than 700 people in its Atlanta office which was established in 1919. Through industry-specific service groups Ernst & Young's client services range from traditional audit and tax services to litigation support and process improvement consulting. In addition to helping their clients achieve their goals, Ernst & Young is actively involved in community enrichment, the firm and its people participating with the Chamber of Commerce, the United Way, the Olympic Opportunities Program, the Woodruff Arts Center and the Atlanta Symphony Orchestra. Send resume to: Ernst & Young Director of Recruiting, 600 Peachtree St., Atlanta, GA 30308.

Federal Reserve Bank of Atlanta
CEO: Robert Forrestal
521-8767. Head office for the Sixth District of the Federal Reserve System, employing over 1,000 people here. Hires recent college graduates and experienced personnel in finance, computing and accounting, business, operations management, audit and banking regulation. Send resume to: FRB Employment, 104 Marietta St., Atlanta, GA 30303-2713.

Federated Systems Group
CEO: Larry Honig

770-448-8900. Information processing division of Federated Department Stores, parent of Atlanta's Rich's Department Stores. Employs approximately 1,400 people here. Send resume to: Federated Personnel, 6801 Governor's Lake Pkwy. Bldg. 200, Norcross, GA 30071.

First Union National Bank of Georgia
CEO: David Carroll
827-7150. Operates 93 branches in the Atlanta area, employing approximately 2,000 people here. Send resume to: First Union Personnel, 999 Peachtree St., Atlanta, GA 30374.

**Ford Motor Company-
Atlanta Assembly Plant 340**
669-1547. This facility assembles Ford Taurus and Mercury Sable cars. Most personnel hiring here is for electrical engineers (trainee and experienced) in manufacturing management, plus some needs in industrial relations. Send resume to: Ford Personnel Office, 340 Henry Ford II Ave., Hapeville, GA 30354.

GTE Personal Communications Services
CEO: Mark Feighner
770-391-8000. Atlanta headquarters of GTE MobilNet employs 1,000 people in Atlanta. Hires mostly experienced personnel in marketing, computing, accounting, and finance, and engineers with concentrations in cellular technology and network operations. Send resume to: GTE Staffing, 245 Perimeter Center Pkwy., Atlanta, GA 30346.

General Electric Computer Services
CEO: Mike Ford
770-246-6200. National headquarters for GE subsidiary that does maintenance, rental and repair of industrial, electrical and test instruments, and computer equipment. Employs approximately 600 people. Most recent college graduates hired are in engineering and computing. Hires experienced personnel in sales and computing. Send resume to: GE Staffing, 6875 Jimmy Carter Blvd., Norcross, GA 30071.

Georgia Institute of Technology
VP: Jerry Dark
894-4592. Third largest university in Georgia and second largest in Atlanta, with 12,000 students and 4,000 employees. Technical and engineering employees should apply to the Georgia Tech Research Institute (see below). This facility seeks office workers, general management, computing and accounting, public relations, public administration, marketing, and finance personnel. No resumes please; apply in person or call for instructions. Georgia Tech Personnel, 955 Fowler St., Atlanta, GA 30332.

Georgia Power Company
CEO: Allen Franklin
526-7655. Largest electric utility in Georgia and a subsidiary of Atlanta's Southern Company (see below). Employs approximately 5,000 people here. Hires recent college graduates with engineering or technical degrees; business positions in the areas of finance, computing and accounting, marketing and management require a business major. Also seeks experienced personnel with technical credentials. Send resume to: Georgia Power Staffing, POB 4545, Atlanta, GA 30302.

Georgia State University
CEO: Dr. Carl V. Patton
651-4270. Georgia's second largest and Atlanta's largest university with more than 20,000 students. Employs approximately 3,300 people. Constant openings but unsolicited resumes are discouraged. Call the above number to learn about current openings or drop in on the Employment Office at University Plaza, 1 Park Place South, Atlanta, GA 30303.

Georgia Tech Research Institute
CEO: Dr. Gerald Clough
894-9412. Operates eight research laboratories. Employs approximately 900 people here. Hires only technical personnel. Accepts applications Monday-Wednesday, 8-5 p.m., or: Send your

resume to: Georgia Tech Human Resources, 955 Fowler St., Atlanta, GA 30332-0435.

Georgia-Pacific Corporation
CEO: A.D. Correll
652-5211. This forest products company, headquartered in Atlanta, is our largest Fortune 500 firm and employs over 3,000 people here. Hires recent college graduates and experienced personnel in many areas including sales, engineering, logistics, transportation and computing. Send resume to: GP Corporate Staffing, 133 Peachtree St., Atlanta, GA 30303.

Grady Health System
616-5627. Atlanta's largest hospital, employing over 6,500 people here. Hires recent college graduates and experienced personnel in computing and accounting, finance, department management and computing. Also seeks many health care specialists. Send resume to: GHS Employment, 80 Butler St., Atlanta, GA 30335.

Hilton Hotels
VP: Jorgen Hansen VP
221-6807. Atlanta's third largest downtown hotel with 1022 rooms and more than 750 employees. Most hiring is for rooms and food and beverage. Apply in person, Monday 9 a.m. to noon or Tuesday 1-4 p.m. Send resume to: Hilton Employment, 255 Courtland St., Atlanta, GA 30303.

Holiday Inn Worldwide
CEO: Bryan Langton
770-604-2000. World's largest motel chain. Headquartered in Atlanta and employing over 1,000 people here. Send resume to: Holiday Inn Employment, 3 Ravinia Dr., Atlanta, GA 30346.

Home Depot
CEO: Bernie Marcus
770-433-8211. Atlanta-based retailer of home improvement and building materials supplies. Operates over 230 stores. Corporate headquarters employs 1,700 people here. Hires recent college graduates and experienced per-

sonnel in computing, buying, merchandising and other people with home building products industry experience. Send resume to: Home Depot Human Resources, 2727 Paces Ferry Rd., Atlanta, GA 30339.

IBM
CEO: William Tom Smith, Jr.
770-835-9000. All hiring for IBM is through its subsidiary Workforce Solutions. Call first; then, Send resume to: Workforce Solutions, 3200 Windy Hill Rd. East Tower, Marietta, GA 30367.

Institute for Strategic Initiatives
VP: Robert L. Copeland
989-2595. A client-oriented consulting firm specializing in strategic planning, long-range planning, and the design, management and audit of information systems and resources. Hires college graduates with graduate degrees in computer and information science and experienced planners and information systems personnel. Send resume to: ISI Human Resources, 2870 Peachtree Rd., # 461, Atlanta, GA 30305.

KPMG Peat Marwick
CEO: Neal Purcell
222-3000. The world's largest computing and accounting firm, KPMG Peat Marwick posts worldwide revenues in excess of $6 billion annually. Established in Atlanta since 1922, it employs over 425 people here. KPMG has three divisions; tax and audit and consulting. Send resume to: KPMG Personnel, 303 Peachtree St., Atlanta, GA 30308.

Kaiser Permanente
CEO: Chris Binkley
233-0555. Nation's largest and Atlanta's largest health maintenance organization (HMO). Regional office here employs over 1,300 people. Kaiser hires recent college graduates and experienced personnel with health care management backgrounds. Send resume to: Kaiser Human Resources, 3495 Piedmont Ave., Atlanta, GA 30305.

Kroger Supermarkets
CEO: Paul Smith
496-7467. Largest supermarket chain in Atlanta. Operates 70 stores in Atlanta area, employing over 15,000 people. Send resume to: Kroger Recruiting, 2175 Parklake Dr., Atlanta, GA 30345.

Lanier Worldwide
CEO: Wesley Cantrell
770-496-9500. Atlanta headquarters sells and services copying systems, fax machines, and dictation systems. Employs approximately 1,000 people here. Send resume to: Lanier Corporate Recruiter, 2300 Parklake Dr., Atlanta, GA 30345.

Law Companies Group
CEO: Bruce Coles
770-396-8000. Atlanta engineering and environmental consulting firm. Employs approximately 1,000 people in Atlanta. Most needs are for engineers and scientists. Send resume to: Law Personnel, 1000 Abernathy Rd., Atlanta, GA 30328.

Lithonia Lighting
CEO: Jim McClung
770-922-9000. Corporate headquarters for the nation's largest lighting firm, manufacturing all types of lighting fixtures for residential, commercial and industrial uses. Employs approximately 1,700 people here. Hires recent college graduates and experienced personnel for corporate and manufacturing functions. Send resume to: Lithonia Human Resources, 1335 Industrial Blvd., Conyers, GA 30307.

Lockheed Aeronautical Systems Company
CEO: John McLellan
770-494-5000. Defense contractor that develops and manufactures aircraft; one of Atlanta's largest employers with 12,000 employees. Seeks recent college graduates and experienced personnel. Has internships in engineering. Send resume to: Lockheed Employment, 86 S. Cobb Dr., Marietta, GA 30063-0530.

MARTA
GM: Richard Simonetta
848-5231. Employs approximately 3,700 people here. Send resume to: MARTA Employment, 2424 Piedmont Ave., Atlanta, GA 30324-3324.

Mobil Chemical Company
CEO: Ed Bates
770-786-5372. Manufactures and sells polyethylene and polystyrene disposable products for consumer, industrial and institutional use. Employs approximately 625 people here, mostly experienced personnel. Send resume to: Mobil Employment, POB 71, Covington, GA 30209.

NAPA Auto Parts
CEO: Paul Scott
770-447-8233. Atlanta distribution center for Atlanta's Genuine Parts Company, an automotive parts distributor and retailer. Employs 475 people here. Seeks management trainees with some business experience. Send resume to: NAPA Personnel, POB 2000, Norcross, GA 30091.

National Data Corporation
CEO: Robert Yellowlees
728-2030. Atlanta data processing company providing data exchange, processing and telecommunications services to a variety of finance and corporate clients. Employs over 1,100 people in Atlanta. Send resume to: NDC Director of Employment, 2 NDC Plaza, Atlanta, GA 30329.

NationsBank
CEO: Hugh McColl
770-491-4530. Fourth largest US bank, headquartered in Charlotte, NC. Atlanta is headquarters for its General Bank Division. Employs approximately 5,000 people in Atlanta. Seeks recent college graduates and experiences personnel. Send resume to: NationsBank Management Recruiting, POB 4899, Atlanta, GA 30302-4899.

Nordson Corporation
CEO: William P. Madar

770-497-3400. North American division headquarters of Ohio's Nordson Corp., a manufacturer of finishing and adhesive application equipment. This office provides marketing and technical support for several Nordson groups. Employs approximately 400 people here. Send resume to: Nordson Manager of Human Resources, 11475 Lakefield Dr., Technology Park/Johns Creek, Duluth, GA 30136.

Norfolk Southern Corporation
GM: T.L. Ingram
529-1300. Employs approximately 1,700 people in Atlanta. Hires recent college graduates and experienced engineers. Send resume to: Norfolk Southern Employment, 125 Spring St., Atlanta, GA 30303.

Northern Telecom Atlanta
Sr. VP: Dianne Napier-Wilson
1-800-676-4636. Atlanta telecommunications company, employing over 700 people here. Hires mostly electrical engineers and business personnel. Send resume to: Northern Telecom Staffing, 40001 E. Chapel Hills, Nelson Hwy., Research Triangle Park, NC 27709.

Northwest Georgia Health System
CEO: Bernard Brown
770-793-7070. Formed in 1993 by merging of Kennestone Hospital and two smaller hospitals. The four-hospital system now employs over 5,500 people here. Send resume to: NGHS Human Resources, 677 Church St., Marietta, GA 30060.

Oglethorpe Power
CEO: T.D. Kilgore
770-270-7600. Nation's largest power generation and transmission cooperative. Employs approximately 550 people here. Hires mostly experienced computer and engineering personnel. Send resume to: Oglethorpe Human Resources, 2100 East Exchange Place, Tucker, GA 30085-1349.

Price Waterhouse
CEO: John H. Cary

658-1800. Their three divisions tax, audit and consulting employ about 400 people in Atlanta. They seek recent computing and accounting graduates and MBA's. Send resume to: Price Waterhouse Human Resources, 50 Hurt Plaza, Suite 1700, Atlanta, GA 30303.

Primerica Finance Services
CEO: Joe Plumeri
770-564-6100. Sells term-life insurance and mutual funds. Employs approximately 1,300 people here. Seeks recent college graduates and experienced personnel in computing and accounting, management, journalism, and liberal arts. Send resume to: Primerica Corporate Recruiter, 3120 Breckinridge Blvd., Duluth, GA 30199-0001.

RaceTrac Petroleum, Inc.
CEO: Carl Bolch Jr.
770-431-7600. Corporate headquarters for gasoline/convenience store retailer. Employs 2,200 people here. Send resume to: RaceTrac Personnel, POB 105035, Atlanta, GA 30348.

Rich's Department Stores
CEO: Russell Stravitz
770-913-5176. Corporate headquarters for one of the largest department store in Atlanta. Employs approximately 5,600 people here. Send resume to: Rich's Executive Recruitment, 223 Perimeter Center Pkwy., Atlanta, GA 30346.

Riverwood International
CEO: Thomas Johnson
770-644-3000. Manufacturer of paperboard and coated board products. Employs 300 people in its Atlanta corporate headquarters. Seeks recent college graduates and experienced personnel are needed in all corporate support functions, including office staff and computer systems. Send resume to: Riverwood Corporate Staffing, 3350 Cumberland Circle, Atlanta, GA 30339.

Robinson-Humphrey Company
CEO: Jerome Sand Jr.
266-6656. Full-service finance services firm

headquartered in Atlanta. Employs approximately 600 people in Atlanta. Send resume to: RHC Human Resources, 3333 Peachtree Rd., Atlanta, GA 30326.

Rollins, Inc.
CEO: Gary Rollins
888-2125. Corporate headquarters for diversified service corporation. Employs approximately 500 people in Atlanta. Seeks recent college graduates, computer personnel and headquarters staffers. Send resume to: Rollins Human Resources Department, 2170 Piedmont Ave., Atlanta, GA 30324.

Rosser International
CEO: Paul Rosser
876-3800. One of Atlanta's largest architectural/engineering firms, employing 350 people here. Hires both recent college graduates and experienced personnel. Send resume to: Rosser Human Resources, 524 W. Peachtree St., Atlanta, GA 30308.

SITA
VP: George Franco
770-612-4866. French telecommunications and data processing company. Employs 350 people in Atlanta. Hires mostly experienced personnel. Send resume to: SITA Human Resources, 310 Cumberland Circle, Atlanta, GA 30339.

Safeco Insurance Company
VP: William T. Lebo
770-498-3142. Major insurance company employing 320 people in Atlanta. Hires recent college graduates. Send resume to: Safeco Personnel, POB A, Stone Mountain, GA 30086.

Sales Technologies
CEO: Ron Brown
841-4000. Designs, develops, installs, markets, and supports software to improve sales force productivity. Employs approximately 400 people in Atlanta. Mires mostly experienced systems and sales personnel. Send

resume to: ST Human Resources, 3399 Peachtree Rd., Atlanta, GA 30326.

Scientific Atlanta
CEO: James McDonald
770-903-5000: Manufacturer of remote sensing ground stations and support equipment and supplier of electronic instruments and control systems for telecommunications, industrial, and government applications. Employs approximately 200 people here, mostly engineers. Hires recent college graduates and experienced personnel. Send resume to: SA Human Resources Director, 1 Technology Pkwy. South. Norcross, GA 30092.

Siemens-Systems Division
CEO: Tom Malott
770-740-3000. Manufacturers variable speed drives, programmable control products, industrial systems, and power systems. Employs approximately 550 people here, mostly engineers, both recent college graduates and experienced. Send resume to: Siemans Human Resources, 100 Technology Dr., Alpharetta, GA 30202.

Simons-Eastern Consultants
CEO: Harry Waterbor
370-3200. Atlanta consultants specializing in the design of industrial manufacturing facilities. Employs approximately 600 people in Atlanta, mostly experienced engineers and designers. Has co-op program for engineering students. Send resume to: Simons Personnel, POB 1286, Atlanta, GA 30301.

SmithKline Beecham
Clinical Laboratories
GM: Larry Morris
770-621-7450. Largest clinical laboratory in the world. Employs approximately 1,000 people in Atlanta. Most needs are for certified medical technologists and technicians. Send resume to: SmithKline Personnel, 1777 Montreal Circle, Tucker, GA 30084.

Snapper

CEO: Jerry Schweiner

770-954-2500: Atlanta manufacturer of outdoor power equipment. Employs approximately 1,450 people here. Hires recent college graduates and experienced personnel in all areas. Send resume to: Snapper Personnel, POB 777, McDonough, GA 30253.

Solvay Pharmaceuticals

CEO: David Dodd

770-578-9000. Clinical research and development center for major pharmaceutical firm. Employ 40 people in Atlanta, mostly those with experience in pre-clinical and clinical research. Send resume to: Solvay Human Resources, 901 Sawyer Rd., Marietta, GA 30062.

Southern Company Services

CEO: William Dahlberg

770-668-3464. Provides engineering, information resources, office and administrative services to subsidiaries. Employs approximately 1,200 people in Atlanta. Hires recent college graduates and experienced personnel. Send resume to: Southern Company Human Resources, 64 Perimeter Center East, Atlanta, GA 30346.

SouthTrust Bank of Georgia

CEO: Thomas Coley

770-951-4010. Alabama bank that operates 86 branches in Atlanta and employs 1,200 people in Georgia. Hires recent college graduates and experienced banking personnel. Send resume to: SouthTrust Human Resources, 2000 RiverEdge Pkwy., Atlanta, GA 30328.

Southwire

CEO: Roy Richards

770-832-4242. Corporate headquarters for the nation's largest wire maker. Employs approximately 2,500 people in Atlanta. Hires college graduates and experienced personnel in all areas. Send resume to: Southwire Employment, 1 Southwire Dr., Carrollton, GA 30119.

Sprint Corporation

VP: Allen Tothill

770-859-8397. The third largest long distance telephone carrier employs 2,000 in Atlanta. Seeks people with experience in telecommunications, large computer systems, as well as the sale and marketing of such systems. Send resume to: Sprint Staffing, 3100 Cumberland Circle, Atlanta, GA 30339.

SunTrust Services

CEO: Tom Ash

588-8877. SunTrust's computer system division handles programming operations for SunTrust Banks. Employs 230 people in Atlanta. Send resume to: SunTrust Employment, 250 Piedmont Ave., Atlanta, GA 30302.

Super Discount Markets

CEO: Preston Slayden

770-732-6800. Corporate headquarters for 13 Georgia supermarkets. Employs approximately 1,900 people in Georgia. Hires recent college graduates and experienced supermarket personnel. Send resume to: SDM Human Resources, 420 Thornton Rd. Suite 103, Lithia Springs, GA 30057.

TBS-Cable News Network

CEO: Robert E. Turner

827-1500. Operates a 24-hour cable news gathering organization, which includes CNN, CNN Headline News, CNN International, CNN Airport Network, and CNN radio, and employs 1,600 people in Atlanta. Hires many recent college graduates for entry level positions. Applicants seeking on-air or correspondent positions need 5-7 years of television experience. Send resume to: CNN Human Resources, 1 CNN Center, POB 105366, Atlanta, GA 30348-5366.

TBS-Corporate Headquarters

CEO: Robert E. Turner

No information is given by phone. TBS employs 2,200 people in Atlanta. Hires experienced personnel in TV sales and computing. Send resume to: TBS Human Resources, 1 CNN Center, POB 105366, Atlanta, GA 30348-5366.

TBS-Turner Network Television (TNT) and (WTBS)

CEO: Robert E. Turner

No information is given by phone. TNT is the entertainment cable operation and WTBS is SuperStation Channel 17; combined employment in Atlanta is 450 people. Hires recent college graduates or other entry-level personnel with TV intern experience, especially in the entertainment sector. Offers non-salaried internships to college juniors and seniors. Send resume to: TBS Human Resources, 1050 Techwood Dr., Atlanta, GA 30318.

Transus

CEO: Blanton Winship

627-7331. Southeastern common carrier and transportation service headquartered in Atlanta. Employs approximately 800 people here. Hires recent college graduates and experienced personnel. Send resume to: Transcus Employment, 2090 Jonesboro Rd., Atlanta, GA 30315.

SunTrust Banks

CEO: James B. Williams

588-7199. The largest bank holding company headquartered in Georgia; assets in excess of $43 billion make it the 20th largest in the nation. Through its principal subsidiaries, SunBanks, Trust Company of Georgia and Third National, SunTrust operates some 658 full-service banking offices and employs over 5,000 people in Atlanta. Recent college graduates may enter one of several training programs. Experienced personnel are hired in all areas. Send resume to: SunTrust Employment Manager, POB 4418 Mail Code 19, Atlanta, GA 30302.

United Parcel Service

CEO: Kent Nelson

770-662-3451: UPS is headquartered in Atlanta and employs 2,100 people here. For entry-level positions, including part-time seasonal, UPS hires extensively through the Georgia Department of Labor's Smyrna and Decatur offices. Experienced personnel should call the employment number above. Send resume to: UPS Human Resources, POB 468568, Atlanta, GA 30346.

Upton's Department Stores

CEO: David Layne

770-662-2500. Headquartered in Atlanta, this apparel chain operates 34 stores in the Southeast; thirteen in Atlanta. Upton seeks both recent college graduates and experienced personnel. Send resume to: Upton's Executive Recruitment, 6251 Crooked Creek Rd., Norcross, GA 30092.

Uxor Press

CEO: Bob Zimmerman

989-2595. Publisher specializing in Southeastern topics and memorabilia. Hires recent college graduates and experienced publishing personnel. A limited number of internships are available for English, marketing and business majors. Send resume to: Uxor Press Human Resources, 541 Tenth St., #161, Atlanta, GA 30318.

WSB-TV

CEO: Gregory Stone

897-7000. Subsidiary of Atlanta's Cox Enterprises, operates TV Channel 2 (ABC), radio AM-750 and FM-98.5. Employs approximately 190 people in Atlanta. Broadcast applicants must have prior experience and should apply directly to their specific area of experience. Also hires several interns for summer and school year programs; internship applicants must be enrolled in a college broadcast or journalism program. Send resume to: WSB Employment, 1601 W. Peachtree St., Atlanta, GA 30309.

Wachovia Bank Of Georgia

CEO: Joseph Prendergast

332-5000. Employs approximately 5,400 people in Georgia. Hires recent college graduates and experienced personnel for all areas of the bank; management training classes begin in June. Send resume to: Wachovia Management Recruiting, 191 Peachtree St., Atlanta, GA 30303.

Winn-Dixie Supermarkets
CEO: J.R. Pownall
346-2400. Division office for second largest supermarket chain in Atlanta. Send resume to: Winn-Dixie Human Resources, 5400 Fulton Industrial Blvd., Atlanta, GA 30336.

Winter Group of Companies
CEO: Robert L. Silverman
588-3300. With headquarters in Atlanta, the Winter Group consists of Winter Construction, Winter Properties and Winter Environmental Services. This growing organization, numbering over 200 people, seeks experienced project managers, project engineers, office and accounting staff, marketing and business developers, safety officers, schedulers, field engineers and project superintendents. Send resume to: Winter Group Employment, 530 Means St., Atlanta, GA 30318-5730.

Wolf Camera And Video
CEO: Charles R. Wolf
633-9000. Atlanta headquarters for the largest camera retailer in the Southeast; operating about 175 stores in 11 states. Employs approximately 550 people in Atlanta. Hires experienced accountants and corporate staff. Send resume to: Wolf Personnel, 1706 Chantilly Dr., Atlanta, GA 30324.

Worldspan Travel Agency Information Services
CEO: Michael A. Buckman
770-563-7400. World's second-largest travel reservations system, headquartered in Atlanta. Employs over 2,000 people here. Send resume to: Worldspan Human Resources, 300 Galleria Pkwy., Atlanta, GA 30339.

Zep Manufacturing Company
CEO: Harry Maziar
352-1680. A subsidiary of Atlanta's National Service Industries, Zep manufactures and sells specialty chemicals and employs approxi-

mately 450 people in its Atlanta headquarters. Send resume to: Zep Employment, 1310 Seaboard Industrial Blvd., Atlanta, GA 30318.

Fun Facts:

- Coca-Cola designed its famous trademark here in 1914 and in 1995 was one of six winners of the America's Corporate Conscience Award for its extensive support, through pro-active job recruitment programs for minorities, youth and women

- The Lockheed aircraft manufacturing facility in Marietta is the largest, under a single roof, in the world.

SECTION V
Metro Atlanta
Cultural Attractions And Organizations

Major Family Attractions, Kidstuff, Plan Ahead Calendar of Annual Festivals and Events. Art Galleries, Bookstores, Colleges and Universities, Private Secondary Schools, Acting Schools, Arts and Crafts Schools, Cooking Schools, Dance Schools, Travel Schools, Summer Camps and Programs, Theaters, Ethnic Atlanta, Foreign Consulates, Ethnic Cultural Associations and Music at the Clubs.

Commentary

Metro Atlanta is overflowing with a rich diversity of cultural resources. If you visited a different resource each day of the year, you would not ever need to visit the same place twice. There are just zillions of outstanding choices, from the great festivals and attractions, to the wondrous museums, art centers and galleries, to the many browse-worthy bookstores and libraries, to the manifold concerts and theaters, to the outstanding universities, colleges and professional art, dance, acting, travel, vocational, cooking and crafts schools.

Major Family Attractions

As many Atlanta attractions have varied admission fees and days and hours of operation, it is always best to call before you depart. Our admission fee listings for attractions, as below, attempts to show the range of variance. Certain attractions, which usually charge an admission fee, do, on occasion, have free admission.

American Adventures. Marietta (I-75 north, exit 113). 250 N. Cobb Pkwy. Designed for families with children under 12 years of age, the 10-acre amusement park features a giant slide, go-carts, miniature golf, rides and a penny arcade. 770-424-9283. Adm: $4.99-$12.99.

APEX Museum. Downtown. Sweet Auburn Historical District at 135 Auburn Ave. Established in 1978, **APEX** is short for the African American Panoramic Experience, a tangible tour of Black history encompassing both triumphs and tragedies. See a model of Georgia's first black-owned drugstore and local history videos at the Trolley Theater. Adm: $2.00-free. 521-APEX.

Atlanta Botanical Garden. Midtown, Piedmont Ave. at The Prado. Resplendent natural beauty abounds at the Dorothy Chapman Fuqua Conservatory, a 16,000 sq. ft. glass building, which houses a dazzling array of endangered tropical plants and arid-climate succulents such as palms, cycads, ferns, orchids and epiphytes (air plants). The outdoor gardens encompass 15 acres of ornamental displays and the **Upper Woodland** and **Storza Woods** contain many acres of serene forest ambiance. Become a member and receive many benefits including free admission, discounts on classes and purchases, the Garden's quarterly newsletter and invitations to member-only parties. Lunch by **Masterpiece Catering** is served from April to October and there is a 24-hour Plant Hotline that anyone with a plant question may call free (888-GROW). Adm: $6.00-Free. 876-5858.

Atlanta Celebrity Walk. Downtown, Chamber of Commerce Plaza at 235 International Blvd. Street inlays honoring famous Atlantans including Hank Aaron, Jimmy Carter, Ray Charles, Bobby Jones and Martha Mitchell. Adm: Free. 586-8550.

Atlanta College of Art Gallery. Midtown. 1280 Peachtree St. Adm: Free. 898-1157.

Atlanta-Fulton County Library. Downtown. One Margaret Mitchell Sq. Atlanta's central library featuring Margaret Mitchell memorabalia and an extensive collection of rare books. Adm: Free. 730-1700.

Atlanta History Center. Buckhead. 130 W. Paces Ferry Rd. Volumes from the past unfold before your eyes at one of the country's largest history museums (83,000 sq. ft.) offering many special programs throughout the year. The museum honors Atlanta's cultural diversity with its splendid permanent exhibit entitled, **"Metropolitan Frontiers: Atlanta 1835-2000."** Rounding out the Center are two historic National Register houses, beautiful period gardens and a research library. Special features include the Tullie Smith Farm (circa 1840), **Swan Woods Trail and Swan House** (circa 1928). Memberships available. Adm: $7.00-free. 814-4000.

Atlanta International Museum. Downtown. 285 Peachtree Center Ave. International crafts and artifacts. Adm: $3.00-free. 688-AIMS.

Atlanta Motor Speedway. Hampton (30 miles south on U.S. 19/41). NASCAR racing. Twice yearly in March and November. Adm: Varies. 770-707-7970.

Atlanta Ballet, Opera and Symphony Orchestra. Midtown. Woodruff Arts Center. In 1988 Yoel Levi was named the orchestra's third music director in its 47-year history. The master season (over 200 performances) runs from September to May and includes an abundance of special subscription series. There is the Young Performers Series (4 concerts), the Champagne Series (6 concerts), the Coffee Series (6 concerts) and the Family Series (3 concerts). There are also numerous special events and holiday concerts including Saturday Matinee Samplers, Halloween Family Concerts, Kids' Christmas Family Concerts, Gospel Christmas and a New Year's Eve Concert. Adm: Varies. 733-4800.

Atlanta State Farmers Market. Forest Park. One of the world's largest. I-75 south to exit 78. Adm: Free. 366-6910.

Big Shanty Museum. Kennesaw. 2829 Cherokee St. Civil War memorabilia, featuring the steam locomotive "The General" used in the movies "The Great Locomotive Chase" and the "Little Red Caboose." Recently donated by Norfolk and Southern RR and renovated by neighborhood Eagle Scouts. Adm: $3.00-$1.50. 770-427-2117.

Bulloch Hall. Roswell. Circa 1840 antebellum mansion of Theodore Roosevelt's mother Mattie Bulloch. Memorabilia depicting the lives of the Bulloch and Roosevelt families. 770-992-1731.

Callanwolde Fine Arts Center. Midtown. 980 Briarcliff Rd. Originally the home of Charles Howard Candler, son of Coca-Cola founder Asa Candler. The 1920 Tudor-style mansion is now a major arts and cultural center for visual and performing artists. Features concerts, recitals, dance, poetry readings, drama productions and children's productions by guest artists and Callanwolde's affiliate groups: the Poetry Committee, Young Singers of Callanwolde, Southern Order of Storytellers, Apprentice Dance Company, and the Community Concert Band. There are also classes, cultural activities, special events and volunteer opportunities. 872-5338. Adm: Free to the center itself. Certain events may charge fees.

Carter Presidential Center, Library and Museum. Downtown. N. Highland and Cleburne Aves. Even Republicans are welcome at this 30-acre landscaped compound replete with a Japanese garden and two lakes. A handsome museum and library feature the presidency of Jimmy Carter, the 39th President of the United States.

Museum visitors may tour the Oval Office, observe a state dinner, attend a White House concert and ask questions of President Carter via a computer-simulated town meeting. Other specific exhibits portray highlights of the Carter presidency, including normalization of relations with China and the Camp David Accords. Library visitors may peruse 27 million pages of White House documents together with numerous photos and video-tapes.

The Carter Presidential Center also houses the offices of the Task Force for Child Survival, Global 2000, the Carter Center of Emory University, and a restaurant. 331-3942. Adm: $4.00.

Centennial Olympic Park/. Downtown. Designated "the gathering place" for the Olympic experience. A 21-acre park built specifically to serve as a welcome and rest area for Olympic visitors. The park will house a temporary 8,000 seat amphitheater that will feature outstanding entertainers and the Olympic Park Superstore where one and all can purchase Olympic memorabilia. Additionally, the Park will host the Festival of the American South, a multi-cultural, multi-media presentation of life in the South.

Coca-Cola Olympic City is designed to complement **Olympic Park** and lies adjacent to it on 12 acres bounded by Simpson and Baker Sts. on the north and south and Techwood and Hull Sts. on the east and west. The sharing of the glory of the Olympic experience is the guiding design concept for this unprecedented attraction. Visitors will compete, one-on-one, with Olympic athletes, be coached by Olympic coaches, score Olympic performances and meet and receive autographs and photos from Olympic athletes.

Center for Puppetry Arts. Downtown. 1404 Spring St. at 18th St. Puppetry prevails with fine performances of Jack and the Beanstalk, Sleeping Beauty, The Velveteen Rabbit, Mr. Ugg Caveman, Raccoon Tails, Little Red Riding Hood, Starry Starry Night and Peter Rabbit. Also see the puppet displays and attend the workshops. 873-3391. Adm: $5.75-$2.00.

Chattahoochee Outdoor Center. 1990 Island Ford Pkwy. Rafting, canoeing and kayaking on the Chattahoochee River. 770-395-6851.

Chattahoochee Nature Center. Roswell (Georgia 400 to Northridge exit). 9135 Willeo Rd. Nestled along the quiet banks of the Chattahoochee River is a place that time forgot. Hear the cries of the native kingfisher rise above the secluded marsh laden with dancing cattails. Try the "Tuesday Evening Float" along the Chattahoochee (May-October, $15.00) and meet the river wildlife (otter, beaver, turtles, herons, and waterfowl) while canoeing down the river with a staff naturalist as your guide. Or pop in to visit the nature trails, ponds, a small habitat. 770-992-2055. Memberships available. Adm: $2.00-$1.00.

CNN Center and Studio Tour. Downtown. Marietta St. at Techwood Dr. MARTA to the Omni Station. Experience first hand the highly-charged environment of the world's foremost news service in action. Watch news in the making at CNN and Headline News where you'll see editors, producers, technicians, writers and on-air journalists pool their talents to produce round-the-clock news coverage every day. Then visit the Superstation TNT, the Cartoon Network and the TBS collection of film classics. 827-2300. Adm: $7.00-$4.50.

Confederate Cemetery. Marietta. Goss St. and Powder Springs Rd. The graves of over 3,000 Southern Civil War soldiers. Adm: Free.

Crawford W. Long Museum. Downtown. 550 Peachtree St. Medical instruments used by the first doctor to use anesthesia. 686-2631. Adm: Free.

Cyclorama. Near Downtown, next to ZooAtlanta in Grant Park at the corner of Georgia and Cherokee Avenues. Step into the pages of history. The Civil War, particularly the Battle of Atlanta, is portrayed in a vast 106-year-old cylindrical painting, which measures 358 ft. in circumference and is 42 ft. high. The total area covered is 15,030 sq. ft; approximately the size of a football field. 624-1071. Adm: $5.00-free.

DeKalb County Historical Society Museum. Decatur at Old Courthouse Sq. Exhibits of Indian and pioneering life, the Cival War and railroading. Adm: Donations accepted. 373-1088.

Discovery Zone. Two locations. Duluth. 923-8889. Marietta. 770-565-5699. Giant playgrounds for age 12 and under featuring obstacle courses, spider walks, monkey bars, trapezes, arcade games, etc. Adm: $5.00-$1.50.

Dixieland Fun Park. Fayetteville. Three go-cart tracks, indoor miniature golf, a large arcade, skee ball, kiddie bumper boats, and a bungee jump. 770-461-9941.

Ebenezer Baptist Church. Downtown. 407-413 Auburn Ave. 100 years of history are manifest in the original pulpit and sanctuary. 688-7263. Adm: Donations appreciated.

Federal Reserve Bank Monetary Museum. Downtown. 104 Marietta St. A history of the evolution of currency in America. See rare gold coins and a 227 lb. gold bar worth over $160,000. Adm: Free. 521-8747.

Fernbank Museum of Natural History, Science Center with Planetarium and Forest. Decatur.

Fernbank Forest. A 65-acre home to hardwood trees (poplars, oaks, pines, beech), shrubs, wildflowers and over 120 species of birds, amphibians and reptiles. Weekday mornings on the two-mile trail are reserved for school field trips. But don't fret, each weekday afternoon (2p.m. to 5p.m.) is set aside for free public use.

Fernbank Museum of Natural History. A superb ediface for the many permanent exhibits that include: "A Walk Through Time in Georgia" portraying the beauty of Georgia and the chronological development of the earth; "Origin of the Universe" examines the big bang theory on a large screen in the Cosmos Theater; "Dinosaur Hall" houses seven lifesize relics of the cretaceous, jurassic and triassic eras; "Okefenokee Swamp Gallery" offers swamp delights; "Spectrum of the Senses" offers 65 handsome exhibits. There is also an IMAX Theater with a huge 3D screen (separate charge). 378-0127. Adm: $5.50-free.

Fernbank Science Center. Home to the Cherry Memorial Planetarium (one of the largest in the country) and its 36" reflecting telescope. There are also many science exhibits including an Apollo Six Command Module, Georgia tektites and meteorites. 378-4311. Adm: $2.00-$1.00.

Fox Theater. Downtown. 660 Peachtree St. Many thanks to the concerned citizens who in 1978 saved the fabulous Fox from certain demolition. Now an Atlanta landmark, this gigantic theatre hosts almost every entertainment imaginable. Ticket prices vary per event. 881-1977. Tour Adm: $5.00-$3.00. The Fox is neatly surrounded with great eateries such as **Mary Mac's** (Nearby on Ponce de Leon), **Adams at the Fox** (on the Corner), **Alon's** and **Basta** (across the street in the Georgian Terrace Hotel), **Pasta da Pulcinella** at 1027 Peachtree St., and, last but not least, **Nikolai's Roof** atop the Hilton. These restaurants are all included in our **"Nifty-Fifty Reviews," see Section IX, Atlanta's Finest Restaurants.**

Georgia Department of Archives and History. Downtown. 330 Capitol Ave. State records and maps dating from the 1700s. Free. 666-2393.

Georgia State Capitol Building. Downtown. Capitol Hill at Washington St. Dedicated in 1889, of classic renaissance design, it incorporates oolitic limestone as its chief exterior material. The famous gold dome was originally 43 ounces of 23 carat Dahlonega gold (since supplemented), crafted into 100,000 3 1/8" veneers. Inside, find paintings and marble busts of many historical figures such as Oglethorpe, Washington, Franklin, Jackson, Hill, Toombs, Jefferson, and Lafayette. Adm: Free. 223-9200.

Georgia Governor's Mansion. Buckhead. 391 W. Paces Ferry Rd. A 30-room Greek revival styled plantation home, furnished with 19th-century paintings and porcelain, and a fine collection of furniture from the federalist period. Call for the time of the guided tour. Adm: Free. 261-1776.

Georgia World Congress Center/Georgia Dome. Downtown. 102,000 sq. ft. of exhibition space, 80 meeting rooms, a 1,740 seat auditorium and nine restaurants seating 1,900 people make it one of the largest such facilities in the country. 223-4636.

Gwinnett History Museum. Lawrenceville Female Seminary. 455 Perry St. Gwinnett County artifacts. Memorabilia from the 1890 Atlanta Exposition, county schools and farms. 770-822-5178. Adm: Free.

Hammonds House. Downtown. 503 Peeples St. A beautiful Victorian house and gardens where opportunies abound to learn about art and meet artists. The "Backyard Symposium Series" develops issues related to art and life for black Americans. Kwanzaa and Juneteenth celebrations affirm the special values and traditions of the African American community. Memberships available. 752-8730. Adm: $2.00-$1.00.

Herndon Home. Downtown. 587 University Place. An elegant symbol of black achievement. Now a museum, Herndon Home was the residence of Alonzo Franklin Herndon, born into slavery, then founder of the Atlanta Life Insurance Company. Built in 1910, the 15-room mansion is a fine example of the Beaux Arts classical style. The Norris B. Herndon Foundation, which owns and operates the museum, continues the family's philanthropic tradition. 581-9813. Adm: Donation-free. 581-9813.

High Museum of Art. Midtown. 1280 Peachtree St. A 135,000 sq. ft. award-winning building designed by Richard Meier. The permanent collections are home to over 10,000 artworks (including American works by Stuart, Durand, Bierstadt, Bellows, Hassam, the Harts, Richards, Haseltine, Hill, Davies, Marin and Hopper; and European works by Bellini, Carpaccio, Breughel, Battista, Tiepolo, Monet, Riemenschneider and Rodin). Also many, many special shows, events and seminars. Adm: $6.00-free. 892-HIGH.

High Museum at Georgia Pacific Center. Downtown. 133 Peachtree St. Traveling exhibits from the High Museum. Adm: Free. 577-6940.

High Museum of Art, Folk and Photographic Galleries. 30 John Wesley Dobbs Ave. Admission-Free. 577-6940.

Johnny Mercer Exhibit. Downtown. 100 Decatur St. The composer's memorabilia. Adm: Free. 651-2476.

Lake Lanier Islands. See also Lake Lanier Islands in Section XIV, Traveling Georgia's Northeast Mountains. Buford. An aquatic wonderland, 45 parks, two golf courses and two hotels occupy the land surrounding this 38,000-acre man-made lake. Year-round you can find everything from cardboard boat races to beach concerts. Boat rental 770-932-7277; camping and picnicking 770-932-7270; beach and water park 770-932-7200; golf 770-945-8787; group outings. Adm: Varies. 770-932-7277.

Martin Luther King, Jr. Birth Home. Downtown at 501 Auburn Ave. Adm: Free. 331-3920.

Martin Luther King, Jr.Center for Non-Violent Social Change. 449 Auburn Ave. 524-1956.Adm: Free.

Margaret Mitchell House. Midtown at Peachtree and 10th Sts. (Fire damaged:restoration is proceeding).

> *"Scarlett had always liked Atlanta...Like herself, the town was a mixture of the old and new in Georgia, in which the old often came off second best in its conflicts with the self-willed and vigorous new."*
>
> — *Margarett Mitchell, from "Gone With the Wind"*

Michael C. Carlos Museum. Emory University. 571 S. Kilgo St. A 45,000 sq. ft. building designed by internationally-renowned architect Michael Graves is home to the permanent collection of over 12,000 pieces from Egypt, Greece, Rome, the Near East, the Americas, Asia, Africa and Oceania. The time frame ranges from the Middle Ages to the 20th-century. Adm: $3.00 suggested donation. 727-4282.

Oakland Cemetery. 248 Oakland Avenue. Marvel at the beauty of John McNamara's ubiquitous angel (an emissary of God confirming life after death). Then visit graves of Margaret Mitchell, golf legend Bobby Jones, and many others in a setting of gothic revival architecture, among neo-classical style mausolea, religious, secular and botanical sculptures and beautiful stained glass on 88 rolling, landscaped acres. Oakland was Atlanta's first public park. Adm: $3.00-$1.00. 688-2107.

Olympic Experience Downtown at Underground Atlanta. Exhibits, Olympic collectibles, and merchandise for the 1996 Centennial Olympic Games. 658-1996. Adm: Free.

Outdoor Activity Center. Downtown. Three miles southwest. 1442 Richland Rd. A natural science research library, 26-acre forest and live animals. Adm: $3.00. 752-5385.

Rhodes Hall. Midtown. 1516 Peachtree St. A 90-year-old Romanesque style castle built as a residence for the Amos G. Rhodes family. One of the finest existing interiors from the late Victorian period. 881-9980. Adm: $2.00.

Road to Tara Museum. Midtown. 659 Peachtree St. at the **Georgian Terrace Hotel**. Road to Tara was the first title Margaret Mitchell gave to "Gone With the Wind." Memorabilia from around the world honoring the memory of a "true lady of the old South." 897-1939. Adm: $5.00.

SciTrek-Science and Technology Museum. Downtown. 395 Piedmont Ave. Georgia's interactive science and technology center. With over 150 permanent exhibits to help you explore light and color, simple machines, perception and illusion, mathematics and emerging technologies. 522-5500. Adm: $7.50-free.

Six Flags Over Georgia Theme Park. Mableton (I-20, 20 miles west). Roller coaster country and other thrilling family rides, water adventures, restaurants and shows. The Viper (the newest addition to the fleet) accelerates from zero to 57 mph in less than six seconds and then sends riders through a 70-degree incline—only to repeat the journey backwards. Over 100 attractions spread over 331 acres. 770-948-9290. Adm: $26.00-$13.00.

Southeastern Railway Museum. Duluth. 3966 Buford Hwy. Railroading collection—locomotives, freight cars, etc. 770-476-2013.

Stately Oaks. Jonesboro. 100 Carriage Lane and Jodeco Rd. A plantation home, circa 1839, and other historically interesting buildings. 770-473-0197. Adm: $5.00-$4.50.

Stone Mountain Park. Stone Mountain. Hwy. 78. Enormously popular with 3,200 acres of hiking trails, golf courses and restaurants. Stone Mountain is the world's greatest mass of exposed granite and host of many festivals and exhibitions including:

- Laser Show (summers)
- Scenic Railroad
- Antique Auto and Music Museum
- Antebellum Plantation
- Confederate Hall
- Memorial Hall

Adm: Daily parking $6.00. Annual parking $25.00. Attractions are $3.50-$2.50. Campsites $17.00-$15.00. 770-498-5702.

Underground Atlanta. Downtown. Wall St., Central Ave., Martin Luther King, Jr. Dr. and Peachtree St. A 12-acre urban market and entertainment center with over 150 shops, restaurants and night spots. Visit the 18 historic sites and markers that help make a visit to Underground Atlanta an unforgettable experience. 523-2311. Adm: Free.

Welcome South Visitors Center Downtown at 200 Spring St., and International Blvd. Spanking new with all sorts of information and services for visitors and businesses, including a gift shop with Olympic merchandise, the film *A Day in Search of the South*, regional books and much, much more. 224-2062. Adm. Free.

Whitewater Park. Marietta (I-75 North to exit 113). 40-acre water theme park featuring daredevil water acrobats, cascading water falls, pools and slides aplenty, a go-kart race

track, mini-golf, a children's play arcade and restaurants. Visit Tree House Island, the Bermuda Triangle, Little Hootch, the Bahama Bob-Slide or the many other tempting attractions. Swimsuits mandatory. Adm: $17.00-$10.00. 770-424-9283.

Woodruff Arts Center. Midtown. 1280 Peachtree St. The home of the Atlanta Symphony Orchestra, Alliance, Atlanta Children's and Studio Theaters, Atlanta College of Art, and the High Museum of Art. Free. 892-3600.

World of Coca-Cola. Downtown, adjacent to Underground Atlanta at 55 Martin Luther King, Jr. Dr. Everything you ever wanted to know about the history of the Coca-Cola Company, maker of the world's best selling soft drink. Memorabilia oozes from every nook and cranny along with free samples of over 20 Coca-Cola products. Adm: $3.50-free. 676-5151.

Wren's Nest. Downtown. 1050 Ralph David Abernathy Blvd. Here lies the 19th-century home of Joel Chandler Harris, creator of Uncle Remus and Br'er Rabbit. Georgian poet Frank Stanton once said of Harris,

"He made the lowly cabin fires Light the far windows of the world!"

Plenty of storytelling and memorabilia. 753-7735. Adm: $4.00

Yellow River Game Ranch. Lilburn (10 miles east of I-285). 4525 Hwy. 78. Open daily, rain or shine. 600 overly-sociable animals mix with the ranch visitors on the mile-long trail that meanders through 24 wooded acres. There are whitetail deer, kid goats, sheep, bunnies and more all waiting to be petted and fed. Newborn fawns in summer months and mountain lions and bear so gentle you can really get up close. The ranch is also home to the largest buffalo herd east of the Mississippi. Bring your camera and a picnic. 770-972-6643. Adm: $4.50-$3.50.

ZooAtlanta. Downtown, Grant Park. Home to over 1000 animals, including elephants, tigers, flamingoes, zebras, giraffes and the world-famous Willie B., the zoo's irrepressible silverback gorilla. 624-5678. Adm: $7.50-$5.50.

Kidstuff

The greater Atlanta area holds numerous fascinations for families. From the history of the South (**Atlanta History Center**), to the origins and struggle of the civil rights movement (**Sweet Auburn, APEX Museum**), to the marvelously evolving **Atlanta skyline**, the **Center for Puppetry Arts**, the **World of Coca-Cola Museum and CNN Center**, to the zillions of special festivals, events, educational opportunities and day trips listed herein.

All of the mega-attractions (**see Attractions below**) and all of the wondrous antebellum towns and villages are all mixed in with lakes, mountains, state parks and the resplendent beaches of the **Golden Isles**. So, whether you're a visitor or a resident, large family or small, you'll find enough family fun for the day, the week or a lifetime.

See, also, *Around Atlanta With Children*, by Denise Black and Janet Schwartz. This book contains a wealth of valuable stuff for families, from major attractions and day trips to the performing arts, classes and summer progams.

Plan Ahead
Calendar of Annual
Festivals and Events

Many of the festivals/events described below are very popular. Also event dates, event sites and admission prices may vary.

You can avoid unnecessary inconveniences by planning ahead. Always double check the event date, location and price by calling the event or consulting your local newspaper.

To avoid parking fees and problems and traffic delays, always think about riding MARTA to the event.

Festivals and events throughout historic Georgia (beyond metro Atlanta), are listed below each town in Section XII, Traveling Historic Georgia.

January

Martin Luther King, Jr. Week. Sweet Auburn (Metro Atlanta). An inspiring tribute to one of the world's most remarkable spiritual leaders. Interfaith services, parades, films, concerts and much more. 524-1956.

Peach Bowl Parade and Game. Downtown. Georgia Dome. Late December or early January. 586-8500.

Super Show. Downtown. Georgia World Congress Center. Sporting goods. 800-327-3736. 223-4000.

February

Black History Month. A month of events throughout Atlanta celebrating black history and achievements. 521-2654.

Atlanta Sports Carnival. Downtown. Georgia Dome. In either January or February the Georgia Dome becomes a huge carnival, replete with midway, rides, games, celebrity sportspeople, team mascots, cheerleaders and clowns. 249-6400.

Hooked On Rugs-February 3-11. Roswell at historic Bulloch Hall, 180 Bulloch Ave. 10 a.m.4 p.m. An amazing display of old and new hooked rugs. 770-992-1731. Adm: $4.00-$3.00.

Great Outdoors Show-February 8-11. Cobb Galleria Center.

Groundhog Day Juggler's Festival. Downtown. Virginia-Highland. A full week of juggling and magic for kids of all ages. 451-4847.

Ringling Brothers Barnum and Bailey Circus. Omni Coliseum. 20 shows. 681-2100.

Cathedral Antiques Show-February 13-15. Cathedral of St. Philip. 2744 Peachtree Rd. A gala list of exhibitors is supplemented with a preview party ($25.00), antique appraisals and "floor talks" presented by a variety of experts. 365-1000. Adm: $6.00.

Big Chill Dance-February 17. Decatur. Holiday Inn Conference Center. 130 Clairmont Ave; 8 p.m. to midnight. Have a red hot time as you dance to the tunes of the 50's, 60's, and 70's with the Bill Patton Band. A fundraiser for the Concerts on the Square. 371-8386. Adm: $10.00.

Mardi Gras Parade. Downtown. The procession begins at Peachtree and Harris Sts. and ends up at the Underground. Zillions of costumed party-goers and lighted floats. Sponsor: Krewe of Phoenix. 223-4636.

Southeastern Flower Show-February 21-25. Downtown. Town Hall Exhibition Center, lower level in City Hall East. Get plenty of ideas for your garden from the best in the business at the southeast's premier horticultural event (dedicated to promoting conservation and awareness of our natural environment through horticultural excellence. three acres of landscaped gardens, educational exhibits, artistic and horticultural competitions, childrens activities, free lectures, and a retail boutique of garden-related merchandise. Benefits the Atlanta Botanical Garden. Five full days of indoor floral beauty with an opening night black-tie preview party. The 1996 theme is "Welcoming the World: Harmony, Radiance and Grace." Many seminars and special events. 888-5638. Adm: $10.00-$5.00.

Fisharama. South Metro Atlanta (I-85, exit 40). Atlanta Exposition Center. All about fishing and boating. Sponsor: Georgia Wildlife Federation. 929-3350.

Trinity School Art Auction. Buckhead. 3254 Northside Pkwy. Second Sunday. Local Georgia artists present their work. 237-9286.

Atlanta Home Show-February 29-March 3. Downtown. Georgia World Congress. Over 400 exhibitors present everything for home decoration and improvement, including appliances, kitchens and baths, floor and wall coverings, home security systems, windows and doors, decorative accents, remodeling kits and instruction, and interior decorating and design. 223-4636. Adm: $7.00-free.

Goodwill Book Sale. Northlake Mall. Atlanta's largest used book sale, over 200,000 volumes at bargain prices. 377-0441.

Rich's Lovett Fashion Show. Buckhead. Lovett School. 4075 Paces Ferry Rd. Third week, Wed.-Thur. 262-3022.

Arbor Day. Outdoor activities sponsored by the various parks departments of the state, city and county on the third Friday.

March

Atlanta Home and Garden Show. Georgia World Congress Center. Four days of gardening and landscaping ideas. 998-9800.

Taste of Roswell-March 2-3. Held at the 1882 Roswell Cotton Mill, 89 Mill St., featuring Roswell's finest restaurants. 770-640-3253.

Hispanic Festival of Music and Art. Spanish and Latin American music and culture. Sponsor: Atlanta Virtuosi. 770-938-8611.

Atlanta Boat Show. Georgia World Congress Center. Five days of almost every boat and marine activity imaginable. 305-531-8410.

St. Patricks Day Parades-March 17.

• Downtown. Don't forget your greenery. A huge event. It begins at Peachtree St. and Ralph McGill Blvd. and ends downtown. See a local paper for details.

• Buckhead. Sponsor: Buckhead Village Merchants Association. Starts at East Paces Ferry Rd. and Bolling Way and ends at Frankie Allen Park. 250-0438.

ACC Craft Fair Atlanta-March 15-16. Downtown. The Georgia Dome. Produced by the American Craft Council (ACC), bring a wheelbarrow to this exhilarating exhibition and sale of the works of 225 of the nation's top craft artists including ceramics, jewelry, glass, furniture and wearable art. Sponsor: The Georgia Trust for Historic Preservation. 881-9980. Adm: $5.00.

Salute to American Craft 1996. The annual opening-night preview party to kick off the ACC Craft Fair. Tickets range from $2,500 for benefactors to $65 for groups of 30 or more. Single admissions are $75.00.

Musical Marathon Family Fest. Midtown. Woodruff Arts Center. Ear plugs unnecessary at this musical extravaganzea. Hosted in February or March by the Atlanta Symphony, this outstanding event for kids will delight one and all. 898-1184.

Kaleidoscope '96-March 18-21. Marietta. Cobb County Civic Center. A massive exhibition of visual and performing arts sponsored by the Cobb County Board of Education, Cobb County Parks, Recreation and Cultural Affairs and the Marietta City Schools.

14th Annual Great American Cover-Up Quilt Show-March 16-24. Roswell. Bulloch Hall at 180 Bulloch Ave. Quilters unite. 150 antique and contemporary quilts (including NBC's official Olympics quilt) from across the nation with most coming from Georgia and neighboring states. Each year the Bulloch Hall Quilt Guild raffles off a quilt of their own

making and provides daily demonstrations of quilting techniques. 992-1731. Adm: $5.00-$3.00.

High Museum of Art Wine Auction. Fund raising dinner and auction. 898-1144.

Motorcraft 500-March 10. Hampton (I-75, exit 77-Griffin). NASCAR Winston Cup Series. Speed and noise prevail. 946-4211.

Antebellum Jubilee-March 28-31. Stone Mountain Park. Step back to the 1860's and experience Southern heritage. A living historical celebration with traditional storytelling (hear Abe Lincoln himself), handcrafts (20 crafters demonstrating techniques of the 1800's), dance the Virginia Reel, old-time traveling magic shows, a Civil War camp with music and entertainment from the 97th Regimental String Band, open hearth cooking (grits, cobbler, cornbread, collard-greens and black-eyed peas) and see the period fashions (belles in corsets, hoops and billowing skirts). Adm: $3.00-$2.00. 498-5702.

Black Expo USA. Downtown. Georgia World Congress Center. 400 exhibitors featuring African-American businesses from across the nation. Seminars and Friday evening gospel music (x'tra charge). 892-2815. Adm: $6.00-$3.00.

Running Fool 5K Rd. Race-March 31. College Park. This fitness walk and run starts at 2 p.m. at the **Woodward Academy**. Age groups from 10 to 60+. Sponsored by the City of College Park Recreation Department, Atlanta Airport and the East Point Rotary Club. Days 669-3773. Evenings 767-2518.

Bargainata Spring Fair. Buckhead. Miami Circle.

April

For Kids' Sake Day. Downtown. Zoo Atlanta. A great day to visit the zoo and benefit needy kids (admission discounted). The animals, of course, storytelling and puppets. Co-sponsored by WXIA, Channel 11 and the Georgia Council on Child Abuse. 624-5600 or 624-5630.

Atlanta Dogwood Festival. Piedmont Park and elsewhere. Fabulous environmental celebration in honor of Earth Day and Atlanta's amazing dogwoods and azaleas. Hot-air balloon racing and plenty of stuff for the kids. 952-9151.

Atlanta Public School Festival of Art, Music and Physical Education. Underground Atlanta. 770-523-2311

28th Annual BellSouth Classic-April 1-7. Marietta. Atlanta Country Club. A landmark regular PGA Tour golfing event that raises over $500,000 for organizations such as Emory University's Egleston Children's Hospital, BellSouth Corporation, aka Southern Bell and South Central Bell co-sponsors with the Atlanta Classic Foundation. 770-951-8777. Adm: Varies.

Mayor's Walk. Piedmont Park. Sponsor: Atlanta Bureau of Recreation. 817-6936.

Spring Plant Sale-April 12-13. Midtown. Piedmont Park. Atlanta Botanical Garden. 876-5858.

International Cultural Festival-April 14. Midtown. Emory University. Some 50 countries ranging from the Easter Islands of Chile to Sri Lanka, Bulgaria and Bermuda display an amazing variety of costumes, banners and ethnic cuisines. There is music, fashion shows and an international array of entertainment. 727-3300. Adm: Free.

Cobb Senior Games. Marietta and county-wide. 528-0463.

WalkAmerica-April 27. A national fundraising event involving over 875,000 people in 1,500 communities across the nation. Sponsored by the March of Dimes Birth Defects Foundation, proceeds finance research into childhood health problems. 352-9255.

Atlanta Storytelling Festival-April 27-28. Sandy Springs, Williams-Payne House . Hear the tallest tales from the glibbest of the glib. Special features include a Liar's Contest, Swapping Grounds, booksigning and puppet and magic hatmaking. 851-9111. Adm: $3.00-free.

Sheep to Shawl-April 13. Buckhead. 130 W. Paces Ferry Rd. Atlanta History Center. Annual shearing of the sheep at the **Tullie Smith Farm** (1840). Shearing (by hand and with electric shears), washing, fleece sorting, carding and spinning, natural dyeing, plying, skeining and weaving a shawl on a 150-year-old loom. Also visit the antebellum **Tullie Smith House**, its outbuildings and period gardens. Scouts may receive credit toward badges. 814-4080. Adm: Varies.

Grand Prix of Atlanta.

Peachtree Street Basketball. An early April four-on-four basketball tournament. 984-9080.

Archifest. A bus tour of Atlanta's architectual achievements. Sponsor: American Institute of Architects. Pricey. 873-3207.

A Taste of Marietta-April 28.

Southside Fool's Day 5K Rd. Race. College Park-downtown. First Sunday in April at the **Woodward Academy.** 669-3773.

Jazz and Heritage Festival. Downtown. Underground Atlanta. 523-2311.

Atlanta Steeplechase-April 6. Cumming (GA 400 to exit 9). Seven Branches Farm. Horseracing and antique autos combine to make this a memorable event. Bring a gourmet lunch and plenty of money. Proceeds benefit the Atlanta Speech School. Advance tickets only. 237-7436.

Peachtree Crossings Country Fair. Peachtree City (I-85 south to Fairburn. 200 exhibitors, barbecue, country crafts and apple dumplings. 770-434-3661.

Atlanta Celtic Festival. Site and date vary. Celtic craftspeople including jewelry makers, potters, spinners, basket makers and blacksmiths demonstrate their skills and sell their wares. Plenty of hearty food and dance. Proceeds to erect a Celtic Heritage Center. 572-8045.

Hot and Spicy Food Festival. Marietta. Dobbins Naval Air Station. Hot food and music make for an appetizing event as more than 50 Atlanta restaurants compete for best of show. There's Cajun, Italian, continental, Mexican Caribbean and American cuisine. Food samples range from free to $2.00. 249-6400. Adm $5.00-free.

Allen the Orangutan's Birthday Celebration-April 26. Downtown. ZooAtlanta. 524-5630.

Smyrna Jonquil Festival-April 27-28. Village Green. Rapidly growing into one of metro Atlanta's favorite celebrations. Featuring over 150 booths of quality, handmade arts and crafts, entertainment and some of the most delicious festival food found anywhere. There are pony rides, a midway and free line-dancing lessons. 770-434-3661. Adm: $1.00-free.

Atlanta Women's Expo. Marietta and Cobb Center Galleria host a women's extravaganza. Almost everything of special interest to women including seminars, demos and exhibits. 222-2064.

Easter Egg Hunts. Finding an Easter egg hunt in greater Atlanta is easier than finding your way home. Wouldn't want to leave any out. Consult local newspapers.

Sweet Auburn Festival. Four days of parades, childrens and cultural activities. 577-0625.

Native American Heritage Day-April 27. Jonesboro. Encounter the life of the Creek Tribe as it was in the 1700s in a recreated Indian village. Partake of corn cakes cooked on a hot rock, venison stew and fresh roasted corn on the cob while watching demonstrations of basket weaving, skin curing, food preparation and arrow making. 770-473-0197. Adm: $3.50-$.50.

Inman Park Festival and Home Tour. Tour some of Georgia's grandest Victorian mansions in a backdrop of jazz, dancing, food and a smattering of arts and crafts. The last weekend of April . Proceeds benefit Inman Park home preservation. 242-4895.

AT&T Challenge. View men's professional tennis with proceeds to charity and the victors. 770-395-3500.

Freaknik. A three-four day annual event whereupon hundreds of thousands of black college students drive to Atlanta to party. Largely local disruptives and disorderlies resulted in rather bad press notices in 1995. Thus, the event may venture elsewhere in 1996.

Georgia Renaissance Festival-April-June. Fairburn (I-85 south, exit 12). From April 20 to June 9 there are knights in shining armor at this county fair demonstrating 16th-century period crafts and foods. A huge event, spread over 30 acres, with hundreds of shows featuring choral groups, jugglers, minstrels and magicians. Shop in the European crafts marketplace. Eight weekends starting the last Saturday in April . 770-964-8575. Adm: $10.95-free.

Fiddlin' Fish Music and Arts Festival. Lake Lanier Islands (I-85 north). Annual music jamboree featuring some of the South's greatest fiddlers in a fiddle-off contest, seafood, arts and crafts and carnival rides. 770-932-7200.

Baby and Kid Festival-April 13-14. Marietta. Cobb Galleria Center. The largest expo of its type in the Southeast offers fun-filled activities and merchandise. There are storytellers and a puppet theater, jugglers, tightrope artists, clowns, balloon artists and face painters. Enter the Beautiful Baby Contest or the Baby Crawl Off. 770-395-7900. Adm: $3.00-free.

18th Annual Druid Hills Home and Garden Tour. Tour fantastic homes to benefit Emory

University scholarships and Druid Hills neighborhood preservation. 727-8687.

MS 75 Bike Tour. Lithonia to Rutledge. Proceeds to Multiple Sclerosis Society. 770-984-9080.

Scandinavian Festival. Cobb Civic Center. Scandinavian culture and cuisine. 321-3203.

131st Annual Confederate Memorial Day. Kingston at the **Kingston Baptist Church** (1853). Church services and a museum tour. Sponsored by the Kingston Women's History Club, this is the nation's oldest Confederate Memorial Day event. 800-733-2280.

Kennesaw Big Shanty Festival-April 21-22. Big Shanty Museum. Civil War activities and festivities. One of the largest arts and craft shows in North Georgia. 770-423-1330.

Atlanta Dog Jog-April or May. Piedmont Park at 10th St. One and two mile races plus costume and owner look-alike contests. Proceeds to Georgia Sundown Surgery Fund for needy pets. 751-1031. Official Dog Jog t-shirts are available to spectators for $12.00. Adm: $15.00.

Fat Tuesday Jazz and Heritage-April 28. Buckhead. 3167 Peachtree Rd. A recreation of the New Orleans Jazz and Heritage Festival featuring outdoor music by local musicians, spicy boiled crawfish and daiquiris. 355-0440. Adm: Free.

May

Spring Moon Stroll-May 2. Midtown. Piedmont Park. Atlanta Botanical Garden (7:30-9:30 p.m.). 876-5858.

Beastly Feast-May 4. Downtown. Zoo Atlanta. 7 p.m.-1 a.m.; 624-5630.

Decorator's Showhouse. Buckhead. Sponsor: Atlanta Symphony Association. 733-4935.

Parish Festival. Buckhead. St. Philips Cathedral Men's Club. 2774 Peachtree Rd. First Sunday. 365-1000.

Dobbins Open House. Marietta. The air base and naval station are host to the entire family. Meet the pilots, marvel at the airshows, view the airplanes and hear the bands. 770-421-5402/770-421-5055/770-421-5406.

Gardens for Connoisseurs Tour. May 11-12. Tour some of Atlanta's finest private gardens on Mother's Day. Proceeds benefit the Atlanta Botanical Garden. 876-5859.

Roswell Antebellum Spring Festival and Colors Art Festival-May 11-12. Visit historic Town Square daily from 10 a.m. to 6 p.m. Featuring fine arts, original crafts, music, performances, BBQ and walking tours of Bulloch Hall and Archibald Smith Plantation Home. Sponsored by the Historic Roswell Convention and Visitors Bureau and the Roswell Jr. Women's Club. 770-640-3243.

Memorial Day Weekend Beach Music Blast. Lake Lanier Islands. 770-932-7200.

American Indian Festival. Lawrenceville. Gwinnett County Fairgrounds at Johnson and Davis Rds. Native American culture, storytelling, dance and song. An entertaining, educational experience for the entire family. 770-963-6522. Adm: $5.00-$3.00.

Memorial Day Blues Fest Weekend. Downtown at Underground Atlanta. Blues devotees flock to hear over 30 regional and local bands. 523-2311. Adm: Free.

18th Annual Geranium Festival-May 18. McDonough. Courthaouse Square is decked out with hundreds of geraniums. There is music, storytelling, arts and crafts exhibitions and antiques for sale. Sponsored by the McDonough Lions Club. 770-957-3306. Adm: Free.

Herb Education Day. Midtown. Piedmont Park. Atlanta Botanical Gardens. Everything you need to know about herbs and potted plants on the first weekend in May. Sponsor: Chattahoochee Herb Society. 876-5859.

Springfest and Lasershow. Stone Mountain Park. Chow down in early May at the annual BBQ pork cookoff. Much entertainment featuring folk and country music, arts and crafts and activities for the kids. Stay for the free fireworks at 9:30 p.m.; (Friday-Sunday only.) 770-498-5702.

Marietta Greek Festival. Marietta. Cobb County Civic Center. Greek food and music aplenty. 770-924-8080. Adm: $2.50-free.

BellSouth Classic. Marietta. A major PGA Tour event at the Atlanta Country Club. 770-951-8777.

Georgia Folklore By Moonlight. Jonesboro. Fireside yarns, music and a tour of Stately Oaks. 770-473-0197.

Cinco de Mayo Celebration. Underground Atlanta. 523-2311.

Kingfest. A free mid-May festival at the Martin Luther King, Jr. Center. International dancers, arts and crafts and food prevail. 798-7785.

Midtown Music Festival. Mid-May at 10th and Peachtree Sts. Two days and nites of music performed by world famous musicians. Also ethnic food, arts and crafts, face painting, circus workshops and activities for the kids. 798-7785. Adm: $15-free.

National Black Family Reunion Celebration Concert. Piedmont Park. A celebration of cultural pride and achievement. 524-6269.

Historic Marietta Arts and Crafts Festival-May 4-5. Marietta Square. 770-528-0627-0616.

Old Times at Crabapple-May 18. Roswell. Sponsored by the Crabapple Antique Association, 100+ dealers present their wares. 770-343-9454. Adm: Free.

Sweetwater Fever Festival. Mableton, Mable House. A fine arts and photograpy competition with food and entertainment, sponsored by the South Cobb Arts Alliance. 770-739-0189.

Decatur Arts Festival and Garden Tour-May 17-27. Decatur.It begins with a juried art show featuring artists from all over the southeast. On May 24 the annual fundraiser is held in the form of a Cajun Street Party with Cajun dance lessons, Cajun food and a crawfish race (5-11 p.m., Adm: $5.00-free). On May 25-26 the arts extravaganza and garden tour kickin, featuring a performing arts stage, children's festival, classic car show, garden tour, global village, music and plenty of food. 371-8386. Adm: mostly free. Garden tour $10.00.

A Taste of the South. Stone Mountain Park. A lively celebration of Southern culture. Sponsored by the Atlanta Journal-Constitution and the Georgia Peanut Commission, the food ranges from jambalaya and key lime pie to BBQ and boiled peanuts. Artisans demonstrate their crafts while Southern music (cajun, country, beach and blues) fills the air. 770-498-5702. Adm: Free.

Sheepshearing Saturday. Lilburn. Yellow River Game Ranch. An annual shearer's contest. 770-972-6643.

Atlanta Peach Carnival-May 23-28. Downtown (various locations). A festival of spectacular color and masquerade bands, featuring Caribbean arts, music, food and dancers. 344-2567.

Atlanta Jazz Festival. Sites usually include Peachtree Center, Catfish Station, Chastain Park Amphitheatre, and Grant Park. Sponsored by the Atlanta Bureau of Cultural Affairs. Jazz devotees flock to picnic and wile away the day and evening listening to local musicians and top stars. Arrive early, stay late. 817-6815. Adm: Free.

June

Kingfest. Downtown. In mid-June Friday is concert night, Saturday is for kids (pony rides, puppet making, etc,) and Sunday is "gospel day." All at Martin Luther King, Jr. Center. 524-1956.

The 1996 Olympic Arts Festival-June-October. The Olympic Arts Festival will run from June to October of 1996. It will feature an international array of artists, musicians, performers, puppeteers, storytellers and playrights presenting their work. 224-1835.

Virginia-Highlands Summer Fest. Downtown. John Howell Park at 855 Virginia Ave. A 5K run, local bands, arts and crafts and a juried art show. 222-8244. Adm: Free.

Friends of the Atlanta-Fulton Public Library Book Sale. Downtown. Central Library at One Margaret Mitchell Sq. Encyclopedias, first editions, new, old and rare books, all at reasonable prices. 730-1710. Adm: Free.

Southern Wood Carvers Show and Competition. Marietta. Cobb Civic Center. Open to amateur and professional carvers and shoppers. 483-0760.

Atlanta Film and Video Festival. A must for film buffs. Two solid weeks of films by many of the country's leading film makers. 352-4225.

1996 Olympic Arts Festival. From June to October with most events occurring from July 19 to August 4. 224-1835. Adm: Varies.

Celebrate Israel. Dunwoody. Zaban Park Branch of the Atlanta Jewish Community. An Israeli marketplace, petting zoo, dancing, singing, pony rides, Sesame St. Theater, Maccabean Games and plenty of ethnic food. 396-3250.

British Summer Festival. Buckhead. Oglethorpe University. Hot air balloon rides and classic British cars. 395-3262.

Georgia Shakespeare Festival-June-August. Buckhead. Oglethorpe University is host.

Purchase a picnic lunch by calling 396-5361, or bring your own. Reserve far ahead. Three or four performances only ranging from mid-June thru August. 264-0200. Adm: Varies.

A Taste of Atlanta. Midtown. At 10th and Peachtree Streets in mid-June be prepared to find sixty of Atlanta's top restaurants presenting many of their best dishes. There is also plenty of live entertainment, cooking demos, arts and crafts and plenty of stuff for the kids. Proceeds benefit the National Kidney Foundation of Georgia. 248-1315.

Willie B's Birthday Party. Downtown. Zoo Atlanta. Say happy birthday to Atlanta's star gorilla. 624-5678.

Stone Mountain Arts and Crafts Festival. Stone Mountain. Over Father's Day weekend hundreds of craftspeople and antique dealers present their goods. 871-4971.

Beach Party-June 21. Decatur. Nobody seems to care that there's no ocean. Curl your toes in the 40 tons of sand, which transforms Courthouse Square into a beach. Watch for the pink flamingos, palm trees and pelicans. Build sandcastles and let your spirits soar. Sponsored by the Decatur Business Association. 371-8386. Adm: $5.00-free.

American Chef's Competion. Downtown. Georgia World Congress Center. Bring your appetite. Amateur and professional chefs conjure up their best with proceeds benefitting Easter Seals and Atlanta's Table, an Atlanta hunger project. 223-4636.

NationsBank Summer Film Festival. Downtown. Presented at the Fox on Monday and Thursday evenings, June-August. Cartoons, organ music and feature films. 881-2100.

Gay Pride Parade. June is National Gay Pride Month. The parade, on the last Sunday in June, caps off the month's festivities. 662-4533.

Eighth Annual Downtown Picking Up. Downtown. City pride brings 1500 friends together in furtherance of a cleaner downtown. Sponsored by the Atlanta Downtown Partnership, volunteers are rewarded with free t-shirts and a great party. 577-0330.

Atlanta Auto Fair. Hampton. Atlanta Motor Speedway. The first weekend in June brings Georgia's largest car show. Legends car racing, Thundercar racing, street rods, swap meet, car corral and antique engines. Adm: $7.00-$3.00. 707-7851.

July

The 1996 Summer Olympic Games. Please turn to Section III which features this once-in-a-lifetime event.

Georgia State Games. Georgia Tech and elsewhere. Amateur athletic competitions, individual and team. Some 25,000 athletes of all ages. Enacted by the Georgia legislature in 1989. 853-0250.

DeKalb International Choral Festival. DeKalb Convention and Visitors Bureau serves as host to this huge event, which takes place throughout DeKalb County and ends with 15 choral groups singing together on the stage at Stone Mountain Park. Call to get the details. 378-2525.

WSB-TV Salute 2 America Parade: A Star-Spangled Celebration-July 4. Join the fun at the nation's largest Independence Day parade, which always draws a huge throng of marchers and spectators. Nearly 80 colorful floats, award-winning marching bands, and giant helium filled balloons and special guests begin the 1.3 mile parade route at Spring and Marietta Sts. Then on to Woodruff Park, then left on Peachtree, ending up at Ralph McGill Blvd. and West Peachtree. Sponsored and televised by WSB-TV/Channel 2. 897-7000.

Other Fantastic July Fourth Celebrations

▪ Lenox Square. Star Spangled Night 233-6767.

▪ Marietta Square. 528-0616.

▪ Stone Mountain Village. 879-4971.

▪ Stone Mountain Park. 498-5702.

▪ Decatur's Pied Piper Fourth. 371-8386.

▪ Lake Lanier's Fourth. 932-7275.

And many others. Consult your local papers.

Peachtree 10K Rd. Race-July 4. Buckhead. Sponsor: Atlanta Track Club. Lenox Square to Piedmont Park via Peachtree Rd. (6.2 miles) with over 50,000 other runners. Finishers earn a t-shirt and help consume over 500,000 cups of water. Wheelchair and seniors divisions. MARTA is suggested. 231-9064.

Run for Life-July 27. Marietta Square. 5K and 10K races for all ages. Sponsored by Life College, with proceeds benefiting the Open Gate Shelter for Abused Children. 770-424-0554, ext. 786.

Pond Society Tour and Expo-July 13. Acworth. Forty homes with splendid ponds, fish and other accoutrements. 770-975-0277. Adm: $5.00

Roswell Antebellum Village-July 19-August 3. To celebrate the time of the Olympics, Roswell will host an Antebellum Village showcasing its historic sites, tours, strolls, fireworks, and entertainment featuring Tracy Lawrence and other popular acts. 770-640-3253.

World Showcase and Festival. Marietta. Cobb Galleria Center. From July 19 to August 4. 770-984-8016.

August

National Black Arts Festival. On even-numbered years only, hundreds of mostly free events celebrating the works of black artists. Plenty for the entire family from theatre and storytelling to puppetry and poetry readings. 730-7315.

AJC Barbecue Fest-August. Buckhead at **Oglethorpe University**, 4484 Peachtree Rd. Atlanta's only festival dedicated to the finger-lickin' barbecue. Co-sponsored by the Atlanta Braves and the *Atlanta Journal-Constitution*, and featuring vendors selling barbecue, grilling equipment and barbecue sauces. 614-2624.

Atlanta Paralympic Games-August 16-25. 4,000 physically disabled athletes from over 100 countries compete. 588-9600.

African Pride Cultural Festival-August. Downtown. Underground Atlanta is host. Continuous entertainment from 10 a.m. to 9 p.m., with African dancers, musicians, and arts and crafts. Adm: Free. 523-6520.

College Park Super Saturday-August. At the College Park Elementary School on Princeton Avenue. This fifth annual event is sponsored by the College Park Housing Authority Drug Elimination Program and features a 5K road race, entertainment, a flea market, and food vendors. Adm: Free. 761-2013.

A Midsummer Night Dream Tour. August 10. View some of Atlanta's finest gardens as they sparkle in the night. A Valentines day in August with soft music and romantic story telling. 770-975-0277.

September

Powers Crossroad Country Fair and Arts Festival-August 31-September 2. Approximately 12 miles west of Newnan. A festival of artists and craftsmen, dedicated to preserving excellence in the arts and crafts. Country fiddlers and high stepping cloggers together with mouth-watering Southern food as provided by local churches and civic groups. 770-253-2011.

Art in the Park-August 30-September 1. Marietta Square. Three days of art exhibitions with music and food. 770-528-0616.

Peachtree Crossings Country Fair. August 31-September 2. I-85 south to exit 12. 250 juried artists and craftsmen, many of them nationally acclaimed, display paintings, sculpture, and old style woodwrighting, blacksmithing and coppersmithing. See a frontier camp straight out of the 1800s and learn how to throw knives and tomahawks and watch muzzleload rifle demonstrations. There's pony and kiddie rides and great country cooking, including fried catfish and hot apple dumplings. 434-3661.

Tour D' Town-September 2. Buckhead. 6, 12, 24, and 48-mile/races comprise a bicycle odyssey on Labor Day. Fun for the entire family to benefit the American Cancer Society. 841-0700.

Atlanta Home Show-September 5-8. Cobb Galleria Center. Over 400 exhibitors present everything for home decoration and improvement, including appliances, kitchens and baths, floor and wall coverings, home security systems, windows and doors, decorative accents, remodeling kits and instruction, and interior decorating and design. 770-223-4636. Adm: $7.00-free.

Blue Sky Concerts at Courthouse Square. September 4, 11, 18 and 25. Old Decatur Courthouse. Jazz, classical, country and rock music at noon on Wednesdays. Bring a picnic lunch or order take-out from a local restaurant. Sponsored by SunTrust Bank. 371-8386. Adm: Free.

Concerts on the Square. September 2, 9, 16, 26 and 30. Old Decatur Courthouse. Bring lawn chairs, quilts and picnic baskets to the Old Courthouse lawn on Saturday nights to hear jazz, reggae, acoustic, country and classical music. Sponsored by Wachovia Bank. 371-8386. Adm: Free.

Atlanta Greek Festival. Clairmont Rd. (I-85 North, then proceed west to the Orthodox Cathedral of the Annunciation). Greek food and culture in abundance at this huge festival. 633-5870.

Buckarama. South Metro Atlanta (I-85, exit 40). Atlanta Exposition Center. All about hunting and camping. Sponsor: Georgia Wildlife Federation. 929-3350.

Atlanta Food and Wine Festival. Buckhead, principally three hotels, Swissotel, J.W.Marriott and Nikko. A huge wine-tasting event. 873-4482.

Folklife Festival. Buckhead. Atlanta History Center presents the daily life of an 1840s family, with weaving, candlemaking and soapmaking. 814-4000.

Sandy Springs Festival-September 21-22. Sandy Springs, Hitson Memorial Ctr. Re-enactment of 1870's farming community with demos of rug hooking, smithing, tatting, quilting and basket weaving. Also 100 fine arts and craft booths, an antique classic car show, a 5K/10K run/walk, a children's park and plenty of food and entertainment. 851-9111. ADM: $3.00-free.

Grant Park Home Tour. Sponsor: Grant Park Neighborhood Association. 525-7004.

Montreux Atlanta Int. Music Festival. Staged at **Piedmont Park** and local theatres, this mostly free musical event features regional and international musicians playing reggae, blues, jazz, gospel and more. Usually four to six days including Labor Day. 817-6815.

Gwinnett County Fair. Snellville. A real county fair with all the fixins'. Beauty contest, fireworks, car raffle, music groups, and plenty of livestock. 770-822-7700.

Roswell Fine Arts Festival-September 21-22. A 30-year tradition, held in historic Town Square. Sponsored by the Roswell Recreation Association. 770-992-0832.

Asian Cultural Experience. Atlanta's Botanical Garden salutes Asian culture. Demos abound, Chinese opera make-up, origami, calligraphy, Japanese embroidery and much, much more. On Saturday evening there's fire-

works, music dancing and a dragon parade. 876-5858.

Nationwide Golf Championship.

Historic Marietta Antique Street Festival. Marietta. September 14.

Yellow Daisy Arts and Crafts Festival. Stone Mountain Park. Over 400 exhibitors. There's also music, storytellers, food, puppets and a flower show. The #1 arts and crafts exhibition in the nation. 871-4871.

Civil War Encampment. Buckhead. The Atlanta History Center. 130 W. Paces Ferry Rd. Re-enactments of various aspects of life on a Civil War battlefield, plus music, food and exhibitions. 814-4000. Adm: $6.00-free.

Garden of Eden Ball-September 28. Midtown. Piedmont Park. The Atlanta Botanical Garden's principal fund-raising event. Enjoy dinner and dancing under a tent on the Great Lawn. 876-5859. Adm: $250.00 $50.00.

Sesame Street Live. Omni Coliseum. 498-5702.

18th Annual Georgia Music Festival. Many free events at various metro Atlanta locations including gospel, jazz, bluegrass, country and rock. 656-3596.

Arts Festival of Atlanta. Piedmont Park in. Huge nine-day event featuring a vast collection of local and international art. 885-1125.

Peachtree Crossings Country Fair. Peachtree City (I-85 south to Fairburn. 200 exhibitors, barbecue, country crafts and apple dumplings. 770-434-3661.

Swan Coach House Flea Market. Buckhead. Atlanta History Center. 3130 Slaton Dr. Sponsor: Forward Arts Foundation. 261-0224.

October

Halloween Atlanta Style

* **Atlanta Botanical Garden.** The Harvest Moon Stroll is ideal for kids, featuring a costume parade, jack-o-lanterns, spooky Halloween music and decorations. 876-5859.

* **ZooAtlanta.** The Great Halloween Caper is a haunted house with realk bats, spiders and snakes. 624-5678.

* **Midtown.** Haunted Castle. Rhodes Hall is a home for ghosts. 881-9980.

* **Little Five Points.** Costumes and entertainment at Bass Field. 522-2926.

* **Stone Mountain Park.** Southern Ghosts emerge as storytelling prevails at the Antebellum Plantation.770- 469-1105.

* **Sandy Springs.** A Ghostly Gathering at the **Williams-Payne House.** 851-9111.

* **The Malls.** Many Atlanta malls offer Halloween activities and safe opportunities for kids to trick-or-treat.

* **Lake Lanier Islands.** The Great Pumpkin Arts and Crafts Festival. 770-932-7200.

Pace Fair. Buckhead. Pace Academy. 966 W. Paces Ferry Rd. 262-1345.

23rd Annual Dunwoody Women's Club Tour of Homes-October 6. First Wednesday. Sponsored by the Dunwoody Woman's Club. Proceeds benefit area charities. 770-396-1548. Adm: $10.00.

Georgia Marble Festival. Jasper. The town's marble industry. Quarry tours, arts and crafts, antiques, music and sculpture exhibitions. 706-692-5600.

Historic Marietta Arts and Crafts Festival. Marietta Square. October 5-6. 770-528-0627-0616.

Athens to Atlanta Roller Skating Marathon. Sponsor: Atlanta Peachtree Rd. Rollers. 634-9032.

Fall Plant Sale-October 11-12. Midtown. Piedmont Park. Atlanta Botanical Garden. 876-5858.

25th Annual Brown's Crossing Craftsmen Fair-October 19-20. 9 miles west of Milledgeville. Thousands of spectators flock from a three-state area to see the crafts and skills of yesteryear. 175 artists and craftsmen present their wares. 912-452-9327.

St. Elias Fall Festival. Druid Hills. Middle Eastern culture including falafel, kibbe', pickled turnips, and a church tour. Sponsor: Antiochian Orthodox Church. 378-8191.

Heritage Festival-October 11. Decatur's Old Courthouse Square. Children are the focus of this all-day event. Hands-on demonstrations of quilting, pottery and candlemaking. Sponsored by the Decatur Business Association, BankSouth and the Decatur Library. 885-1125. Adm: Free.

Old Times at Crabapple-October 19. Roswell. Sponsored by the Crabapple Antique Association; 100+ dealers present their wares. 770-343-9454. Adm: Free.

Festival of Cultures. Downtown. Underground Atlanta. Sponsors: The World of Coca-Cola and Underground Atlanta. Four weekends, each featuring a different culture. Unique ethnic entertainment, a one-of-a-kind Kidfest, travel showcase and business exposition. Plenty of imported food and beverage, music and arts and crafts. 817-0800.

University Women's Book Fair. Buckhead. Lenox Sq. Mall. Proceeds to fund scholarships for women. 355-1861.

Folklife Festival. Buckhead. Atlanta History Ctr. 130 W. Paces Ferry Rd. Georgia life and crafts from the 1840s. 814-4000.

Italian Heritage Festival. Galleria. Italian culture including opera, food and classical music. 770-988-8085.

Chili Cookoff. Stone Mountain Park. Chili, chili and more chili. 770-498-5702.

Atlanta International Wine Festival.

Fall Moon Stroll-October 24. Midtown. Piedmont Park. Atlanta Botanical Garden (7-9 p.m.). 876-5858.

Gold Rush Days. Dahlonega. On the third weekend help celebrate Dahlonega's gold rush days by panning for gold and marching in the parade. Many activitities for kids. 706-864-3711.

Great Pumpkin Arts and Crafts Festival. Lake Lanier Islands. A two day event featuring 100 arts and crafts exhibitors, live entertainment, children's activities, fall foliage boat rides, pony rides and hay rides. It all starts at 2 p.m.; Adm: Free, but there is a charge to enter the islands.

Vacation World. Downtown. Georgia World Congress Center. Exhibitors present vacation packages with special attention to seniors and those with special needs. 223-4636.

Scottish Festival and Highland Games. Stone Mountain Park. Scots display their Celtic culture. Regimental kilts, caber toss, and highland dancing. 634-7402.

Wok-a-Thon. Buckhead. Hotel Nikko. Pacific Rim cuisine to benefit the Deen Terry Memorial Culinary Scholarship. Sponsor: American Institute of Wine and Food. Adm: Pricey. 399-9781.

Smyrna Jonquil Festival-October 26-27. Village Green. Rapidly growing into one of metro Atlanta's favorite celebrations. Featuring over 150 booths of quality, handmade arts and crafts, entertainment and some of the most delicious festival food found anywhere. There are pony rides, a midway and free line-dancing lessons. 770-434-3661. Adm: $1.00-free.

Jonesboro Fall Festival. Jonesboro. Stately Oaks Plantation. Reenactment of the Battle of

Jonesboro. Also tours, antiques, arts and crafts. 770-473-0197.

Georgia Renaissance Fall Festival. (A repeat of the April event).

Fall Gardening Festival-October 5. Midtown. Piedmont Park. Atlanta Botanical Gardens teaches its garden crafts. 876-5858.

Atlanta Mini Gran Prix. Buckhead. Arthritis Foundation. 237-8771.

November

A Meal to Remember-November 1. Buckhead. Feast at the Ritz-Carlton on the first Friday in November. International chefs donate food and services. Sponsored by the Senior Citizen Services of Metropolitan Atlanta to benefit Meals on Wheels Atlanta. 881-5950. Adm: $2,500-$600.

World On Ice. Downtown. Omni. Clan Disney hits the ice. 249-6400.

Heaven Bound. Downtown. A religous musical pageant sponsored by Big Bethal AME Church. Usually two nights the first weekend in November. 659-0248.

Veteran's Day Parade-November 11. Buckhead. The November 11 armada hits the road at 11 a.m. from Lenox Square and heads south. The 1995 theme is "A Grateful Nation Remembers WWII Veterans and Homefront." There is also a dinner/dance and banquet. 416-0377.

Atlanta Marathon. Thanksgiving morning. Starts in Lithonia. Ends 26+ miles later in Piedmont Park. Also a 1/2 marathon. All ages. Plenty to be thankful about when you finish this one. Sponsor: Atlanta Track Club. 231-9065.

High Museum Antique Show and Sale. Buckhead. 50 international antique dealers peddle their wares and conduct luncheons and home tours. Phipps Plaza hosts. 898-1152.

Or VeShalom. Brookhaven. Sephardic cuisine and culture is displayed . 633-1737.

Great Tree Lighting. Downtown. Underground Atlanta.

Fidelity Tree Lighting and Concert-November 29. Downtown Decatur at the corner of Commerce Dr. and Clairmont, 7-8 p.m. Watch the 60-foot tree atop the Fidelity National Bank as its 10,000 lights brighten Decatur's sky. There's a choral concert, sing-alongs and a giant screen. 371-8386. Adm: Free.

December

Atlanta's Symphony, Ballet and Opera. Each art form usually presents special holiday programs such as Handel's Messiah, the Nutcracker Suite and Amahl and the Night Visitors.

Symphony............	876-HORN
Ballet.................	873-5811
Opera	355-3311

ZooAtlanta's Breakfast and Supper with Santa. Facepainters, storytellers and Santa, not to mention all of those animals. 624-5678.

Teddy Bear Tea. Downtown. Ritz-Carlton lobby. Tea, hot chocolate and Santa to benefit the Egleston Children's Hospital. 659-0400.

Stone Mountain Holiday Celebrations. Candlelight shopping. 498-5702. Great Tree Lighting. 770-523-211.

Christmas on the Square-December 5. Marietta Square.

Marietta Pilgrimage-December 7-8. Marietta Welcome Center. Christmas home tour of six private homes and at least as many public buildings. Concerts and a quilt show are included with proceeds benefitting the Cobb Landmarks and Historical Society. 770-429-1115.

Memories of Christmas Past. Mableton. Mable House is transformed into a wondrous Christmas House replete with decorated trees, antiques and an artists market featuring handmade goods. 770-739-0189.

Governor's Mansion Tree Lighting. Buckhead. The governor and his wife are host to the lighting and a tour of the mansion's public areas. It's all free and a great way to kick off the holiday season. 261-1776.

Decatur Holiday Celebrations.

- Fidelity Tree Lighting-November 29.
- Candlelight Tour of Homes-December 6-7.
- Bonfire-Christmas Carol Sing-Along December 12.
- Breakfast with Santa-December 14.
- Decorate Decatur-December 15. 371-8386.

Christmas at Callanwolde. Midtown. The mansion at the Callanwolde Fine Arts Center is marvously decorated and there are concerts and Santa knee-sitting. 872-5338.

Grant Park Learning Center Candlelight Tour of Homes. Downtown. Grant Park Learning Center. Visit eight renovated homes. Usually held the first weekend in December. 521-0418.

Country Christmas-December 1. Midtown. Piedmont Park. Atlanta Botanical Garden. Chestnuts roast in an open fire at this traditional Christmas display. Christmas spirit is pervasive with distinguished decorations, carolers, bellringers, horse-drawn carriages, wreathmaking, homemade bread and imaginative, handcrafted gifts. 876-5858. Adm: Free.

Egleston Xmas Parade and Festival of Trees. The parade on the first Saturday in December begins at 10:30 a.m. The nine-day festival follows. Proceeds benefit the Egleston Children's Hospital. 325-NOEL.

Peach Bowl Football at the Georgia Dome. 223-9200.

New Year's Eve

Firstnight Atlanta. Midtown. Alcohol-free, family-oriented on Peachtree St. 872-4782.

Underground Plaza. Downtown. The gang's all here as an electrified peach wends its way down the tower. 523-2311.

Sugar Plum Festival.

Wren's Nest Christmas Open House.

Kuppenheimer Basketball Tournament.

Other activities too numerous to list. Consult your local papers. Also, call 523-2311.

Concert Series

Classic Chastain Series. Buckhead. Chastain Park Amphitheater. June-August. 733-5000.

Classic Country Series. Buckhead. Chastain Park Amphitheater. June-July. 733-5000.

Decatur Concerts on the Square. Decatur. 371-8386.

Georgia Mountain Fair. June-October. 706-896-4191.

Glover Park Concert Series. Marietta. June-August. 770-528-0615.

Lanierland Concerts in the Country. Cumming. Lanierland Music Park. 6115 Jot-Em Down Rd. June-August 681-1596.

Michelob Light/Coca-Cola Concerts. Buckhead. Chastain park Amphitheater. June-July. 249-6400.

Roswell Mill Concerts. Roswell. Grass Roots. GA 120 and Roswell Rd. 770-644-0602.

Russian Music Concert Series. Marietta. Cobb Galleria Center. July. 770-955-9100.

Six Flags Concert Series. Tucker (I-20 to Six Flags exit). May-Sept. 249-6400.

Art Centers

800 East. Downtown at 800 East Ave. Adult-oriented, privately sponsored, cutting edge art exhibitions. Definitely not for children, the feighthearted and certainly not for traditionalists. 522-8265.

Callanwolde Fine Arts Center. Midtown at 980 Briarcliff Rd. Originally the home of Charles Howard Candler, son of Coca-Cola founder Asa Candler. The 1920 Tudor-style mansion is now a major arts and cultural center for visual and performing artists. Features concerts, recitals, dance, poetry readings, drama productions and children's productions by guest artists and Callanwolde's affiliate groups: the Poetry Committee, Young Singers of Callanwolde, Southern Order of Storytellers, Apprentice Dance Company, and the Community Concert Band. There are also classes, cultural activities, special events and volunteer opportunities. 872-5338. Adm: Free to the center itself. Certain events may charge fees.

King Plow Art Center. Downtown West. 887 W. Marietta St. Once a 165,000 sq.ft. plow factory, the King Plow Arts Center, circa 1991, is overflowing with artists and galleries, including some for the commercial arts. The **Actor's Express Theater** also performs here. 885-9933.

Art Galleries

Abstein Gallery
558 14th St., Midtown.
872-8020.
Ongoing exhibits of original paintings, drawings, sculptures and watercolors.

Ariel Gallery
75 Bennett St., Midtown.
352-5753.
Features contemporary and abstract art, sculptures, glass, and wall-hangings.

Art Station
6384 Manor Dr., Stone Mountain.
770-469-1105.
Ongoing exhibits of African-American artists

featuring original watercolors, sculptures, drawings and paintings.

Berman Gallery
3261 Roswell Rd. Buckhead.
261-3858.
Awarded as best folk art gallery, owner Rick Berman continues to inform the public with masters of Southern self-taught art such as Bill Traylor and Thornton Dial.

Bobo's Monkey
441 Seminole Ave., Little Five Points, Downtown.
522-4123.
An eclectic mixture of pottery, steel, glass and canvas.

City Art Works
2140 Peachtree Rd., Buckhead.
605-0786.
Unique and distinctive gift gallery of jewelry, ceramics, furnishings and art pieces.

Coyote Trading Company
419 Moreland Ave., Little Five Points, Downtown.
221-1512.
Wonderful selection of Native American handicrafts featuring pottery, weavings, carvings, sand paintings and sterling jewelry.

The Cricket Gallery
5525 Glen Errol Rd., Sandy Springs.
252-0021.
Specializing in animated art from Walt Disney, Warner Bros., Hanna-Barbera and more.

Dorothy McRae Gallery
3193 Roswell Rd., Buckhead.
266-2363.
Featuring contemporary crafts, national and international, three-dimensional metals and sculptures.

Eclectic Electric Gallery
1393 N. Highland Ave. Virginia-Highlands.
875-2840.
Light up your life with creations from artists that use light as an medium. Art work in the

form of copper sconces, ceramic candlesticks, and neon wall sculptures are some of the samples.

Fishbone Gallery
500 Means St. Midtown.
522-3425.
Art filled renovated loft space in the historic Allied Factory Building featuring heart pine floors and beams, exposed brick, unusual custom aquariums, furniture and colorful ceramics. Available for private functions, art shows and photo shoots.

Form and Function Gallery
784 N. Highland Ave., Virginia-Highlands.
892-3193.
Functional art by local and national artists featuring furnishings and decorative arts.

Frabel Gallery
3393 Peachtree Rd., Lenox Square, Buckhead.
233-8129.
Internationally know German artist, Hans-Godo Frabel creates glass hand-crafted sculptures, Absolute Vodka artist of 1989.

Goldsmiths Gallery for Fine Art and Jewelry
247 Buckhead Ave., Buckhead.
841-9264.
Handcrafted select jewelry handcrafted by European goldsmiths and designers.

Heath Gallery
416 E. Paces Ferry Rd., Buckhead.
262-6407.
Exhibiting regional and traditional paintings and drawings.

Human Arts Gallery
887 W. Marietta St., Marietta.
770-724-9141.
Exhibits of contemporary to abstract oils on canvas, outdoor and indoor sculptures and decorative art

Ichiyo Art Center
432 E. Paces Ferry Rd., Buckhead.
233-1846.

Contemporary Japanese exhibitions of wood-block prints, silkscreens, books, Japanese art supplies and bonsai supplies.

Illumina
3500 Peachtree Rd., Phipps Plaza, Buckhead.
233-3010.
Specializing in handcrafting fine jewelry with exotic colored gemstones and unique settings designed by over 50 artists.

Jackson Fine Art
3115 E. Shadowlawn Ave. Buckhead.
233-3739.
Vintage and 20th-century photographic art, showing quality and integrity, featuring well-known Harry Callahan as well as new young talent.

Koolhipfunkystuff
1030 Monroe Dr., Piedmont Park Area.
607-1095.
Featuring an collection of canvas, watercolors, pottery and jewelry from local artists. Proceeds to Good Samaritan Aid of Atlanta Project.

Lansdell Galleries
3177 Roswell Rd., Buckhead.
231-2190.
Exhibiting contemporary to traditional by young talent featuring the figurative to landscapes.

Marcia Wood Gallery
1198 N. Highland Ave., Virginia-Highlands.
885-1808.
Presenting contemporary paintings, drawings and prints from promising young artist such as Deborah Maebroad, Mary Carmichael and Don Pollack.

Modern Primitive Gallery
1402 N. Highland Ave. Virginia-Highlands.
892-0556.
For both the casual shopper and serious collector, the gallery offers the finest of American folk, outsider and self-taught art.

Nexus Contemporary Art Center
535 Means St. Midtown.
688-1970.
Nexus Contemporary Art Center's mission is to promote experimentation, excellence and education in the visual, performing and book arts. Founded in 1973, it operates in a historic warehouse complex presenting six exhibition periods as well as special projects throughout the year; Nexus also presents Atlanta's largest annual art party the weekend after Labor Day.

O'Karma-Jones Gallery
450 14th St., Midtown.
874-9461.
Traditional oils, prints and watercolors. Also antique engravings.

Photography Center of Atlanta
1769 Cheshire Bridge Rd.,
Buckhead/Midtown.
872-7262.
Featuring the fine art of contemporary photography with seasonal exhibits, photography books and classes.

Ray's Indian Originals Gallery
90 Avondale Rd., Decatur.
292-4999.
Specializing in fine contemporary southwest American-Indian art, Pueblo pottery, historical baskets, Hopi dolls, weaving and jewelry.

The Russian Art House
2300 Peachtree Rd., Buckhead.
605-0097.
Unique gallery of Russian art, sculptures, jewelry, nesting dolls and many other collectibles.

Shrine of the Black Madonna
946 Ralph D. Abernathy Blvd., SW Atlanta.
752-6125.
Specializing in imported African sculpture and artifacts. Also Atlanta's largest African-American bookstore.

The Silver Sun Gallery
76 Alabama St., Downtown.
614-0610.

Specializing in Native American art, jewelry and Kachina dolls.

Soapstone Center for the Arts
2853 Candler Rd., Decatur.
241-2453.
Fine selection of soapstone pieces.

Studio Five
439 Seminole Ave., Little Five Points.
524-5223.
Specializing in functionally pottery, jewelry and folk art by American and regional artists.

TULA Foundation Gallery
75 Bennett St., Midtown.
351-3551.
Renovated warehouse which today features artists studios, galleries and art-related business.

Urban Nirvana Gallery & Gardens
15 Waddell St., Inman Park.
688-3329.
Contrary to the ordinary outdoor garden sculptures, many with a spiritual theme, and English traditional by local artist, Christine Sibley.

V. Reed Gallery
780 N. Highland Ave., Virginia-Highlands.
897-1389.
Presenting the finest hand-blown glass, jewelry, ceramics and handcrafted furniture.

William Tolliver's Art Gallery, Inc.
2300 Peachtree Rd. Buckhead.
350-0811.
Specializing in originals, limited editions, paintings, pastels, watercolors, etchings and more, by William Tolliver.

Metro Atlanta Libraries

Call first for hours and policies. Not all libraries, unfortunately, are open to the public.

Atlanta Central 730-1700
Cobb County Central 770-528-2320
Gwinnett County Central . . 770-729-0931

Atlanta History Center 814-4000
Jimmy Carter Library 331-3942
**Georgia State
University Library** 651-2172
Georgia Tech Library 894-4529
**Emory University
Health Library** 727-5810
**Emory University
Law Library** . . . . '727-6824
**Emory University
Main Library** 727-6868

Bookstores

One important distinguishing characteristic of a thriving community is the number and quality of its book shops. By this measure, in a world experiencing declines in independent book shops and readership, Atlanta is booming, booming, booming. Wherever you turn you'll find one or more of Atlanta's magnificent book emporiums. Autochton prevails. Borders, Oxford and Chapter 11 are huge Atlanta phenomena, replete with zillions of titles (new and used), audacious discounts, vast displays of local, national and international magazines and newspapers, and a kindly predilection toward local writers and publishers.

Also, read *The Booklover's Guide to Atlanta* by librarians Cal Gough and Celeste Tibbets. Borders and Oxford usually carry it or call the authors at 377-0476.

A Cappella Books. Owner: Frank Reiss. Little Five Points. 1133 Euclid Ave. New, used literature and collectibles, especially books about folk, country and jazz music. 681-5128.

Ageless Books. Owner: Tom Vail. 3369 Buford Hwy. Mostly used books and first editions. Histories of America, the South and Georgia predominate. 321-3369.

AIA/Architectural Book Center. Manager: K. C. Culbreth. Downtown. 231 Peachtree St..

Architecture, art and interior design and decor predominmate. 222-9920.

Atlanta Book Exchange. Owner: Tom Henson. Virginia-Highlands. 1000 N. Highland Ave. New and used books for the artsy, intellectual reader. 872-2665.

Aspen Book Shop. Owner: Paul Blicksilver. Downtown Atlanta. 5986 Memorial Dr. Used and rare books. 296-5933.

Atlanta Tech Metro/Bookstore. VP: Doug Robinson. Books for professionals in business, medicine, mechanics, computing, building, electronic and more. 1560 Stewart Ave. 756-3817.

Atlantis Connection. Owners: Mary and Tim Morris. Virginia-Highlands. 1402 N. Highland Ave. New age books and paraphenalia. 881-6511.

Auto Motif. Owner: Milton Hill. Smyrna. 2941 Atlanta Rd. SE. Auto books and gadgets. 770-435-5025.

Avalon Book Center. Owner: Charles Whor. Buckhead. 211 Pharr Rd. 233-1611. New Age, metaphysical books and tools. 233-1611

B. Dalton Booksellers. A full-service establishment with numerous locations including:

Peachtree Center. 231 Peachtree Rd.
Manager: Ed Gutierrez. 231-8526.
Buckhead. Lenox Sq. Mall.
Manager: Mark Williams. 231-1183.
N. Druid Hills. 2968 N. Druid Hills Rd.
Manager: Becky Klebe. 634-4461.
Dunwoody Perimeter Mall.
Manager: Ariel Doughty. 770-394-4185.
Decatur. S. DeKalb Mall.
Manager: Angela Moore. 244-7705.
Morrow. Southlake Mall.
Manager: Gretchen Anderson. 770-923-4484.
Duluth. 2100 Pleasant Hill Rd.
Manager: David Denssord. 770-476-8742.
Kennesaw. 400 Ernest Barrett Pkwy.
Manager: Kim McGowan. 770-425-2817.
Northlake Mall.

Manager: Harrison Hicks III. 770-934-9292.
The Crossings at Roswell.
Manager: Ty Threadwell. 770-998-7820.
Cumberland Mall.
Manager: Mark Hughs. 770-435-3297.
Norcross. Greens Corner Shopping Center.
Manager: Judy Murphy. 770-923-4484.

Barnes and Noble. A full-service emporium with zillions of books and magazines, domestic and foreign.
Buckhead. 2900 Peachtree Rd.
Manager: Kim Phillip. 261-7747.
Dunwoody. 4776 Ashford-Dunwoody Rd.
Manager: Mike Crumpton. 770-393-9277.
Alpharetta. 7660 Northpoint Pkwy.
Manager: Brenda Hill. 770-993-8340.

Berean Christian Stores. Christian books, videos, music and school supplies.
Atlanta. 441 Cleveland Ave.
Manager: Jane Ross. 767-7514.
Smyrna. 3201 S. Cobb Dr.
Manager: Linda Hoss. 770-436-0077.

Books and Bytes. Owner: Carol Berg. Lawrenceville. Five Forks Village. 850 Dogwood Rd. Books for every person with special sections for children and computer buffs. 770-985-0812.

Book Nook. Owner: Alex Nunan. A must for music lovers and comic book devotees. New and used paperbacks, records and CDs. Swaps and trades.

Chamblee. 3342 Clairmont Rd. 770-633-1328
Lilburn. 4664 Lawrenceville Hwy. 770-564-9462

Book Warehouse of Georgia. Owner: Howland Ware. Zillions of used books in every imaginable category. All profits go to Emory University's M. Ware Cancer Research Laboratories.

Buckhead. 1851 Peachtree Rd. 352-8000
Stone Mountain. 5370 Hwy 78. 770-498-8077

Books Plus. Owner: John Behnken. Full-service bookstore. Dunwoody. 2482 Jett Ferry Rd. 770-804-0987.

Books and Things. Owner: Ricky Jones. Decatur. 3182B Glenwood Rd. 289-8959.

Bookstar. Manager: Maree Reylly. Marietta. 4101 Roswell Rd. Over 100,000 titles with a giant children's department and a complete newstand. 770-578-4455.

Borders Bookshops. Manager: Robert McCormick. Buckhead. 3637 Peachtree Rd. A huge array of books (over 90,000 titles) and out-of-town newspapers and magazines, plus an extensive children's section. Sales and discounts prevail. 237-0707.

Brentano's Bookstore. Manager: Lee Titus. Perimeter Mall. 770-394-6658.

C. Dickens/Books. Owner: Tom Hamm. Buckhead's Lenox Sq. Mall. 231-3825.

Chapter 11 Discount Books. A full-service, heavy discount book store.

Ansley Mall.
Manager: Toni Vess. 872-7986.
Alpharetta. Saddlebrook Mall.
Manager: Mike Susman. 770-667-0023.
Decatur. Emory Commons.
Manager: Jack Hile. 325-1505.
East Cobb's Highland Plaza.
Manager: Bob Workman. 770-971-0744.
Northlake's Briarcliff Village.
Manager: Bill Browning. 770-414-9288.
Sandy Springs Plaza.
Manager: Tim Hayes. 256-5518.
Snellville Plaza.
Manager: Lisa Tilleman-Cuff. 770-736-0502.

Charis Books. Owners: Linda Bryant and Sherry Emory. Little Five Points. 1189 Euclid Ave. Feminist literature. 524-0304

Chattahoochee Tech. Marietta. 980 S. Cobb Dr. Technical schoolbooks. Manager: John Waddle. 770-528-4560.

Civilized Traveller. Owner: Allen Vollweiler. Buckhead. Phipps Plaza Mall. Travel books. 264-1252.

Cokesbury Religious Books. Manager: Marian Badgett. Decatur. 2495 Lawrenceville Hwy. 770-320-1034.

Coles The Book People.
Decatur. Market Square
Manager: Wayne Smith. 634-2616.
Kennesaw. 1604 Town Center.
Manager: Maria Garcia. 770-423-1579.

Doubleday Bookshops. A full-service book store.
Downtown. the Underground.
Manager: William Adams. 681-1797.
Buckhead. Phipps Plaza Mall.
Manager: Tara Cook. 816-1755.

Eastern Associates Bookstore. Downtown. Grant Park at the Cyclorama. Civil War books and maps. Manager: Zoeda. 622-6264.

Emory Village Bookstore. Decatur. 1401 Oxford Rd. College textbooks. Manager: Todd Urbanski. 378-9415.

Engineer's Bookstore. Midtown. 748 Marietta St. Everything a Georgia Tech student ever wanted to know about engineering and computers. Manager: Pat Cunningham. 221-1669.

Family Bookstores. Religious books, music and gifts.
Duluth. Crossroads Shopping Mall.
Manager: Glenna Silvers. 770-497-9368.
Dunwoody Village.
Manager: Mark Cox. 770-392-1662.
Jonesboro. 7977 Tara Blvd.
Manager: Tim Barbee. 770-471-1962.
Kennesaw. Town Center.
Manager: Ty Moses. 770-499-1849.
Morrow. Southlake Mall. 770-961-7962.
Roswell. Market Center.
Manager: Trey Kongenecker. 770-518-0279.
Roswell. Winn-Dixie Marketplace.
Manager: Steve Burress. 770-998-8073.

Shannon Southpark Mall.
Manager: Ricky Walden. 770-964-6653.
Stone Mountain Square.
Manager: Julian. 770-498-1728.

Georgia Book Store. New and used college texts and law texts. Downtown. 124 Edgewood Ave. Manager: Thomas Thrower. 659-0959.

Greater Atlanta Christian Bookstore. Norcross. 1575 Indian Trail. Manager: Peggy Walker. 770-923-9285.

Hakim's Book Store. Owner: Dawud Hikim. Downtown. 842 Martin Luther King Jr., Dr. Specializing in African American history and children's. 221-0740.

Hobbit Hall. Owner: Ann Ginkel. Roswell. 120 Bulloch Ave. Vast selection of childrens' books. 770-587-0907.

Joshua's Christian Bookstores.
Douglasville. 5963 Stewart Pkwy.
Manager: Crystal Francis. 770-942-5286.
Dunwoody. 4478 Chamblee-Dunwoody Rd.
Manager: Dennis Loggins. 770-451-3137.
Duluth. 3505 Gwinnett Place Dr. 770-476-0380.
Kennesaw. 440 Barrett Pkwy.
Manager: Mary O'Rourke. 770-425-5030.
Marietta. 270 Cobb Pkwy.
Manager: Joe Cantello. 770-429-8283.
Morrow. 1377 Morrow Industrial Blvd.
Manager: Jamy Kent. 770-961-1206.
Stone Mountain. 937 N. Hairston Rd.
Manager: Tim Bacon. 770-879-6746.

Macy's Bookstore. Downtown. 180 Peachtree St. Featuring best sellers, cookbooks and works by local writers.221-7221.

Majors Scientific Books. Downtown. 141 North Ave. Medical books and supplies. Manager: Rosemary Puckett. 873-3229.

Medu Bookstore. Owner: Nia Damali. Afro-American titles and how to books. 2841 Greenbriar Pkwy. 346-3263.

News Center. Owner: Alton Lewis. Books, magazines and newspapers.
Forest Park. Forest Square Shopping Center. 4903 Jonesboro Rd. 361-9340.
Marietta. Parkway Plaza Shopping Center. 667 S. Marietta Pkwy. 770-590-0688.

North Metro Tech. Acworth. 5198 Ross Rd. Technical schoolbooks. Manager: Mike. 770-975-4010.

Notre Dame Book Shop. Doraville. Pinetree Plaza. 5273 Buford Hwy. Religious books and supplies. Book Buyer: Ann May. Manager: Jane. 770-458-1779.

Old New York Book Shop. Midtown. 1069 Juniper St. An amazing array of first editions. Manager: Cliff Graubart. 881-1285.

Outwrite Books. Owner: Philip Rafshoon Downtown. 931 Monroe Dr. Alternative lifestyle literature. 607-0082.

Oxford Book Stores. Replete with a huge art book collection and an expresso cafe. A vast selection of books and magazines on almost every conceivable subject.
Buckhead. 360 Pharr Rd.
Manager: Gregg Norton. 262-3333.
Buckhead. 2345 Peachtree Rd.
Manager: Kitty Moon. 364-2700.

Oxford Too. Buckhead. 2395 Peachtree Rd. Used books, records and CDs supplemented by first editions and remainders. Manager: Trina Jones. 262-3411.

Phoenix and Dragon Bookstore. Owner: Candice Apple. Sandy Springs. 300 Hammond Dr. New age books and music. 255-5207.

Presbyterian Bookstore. Owner: Camille Gaffron. N. Druid Hills. 1455 Tullie Rd. 728-9985.

Science Fiction and Mystery Bookshop. Owner: Mark Stevens. Specializes in the best of Atlanta and mystery, horror and science fiction. Cheshire Pointe Shopping Center, 2000-F Cheshire Bridge Rd. 634-3226.

Scribner's Bookstore. Buckhead. Lenox Sq. Mall. A classic American bookstore. Manager: Mark Williams. 231-1183.

Shepherd's Staff Christian Bookstore. Owners: Nancy and Ken Fowler Roswell. 2880 Holcomb Bridge Rd. 770-998-6009.

Soul Source. Owner: James P. Wilbur. Afrocentric bookstore and cafe located on the campus of Atlanta University. 577-1346.

Sound Principle Christian Bookstore. Owner: John Ackerman. Smyrna. 2443 Spring Rd. 770-436-4602.

Sphinx Bookstore. Owner: Tom Poole. Ansley Square. 1510 Piedmont Ave. Metaphysics. 875-2665.

St. Mary's Bookstore. Owner: Jean Dortch Buckhead. 2140 Peachtree Rd. Catholic books and religious items. 351-2865.

Tall Tales Book Shop. Owner: Molly Zeiler 2999 N. Druid Hills Rd. at the Toco Hills Shopping Center. A full-service independent book store. 636-2498.

Truth Bookstore. Owner: Sharon Warner. Downtown. 56 Marietta St. Afro-centric books and games. 523-3240.

U.S. Government Bookstore. Downtown. 999 Peachtree St. Manager: Ann Owenby. 331-6947.

Unity Bookstore. Owner: Kathy Lumberg. Chamblee. 4146 Chamblee-Dunwoody Rd. Self-discovery and the metaphysical, books and audio. 770-457-9888.

Waldenbooks. A full-service bookstore. Alpharetta. North Point Mall. Manager: Steve Lanning. 770-740-8341. Buckhead. Lenox Sq. Mall. Manager: Laurel. 261-2781 Marietta. Cumberland Mall. Manager: Louis Mancill. 770-432-3288. Town Center at Cobb. Manager: Kelly. 770-427-7810 Norcross. Spalding Woods Village.

Manager: Beth Pickens. 770-448-7539. Northlake Mall. Manager: Laura O'Donnell. 770-938-2441. Duluth. Gwinnett Place Mall. Manager: Tom. 770-476-7410. Stone Mountain. 5251 Memorial Dr. Manager: Krys Bondello. 770-297-8865.

West Campus Book Store. Georgia Tech area. 529 10th St. Engineering and computer books. Manager: Mark Singletary. 881-8009.

Yesterday Book Shop. Owner: Polly Fraser. Buckhead. 3201 Maple Dr. Just what you would expect. Hard to find Georgia and American history, art books, maps and a friendly, helpful staff. 237-0163.

Commentary

Metro Atlanta's Vast Educational Arena. Included in this section are most of metro Atlanta's colleges and universities, private sschools, professional schools of art, acting, dance, travel, cooking, summer camps and crafts.

Colleges and Universities

Agnes Scott College
11 East College Ave.
Decatur, GA 30030
638-6279.
A four-year college with 600 students.

The American College for the Applied Arts
3330 Peachtree Rd.
Atlanta, GA 30326
231-9000.
A four-year private college with 740 students.

Atlanta Area Technical Institute
1560 Stewart Ave.
Atlanta, GA 30310
756-3778.
A public technical institute with 1,639 students.

Atlanta Christian College
2605 Ben Hill Rd.
East Point, GA 30334
669-2095.
A four-year private college with 250 students.

Atlanta College of Art
1280 Peachtree St.
Atlanta, GA 30309
733-5200.
A four-year private college with 400 students.

Atlanta Metropolitan College
1630 Stewart Ave.
Atlanta, GA 30310
756-4038.
A two-year public college with 1,711 students.

Bauder College
3500 Peachtree Rd.
Atlanta, GA 30326
237-7573.
A two-year private college with 500 students.

Beulah Heights Bible College
892 Berne St.
Atlanta, GA 30316
627-2681.
A four-year private seminary with 300 students.

Brenau University
6745 Peachtree Industrial Blvd.
Atlanta, GA 30360
770-446-2900.
A private liberal arts university with 650 students.

Carver Bible Institute and College
437 Nelson St.
Atlanta, GA 30313
527-4523.
A five-year private seminary with 115 students.

Carroll Technical Institute
997 South Hwy.16
Carrollton, GA 30117
770-836-6800.
A public technical institute with 1,000 students.

Chattahoochee Technical Institute
980 South Cobb Dr.

Marietta, GA 30060
770-528-4545.
A public technical institute with 1,700 students.

Clark Atlanta University
James P. Brawley Dr.
Atlanta, GA 30314
880-8017.
A private historically black Methodist-affiliated university with 4,480 students.

Clayton State College
5900 North Lee St.
Morrow, GA 30260
770-961-3550.
A four-year public college with 4,548 students.

The Creative Circus
1935 Cliff Valley Way
Atlanta, GA 30329
633-1990.
A two-year private college with 100 students.

Columbia Theological Seminary
301 Columbia Dr.
Decatur, GA 30031
378-8821.
A seminary of the Presbyterian Church with 602 students.

DeKalb College
3251 Panthersville Rd.
Decatur, GA 30034
244-5090
A two-year public college with 16,000 students.

DeKalb Technical Institute
495 North Indian Creek Dr.
Clarkston, GA 30021
297-9522.
A two-year public technical institute with 5,000 students.

DeVry Institute
250 North Arcadia Ave.
Decatur, GA 30030
292-2645.
A four-year private college with 2,824 students.

Emory University
200 Oxford Rd.

Atlanta, GA 30322
874-0999.
A private Methodist university with 9,958 students.

Georgia Baptist College of Nursing
303 Parkway Dr.
Atlanta, GA 30312
265-4800.
A four-year Baptist professional college for women with 336 students.

Georgian Institute of Technology
225 North Ave.
Atlanta, GA 30332
894-3378.
A public university with 12,814 students.

Georgia State University
University Plaza
Atlanta, GA 30303
651-3456.
A public university with 24,024 students.

Grady Memorial Hospital Professional Schools
80 Butler St.
Atlanta, GA 30335
616-3610.
A hospital-based professional school with 43 students.

Gwinnett Technical Institute
1250 Atkinson Rd.
Lawrenceville, GA 30246-1505
770-962-7580.
A public technical institute with 20,340 students.

The Howard School
Central Campus
1246 Ponce de Leon
Atlanta, GA 30306
377-7436.
A private special education school with 140 students.

Institute of Paper Science and Technology
500 - 10th St.
Atlanta, GA 30318

853-9525.
A graduate school with 79 students.

Interdenominational Theological Center
671 Beckwith St.
Atlanta, GA 30314
527-7707.
A interdenominational seminary with 343 students.

Keller Graduate School
Two Ravinia Dr. #250
Atlanta, GA 30346
671-1744.
A private graduate school with 150 students.

Kennesaw State College
3455 Frey Lake Rd.
Marietta, GA 30061
770-423-6400.
A comprehensive public college with 11,670 students. Degrees: Nursing, four-year; post-graduate in Business and Education.

Life College
1269 Barclay Circle
Marietta, GA 30060
770-424-0554.
A private college with 3,051 students.

Luther Rice Seminary
3038 Evans Mill Rd.
Lithonia, GA 30038
770-484-1204.
A four-year seminary with 150 students.

Massey Business College
3355 Lenox Rd.
Atlanta, GA 30326
816-4533.
A two-year public college with 225 students.

Mercer University
3001 Mercer University Dr.
Atlanta, GA 30341
986-3375.
A private Baptist university with 6,348 students.

Mercer University-Southern School of Pharmacy
3001 Mercer University Dr.

Atlanta, GA 30341
986-3300.
A private professional Baptist school with 484 students.

Morehouse College
830 Westview Dr.
Atlanta, GA 30314
681-2800.
A private historically black four-year men's college with 2,992 students.

Morehouse School of Medicine
720 Westview Dr.
Atlanta, GA 30310-1495
752-1500.
A private professional school with 157 students.

Morris Brown College
643 Martin Luther King Jr. Dr.
Atlanta, GA 30314
220-0205.
A private four-year African Methodist Episcopal-affiliated college with 2,050 students.

National Louis University
1777 Northeast Expressway, #250
Atlanta, GA 30329
633-1223.
A four-year private institution with 300 students.

North Metro Technical Institute
5198 Ross Rd.
Acworth, GA 30102
770-975-4000.
A public technical institute with 675 students. Degrees: diploma, associate degrees and continuing education classes.

Oglethorpe University
4484 Peachtree Rd.
Atlanta, GA 30319
364-8383.
A four-year private liberal arts college with 1,100 students.

Oxford College of Emory University
100 Hamill St.
Oxford, GA 30209
727-4390.

A two-year private Methodist-affiliated college with 550 students.

Portfolio Center
125 Bennett Street
Atlanta, GA 30309
351-5055.
A two-year private school with 100 students.

Psychological Studies Institute
2055 Mt. Paran Rd.
Atlanta, GA 30327
233-3949.
A two-year public institute with 100 students.

Reinhardt College
P.O. Box 128
Waleska, GA 30183
770-479-1454.
A two-year private Methodist-affiliated college with 864 students. Degrees: two-year Liberal Arts, four-year Business.

Shorter College
1950 Spectrum Circle, #B-190
Marietta, GA 30067
770-951-1950.
A four-year private college with 500 students.

Southern College of Technology
1100 South Marietta Pkwy.
Marietta, GA 30060
770-528-7240.
A comprehensive technical college with 3,922 students.

Spelman College
350 Spelman Lane
Atlanta, GA 30314
681-3643 ext.2171.
A four-year private women's college with 1,984 students.

West Georgia College
1600 Maple Street
Carrollton, GA 30118
770-836-6416.
A comprehensive public college with 7,717 students.

Private Secondary Schools

Atlanta International School
4820 Long Island Dr.
Atlanta, GA 30342
843-3380.
Grades K-12 with 556 students.

Brandon Hall School
1701 Brandon Hall Dr.
Dunwoody, GA 30350
770-394-8177.
Grades 4-12 with 160 students.

Brimarsh Academy
1565 Holcomb Bridge Rd.
Roswell, GA 30076
770-992-0416.
Grades PreK-8 with 200 students.

Cherokee Christian
209 Hames Rd.
Woodstock, GA 30188
770-516-0922.
Grades K-9 with 145 students.

The Children's School
345 Tenth St.
Atlanta, GA 30309
873-6985.
Grades 3-6 with 230 students.

Community Christian
Hwy. 5 S.
Canton, GA 30114
770-479-9535.
Age 3-1st grade with 45 students.

Counterpane School
Montessori Community School, Inc.
839 Hwy. 314, P.O. Box 898
Fayetteville, GA 30214
770-461-2304.
Grades PreK-12 with 150 students.

Epstein School
335 Colewood Way
Atlanta, GA 30328

843-0111.
Grades 2-8 with 585 students.

First Montessori School of Atlanta
5750 Long Island Dr.
Atlanta, GA 30327
252-3910.
Ages 18 months-12 years with 145 students.

Galloway School
215 W. Wieuca Rd.
Atlanta, GA 30342
252-8389.
Age 2 years-12th grade with 580 students.

Greater Atlanta Christian Schools
1575 Indian Trail Rd.
Norcross, GA 30093
770-923-9230.
Age 4 years-12th grade with 1,025 students.

Harvest Christian Academy
1573 Alabama Rd.
Acworth, GA 30101
770-974-9091.
Age 4-12th grade with 45 students.

The Heiskell School
3260 Northside Dr.
Atlanta, GA 30305
262-2233.
Age 2-7th grade with 450 students.

Holy Innocents' Episcopal School
805 Mt.Vernon Hwy.
Atlanta, GA 30327
255-4026.
Age 3-12th grade with 1,140 students.

The Lovett School
4075 Paces Ferry Rd.
Atlanta, GA 30327
262-3032.
Age 4-12th grade with 1,446 students.

Marist School
3790 Ashford Dunwoody Rd.
Atlanta, GA 30319
770-457-7201.
Grades 7-12 with 1,008 students.

Mill Springs Academy
6955 Brandon Mill Rd.
Atlanta, GA 30328
255-5951.
Age 5years-12th grade with 145 students.

Mount Vernon Christian Academy
4449 Northside Dr.
Atlanta, GA 30327
256-4057.
Grades 8-12 with 125 students.

Pace Academy
966 West Paces Ferry Rd.
Atlanta, GA 30327
262-1345.
Grades K-12 with 825 students.

Paideia School
1509 Ponce de Leon Ave.
Atlanta, GA 30307
377-3491.
Age 3-12th grade with 715 students.

St.Martin in the Fields Episcopal School
3110-A Ashford Dunwoody Rd.
Atlanta, GA 30319
237-4260.
Age 2-8th grade with 450 students.

St.Pius X Catholic High School
2674 Johnson Rd.
Atlanta, GA 30345
636-3023.
Grades 9-12 with 1,000 students.

Trinity School
3254 Northside Pkwy.
Atlanta, GA 30327
231-8100.
Age 2-6th grade with 507 students.

The Walker School
700 Cobb Pkwy. N.
Marietta, GA 30062
770-427-2689.
Age 4-12th grade with 600 students.

Wesleyan Day School
86 Mt.Vernon Hwy.
Atlanta, GA 30328

255-8557.
Grades 3years-9th grade with 375 students.

The Westminster School
1424 West Paces Ferry Rd.
Atlanta, GA 30327
355-8673.
Grades K-12th with 1,700 students.

Woodward Academy
P.O. Box 87190
College Park, GA 30337
765-8250.
Grades 5-12 with 1,817 students.

Acting Schools

Actor's Express 607-7469
Alliance Theater School 898-1131
Callanwolde Fine Arts Center . . 872-5338
Jeff Justice's
   Comedy Workshops 262-7406
Stage Door Players
   Theater School 396-1726

Arts and Crafts Schools

Freemanville Woodworking
   Shop 770-476-5452
Highland Hardware 872-4466
Home Depot 433-8211
National Institute of
   Home Builders 257-1211
Southface Energy Institute 525-7657

Cooking Schools

Diane Wilkinson's
   Cooking School 233-0366
East 48th Street Market 446-8256
Kitchen Fare 455-7304
Nathalie Dupree 881-6299
Ursula's Cooking School 876-7643
Wine Sips 901-9433

Dance Schools

Academy of Sports 981-8000
Atlanta Cajun Dance Assn. 451-6611
Atlanta Tap and Dance Center. 634-9494
Ballethnic Dance Company 933-9050
Dancer's Studio Backstage 993-2623
Decatur School of Ballet 378-3388
Lee Harper Dancers' Studio . . . 261-7416
Mulligan School of Irish Dance. 426-5521
Room to Move. 847-0453
Royal Scottish Country
   Dancing Society 982-9438
Rotaru Ballet School 662-0993
Ruth Mitchell Dance Studio . . . 426-0007
School of the Atlanta Ballet. . . . 874-8695

Square Dancing

Cathedral Squares 874-0320
Dixie Squares 770-668-9954
Lads and Lassies. 770-474-3391
Shufflin' Shoes 688-0628
South Cobb Yellow Rocks . . 770-489-9901
Y Knot Club 770-509-2737
Terpsichore Dance
   Expressions. 874-8755
Total Dance Theater. 892-8486
Village Clogging Center. . . . 770-498-5953

Travel Schools

Advanced Career Training
1 Corporate Square #110
Atlanta, GA 30329
321-2929.
A comprehensive six-month program.

Executive Travel Institute
1150 Lake Hearn Dr. #260
Atlanta, GA 30342
303-2929.
A compensive six-month program.

Omni School of Travel
1150 Hammond Dr. #1190, Bldg.A
Atlanta, GA 30328

395-0055.
A comprehensive three-month program

Summer Camps

Athens YWCO
706-754-8528.

Circus Arts Camp
892-2727.

Georgia Tech Tennis Camp
894-0459.

Rabun Gap-Nacoochee School
800-543-7467.

Suzuki Talent (pre-school music) Camp
352-0803.

Alliance Theater Summer Drama Camp
733-4700.

Westminster Summer Camp
355-4084.

SciTrek Summer Camp
522-5500 ext.298.

Camp Kingfisher
770-992-2055.

National Computer Camps
364-8423.

**Briarlake Baptist Church-
Children's Summer Camp**
325-9638.

Summer Safari Day Camp
624-5822.

Wilderness Adventure
800-782-0779.

Valley View Ranch(girls equestrian) Camp
706-862-2231.

Summerscape (science enrichment program)
894-0777.

Southeast Music Camp
770-840-9172.

Theaters

Actors Express 221-0831
Agatha's, A Taste of Mystery . . . 875-1610
Alliance Theater 892-2414
Atlanta Shakespeare Tavern. 874-5299
A.R.T. Station. 469-1105
DeKalb Center for the
  Performing Arts. 289-ARTS
Down Right Theater. 476-7926
Horizon Theater Company. 584-7450
Jomandi Productions 876-6346
Neighborhood Playhouse 373-5311
Onstage Atlanta 897-1802
Roswell Village Theater. 770-998-3526
Seven Stages. 523-7647
Shakespeare Tavern 874-5299
Southern Fried Productions 378-8646
Stage Door Players. 770-396-1726
Theater in the Square 770-422-8369
Theater Gael 876-1138
Theatrical Outfit 872-0665
Tri Cities Community Theater . . . 681-6091

Ethnic Atlanta-
An Evolving Multiculturalism

At every turn in the road you will experience
and marvel at the evolving cultural diversity
that is transforming Atlanta into a world-class
city. Below is a list of Atlanta's foreign consulates followed by a list of Atlanta's numerous cultural associations.

Foreign Consulates

Consulate of Argentina. 880-0805
Consulate of Austria. 264-9858
Consulate General of Belgium . . . 659-2150
The British Consulate General . . . 524-5856
Canadian Consulate General 577-6810
Honorary Consulate of Chile . 770-804-9067
Consulate General of Colombia. . 237-1045
Consulate General of
  Costa Rica 770-951-7025
Honorary Consulate of the
  Republic of Cyprus 770-941-3764

Honorary Consulate of Denmark . 614-5207
Honorary Consulate
  General of Ecuador. 770-491-6026
Honorary Consulate of
  El Salvador 252-8425
Honorary Consulate
  of Finland 770-993-6696
Consulate General of France. 522-4226
Consulate General of the
  Federal Republic of Germany . . . 659-4760
Consulate of Greece 261-3313
Honorary Consulate of Guatemala 255-7019
Honorary Consulate of Haiti 847-0709
Honorary Consulate of the Republic of Hon-
duras....482-1332
Honorary Consulate General
  of Iceland. 321-0777
Consulate General of Israel. 875-7851
Honorary Consulate of Italy 355-6994
Honorary Consul
  of Jamaica. 770-593-1500
Consulate General of Japan. 892-2700
Consulate General of the
  Republic of Korea 522-1611
Honorary Consulate of Liberia . . . 753-4753
Honorary Consulate of
  Luxembourg 770-668-9811
Consulate of Mexico 266-2233
Honorary Consulate
  General of Nepal 892-8152
Consulate of the Netherlands 525-4513
Royal Norwegian Consulate 239-0885
Consulate General of Panama 525-2772
Honorary Consulate of
  the Philippines 233-9916
Honorary Consul of Senegal 794-6836
Consulate of the Republic
  of Sierra Leone 770-785-9990
Honorary Consulate of Sweden . . 261-1187
Consulate General of Switzerland. 870-2000
Royal Thai Consulate 770-988-3304
The Honorary Consulate of
  the Republic of Turkey. . . . 770-913-0900

Ethnic Cultural Associations

The organizations and telephone numbers listed below have been subject to frequent change. If you have trouble reaching any of these numbers, dial the information operator or contact the appropriate consulate.

Afghan
Afghan Council 875-0201
African-American
Africa Association of Georgia . . . 239-8183
Arts Exchange 624-1572
Atlanta Kidst Mariam Orthodox
  Tewahido Church 770-991-4935
First Baptist Church of Atlanta . . 347-8203
MLK Center for Non-Violent
  Social Change 524-1956
Metro Atlanta Kwanzaa
  Association 688-3376
NAACP 688-8868
Pan African Orthodox
  Christian Church 752-5490
Shrine of the Black Madonna
  Cultural Arts Center 752-6125
Soapstone Center for the Arts . . . 241-2453
Arab
Arab-American
  Women's Society 770-448-9190
National Association of
  Arab Americans. 770-493-4725
Armenian
Armenian Cultural
  Association 770-971-8368
Australian
Australian Women's
  Association 770-457-8734
Barbados
Barbados-American Cultural
  Association 770-593-1832
Belgian
Belgian Chamber of
  Commerce 870-8085
Bolivian
Bolivian Association 373-2985
Brazilian
Brazilian-American Society 351-6791

Buddhist
Atlanta Soto Zen Center 659-4749
Buddhist Instructional
  Retreat 770-772-9927
British
Daughters of the
  British Empire 770-482-7252
English Speaking Union 636-4009
Cajun
Atlanta Cajun
  Dance Association 770-451-6611
Louisiana Club 770-962-2492
Cambodian
Cambodian Buddhist
  Society 770-482-5563
United Cambodian Society . . 770-991-9146
Canadian
Canadian-American Society 221-0617
Canadian Women's Club . . . 770-564-9986
Caribbean
Atlanta Caribbean
  Assocation 770-482-6781
Dunham Community Center 523-4474
Chinese
Cantonese Association
  of Atlanta 770-993-1017
Chinese-American Lions Club . . . 249-5361
Chinese Community Center . 770-451-4456
Hakka Association of Atlanta 325-9226
Kwong Tung Association
  of Atlanta 770-993-1017
National Association of
  Chinese Americans. 770-394-6542
Organization of Chinese-
  Americans. 770-594-7836
Cuban
Cuban Club 770-451-3477
Cyprian
Cyprus Friendship
  Association. 770-941-3764
Druze
American-Druze Society. 633-1161
Dutch
Holland Club. 812-0990
Ecuadorian
Ecuadorian Association. 770-498-5482
Eriteans
Eritean Community Association . . 752-1667
Ethiopians

Ethiopian Christian Fellowship . . 551-9446
Ethiopian Job Counseling 875-0201
Filipino
Filipino-American
Association 770-478-2057
Finnish
Suomi-Finland Society. 770-448-4608
French
Alliance Francaise 875-1211
French Chamber of Commerce . . 874-2602
German
Goethe Institute 892-2388
Friends of German Language
and Culture 770-422-9956
Salzburger Society 770-427-2287
Ghana
Ghana Association 880-8151
Greek
Greek Orthodox Cathedral
of the Annunciation. 633-5870
Hellenic Community Center. 636-1871
Holy Transfiguration Greek
Orthodox Church. 770-924-8080
Haitian
Haitian Community Church
of God 762-9144
Haitian Ministry Theophile
Church In Christ 624-9432
Hindu
Atlanta Vedic Temple
Society. 770-564-3003
Hindu Temple of Atlanta 770-907-7102
Vishwa Hindu Parishad
of America. 770-458-2661
Hmong
Asian Community Service . . . 770-908-2021
Hungarian
Hungarian Cultural Foundation . . 377-2601
Indian
India-America Cultural
Association 770-436-3719
India Cultural and Religious
Center 770-436-4272
International
Amnesty International 876-5661
Atlanta Sister City Committee . . . 894-4590
Catholic Social Services. 888-7841
Christian Council of
Metropolitan Atlanta 622-2235

Club International 250-5201
Friendship Force 522-9490
Georgia Council for
International Activities. 240-0042
Georgia Mutual Assistance
Association. 763-4241
International Club of Atlanta 315-1766
International Women's Club
of Atlanta 252-2728
International Rescue Committee. . 292-7731
Save the Children Refugee Project 885-1578
Southern Center for
International Studies. 261-5763
Iranian
Persian Community Center. . 770-409-8966
Irish
Children's Friendship Program
for Northern Ireland 770-427-3968
Hibernian Benevolent Society. . . . 299-9399
Islamic
Al-Farooq Masjid of Atlanta. 874-7521
Atlanta Masjid of Al Islam 378-1600
Community Masjid of
the West End 758-7016
Ismali Center 770-996-0755
Masjid Al-Hidayah 770-953-6806
World Relief Refugee Services. . . 294-4352
Israeli
American-Israeli Chamber
of Commerce 874-6970
Jewish Community Center . . 770-396-3250
Italian
Italian Cultural Society 634-8690
Italian Friendship Club 770-434-1459
La Societa Italiana. 770-392-1499
Sons of Italy 770-333-3113
Jamaican
Atlanta Jamaican
Association. 770-593-9290
Jamaican Cultural Society. . . 770-808-1869
Japanese
Japan-America Society 524-7399
Japanese Women's
Garden Club 770-961-5466
Let's Speak Japanese Club 526-5313
Kenyans
Kenyan-Atlanta Community
Organization. 262-7821
Korean

Korean-American
Wives Association 361-8070
Korean Association 770-458-7798
Korean Community
Service Center 770-936-0969
Society of 87 763-4473
Laotian
Asian Community Service . . . 770-908-2021
Lao Buddhist Community
Temple 770-994-9270
Lao Friendship Association . . 770-996-5820
Latino
Atlanta Hispanic Chamber
of Commerce 264-0879
Briarlake Congregacion
Hispana Bautista 634-2460
Centro Catholico Chamblee . . 770-454-8437
Georgia Hispanic Alliance 885-1386
Georgia Partners of the Americas 525-1168
Good Samaritan Center 885-1386
Hispanic-American Circle 292-1903
Iglesia Bautista
Hispana Americana 770-381-8032
Image 266-1956
Juventud Catolica de Atlanta 888-7839
Latin American Association 638-1800
Our Lady of the Americas 332-0103
Latvian
Atlanta Latvian Community 292-6779
Lebanese
Cedar Club of Atlanta 770-498-2597
National Alliance of
Lebanese Americans 770-493-1670
Lithuanian
Lithuanian Community 770-454-7629
Mexican
Friends of Mexico 688-3278
Mexican Center of Culture 264-1240
Native Americans
Oglewanagi Gallery and
American Indian Center 872-4213
Nigeria
Igbo Union U.S.A. 767-6932
OTU Imunne 770-991-6805
Norwegian
Ladies of Norway Club 770-483-0378
Nordic Lodge 770-457-5560
Panamanian
Panamanian Society 284-3434

Peruvian
Cambio 90 292-1903
Honorable Society of the
Friends of Peru 727-6562
Polish
Komitet Parafialny 770-642-6542
Polish-American Heritage
Society 770-972-0503
Puerto Rican
Atlanta Puerto-Rican
Association 770-436-5750
Scandinavia
Scandinavian-American
Foundation 522-1458
Scottish
St. Andrews Society
of Atlanta 770-751-3885
Sierra Leonians
Association of Sierra Leonians . . . 752-1712
Swedish
Svenska Damklubben (women) . . 237-1517
Swiss
Swiss-American Society 770-418-3225
Taiwanese
Atlanta-Taiwanese
Association 770-449-8649
Atlanta Taiwanese Chamber
of Commerce 766-5710
Thai
Thai Association 770-493-1175
Wat Buddha Temple 284-2416
Tibetan
Losel Shedrup Ling Tibetan
Buddhist Center 231-4128
Ukranian
Ukranian Association 770-475-1084
Vietnamese
Georgia Association for Vietnamese-
American Education 89-4556
Vietnamese Buddhist Association 624-9782
World Relief's Operation
Homecoming 294-4352
Welsh
St. David's 953-1040

Atlanta Outreach

The International Friendship Force, comprised of 1,500,000 volunteer citizen-ambassadors, reaches out to 42 countries around the world. Call 522-9490 for more information.

Atlanta also participates in the Sister City Program reaching out to Brussels, Rio de Janeiro, Newcastle-Upon-Tyne, Montego Bay, Lagos, Port-of-Spain, Toulouse and Tbilisi.

Cinemas and Film Societies

AMC	816-4262
Atlanta African Film Society	525-1136
Black Cinematheque	792-2167
Brannon Sq. Twin Cinema	986-5050
Buckhead Art Cinema	237-2436
Buford Hwy Twin	458-5234
Capital Cinemas	594-4593
Cinefest Film Theater	651-2463
Cinemark Theaters	460-7998
Cineplex Odeon	986-5050
Fox Theater	249-6400
General Cinemas	851-1890
Georgia Theater Company	971-1200
Goethe Institute Atlanta	892-2388
Greenbriar Cinema	629-9999
High Museum of Art	892-3600 ext.391
Hilltop Family Theater	941-2233
Image Film and Video Center	352-4225
LeFont Theaters	266-2202
Litchfield Luxury	662-6680
Metropolitan Film Society	729-8487
Movies 8-Buford	945-5066
Northeast Plaza Cinema	248-0624
North Springs Cinema Grill	395-0724
Regal's	840-7300
Silent Film Society of America	633-5131
Storey Theaters	762-9636
Toco Hills Theater	636-1858
Town and Country	977-6887
United Artists	827-4000

Music at the Clubs

Commentary

Clubs listed below range from old and established to recently opened. Hours and acts tend to vary considerably. Always call ahead. Also check the Leisure Section of the *Atlanta Journal/Constitution* and *Creative Loafing*.

Blues/Jazz Clubs

Belcastro's	954-9826
B'L'T's	897-5656
Blind Willie's	873-2583
Blues Harbor	606-0661
Bourbon Street Cafe	980-1900
Cafe 290	256-3942
Catfish Station	875-2454
Concorde Bar and Grill	209-9999
Cooley's Cafe and Bar	607-7736
Daddy D'z	222-0206
Dailey's	681-3303
Dante's Down the Hatch Nightclub	266-1600
Dante's Down the Hatch Underground	577-1800
Delights of the Garden	876-4307
Fat Sam's	843-1260
Java Blues	419-0095
Jeryl's Topaz	250-9888
Just Jazz	355-5423
Lou's Blues Revue	249-7311
Meno's New Orleans Cafe	377-4405
Metropolitan Pizza Bar	264-0135
Morgan's Supper Club	636-2630
Northside Tavern	874-8745
Omega International House	349-2149
Otto's	233-1133
Ray's on the River	955-1187
Red Hot and Blue	814-0066
Red Light Cafe	874-7828
Ritz-Carlton/Buckhead	237-2700
Rooster's	949-3343
Teddy's Live	653-9999
Yin Yang Cafe	607-0682

Country

Buckhead Country Music
  Showcase 955-7340
Country Music Showcase 955-7340
The Country Club 972-7545
Cowboys in the Country 972-7545
Crystal Chandelier 426-5006
Gregory's Lounge 691-4100
Mama's Country Showcase 288-6262
Miss Kitty's 424-6556
Rhett Butler's Lounge 952-6558
Southern Comfort 361-5675
Two Steps West 458-9378
Yellow Rose Saloon 949-7706

Comedy Clubs

Brass Rail and Grill 723-0077
Manuel's Tavern 717-4714
The Punchline 252-5233
Uptown Comedy Corner 350-6990

Acoustic

Eat Your Vegetables 523-2671
Freight Room 378-5365
Sylvia's Art of this Century 522-3666

Classical

Cannon Chapel 727-6666
Spivey Hall 961-3683
Symphony Hall 733-5000

Coffeehouses

Cafe Diem 607-7008
Espresso Cafe 266-8350
Homage Coffee House 681-2662
Hungry Ear Coffee House 955-1408
Java Jive 876-6161
Javaco 872-6676
KaLo's Coffee House 325-3733
Red Light Cafe 874-7828

Variety

Churchill Arms 233-5633
C.J.'s Landing 237-7657
Club 20 Grand 907-9200
Cue Club 261-0660
Dave and Buster's 951-5554
Fanny Moon's Beer Hall 521-2026
Jellyrolls 261-6866
Johnny's Hideaway 233-8026
The Odyssey 261-8476
Park Place Cafe 399-5990
Rupert's 266-9834
Zasu's 237-6848

Rock/Pop

Dark Horse Tavern 873-3607
Have a Nice Day Cafe 351-1401
Midtown Music Hall 872-0060
The Point 659-3522
The Roxy 233-7699
The Scrap Bar 724-0009
Smith's Olde Bar 875-1522
Somber Reptile 842-0700
Velvet 681-9936
Wreck Room 874-8544

Piano Bars

Dailey's 261-6866
Filamia's 279-7818
Jellyrolls 261-6866
Ottley's 262-3344
Park Place Cafe 399-5990

Miscellaneous Clubs

Abri 237-6848
Baja 814-0808
Bell Bottoms 816-9669
Club USA 255-4276
Dottie's Food and Spirits 523-3444
Eddie's Attic 377-4976
Frijoleros 892-8226
Fuzzy's Place 321-6166
International Ballroom 936-9497
Loretta's 874-8125
Miracle Theater 594-4484

Oxygen	816-6522
Paschal's La Carousel Lounge . . .	577-3150
Royal Peacock	880-0745
Sanctuary	262-1377
Sloppy Joe's	239-0882
Tongue & Groove	261-2325
Whiskers Tavern	992-7445

Fun Facts:

- Georgia became the fourth state on January 2, 1788.

- Chartered in 1785, the University of Georgia is America's oldest state-chartered university.

- The "Augusta Journal," founded in 1785, is Georgia's oldest continuously published newspaper.

Fun Facts:

- Georgia has more counties, 159, than any other state except, of course, Texas. Peach County is the latest entry, established in 1924.

- Georgia's land mass covers 58,910 sq. miles, 21st in the nation with the highest elevation occurring at Brasstown Bald Mountain (4,784 ft.

SECTION VI
The Metro Atlanta Health Care System

Commentary

Atlanta is the South's regional center for state-of-the-art health care and services. As you will see in the brief list below, Atlanta is blessed with an abundance first-rate trauma centers and world-class hospitals. Also, do consult your local *Yellow Pages* under Clinics, Hospitals, Emergency Minor Medical Care, Hospices, Physicians, Dentists, Chiropractors, and the like. But, before you venture forth, in an effort to reduce the demands on health care providers and the costs of health care, please peruse the self-help list that follows.

Self-Help:
Ancient and Nouveau
Home Remedies

Achy Feet-Get a better pair of sneakers, or soak feet in a hot white oak bark and water mixture for 15 minutes.

Arthritic Pain Minor-Add a couple of aspirin or Aleve to ginseng, goldenseal and barbell stem tea. Mix 'em up, or one at a time.

Asthma-Breathe deeply through your ears or scavenge up a batch of inner yellow plum tree bark, and some mullein leaves. Add some sage leaves and boil for 20 minutes. Add a tablespoon of alum to each quart. Drink sparingly, each morning and evening.

Burns-Apply either baking soda or castor oil and stop playing with matches.

Cat Allergies-Don't breathe in cat-infested areas.

Chest Congestion-If catnip tea doesn't do it, spread mutton tallow salve on your chest and back.

Cluster Headaches-Get more oxygen into your system either by jogging or using an oxygen inhalant. Also see migraine headaches.

Constipation-Castor oil or senna leaf tea and a letter to the city council.

Common Colds-Try some stiff chicken soup, or onion soup, or some ginger and sugar in hot water.

Common Cough-Hot ginger tea with plenty of local honey unless it were he or she who gave it to you.

Common Headache-If aspirin won't work, quit your job, chuck your golf clubs or both.

Common Hives-Try beekeeping or drink catnip tea.

Crankiness-Get a grip, take opera singing lessons and see listlessness.

Diarrhea-Drink tea made from blackberry root or lady-slipper plant and if you must leave home take extra clothing with you.

Earache-Turn down the sound system or a few drops of extracted walnut oil or Vicks.

Fever-If you're out of aspirin, try rabbit tobacco tea.

Heartache-Dandelion tea and ten good deeds a day until it goes away.

Hiccups-Hold breath and swallow 10 times.

Hemorroids-Stand up and apply ground garlic clove to the afflicted area.

High Anxiety-See common headache and nervous tension.

High Blood Pressure-Try sarsaparilla tea, losing weight and see nervous tension below.

Migraine Headaches-Try the herb feverfew. See. also, common and cluster headaches above.

Nervous Tension-Quit your job and chuck the golf clubs.

Nosebleed-Stop pruning your nasal hair and get a life.

Listlessness-Start thinkin' like Jimmy Carter.

Persistent Stuffed Nose-Call the drug crisis hotline.

Poisons, Ivy, Sumac, Oak-Hold under hot, not scalding, water and then apply a solution of sulphur or calamine.

Pollen Poisoning-Join the Atlanta Botanical Garden; move to the desert; or climb a tree or wear a surgical mask.

Red or Itchy Eyes-Any combination of Visine, sleep and a good pair of goggles.

Sleeplessness-Insert ear plugs and read any page or two from any book authored by Immanuel Kant.

Snakebite-Don't turn the other cheek, bite back.

Spring Fever-Take a cold shower and/or read the collected works of Soren Kierkegaard.

Stomachache-Stop drinking Clorox and start drinking Coke.

Summer Weather Cautions

Sizzling summer days are dangerous. Without appropriate safeguards, high temperatures will result in heat cramps, heat exhaustion and heat stroke.

Heat cramps are muscular pains or cramps usually in the leg or abdomen, resulting from heavy exertion and loss of water. Move the afflicted person to a cool place to rest and stretch the affected muscles. Have the person drink a half glass of water every 15 minutes. Strictly avoid drinking anything with caffeine or alcohol.

Heat exhaustion is a result of water loss from heavy activity. Symptoms include weakness, nausea, dizziness and fatigue. The skin becomes clammy, cool and pale. If not treated promptly and properly the heat exhaustion condition may deteriorate into heat stroke. Move the afflicted person to a cool place and remove all tight clothing. Cool the body by applying wet towels. Have the person drink a half glass of water every 15 minutes and avoid caffeine and alcohol. Watch closely to make sure no adverse change in condition occurs.

Heat stroke is life threatening. Call 911 immediately. Heat stroke is a breakdown of the body's ability to perspire. The afflicted person will have an extremely high body temperature, a rapid and strong pulse, hot, red, dry skin and may lose consciousness. Immediately move the afflicted person to a cool place, lay them down and apply cool water (or place in a cool tub) until body temperature is lowered. Have them drink cool water but avoid food, alcohol and caffeine. Wait for medical help to arrive.

All of these conditions can easily be avoided with these precautions:

▪ Slow down and avoid strenuous activity when the weather is hot.

▪ If you must do strenuous activities, do them during the coolest part of the day.

▪ Stay indoors whenever possible with air conditioning or a fan.

▪ Wear lightweight, light-colored clothing.

▪ Drink plenty of water regularly and often, even if you do not feel thirsty. Avoid drinks with alcohol or caffeine in them. They actually dehydrate the body.

▪ Eat small, healthy meals, often.

For more information on hot weather safety, call the American Red Cross at 262-7010.

Walk-In Clinics

Walk-in clinics provide immediate care for a wide variety of needs, often with extended hours, some as late as 9 p.m., seven days a week. If required, patients are quickly transported to the clinic's affiliate hospital. Check your *Yellow Pages* under "Emergency" or "Clinics" for a complete list of these facilities.

General Hospitals

Atlanta has strategically located trauma centers. Level I trauma care is designed to meet serious health emergencies 24 hours a day. Level II facilities also offer 24-hour trauma facilities with the emphasis on surgery and specialty care. Level III facilities are designed to meet less urgent needs for surgery and specialty care.

**Crawford Long Hospital
of Emory University**
Downtown. 555 Peachtree St. 686-4411. Crawford Long is host hospital for the 1996 Olympic Games. Part of the Emory University Hospital System of Health Care.

**Emory University Hospital
System of Health Care**
1364 Clifton Rd., NE. 712-7021. Spread out throughout Atlanta, this teaching and research institution is ranked 9th nationally in heart care. Emory provides just about every type of specialized care with specialties in multiple organ, tissue and bone marrow transplants, oncology, hematology, neurosurgery and cardiac care. Consult the *Yellow Pages* for their manifold facilities.

Georgia Baptist Medical Center
303 Parkway Dr. 265-4000. A general acute care institution that provides heart, cancer, orthopaedics and maternal-child care. It is also Atlanta's only hospital-based aeromedical service. Its LifeFlight program travels a 100-mile radius and is fully staffed for extreme emergencies.

Grady Memorial Hospital
Downtown. 80 Butler St. 616-4307. A general and acute care facility, Grady is one of the nation's best emergency and trauma care centers and meets the most stringent requirements of a Level I Trauma Center. Grady also provides round-the-clock care in surgery, anesthesia and specialized services such as neurosurgery and obstetrical surgery. A full range of services includes a regional prenatal center for high-risk mothers and babies, a diagnostic imaging center and a radiation therapy center. Designated a regional burn center and long-term care facility, neonatal intensive care nursery, diabetes detection and control center, sickle cell center and a rape crisis center. The Grady Health System infectious disease program has set national standards in providing comprehensive health care for HIV-positive and AIDS patients.

Metropolitan Hospital
3223 Howell Mill Rd. 351-0500. A community hospital offering a variety of medical services combined with in-town convenience. Specialty areas include Women's Services, a Sports Medicine Clinic, a Sinus Center, an Eye Care Center and treatment for impotence and urological problems.

North Fulton Regional Hospital
Roswell. 3000 Hospital Blvd. 770-751-2500. A full-service medical/surgical community hospital with a Level II Trauma Center, that provides seven-day, 24-hour in-house anesthesia and operating room coverage and general acute care. Treatment for cancer and heart problems, nuclear medicine, women's services, orthopaedic services, diagnostic radiology and renal dialysis. The Renaissance Rehabilitation Center focuses on progressive care, a neonatal care unit treats pre-term infants. Also a sports medicine program and a sleep disorder center.

Northside Hospital
1000 Johnson Ferry Rd. 851-8000. A general hospital with specialties in high-risk pregnancies, cancer detection, treatment and control of sleep disorders.

Piedmont Hospital
Buckhead. 1968 Peachtree Rd. 605-5000. An acute and extended care facility providing medical services in every major category of medicine. Specialty areas include obstetrics and women's services, ophthalmology, cardiology, microsurgery, neuroscience and cardiology.

Saint Joseph's Hospital
5665 Peachtree Dunwoody Rd. 851-7001. Atlanta's first hospital (1880). Specialty areas include cardiac, orthopaedic and cancer care.

South Fulton Medical Center
1170 Cleveland Ave. East Point. 305-3500. Provides full-service cardiology and cancer care. Other specialty areas include a Small Wonders Newborn Center, a Diagnostic Imaging Laboratory and a center for rehabilitation. South Fulton also offers vascular laboratory and renal dialysis services, and outpatient surgery.

Southwest Hospital and Medical Center
501 Fairburn Rd. 699-1111. Since 1943 one of ten such institutions in America that is owned, governed and managed by African-Americans. The facility's Primary Care Center specializes in the treatment of children and adolescents. The full range of services includes laparoscopic surgery and maternity care. Southwest offers respiratory therapy, a department of urology, EKG and EEG testing, rehabilitation and physical therapy, as well as an asthma intervention and education program.

Specialized Hospitals

**The Carter Center of
Emory University Centers**
for Disease Control and Prevention
1600 Clifton Rd. 639-3534. Popularly known as the Center for Disease Control (CDC). A public health agency, its responsibilities have expanded from prevention of communicable diseases to assessing environmental hazards, workplace dangers and chronic illness.

Cobb Hospital and Medical Center
Austell. 3950 Austell Rd. 732-4000. Cobb enables mother and baby to be cared for in one private birth suite from admission to discharge. For babies with special needs, Cobb offers advanced care in its Level II nursery. With more than 1,000 employees, Cobb Hospital is a full-service facility.

DeKalb County Decatur Hospital
Decatur. 450 N. Candler St. 377-0221. This 120-bed hospital offers advaced medical technology for general acute care. Considered a leader in laser surgery for the eye, general surgery and gynecological problems. There is a comprehensive adult alcohol and chemical dependency program and a program for eating disorders.

Dunwoody Medical Center
4575 N. Shallowford Rd. 770-454-2000. Services provided include an intensive care unit, a coronary care unit, a gastroenterology lab and a cardiac catheterization lab. The 24-hour Level III Emergency Services offer cardiac monitoring, radiology services, advanced cardiac life support and advanced trauma support. A Women's Pavilion features 10 labor/deliver/recovery suites and a Mother-Baby Unit with 28 private rooms. The hospital's Neonatal Intensive Unit is under the supervision of a board-certified neonatologist.

**Egleston Children's Hospital
at Emory University**
Midtown. 1405 Clifton Rd. 325-6000. Egleston treats over 100,000 children each year and is nationally renowned for its Childhood Cancer and Heart Centers. Egleston provides comprehensive pediatric care, heart surgery and organ transplants. As a clinical, teaching and research institution, the hospital offers an extensive array of clinical care services.

Fulton County Charter Peachford Hospital
2151 Peachford Rd. 455-3200. Offers care of psychiatric illnesses and addictive disease in adults, adolescents and children, including programs for the treatment of alcohol and substance abuse and specialized plans for patients with dual diagnoses, chronic pain and eating disorders.

Gwinnett Medical Center of Lawrenceville
1000 Medical Center Blvd. 770-995-4321. Opened in 1984, the Medical Center is a 190-bed acute care hospital offering all general medical, surgical and diagnostic services. It houses a Level III 24-hour Emergency Department that is the trauma triage center for Gwinnett County. The Center also provides cardiac lithotripsy, catheterization, and magnetic resonance imaging. The DaySurgery houses the GHS Laser Institute which specializes in advanced outpatient laparoscopic and laser surgery. The Scottish Rite Children's Emergency Center serves pediatric emergency cases.

Gwinnett Women's Pavilion
Lawrenceville. 700 Medical Center Blvd. 770-995-3600. The 34-bed facility is situated on the Gwinnett Medical Center campus. It offers maternity, diagnostic and educational services to women of all ages. The diagnostic center provides mammography, ultrasound and osteoporosis screening.

Hughes Spalding Pediatric Hospital
35 Butler St. 616-6600. Provides for a full range of children's medical needs. It is also the site of Georgia's Poison Control Center, which provides emergency advice by phone to almost 10,000 parents and medical professionals a month.

Joan Glancy Memorial Hospital
Duluth. 3215 McClure Bridge Rd. 770-497-4800. This 90-bed general hospital offers medical, surgical, diagnostic and 24-hour emergency services. Twenty of the hospital's beds are dedicated to the Glancy Rehabilitation Center for the treatment of accident and stroke patients.

Laurel Heights Hospital
934 Briarcliff Rd. 888-7860. Offers intensive residential care for children and adolescents, ages 5-17, and their families. The hospital provides special care tracks as dual-diagnosis chemical dependency track, sexual abuse track, substance abuse track and a track for children who are fire setters. Year-round schooling is offered so patients can continue their education.

Northlake Regional Medical Center
1455 Montreal Rd. Tucker 270-3000. Offering general acute care in a broad range of medical services and general surgery, neurosurgery, podiatric reconstructive surgery, plastic reconstructive surgery, vascular and orthopaedic surgery as well as maternity care, oncology, cardiology, orthopaedics and podiatry. There is a newborn intensive care unit. Northlake's extensive rehabilitative programs include physical therapy, respiratory therapy and occupational and speech therapy. For women, the Womancare Breast Diagnostic Center provides comprehensive care. The hospital is home to the Advanced Georgia Laser Center, a diabetes treatment center and an industrial medicine program. A 24-hour emergency department is staffed with board-certified doctors.

The Promina Windy Hill Hospital
Marietta. 2540 Windy Hill Rd. 644-1000. Another member of Northwest Georgia Health Systems, Windy Hill Hospital is a115-bed

hospital for acute care. Among the wide range of medical services are women's programs such as low-dose mammography and breast ultrasound, treatment for substance abuse, and a combined medical/psychiatric program. Comprehensive care is available through Kennestone at Windy Hill's pain management program, occupational health clinic, headache clinic and rehabilitation/evaluation program.

Scottish Rite Children's Medical Center
1001 Johnson Ferry Rd. 256-5252. A Level I trauma and multi-specialty pediatric center with national recognition in the fields of orthopaedics and plastic and reconstructive surgery.

Shepherd Center
2020 Peachtree Rd. 352-2020. The largest facility in the nation dedicated exclusively to treating paralyzing spinal cord injuries and neuromuscular diseases. Other services include a comprehensive Multiple Sclerosis Center, a Fertility Clinic for men and a career planning placement program to assist patients in finding employment.

Smyrna Hospital
3949 S. Cobb Dr. 434-0710. Providing general acute care in a 100-bed facility. Emory otolaryngologists have associated with Smyrna Hospital's Sinus Center, offering expanded treatment of all conditions of the ear, nose, throat and neck. There is also a Foot and Ankle Center.

Summit Ridge
Lawrenceville. 250 Scenic Hwy. 770-822-2222. The hospital provides psychiatric and chemical dependency treatment for adults and adolescents. Services are available for inpatient, partial hospitalization and outpatient care as well as aftercare programs.

Vencor Hospital
705 Juniper St. 873-2871. A long-term acute care hospital specializing in extended care for the medically complex patient, including pulmonary services for the ventilator-dependent

patient, renal dialysis, orthopaedic care and diagnostic radiology.

V.A. Medical Center
Decatur. 1670 Clairmont Rd. 321-6111. Provides acute care in addition to a wide range of other services.

Wesley Woods Geriatric Hospital
1821 Clifton Rd. 728-6200. A teaching and research hospital, its outpatient services include geriatric primary care, neurology, ophthalmology and dentistry.

West Paces Medical Center
3200 Howell Mill Rd. 351-0351. A general acute care center offering psychiatric, rehabilitation and alcohol and substance abuse programs. The Cancer Center at West Paces offers comprehensive care for patients from diagnosis to all stages of treatment. There is also advanced insulin therapy at the Diabetes Center, a Center for Mental Health, a Center for Women, and a Wound Care Center. The hospital's Greater Atlanta Sports Medicine program offers education and research, orthopaedic evaluation, treatment and rehabilitation.

Atlanta's Hospice Care
There are several hospice care facilities in the metro Atlanta area. All are listed under "Hospice Care" in your *Yellow Pages Directory*.

Plastic Surgery

Vinings Surgery Center
Dr. Robert A. Colgrove, Jr.
4200 Paces Ferry Rd., Atlanta
770-432-2191

Vinings Surgery Center offers highly-skilled plastic, cosmetic and reconstructive surgery on an out-patient basis. The Center's Chief Surgeon, Dr. Robert A. Colgrove Jr., is Board Certified by the American Board of Plastic Surgery, and has been a licensed M.D. since 1981, specializing in plastic, cosmetic and reconstructive surgery. Center specialties include facelifts, nose, chin and ear surgery; lip, chin and breast enlargement and reduction; liposuction of face, neck and body; implants for chest and calves, scar revision, tattoo, lesion, mole and cyst removal; and chemical peel, dermabrasion, fat transplants, laser skin resurfacing, and minimally invasive endoscopic surgery.

The Center uses Computer Video Imaging, an advanced computer technology that allows the doctor and the patient to see and discuss surgical options and desired changes.

The Center's operating room personnel are specially trained in outpatient surgery and recovery care and the surgery unit meets rigorous standards for high quality and safety. The cost of in-patient procedures performed at the Center are generally 40% to 50% less than out-patient hospital charges.

Health Insurance and HMO's

BlueCross BlueShield of Georgia
3350 Peachtree Rd., NE
Atlanta, GA 30326
842-8875.

An independent Licensee of the Blue Cross and Blue Shield Association offers two major coverages. Flexplus is the major medical plan that covers physician's visits, prescription drugs and hospitalization and is designed for families who visit physicians on a regular basis. As a member, you are eligible to participate in the Value-Dent program, offering discounts on preventive and diagnostic dental care; Express Pharmacy Services, a low cost delivery system for maintenance prescription drugs for the treatment of chronic or long-term conditions; and VisionCare providing instant savings on eye care, frames, contact lenses and eye examinations. The Hospital Surgical plan is hospitalization coverage only designed for individuals who want catastrophic coverage in

case of an emergency. Choose the health plan designed to satisfy your health coverage needs with ready assistance.

Kaiser Foundation Health Plan of Georgia, Inc.
Nine Piedmont Center,
3495 Piedmont Rd., NE
Atlanta, GA 30305-1736
261-2590.

For fifty years Americans have felt secure with the benefits of the nation's largest and most experienced managed care, Member of the Nationwide Kaiser Permanente. Committed to providing quality medical care and service, in a personal manner and at a affordable cost. Select from one of three plans to fit you individual health care needs and choose from many medical office locations all provided with in-house pharmacy that buys drugs at substantial savings, passing it on to you. Kaiser Permanente builds its reputation on highly qualified physicians, choice of physician, convenience of many locations, cost at its minimal, if any, holding true for all types of medical care, from routine checkups to major surgery. Kaiser Permanente, good people, good medicine.

MetLife
1130 North Chase Pkwy.
Marietta, GA 30067
770-618-2440.

Formed in 1868 as The Metropolitan Life Insurance Company, and a forerunner in health care, safety and educations since 1909 MetLife HMO benefits score high nationwide for word-wide emergency care coverage, full coverage for periodic physicals and well-child care, minimal, if any, out-of-pocket expense and virtually no claim forms. A continues member satisfaction survey shows high scores in skilled physicians, friendliness, obtaining an appointment in a reasonable amount of time and convenient location of participating doctor's office, and hospitals.

Additional to a full array of medical benefits, MetLife HMO memberships include many educational and monitoring programs to promote wellness. From MetLife HMO's Healthy Pregnancy Program, Women's Health Initiative Program to Child Health and Men's Health Initiative Programs, combined with information on fitness walking, healthy nutrition, smoke cessation and stress management. Offering you a partnership caring about good health, get Met, it pays.

United HealthCare of Georgia
2970 Clairmont Rd., #300
Atlanta, GA 30329-1634
982-8887.

One of the area's largest managed care companies, United HealthCare has been taking care of Georgia since 1980. Providing affordable quality health care with freedom and flexibility choose from any doctor within the network, benefits with no hidden costs or annual deductions. Choose any specialist without a referral or emergency care convenient to you, if a non-participating hospital you may share a portion of the cost. You are always covered with preventive care, prescriptions, hospital services and prenatal care. When using a network provider there are no bills or claim forms to file, and always a friendly representative available ready to assist you. Enjoy a managed health care plan where the decisions are made by you, not for you.

Fun Facts:

- By a 1823 ordinance Savannah, Georgia homeowners must air out unoccupied houses at least once a week.

- In 1994 Atlanta was the fourth busiest convention site in America.

- Georgia is named after England's King George II (so was my father) by James Edward Oglethorpe, who brought English settlers here in 1733.

Georgia's State Motto

-Wisdom, Justice, Moderation

Georgia's State Song

In 1979 "Georgia On My Mind," with music by Hoagy Carmichael and lyrics by Stuart Gorell was officially designated Georgia's state song.

Georgia On My Mind

Melodies bring memories

That linger in my heart

Make me think of Georgia

Why did we ever part?

Some sweet day when blossoms fall

And all the world's a song

I'll go back to Georgia

'Cause that's where I belong.

Georgia, Georgia, the whole day through

Just an old sweet song keeps Georgia on my mind.

Georgia, Georgia, a song of you

Comes as sweet and clear as moonlight through the pines.

Other arms reach out to me

Other eyes smile tenderly

Still in peaceful dreams I see

The road leads back to you.

Georgia, Georgia, no peace I find

Just an old sweet song keeps Georgia on my mind.

Hank Aaron

SECTION VII
The Sporting Life

Sports Facilities and Organizations, Pro Sports Teams, Collegiate Sports, Nature and Wildlife Trails, Georgia's Game and Fish Offices, Georgia's State Parks, and Historic Sites

Sports Facilities and Organizations

Georgia is blessed with an abundance of sporting resources. From aerobics to waterskiing, and even a bit of snow skiing, just about every popular indoor and outdoor sporting activity is at hand. Great camping, fishing, swimming, numerous golf and tennis facilities, horseback riding, hiking and rafting, it's all there waiting for you.

*For a wealth of information regarding outdoor activites throughout Georgia see the *"Outdoor Activity Guide"* by Carol and Dan Thalimer. Also call your local department of parks and recreation and the YMCA/YWCA.

Aerobics

Australian Body Works 365-9696
Jeanne's Body Tech 261-0227

Archery

Buckskin Archery. 425-2697
Henry County Archery
   Association 474-3345
Japanese Archery Association . . . 373-0546

Badminton

GA State Badminton Association 876-3626

Baseball/Softball

Atlanta Semi-Pro Association . . . 751-0081
Cherokee Batting Range. 591-4778
Green Ways 361-0218
Heritage Hills 434-6727

Hidden Valley 636-0406
Malibu 514-8081/416-7630
McDivots. 740-1674
Metro Atlanta Softball. 344-3414
Softball Country Club 299-3588
Stone Mountain Sports Complex . 413-5301

Basketball

Atlanta Basketball Classics 817-6937

Bicycling

Try the 400+ mile Atlanta to Savannah bicycle ride (Bicycle Ride across Georgia, 279-9797) or any of the less arduous routes listed below. Most rent bikes.

Callaway Gardens 800-282-8181
Chattahoochee National
   Recreation Area at Dunwoody. . 394-7912
Chattahoochee National Forest
   at Chatsworth (Cohutta Ranger
   District). 706-695-6736
Chattahoochee National Forest
   at Blue Ridge (Toccoa Ranger
   District). 706-632-3031
Lake Lanier Islands 932-7233
Skate Escape 892-1292
Stone Mountain Park. 413-5301

Bicycle Racing and Riding

Cerrato Bicycle Co 417-1821
Chattahoochee River Trail 394-8335
Cycle South 991-6642
Dick Lane Velodrome 765-1085
Free Flite 422-5237
Georgia Bicycle Motorcross
   Association 706-599-8420
Piedmont Park 872-1507
Road Atlanta (see Motor Racing).
Road Wolves Cycling Club. 998-2550
Roswell Bicycles. 642-4057
Southern Bicycle League 594-8350
Stone Mountain Park. 770-498-5633

Billiards/Pool

Buckhead Billiards 237-3705
Cue Club. 237-POOL
Players Billiards 859-9353

Bird Watching

St. Simons Island 912-638-3214
Okefenokee Wildlife Refuge   912-283-0583
Sea Island 638-9354

Boxing

Doraville Boxing Team 457-0003
Knights Boxing Team 432-3632

Bowling

(Many facilities; please consult your
Yellow Pages.)

Bungee Jumping

Dixie Land Fun Park 460-5862

Camping

(See also listings under
State Parks and Wildlife Trails.)

Georgia's numerous state parks (800-3GA-PARK) and lakes (331-6715) provide an unbelievable diversity of camping opportunities for every level of happy camper. From the primitive sites at the shores of Cumberland Island and the Okefenokee National Wildlife Refuge to the manicured facilities at Lake Lanier Islands and Jekyl Island, Georgia's wilderness awaits you.

Allatoona Campground 974-3182
Amazon Adventure 332-0970
Cumberland Island 912-882-4335
Jekyl Island. 912-635-3021
Lake Lanier Islands 945-6701
Okefenokee. 912-496-3331
Stone Mountain Park 770-498-5700
Unicoi State Park 656-3530

Canoeing

Atlanta Whitewater Club 299-3752
Chattahoochee 998-7778
Chattahoochee Outdoor Center . . 395-6851

Georgia Canoeing Association . . . 421-9729
Southeastern Expeditions 29-0433
Stone Mountain Park. 498-5683

Caving

Cave Springs 706-386-0576
Lookout Mountain Caverns . 615-821-2544

Cricket

Atlanta Cricket Association 263-6430
Atlanta Gymkhana. 822-5755
Cosmos Cricket Club 292-8226
Metropolitan Cricket Club 241-1348
Peachtree Cricket Club 813-8809

Croquet

Atlanta Mallet Club. 939-7829

Equestrian

(see, also Horseback Riding)
Atlanta Steeplechase 237-7436
GA International Horse Park. 785-6900
Polo Club of Atlanta 396-9109

Fencing

Atlanta Fencer's Club 892-0307
Fayette Fencing Academy. 461-3809

Field Hockey

Georgia Field Hockey Assn. 262-1633
GFHA Men's Team. 255-6540
GFHA Women's Team 565-9636
GFHA Youth Team. 475-1001

Fishing

Call the Fishing Division at the Georgia Department of Natural Resources (656-3524) to learn everything you ever wanted to know about fishing and crabbing in Georgia's numerous waterways. From the deep sea sharks, blues, king mackerel, snapper and grouper, to the red bass, croaker and sea trout in the surf, to the sunfish, trout, large-mouth bass, catfish, bluegills and zillions of others that populate the lakes, rivers and streams, there are probably a million beautiful acres plus the deep sea set aside for your fishing pleasures. Call 770-493-5770 for fishing license information.

Flying

Sky Warriors. 699-7000

Football

Atlanta Colt
  Youth Association. 770-551-8956
NAFFA Flag Football 223-9800

Frisbee

Atlanta Flying Disc Club 351-0914
Identified Flying Objects 524-4628

Gliding

Atlanta Soaring Club 770-336-5006
Mid-Georgia Soaring 770-621-0522

Golf

(see Section IX entitled Golf Courses)

Golf Associations

Atlanta Jr. Golf Association. . 770-850-9040

Gymnastics

Atlanta School
  of Gymnastics 770-938-1212
Circus Arts Studio 378-4582
Emory University's Summer
  Sports Fitness Camp 727-6547

Hang Gliding

Hang Glider Heaven. 770-782-9908
Lookout Mountain 800-688-LMFP

Hiking

(See also Nature Trails and Wildlife Trails)

The king of hiking trails, the famous Appalachian Trail (78 miles in Georgia) begins at Springer Mountain in Northern Georgia. Happily, the king has a zillion descendents. There are trails for every level of hiker from the concrete walkways of Atlanta's pristine parks to the wilderness of the national forests. Contact the U.S. Forest Service (347-2384) and

the Georgia Sierra Club (770-476-8807) to gain valuable insights into hiking Georgia.

Also read the Hiking Section in the *Georgia Outdoor Activity Guide* by Carol and Dan Thalimer.

Horseback Riding

Atlanta Equestrian Society . . 770-475-5551
Chastain Park Stables 257-1470
Fox Hollow Farm 770-971-3437
Georgia Training Association 770-926-3870
Georgia Horse Foundation 261-0612
Georgia Pony Club 893-3751
Huntcliff Stables 770-993-8448
January Serafy's Riding Camp . . . 355-5519
Lake Lanier Islands. 770-932-7233
Little Creek Farm School 634-9209
Pounds Stables. 770-394-8288
Quarter Horse Association . . 770-483-2818
Wills Park Equestrian Center 770-740-2400

Hot Air Ballooning

Atlanta Hot Air Promotions . 770-452-0033
Bulldawg Balloon Tours. 366-5891
Georgia Balloon Association 770-963-0149
Sundance Balloon 875-3419
U.S. Hot Air Balloon Team. 659-0919

Ice Hockey

USA Hockey 770-419-0349

Ice Skating

Parkaire Olympic Ice Arena . 770-973-0753

In-Line Skating

In-Line Skating Association 728-9707
Peachtree Roadrollers 634-9032
Skate Atlanta 770-59-0605
Southern In-Line Hockey . . . 770-528-9809

Jetskiing

Atlanta Water Ski Club. 770-425-7166
Lake Lanier Islands. 770-932-7255

Jogging

Atlanta Track Club 231-9034

Kayaking

Atlanta Whitewater Club 299-3752
Chattahoochee
  Outdoor Center 770-395-6851
Georgia Canoeing
  Association 770-421-9729
Southeastern Expeditions 329-0433
Stone Mountain Park 770-498-5683

Lacrosse

Atlanta Lacrosse Foundation . 770-992-7231
Atlanta Lacrosse Men's Club. 770-926-6920
Atlanta Women's Lacrosse 303-1160
Georgia Tech Lacrosse. 872-6082

Martial Arts

Atlanta Karate Club 892-7138
Dogwood Aikikai 364-0005
Hapkido 770-448-0564
Lake Lanier Islands 770-932-7233
Peachtree City Judo Club 770-631-4726

Miniature Golf

(Many facilities; please consult your
Yellow Pages.)

Motor Racing

Atlanta International
  Raceway 770-946-4211
New Atlanta Dragway 706-335-2301
Road Atlanta. 881-8233/872-4809

Pool

(see Billiards)

Quail Hunting

Covington-Starrsville
  Plantation. 770-495-2307
McDonough-Dogwood
  Plantation. . . . . 770-957-7005.
Newnan-Gunby Shooting
  Preserve 525-2033/255-1684

Racquetball

Eastlake. 373-3500

Rafting

(See also Canoeing)

Atlanta Whitewater Club. 299-3752
Chattahoochee
  Nature Center 770-992-2055
Chattahoochee
  Outdoor Center. 770-395-6851
Georgia Canoeing
  Association. 770-421-9729
Southeastern Expeditions 329-0433
Stone Mountain Park. 770-498-5683

Rock Climbing

Atlanta Climbing Club 770-621-5070
Women's Rock Climbing Club. . . 876-9916
Kid's Rock Climbing Club . . 770-992-5400

Roller Skating

(See also In-Line Skating.)

All American Skating Center   770-469-9775
Roswell Roller Rink 770-998-9700
Screaming Wheels. 752-5595

Rowing

Atlanta Rowing Club. 770-993-1879
U.S. Rowing Association 317-5656

Rugby

Atlanta Renegades RFC 365-2442
Atlanta RFC. 303-5855
Georgia State Panthers RFC 364-6008

Running

Atlanta Hash House Harriers   770-455-6952
Atlanta Singles 770-509-7961
Atlanta Track Club 231-9064

Sailing

Barefoot Sailing Club 770-513-3851
Hobie Cat Sailing Club 770-781-3762
Lake Lanier Sailing Club . . . 770-967-6441
Lanier Sailing Academy 770-945-8810
Southern Sailing Club. 296-5600
Windsong Sailing Academy 256-6700

Scuba Diving

Atlanta Reef Dwellers 770-477-5176
Atlanta Scuba Club. 770-879-9923
Atlanta Scuba and Swim
  Academy 770-973-3120
Bottom Time Scuba Club. . . . 770-979-9196
YMCA National
  Scuba Program 770-662-5172

Skateboarding

Surf's Up Street Waves 770-482-7471
Skate Zone Skateboard Park . 770-491-0656

Skeet and Trap Shooting

Callaway Gardens Gun Club . 706-663-5129
Georgia Skeet Shooting Assn. 770-979-6364
Wolf Creek Skeet and
  Trap Club. 346-8382

Skidiving

Peach State Skydiving 770-786-JUMP

Snow Skiing

Atlanta Ski Club 255-4800

Soccer

All American Indoor 770-578-6001
Cobb's Women's
  Soccer Association 770-432-2888
Fayetteville 770-460-8785
Georgia Amateur
  Soccer Association 770-452-0505
Lightning Soccer Club 770-460-8070
Soccer Academy. 770-925-4404
Summer Soccer Camps 770-431-6111

Swimming Pools and Beaches

Atlanta Mariott Northwest . . . 770-952-7900
Century Swim. 770-698-8020
Chastain Memorial Park. 817-6785
D.A.M.P 770-698-8020
Dynamo Swim Center 770-451-3272
Grant Park. 622-3014
Lake Allatoona 770-974-5182
Lake Lanier Islands 770-932-7200
M.L. King North. 688-3791
M.L. King South. 658-6099

Piedmont Park 876-2040
Stone Mountain 770-469-9831
Sun Valley Beach 770-943-5900

Table Tennis

Atlanta Table
  Tennis Association. 770-962-0602

Team Handball

Georgia Team Handball 262-7811

Tennis/Courts/Centers

Atlanta Lawn
  Tennis Association. 770-399-5788
Atlanta City Courts 658-7277
Bitsy Grant 770-531-2774
Blackburn 770-451-1061
Chastain Park. 255-1993
Clayton County 770-477-3766
Cobb County 770-424-0204
DeKalb. 325-2520
DeKalb County 371-2548
East Lake 373-3500
Fulton County 572-2526
Georgia Tech. 894-8371
Gwinnett County 770-448-4464
Hudlow 770-417-2210
McGhee 752-7177
North Fulton 256-2377
Piedmont Park 872-1507
South Fulton 770-306-3059
Stone Mountain 770-498-5728
Washington Park 523-1169

Volleyball

Atlanta Club Sports 842-0317

Walking

(See also Nature Trails, Wildlife Trails,
  Atlanta's Parks, Jogging and Bicycling)
Georgia Walkers 770-961-0109
Walking Club of Georgia 847-WALK
Roswell Striders 770-641-3760
Walkers Club of Georgia . . . 770-593-5817

Also, for detailed info see "*Atlanta Walks,*" a
book by Helen and Ren Davis.

Water Polo

Atlanta Water Polo Club 351-4155

Waterskiing

Atlanta Water Ski Club 770-425-7166

Spectator Sports Atlanta

The Olympics
Tickets
224-1996/658-1996.
Prices-$6.00 to $600.00.

Pro Sports Teams

Baseball Atlanta Braves
Fulton County Stadium
Season: April-October
The bleacher seats at $2.50 are a great bargain, but bring your binoculars. Adm: $15.00-$1.00.
249-6400.

Football Atlanta Falcons
Georgia Dome
Season: August-December
Adm: $27.00.
945-1111/223-8000.

Soccer Atlanta Attack
Omni Coliseum
Season: November-March.
431-6111.

Basketball Atlanta Hawks
Omni Coliseum
Season: October-March
Adm: $30.00-$10.00.
827-DUNK.

Hockey Atlanta Knights
Omni Coliseum
Season: October-April
Adm: $16.00-$8.00.
525-8900.

Roller Hockey-Atlanta Fire Ants
Omni Coliseum
Adm: Varies.
521-ANTS.

Team Tennis Atlanta Thunder
Peachtree World of Tennis
6200 Peachtree Corners Circle
Norcross. Adm: Varies.
770-449-6060/250-3428.

Collegiate Sports

Georgia Tech
Yellow Jackets Basketball
Georgia Tech Coliseum
Season: November-February
Adm: $21.00-$15.00.
894-5425.

Yellow Jackets Football
Bobby Dodd Stadium
Season: September-December
Adm: $20.00.
894-5420.

Other Tech Sports: 894-5445.

University of Georgia
Bulldogs Football
Sanford Stadium-Athens
Season: September-December
706-542-1231.

Bulldogs Basketball
UGA Coliseum-Athens
Season: November-February
706-542-1231.

Other Sports: 706-542-1231.

Georgia State University
GSU men's and women's baseball and basketball.
651-2772.

Emory University
Many varsity sporting events.
727-6547.

Clayton State College
Men's and women's
basketball and soccer.
770-961-3450.

Kennesaw State College
Baseball, basketball and others.
770-423-6284.

Nature Trails

Alpharetta

Providence Park 770-740-2419

Atlanta

Atlanta Botanical Garden 876-5859
Atlanta History Center
Bush Mountain Outdoor Activity Center.
ator Wooford Memorial Garden . 377-3836
Chastain Park 653-7160
Chattahoochee River National
   Recreational Area 770-992-2055
Cochran Mill Park 770-306-0914
Dunwoody Nature Center 394-3322
Fernbank Nature Trails. 378-4311
Grant Park. 624-0697
Piedmont Park 892-0117
ZooAtlanta 624-5600

Lake Allatoona

Red Top Mountain State Park 770-975-4203

Lithia Springs

Sweetwater Creek State Park 944-1700

Lithonia

Davidson-Arabian Mountain
   Nature Preserve 770-593-5864

Loganville

Vines Botanical Gardens 466-7532

Marietta

Al Burruss Nature Park 770-528-0615
Kennesaw Mountain National
   Battlefield Park 427-4686

Morrow

West H. Reynolds Memorial
   Nature Preserve 961-9257

Roswell

Big Trees Forest Preserve 594-9367
Chattahoochee Nature Center 992-2055

Rutledge

Hard Labor Creek
   State Park 706-557-2863

Stockbridge

Panola Mountain State
   Conservation Park 770-389-7801

Stone Mountain

Stone Mountain Park. 770-498-5600

Wildlife Trails

Commentary

The following wildlife trails are divided into
three geographic regions: North Georgia,
Central Georgia and South Georgia.

Northern Georgia Trails

**Crockford-Pigeon Mountain Wildlife
Management Area.** Seven separate trails of
differing difficulty at the extreme northwest
corner of Georgia in Walker County. From
Lafayette take GA.193 west 2.5 miles to
Chamberlain Rd; turn left, three miles to
Rocky Lane Road; right 0.5 miles to the
checking station.

1. Rocktown Trail. One mile. Low difficulty.
Leads to undisturbed area of huge sandstone
boulders. Hikers only.

2. South Pocket Trail. 3.1 miles. Scenic, but
strenuous. Surrounded by steep mountain
slopes. Passes beautiful waterfall and abundant wildflowers. Hiking, biking, horseback
riding.

3. North Pocket Trail. 3.5 miles. Scenic. Moderate difficulty. Overlooks the Pocket. Hikers, bicyclists, horseback riders.

4. Atwood Trail. 4.1 miles. Scenic, rustic. Moderate difficulty. Mountain views, wildflowers. Hiking, bicycling, horseback riding. Primitive camping area.

5. West Brow Trail. Six miles. Begins at Rape Gap. Moderate difficulty. Overlooks beautiful views of McLemore Cove. Hiking, bicycling, horseback riding.

6. Estelle Mine Trail. 2.4 miles. Moderate difficulty. Typical mountain scenery. Hiking, bicycling, horseback riding. Near old mountain mining camp. Particularly popular for horseback riding. Primitive camping.

7. Cane Trail. 2.5 miles. Moderate difficulty. Hiking, bicycling, horseback riding. Primitive camping area nearby.

Arrowhead Wildlife Interpretive Trail

Northeast Floyd County, 11 miles north of Rome on Floyd Springs Rd. 2.2 miles. Easy to walk. Education center. Classroom, lab and interpretive specialist available for local school programs.

Amicalola Wildlife Interpretive Trail

Dawson Forest, six miles west of Dawsonville at Amicalola River Bridge on Ga.53. 3.5 miles. Moderate difficulty. Some steep slopes, rocky areas. Passes well-known Class IV "edge of the world" rapids. Interpretive stations. Foot traffic only. Maps and brochures at trailhead.

Lake Burton Trail

Fifteen miles west of Clayton off Ga.197 near Lake Burton, adjacent to Burton Fish Hatchery and Moccasin Creek State Park on U.S. Forest Service lands. One mile. Easy to walk. Interpretive stations. Hikers only.

Central Georgia Trails

Walton Environmental Education Trail

Walton County. I-20 to exit 48. Then north three miles on U.S.278. Two, 1/2-miles, interconnected loops. Easy to walk. Variety of Piedmont habitats; 25 interpretive stations. Side trail through facility's "backyard habitat" of native plants.

Keg Creek Wildlife Management Area

Sixteen miles north on I-20 on Ga.104 at Pollards Corner in Columbia County. One mile; moderate difficulty. Upland pines, hardwoods, old fields, lake shore habitat. Interpretive stations, observation deck. Foot traffic only.

Clarks Hill Trail

Seven miles north of Thomson on Clarks Hill Wildlife Management Area off Ga.78. One mile. Moderate difficulty. Upland pines, creek-bottom hardwoods, old fields, wetlands. Two observation decks, interpretive stations.

Oconee Wildlife Interpretive Trail

Fifteen miles east of Eatonton on Ga.16, just before Oconee River Bridge. 1.9 miles. Easy to walk. Piedmont uplands, bottomlands; skirts edge of waterfowl impoundments; observation platform allows views during fall and winter, possibly including bald eagles. Foot traffic only. Organized school tours encouraged.

Rum Creek Nature Trail

West Monroe County. From Atlanta, take I-75 south to Ga.18 (exit 60), and go seven miles east toward Gray; turn left at Rum Creek sign; 200 yards. 0.4 mile. Easy to walk. Limited handicapped access. Upland hardwood forests, thinned and burned pine forests, wildlife openings. Ends at marshlike cove of Lake Juliette. Interpretive stations. Foot traffic only. Restrooms, water.

Blanton Creek Wildlife Trail

Ten miles south of West Point on Hwy.103 in Harris County. 1.4-miles. Easy to walk. Mature upland hardwoods, beaver pond, pine regeneration area, wildlife openings, thinned and burned pine stand. Interpretive stations. Observation deck overlooks beaver pond. Picnic tables. Foot traffic, all-terrain wheelchairs only.

Tuckahoe Horse Trail

Screven County. From Sylvania take East Ogeechee 2.2 miles to junction of Buck Creek and Brannen's Bridge Road; 8.6 miles to checking station. 8.5 miles. Habitats adjacent to Savannah River; two oxbow lakes. Camping, bath house two miles away. Water for horses.

Southern Georgia Trails

Big Hammock Natural Area Hiking Trail

Tattnall County, three miles north of Altamaha River Bridge on County 144, east of Ga.169. Easy to walk. 1.3 miles. Turkey oak-longleaf pine forest, bay swamp, xeric broadleaf-evergreen forests, flatwoods, cypress-gum forest. Excellent example of vanishing sandhill habitat. National Natural Landmark. Largest known population of Georgia plume a rare, state-protected plant. Numerous gopher tortoise burrows. Foot traffic only.

Grand Bay Canoe Trail

Ten miles north of Valdosta on Ga.221. Five miles. Blackgum swamps and open bay, similar to Okefenokee Swamp. Easy to walk.

Handicapped access, parking, landing, bathrooms, shelters.

Albany Nursery Wildlife Trail

Eleven miles west of Albany on Ga.234. Right on Tallahassee Road, then 1.2 miles to sign. Two miles. Easy to walk. Mature, lowland and hardwood forest. Interpretive stations. Hikers only.

Champney Island Wildlife Trail

Two miles south of Darien on west side of Champney Island on Altamaha Wildlife Management Area. One mile. Easy to walk. Dikes surrounding manmade lake. Often affords sights of waterfowl. Interpretive stations. Foot traffic only. Parking area, observation deck; restrooms nearby at county park.

Game and Fish Offices Georgia Department of Natural Resources

Albany Game and Fish Office
2024 Newton Rd.
Albany, GA 31708
912-430-4252.

Brunswick Game and Fish Office
1 Conservation Way
Brunswick, GA 31520
912-264-7237.

Calhoun Game and Fish Office
POB 786
Calhoun, GA 30703-0786
706-629-8674.

Demeries Creek Game and Fish Office
Rt. 2, Box 219R
Richmond Hill, GA 31324
912-727-2111.

Gainesville Game and Fish Office
Route 13, Box 322A
Gainesville, GA 30824
706-595-4211.

Manchester Game and Fish Office
601 3rd Ave.
Manchester, GA 31816
706-846-8448.

Metter Game and Fish Office
Rt. 2, Box 48
Metter, GA 30439
912-685-2145.

Thomson Game and Fish Office
142 Bob Kirk Rd.
Thomson, GA 30824
706-595-4211.

Walton Game and Fish Office
2109 U.S. 278 SE.
Social Circle, GA 30279
706-557-2227.

Waycross Game and Fish Office
POB 2089
Waycross, GA 31501
912-285-6093.

Georgia's State Parks

Mountain Region

Amicalola Falls Park and Lodge
Dawsonville, 16 miles northwest via Ga.183 and 52.
Star Route, Box 215,
Dawsonville, GA 30534
706-265-8888.

Black Rock Mountain Park
Clayton, three miles north via US.441
P.O. Drawer A,
Mountain City, GA 30562
706-746-2141.

Cloudland Canyon Park
Lafayette, 25 miles northwest off Ga.136

Route 2, Box 150,
Rising Fawn, GA 30738
706-657-4050.

Fort Mountain Park
Chatsworth, eight miles east via Ga.52
181 Ft. Mountain Park Rd.,
Chatsworth, GA 30705
706-695-2621.

Hart Park
Hartwell, three miles north off US.29
1515 Hart Park Rd.,
Hartwell, GA 30643
706-376-8756.

James H. "Sloppy" Floyd Park
Summerville, three miles southeast off US.27
Route 1, Box 291,
Summerville, GA 30747
706-857-5211.

Moccasin Creek Park
Clarkesville, 20 miles north on Ga.197
Route 1, Box 1634,
Clarkesville, GA 30523
706-947-3194.

Red Top Mountain Park and Lodge
Cartersville, one 1/1 miles east of I-75 exit 123
653 Red Top Mountain Rd. SE.,
Cartersville, GA 30120
404-975-0055.

Tallulah Gorge Park and Terrora Park and Campground
Tallulah Falls, city limits on US.441
POB 248,
Tallulah Falls, GA 30573
706-754-8257/706-754-6036.

Tugaloo Park
Lavonia, six miles north off Ga. Hwy.328
1763 Tugaloo State Park Rd.,
Lavonia, GA 30553
706-356-4362.

Unicoi Park and Lodge
Helen, two miles north on Hwy.356
POB 849,

Helen, GA 30545
706-878-2201.

Victoria Bryant Park
Royston, four miles west off US.29
1105 Bryant Park Rd.,
Royston, GA 30662
706-245-6270.

Vogel Park
Blairsville, 11 miles south via
U.S. Hwy.19/ 129
7485 Vogel State Park Rd.,
Blairsville, Ga 30512
706-745-2628.

Central Region

A.H. Stephens Historic Park
Crawfordville, two miles north of I-20
POB 283,
Crawfordville, GA 30631
706-456-2602.

Bobby Brown Park
Elberton, 21 miles southeast off Ga.72
2509 Bobby Brown State Rd.,
Elberton, GA 30635
706-213-2046.

Elijah Clark Park
Lincolnton, seven miles east off US.378
2959 McCormick Hwy.,
Lincolnton, GA 30817
706-359-3458.

**Fort Yargo Park and   •
Will-A-Way Recreation Area**
Winder, one mile south on Ga.81
POB 764,
Winder, GA 30680
867-3489/867-5313.

Hamburg Park
Sandersville, 16 miles northeast
on Hamburg Rd.
Route 1, Box 233,
Mitchell, GA 30820
912-552-2393.

Hard Labor Creek Park
Rutledge, two miles north off US.278
POB 247,
Rutledge, GA 30663
706-557-3001.

John Tanner Park
Carrollton, six miles west on Ga.16
354 Tanner's Beach Rd.,
Carrollton, GA 30117
770-830-2222.

Mistletoe Park
Appling, 7.9 miles north of I-20 at exit 60
3723 Mistletoe Rd.,
Appling, GA 30802
706-541-0321.

Panola Mountain Conservation Park
Atlanta, 18 miles southeast on Ga. Hwy.155
2600 Hwy.155, SW.,
Stockbridge, GA 30281
770-389-7801.

Richard B. Russell Park
Elberton, 10 miles north off Ga.77
on Ruckersville Rd.
2650 Russell State Park Rd.,
Elberton, GA 30635
706-213-2045.

Sweetwater Creek Conservation Park
Atlanta, 15 miles west off I-20, exit 12
POB 816,
Lithia Springs, GA 30057
770-732-5871.

Watson Mill Bridge Park
Comer, six miles south on Ga.22
Route 2, Box 190,
Comer, GA 30629
706-783-5349.

Southern Region

Franklin Delano Roosevelt Park
Pine Mountain, five miles southeast on
Ga.190
2970 Ga. Hwy.190,

Pine Mountain, GA 31822
706-663-4858.

Florence Marina Park
Lumpkin, 16 miles west at end of Ga.39C
Route 1, Box 36,
Omaha, GA 31821
912-838-6870.

George T. Bagby Park and Lodge
Fort Gaines, four miles north off Hwy.39
Route 1, Box 201,
Fort Gaines, GA 31751
912-768-2571.

Georgia Veterans Park
Cordele, nine miles west via U.S.2
2459-A U.S. Hwy.280 W.,
Cordele, GA 31015
912-276-2371.

High Falls Park
Forsyth, 10 miles north off I-75 exit 65
Route 5, Box 202-A,
Jackson, GA 30233
912-994-5080.

Indian Springs Park
Jackson, five miles south on Hwy.42
678 Lake Clark Rd.,
Flovilla, GA 30216
770-775-7241.

Kolomoki Mounds Historic Park
Blakely, six miles north off Hwy.27
Route 1, Box 114,
Blakely, GA 31723
912-723-5296.

Providence Canyon Conservation Park
Lumpkin, seven miles west on Ga.39C
Route 1, Box 158,
Lumpkin, GA 31815
912-838-6202.

Reed Bingham Park
Adel, six miles west on GA.37 via I-75 exit 10
Route 2, Box 394 B-1,
Adel, GA 31620
912-896-3551.

Seminole Park
Donalsonville, 16 miles south via Ga.39
Route 2,
Donalsonville, GA 31745
912-861-3137.

Coastal Region

Crooked River Park
St.Mary's, seven miles north on Ga.Spur 40
3092 Spur 40,
St.Mary's, GA 31558
912-882-5256.

Fort McAllister Historic Park
10 miles east of I-95 and US.17 on Spur 144
Route 2, box 394-A,
Richmond Hill, GA 31324
912-727-2339.

General Coffee Park
Douglas, six miles east on Hwy.32
Route 2, Box 83,
Nicholls, GA 31554
912-384-7082.

George L. Smith Park
Twin City, four miles southeast
off Ga.Hwy.23
POB 57,
Twin City, GA 30471
912-763-2759.

Gordonia-Alatamaha Park
Reidsville, city limits off US.280
POB 1047,
Reidsville, GA 30453
912-557-6444.

Laura Walker Park
Waycross, 10 miles southeast on Ga.177
5653 Laura Walker Rd.,
Waycross, GA 31503
912-287-4900.

Little Ocmulgee Park and Lodge
McRae, two miles north off Hwy.441
POB 149,
McRae, GA 31055
912-868-7474.

Magnolia Springs Park
Millen, five miles north on US.25
Route 5, Box 488,
Millen, GA 30442
912-982-1660.

Skidaway Island Park
Savannah, six miles southeast
off Diamond Causeway
52 Diamond Causeway,
Savannah, GA 31411-1102
912-598-2300/912-598-2301.

S.C. Foster Park
Fargo, 18 miles northeast via Ga.177
Route 1, Box 131,
Fargo, GA 31631
912-637-5274.

State Historic Sites

Mountain Region

Dahlonega Gold Museum
Dahlonega, Public Square
Public Square,
Dahlonega, GA 30533
706-864-2257.

New Echota Cherokee Capital
Calhoun, one mile east of I-75
exit 131 via Ga.225
1211 Chatsworth Hwy.,
Calhoun, GA 30701
706-629-8151.

Traveler's Rest
Toccoa, seven miles east off U.S.123
Route 3, Box 516,
Toccoa, GA 30577
706-886-2256.

Chief Vann House
Chatsworth, at intersection of
Ga.52 and Ga.225
Route 7, Box 7655,
Chatsworth, GA 30705
706-695-2598.

Central Region

Etowah Indian Mounds
Cartersville, 5.5 miles southwest
of I-75 off Ga.61
813 Indian Mounds Rd.,
Cartersville, GA 30120
404-387-3747.

Pickett's Mill Battlefield
Dallas, five miles NE.
2640 Mt. Tabor Rd.,
Dallas, GA 30132
770-443-7850.

Robert Toombs House
Washington, city limits
POB 605,
Washington, GA 30673
706-678-2226.

Southern Region

Jarrell Plantation
Juliette, 18 miles east of I-75
at exit 60 off Ga.18
Route 2, Box 220,
Juliette, GA 31046
912-986-5172.

Lapham-Patterson House
Thomasville,
626 North Dawson St.,
Thomasville, GA 31792
912-225-4004.

Little White House
Warm Springs, 1/4 miles south on Ga.85W
Rt. 1, Box 10,
Warm Springs, GA 31830
706-655-5870.

Coastal Region

Fort King George
Darien, three miles east of I-95 at exit 10
POB 711,
Darien, GA 31305
912-437-4770.

Fort Morris
Midway, seven miles east of I-95 exit 13
Route 1, Box 236,
Midway, GA 31320
912-884-5999.

Hofwyl-Broadfield Plantation
Brunswick, one mile east of I-95 exit 9
5556 U.S. Hwy.17 N.,
Brunswick, GA 31525
912-264-9263.

Wormsloe
Savannah, eight miles southeast
via Skidaway Rd.
7601 Skidaway Rd.,
Savannah, GA 31406
912-353-3023.

Park Office Hours:8:00-5:00p.m. daily, may
vary at some parks.

Park Hours:7:00a.m.-10:00p.m. daily, may
vary at some parks.

Historic Sites:vary, please call for times.

Source of above information,
Georgia State Parks and Historic Sites
operated by the Parks, Recreation and Historic
Sites Division of the Georgia Department
of Natural Resources.

Fun Facts:

- On April 8, 1974, while playing the Los Angeles Dodgers, Atlanta Brave Hank Aaron shattered the unshatterable, breaking Babe Ruth's lifetime home run record.

- In 1982 Georgia Bulldog running back Herschel Walker was awarded the prestigious Heisman Trophy.

- A St. Simon Islander, Cleveland Browns' fullback Jim Brown led the NFL in rushing yardage in eight of his nine seasons of play.

- Four types of poisonous snakes inhabit Georgia, the coral, copperhead, rattler and water moccasin. So, what's fun about that.

SECTION VIII
The Cuisines of Atlanta and Beyond

Southern Food and Hospitality

From conception through service, Southern hospitality is pervasive in the Southern dining experience, particularly in the preparation and presentation of the Southern cuisines (traditional, nouveau, barbecue, low-country, Cajun and Creole). While most of Atlanta's historic tea rooms have vanished (**Mary Mac's** is still going strong), traditional Southern food lives on side-by-side with all of the nouveau Southern cuisines that have evolved. There's still plenty of finger lickin' fried chicken and catfish, barbecue, grits, yams, collard and turnip greens in Atlanta and throughout Georgia but these are now vastly supplemented, (as you will see in the section on restaurants), with the many glorious cuisines of the new South.

Atlanta's Premier Restauranteur

Many Atlantans, especially chefs and owners, attribute the spectacular growth of fine dining in metro Atlanta to the pioneering efforts of **Pano Karatassos.** Atlanta is now blessed with a multitude of fine restaurants that together present a global menu. Every major and many lesser-known cuisines are now readily found in metro Atlanta, and, in themselves, they are a special form of welcome to visitors from around the world and a blessing to Atlantans.

Zoning in on Atlanta's Diet and Calorie Consciousness

For the most part Atlantans are not overly thin, in part because of the abundance of fine Southern food and in part because of strict adherence to the following ten iron rules of dieting.

The Ten Step Atlanta Diet

1. Dieting is a good thing to think about every once-in-a-while.
2. Calories consumed while thinking about dieting do not count.
3. Calories from authentic Southern food and sweet tea do not count.
4. Calories consumed while snacking, dining out or watching TV also do not count.
5. Beer and mouth-watering Southern desserts are essential, calorie-free, food products.
6. Medicinal alcohol such as likker and brandy are also calorie-free.
7. It is better to plan to diet than to not plan at all.
8. Eatin' is vastly superior to not eatin' and eatin' out usually beats eatin' in.
9. There are fewer calories in large portions than in small portions.
10. To eat or not to eat is definitely not the question.

Georgia's Seafood

Much of the seafood you'll find in Georgia is described here. Visit one of our recommended sushi restaurants, such as **Ru San** or **Shiki** and sample such exotic fare as shark, octopus, squid, sea urchin and others are sure to catch your eye.

Amberjack-A firm fish with a moderate flavor, generally charbroiled, smoked or in chowder.

Catfish-Found in rivers or cultivated in farms, this moist but firm fish is served whole or filleted, normally deep-fried.

Blue Crab-A flaky white meat that has a sweet taste, served boiled or steamed in its hard shell.

Dolphin (Mahi Mahi or Dorado)-A firm, flaky, textured white-meat fish with a mild taste, prepared in virtually every manner.

Flounder-A delicate, white fish with a mild flavor; often fried, broiled or stuffed with crab meat.

Grouper-A lean, firm, moist white fish with a sweet flavor. Grilled, broiled or sauteed are good choices.

King Mackerel-A delicate dark-meat sportsfish with a distinctive taste; served charbroiled or barbecued.

Oysters-A shellfish prepared countless ways:raw or steamed on the half-shell, fried or in stew. Local oysters are generally available during months with "Rs" in them.

Red Snapper-A medium-firm, flaky fish with a sweet, mild flavor; usually baked, broiled or sauteed.

Scallops-A shucked mussel, called the "fruit of the sea." A sweet, delicate, white meat often served deep-fried or sauteed.

Sea Trout-A white, lean fish with sweet, delicate flavor; generally sauteed or deep-fried.

Shrimp-Everyone's favorite whether fried, sauteed, steamed, stuffed or broiled.

Swordfish-A lean, firm fish, usually served steak-cut and charbroiled.

Tuna-A distinctive, dark, firm fish with a not-like-the-can taste; especially good charbroiled or smoked.

Delicate Texture
Mild Flavor
Flounder/Sole
Orange Roughy
Skate
Sea Trout

Moderate Flavor
Butterfish
Whiting/Hake
Pink Salmon

Full Flavor
Eel
Smelt
Herring/Sardine

Medium/Firm Texture
Mild Flavor
Cod
Haddock
Halibut
Tilefish
Grouper
Snapper
Tilapia
Dolphin

Moderate Flavor
Perch
Ocean Perch
Striped Bass
Chum Salmon
Drums
Amberjack
Pompano
Atlantic Pollock
Sea Bass
Porgy/Scup

Full-Flavor
Atlantic Salmon
King Salmon
Mackerel
Yellowtail
Sockeye Salmon
Carp
Bluefish

Firm Texture
Mild Flavor
Monkfish
Kingklip
Moderate Flavor
Catfish
Shark
Sturgeon
Full Flavor
Swordfish
Tuna

A Wine Sampler

Many of the restaurants reviewed offer a fine selection of domestic and international wines. A wine need not be expensive to be good. Usually any bottle priced between $15.00 and $30.00 will prove more than sufficiently pleasing to the palette. Try a glass before ordering the full bottle and don't hesitate to ask your server for suggestions.

White Wines

Chardonnay-Perhaps the most popular white wine in the world. Very pleasing before dinner and with seafood.

Pinot Blanc-A medium-bodied white that goes well with seafood.

Sauvignon Blanc-A light to medium-bodied white that also goes well with seafood.

Red Wines

Cabernet Sauvignon-Many red wines from with varying characteristics fall within this category. An excellent accompaniment to a rich meat entree.

Gamay/Beaujolais-Lighter than Cabernet, it goes well with grilled fish and meat.

Merlot-Rising rapidly in popularity, this medium-bodied red wine is excellent with lamb, game and cured meats.

Red Zinfandel-This medium to full-bodied red wine, which originated in America, is

great with pasta, grilled meats and blackened entrees.

How to Cook a Husband

A good many husbands are spoiled by mismanagement. Some women blow them up; others keep them constantly in hot water; others let them freeze by their carelessness and indifference. Some keep them in a stew by irritating ways and words, others roast them, and some keep them in a pickle all their lives.

It cannot be supposed that any husband will be tender and good - managed in this way, but they are delicious when properly treated.

In selecting your husband, you should not be guided by the silvery appearance, as in buying mackerel; nor by golden tint, as if you wanted salmon. Be sure to select him yourself as tastes differ. Do not go to market for him as the best are always brought to your door.

It is far better to have none unless you will patiently learn how to cook him. A preserving kettle of the finest porcelain is best, but if you have nothing but an earthenware pipkin, it will do. See that the linen in which you wrap him is nicely washed and mended with the required number of buttons and strings tightly sewed on. Tie him in a kettle with a strong silk cord called comfort, as the one called duty is apt to be weak. They are apt to fly out of the kettle and be burned and crusty on the edges since, like crabs and lobsters, you have to cook them while alive. Make a clear, steady fire out of love, neatness, and cheerfulness. Set him as near this as seems to agree with him. If he sputters and fizzes, do not be anxious; some husbands do this until they are quite done.

Add a little sugar in the form of what confectioners call kisses, but no vinegar or pepper on any account. A little spice improves them, but it must be used with judgement. Do not stick sharp instruments into him to see if he is becoming tender. Stir him gently, watching the while lest he lies too flat and close to the kettle and so becomes useless. You cannot fail to know when he is done. If thus treated, you will find him very digestible, agreeing with you; and he will keep as long as you want, unless you become careless and set him into a cool place.

— *Social Circle Cook Book (1920)*

Dining Out

Commentary

It's usually a good idea to call ahead to make a reservation, request seating (no smoking or smoking section), elicit specials of the day, and check driving directions.

Love Atlanta Picks Metro Atlanta's Nifty Fifty

From the zillions of eateries in metro Atlanta our food editors have selected their "Nifty Fifty." These restaurants offer the diner outstanding value as expressed by the number of hearts they have been awarded.

Hearts are awarded both objectively and subjectively based on our editors' evaluation of the taste and presentation of menu items, price, ambiance and service. Our editors have reviewed a good number of different cuisines, established eateries as well as new restaurants. They talk to everyone they meet, including restaurant owners and chefs, and read the media's reviews in an ever-vigilant effort to discover something new and exciting. We urge you to send us your views on the "Nifty Fifty," and listings of your favorite restaurants.

Love Atlanta's Heart Value System

♥♥♥♥   Excellent

♥♥♥   Very Good

♥♥   Good

Love Atlanta's Restaurant Value Ratings

Commentary

Detailed write-ups of the following restaurants are found below, by cuisine type, under the sections entitled **Metro Atlanta's Nifty Fifty** and **Other Nifty Restaurants Outside the Metro Atlanta Area**. There are plenty of fine restaurants not yet reviewed by *Love Atlanta's* food editors. Many of these restaurants are listed below, by cuisine type, under the section entitled **Other Metro Atlanta Restaurants**.

Metro Atlanta's Nifty Fifty

♥♥♥♥

1848 House
A Taste Of New Orleans
The Abbey
Basil's Mediterranean Cafe
Brooklyn Cafe
Horseradish Grill
La Grotta
Lombardi's
Mary Mac's Tea Room
Nikolai's Roof
Ru San's
Shiki Japanese Restaurant
South City Kitchen
Sprayberry's Barbecue
Sundown Cafe
The Grille Room
The Restaurant
Van Gogh's

♥♥♥
Adams At The Fox
Alfredo's
Amici
Anis Cafe and Bistro
Azalea
Babette's Cafe
Basta
Bertolini's
Dimitri's
Hal's on Old Ivy
Heera of India
House of Chan
Indigo Coastal Grill
La Strada
Luna Si
Nuevo Laredo Cantina
The Orient at Vinings
Pasta da Pulcinella
Pleasant Peasant
Sylvan's on Lanier
Taste of Thai
Tribeca Cafe
Yesterday's Cafe

♥♥
Cassis
Chicago's
Dailey's
Dominick's
Down East Bar-B-Que
French Quarter Grocery
Kamogawa
Mark's Seasons Bistro
Mambo
Little Szechuan
South of France
Surin of Thailand

Commentary: The metro Atlanta **Nifty/Fifty** restaurants are presented in alphabetical order by cuisine type. We lead off with the Southern cuisine out of a deep sense of chauvinism.

Southern Cuisine

The 1848 House
780 South Cobb Dr.
Marietta, Georgia 30060
770-428-1848
Location: At Bushy Park Plantation
Seating: 300
Owner: William B. Dunaway
Chef: Tom McEachern
Cuisine: Contemporary Southern
Opened: 1992
Overall Rating: ♥♥♥♥

Commentary: Step back into time and allow the old South to envelop as you ascend the veranda steps into an authentic Greek revival plantation home. Bill Dunaway, a most gracious host, will greet and encourage you to wander about and absorb the history of the authentic grandeur dining rooms, some with fireplaces. Gaze through large windows onto a lovely garden flourishing with trees and flowers while daydreaming the sound of rustling gowns and snapping fans. Then, relax and ease into a delectable menu of house smoked trout or sauteed peppered duck served with delectible chutneys, as proficient service will cater to all your needs. Complete your Southern journey with an incredible creme brulee.

Dress Code: Not quite casual to formal.
Appetizers: . . . . $3.95-$7.95
Entrees: . . . . $13.95-$22.95
Desserts: $4.50
House Specialties and Menu Items:
Pan-Fried Crab Cake with Dijon. . . . . $ 6.95
House Smoked Trout Appetizer. . . . . $ 7.95
Buttermilk Batter Fried Quail Salad . $ 6.95
Sauteed Venison on Onion
   Marmalade $22.95
Pork Tenderloin Lightly Smoked . . . $18.95
Grilled Chicken over Crawfish Rice . $15.95
Sauteed Peppered Duck with
   Brandy Sauce $18.95
Sweet Potato Pecan Pie with
  Ice Cream . . . . $ 4.50

Warm Fruit Cobbler w/Cinnamon
Ice Cream. $ 4.50
Days and Hours of Operation:
Tuesday-Sunday 6:00-9:30
Brunch Sunday 10:30-2:30

A Taste Of New Orleans

889 W. Peachtree St.
Atlanta, GA 30309
874-5535
Location: Midtown
Seating: 75
Owner/Chef: John Beck
Cuisine: Southern Cajun
Opened: 1986
Overall Rating: ♥♥♥♥

Commentary: Whether its business or pleasure, treat yourself to delicious Cajun food in Atlanta at this intimate, friendly and well-run restaurant. Small tables, murals on the wall and efficient staff will have you relishing each bite as you venture from outstanding mildly spicy crabcakes, brisk seafood gumbo, to a knock-your-socks-off Cajun velvet pie. Together with a friendly winelist, you will come again and again.

Dress Code: Casual to jackets.
Appetizers: . . . . $2.95-$4.95
Entrees: . . . . $8.95-$16.95
Desserts: . . . . $2.95-$3.50
House Specialties and Menu Samples:
Oysters en Brochette,
Bacon Wrapped. . . . . $ 4.95
Sweet and Spicy Shrimp, ... $ 3.75
Seafood Gumbo . . . . $ 3.50
Seafood Baked Eggplant, Shrimp,
Crab,Crawfish $14.95
Cajun Cordon Blue, Blackened
Chicken Breast $12.95
Seafood Cakes, w/Jalapeno
Tartar Sauce. $14.95
Etouffee Seafood, Fresh Seafood
Pan-Sauteed. $14.95
Seafood Pasta, Shrimp, Crawfish,
Scallops $14.95
Cajun Velvet Pie, Peanut Butter
Mousse. . . . . $ 2.95

French Silk Pie, Creamy
Chocolate Mousse . . . . $ 2.95
Days and Hours of Operation:
Monday-Friday 11:30-2:00
Monday-Thursday 6:00-10:00
Friday and Saturday 5:30-11:00

Adams At The Fox

654 Peachtree St.
Atlanta, Georgia 30308
881-0223
Location: Midtown
Seating: 150
Owner: J.T. Adams
Chef: Joey Ahn
Cuisine: Nouveau Southern with Continental Accents
Opened: November 1994
Overall Rating: ♥♥♥

Commentary: Decorous and bright, with tunes of Broadway coming from the baby grand. A contemporary setting, with red tile floors, high ceilings and large windows makes this split-level restaurant a good choice for quiet business lunches, or romantic, pre and post theater dinners. Add dimension to your Fox Theater outing with a delectable array of appetizers such as Camembert salad, smoked salmon ravioli, and such entrees as delicately grilled rosemary lamb steak or pan-seared spicy jumbo shrimp. A competent staff will attend to your needs and make sure you'll be on time for the show.

Dress Code: Casual to jackets.
Appetizers: . . . . $4.95-$7.95
Entrees: . . . . $11.95-$18.95
Desserts: $4.95
House Specialties and Menu Samples:
Crispy Sweet and Sour Calamari . . . . $ 6.95
Fresh Tuna Carpaccio with Sake . . . . $ 5.95
Camembert Salad
w/Organic Baby Greens. . . . . $ 6.95
Black and White Bean Soup . . . . $ 3.95
Grilled Portabella Mushroom Steak . $12.95
Roasted Center Cut Pork Chop. $14.95
Pan-Seared Spicy Jumbo Shrimp . . . $15.95
Grilled Rosemary Lamb Steak $18.95
Bittersweet Chocolate Mousse Cake. . $ 4.95

Luscious Cheesecake of the Day . . . . $ 4.95
Days and Hours of Operation:
Monday-Friday . . . . 11:30 to midnight
Saturday-Sunday . . . . 5:00 to midnight

French Quarter Grocery
2144 Johnson Ferry Rd.
Atlanta, GA 30319
458-2148
and
923 Peachtree St.
Atlanta, GA 30305
875-2489
Locations: Sandy Springs and Midtown
Seating: 75 and 100
Owners: Melissa and Tony Privat
Chef: Brady Privat
Cuisine: Cajun/Creole
Opened: 1990
Overall Rating: ♥♥

Commentary: You haven't eaten authentic Cajun until you've stopped at this spartan but clean hole-in-the-wall cafe and patio. Large ceiling fans, mardi-gras masks on the wall and taped jazz in the background lend authenticity to the surroundings. Plan on getting your hands dirty eating racy Louisianna home-grown crawfish, jambalaya, etouffee, and bread pudding that should receive an Oscar. Try a blackened voodoo lager and have a good time being served by the cheerful staff.

Dress Code: Anything goes.
Appetizers: . . . . $2.95-$6.95
Entrees: . . . . $5.95-$13.95
Desserts: . . . . $2.25-$3.25
House Specialties and Menu Items:
Oyster or Shrimp Appetizer
   w/Remoulade . . . . $ 4.95
Shrimp Remoulade on Fresh Greens . $ 6.95
Catfish Po-Boys (Variety of Fish) . . . $ 6.95
Jambalaya w/Secret
   Seasonings/Spices . . . . $ 7.95
Chicken Tasso Grilled with
   Tasso Cream . . . . $ 8.95
Etouffee (Seasonal Seafood) market
Seafood Platter: Shrimp, Oyster,
   Catfish, Stuffed Crab and
   Frog Legs $13.95

New Orleans Bread Pudding . . . . $ 2.25
Pecan Praline Cheesecake . . . . $ 3.25
Days and Hours of Operation:
Monday-Thursday 11:00-10:00
Friday-Saturday 11:00-11:00

Horseradish Grill
4320 Powers Ferry Rd.
Atlanta, GA 30342
255-7277.
Location: Chastain Park
Seating: 174
Owners: Steve and Renee Alterman
Chef: Scott Peacock
Cuisine: Southern Contemporary
Opened: November 1993
Overall Rating: ♥♥♥♥

Commentary: With its high open-beam ceiling and massive stone fireplace, Horseradish Grill evokes the feeling of a stylish, yet comfortable, mountain lodge; previously it was a horse barn. The view is a lush vegetable garden on one side, and a treed terrace on the other. Commended by *Bon Appetit*, *James Beard* and *Atlanta Dining*, the seasonal menu offers such mouth-watering morsels as grilled Georgia mountain trout, skillet-fried chicken, the thickest, most tender porkchop, and home-smoked turkey, accompanied by either rich skillet gravy and mashed pototoes, a relish of black-eyed peas or killer biscuits, followed by either the lemon chess pie, or the homemade peanut brittle ice cream.

Dress Code: Casual to jackets.
Appetizers: . . . . $4.50-$7.95
Entrees: . . . . $10.95-$18.95
Desserts: . . . . $3.75-$4.95
House Specialties and Menu Items:
Hot Georgia Browns, Thin
   Sliced Smoked Turkey . . . . $ 5.25
Southern Flatbread,
   w/Carmelized Onions . . . . $ 4.75
Wood Grilled Fish Salad market
   Skillet Fried Chicken,
   w/Blackeyed Peas $11.50
Grilled Whole Georgia
   Mountain Trout $13.50
Thick Cut Fresh Pork Chop $13.95

Wood Grilled Loin Lamb Chops $19.95
Prime Veal Chop, Grilled over
   Hickory and Oak $18.95
Peanut Brittle Ice Cream . . . . $ 3.95
Lemon Chess Pie . . . . $ 4.25
Days and Hours of Operation:
Monday-Saturday 11:30-5:00
Sunday 5:00-9:00
Monday-Thursday 5:00-10:00
Friday and Saturday 5:00-11:00

Mary Mac's Tea Room

224 Ponce de Leon Ave.
Atlanta, GA 30308
876-1800
Location: Midtown
Seating: 350
Owner: John Ferrell
Cuisine: Southern
Opened: 1945
Overall Rating: ♥♥♥♥

Commentary: Southern hospitality and historic recipes are the foundation of Mary Mac's continuing success story. The real Southern cooking featuringe made-from-scratch meals together with the warm and gracious atmosphere attract a zillion locals and people the world over, including Hillary Clinton. After decades of devotion from now retired Margaret Lupo, John Ferrell has taken over this historical landmark. Four dining rooms, each distinctive, with tin ceilings, old wooden floors and photos of celebrities on the walls. Following a Southern tradition, friendly waiters will offer "Table Wine of the South" (sweetened iced tea) and fresh homemade rolls. Fill-out your own order ticket and sample crispy fried chicken, soothing turnip greens with pot likker, or sweet fried okra and leave a little room for a yummy Georgia peach cobbler. By dinner's end you'll know why Mary Mac's remains a Southern icon.

Side Dishes: Included
Entrees: . . . . 5.00-$10.00
Desserts: Included
House Specialties and Menu Items:
Chicken and Dumplings w/Fried Okra

Fried Catfish and Hushpuppies
Homestyle Meatloaf and Field Peas
Fried Chicken and Turnip Greens
Beef Tips on Noodles w/Squash Souffle
Pork Barbeque w/Brunswick Stew
Georgia Peach Cobbler
Carter Custard
Days and Hours of Operation:
Monday-Friday 11:00-9:00
Saturday 5:00-9:00
Sunday Brunch 11:00-3:00

South City Kitchen

1144 Crescent Ave.
Atlanta, GA 30309
873-0317
Location: Midtown
Seating:130
Owner: Chris Goss and Steve Simon
Chef: Scott Walker
Cuisine: Innovative Southern Cuisine
Opened: June 1993
Overall Rating: ♥♥♥♥

Commentary: Located on a quiet street in an elegant reclaimed Southern home; invites diners to a snug outdoor patio, or a bright, airy, dining room with umpteen windows. The atmosphere is set with an open kitchen and bar, wood floors, warm colors mixed with crisp linen, friendly staff attired in denim shirts, and imaginative presentation. A growing winelist attracts early crowds. Feast from fresh mussels in vermouth to robust pan-fried catfish to name a few.

Dress Code: Casual and dressy.
Appetizers: . . . . $4.50-$7.95
Entrees: . . . . $6.25-$18.95
Desserts: $4.95
House Specialties and Menu Samples:
Stuffed Collard Greens with Lamb . . . $ 5.95
Steamed Mussels w/Vermouth . . . . . . $ 6.50
Edisto Crab Cakes w/Cajun
   Hollandaise market Grilled Tuna
   Salad . . . . $ 8.50
Spicy Shrimp and Chicken
   Jambalaya . . . . $ 8.95
Pan-Fried Catfish w/Cabbage
   and Potato Cake . . . . $ 8.95

Grilled Midtown Meatloaf
  w/Garlic Mash Potato $13.50
Sauteed Shrimp and Scallops
  and Garlic Gravy $11.25
Chocolate Pecan Pie . . . . $ 4.95
Homemade Blueberry Cobbler/
  Seasonal Fruit . . . . $ 4.95
Days and Hours of Operation:
Sunday-Thursday 11:00-11:00
Friday and Saturday 11:00-midnight

American Cuisine

Azalea
3167 Peachtree Rd.
Atlanta, GA 30305
237-9939.
Location: Buckhead
Seating: 130
Owner: Tom Kane
Chef: Ricardo DeLeon
Cuisine: American Contemporary
Opened: August 1990
Overall Rating: ♥♥♥

Commentary: Enter a sophisticated capacious open dining and kitchen space, buzzing with energy from customers and staff alike. With open bar, black and white deco, this restaurant prides itself on fresh products, deft service, and great presentation. Enjoy a diverse winelist and graze from fresh North Carolina catfish, healthy spinach ravioli, pan-seared smoked salmon to luscious desserts.

Dress Code: Casual to jackets.
Appetizers: . . . . $3.95-$10.95
Entrees: . . . . $7.95-$21.95
Desserts: . . . . $4.95-$5.95
House Specialties and Menu Items:
BBQ Shrimp Enchilada . . . . $ 5.95
Carpaccio of the Day
  (Fresh Meat or Fish) . . . . $ 6.95
Whole Sizzling Catfish. $10.95
Spinach Ravioli w/Seared
  Scallops $16.95
Heart Healthy Special of
  the Day. $16.95

Lobster Ravioli w/Blackened
  Scallops $17.95
Hot Smoked/Seared Salmon in
  Potato Crust $16.95
Coriander Cured Lamb Chops $21.95
Creme Brulee Trio. . . . . $ 5.95
Almond-Sesame Lace Basket
  w/Heathbar Ice Cream . . . . $ 5.95
Days and Hours of Operation:
Sunday-Thursday 5:00-11:00
Friday and Saturday 5:00-midnight

Dailey's
17 International Blvd.
Atlanta, GA 30303
681-3303.
Location: Downtown
Seating: 200
Owners: Steve Nygren and Dick Dailey
Cuisine: American
Opened: 1981
Overall Rating: ♥♥

Commentary: Remaining rock-solid in popularity, Dailey's serves hardy American fare with generous portions. High-energy service amidst a decor consisting of fantastic high beamed ceilings, vintage lamp posts, carousel horses, and unique train station globe lamps. Downstairs is a comfortable bar with piano player, and up the wide, carpeted stairs, a grand dining area. Select from such favorites such as French onion soup, rice paper salmon, and black-peppered swordfish. Then put the diet on hold while choosing a king-size dessert from the dessert bar.

Dress Code: Casual to jackets.
Appetizers: . . . . $5.50-$8.95
Entrees: . . . . $16.50-$24.50
Desserts: . . . . $3.95-$5.50
House Specialties and Menu Items:
French Onion Soup,
  Baked w/Cheese . . . . $ 5.50
Oregano Grilled Tuna, Marinated. . . $19.95
Apple Brandy Duckling $17.95
Swordfish Au Poivre,
  House Special. $22.95
Rack of Lamb, w/Peach
  Pecan Glaze $22.95

Rice Paper Salmon w/Vegetables . . . $20.95
Bourbon Strip Steak
   w/Fried Onions $23.75
Filet Mignon, Chargrilled. $24.50
Georgia Pecan Ice Cream Pie
   w/Ginger . . . . $ 5.50
Chocolate Charlotte . . . . $ 5.50
Days and Hours of Operation:
Monday-Friday. 11:00-2:30
Sunday-Thursday 5:30-11:00
Friday and Saturday 5:30-midnight

Pleasant Peasant

489 Peachtree St.
Atlanta, GA 30308
872-1400
Located: Midtown, close to the Fox
Seating: 77
Owner: Steve Nygren, Dick Daily
Chef: Alvin Hambersham
Cuisine: American
Opened: 1974
Overall Rating: ♥♥♥

Commentary: Formerly a pharmacy; now an intimate bistro with wrought iron chandeliers, red brick walls and a vintage mosaic tile floor. Even when crowded, its friendly staff and vivacious manager Candice provide a memorable dining experience to an eclectic clientele. Known for large portions, the menu varies from a homey plum pork medallion with sweet potato, to a sophisticated black angus beef tenderloin with fried tobacco onion rings.

Dress Code: Casual.
Appetizers. . . . . $ 4.75- 8.75
Entrees $10.95-21.95
Desserts. . . . . $ 4.25- 5.50
House Specialties & Menu Samples:
Shrimp Southwestern in Phyllo . . . . . $ 7.95
Baked Elephant Garlic . . . . $ 8.50
Plum Pork, tenderloin
   w/Sweet Potato $15.75
Juniper Berry Salmon, Grilled $18.95
Lemon Caper Chicken,
   w/Roast Tomato $14.95
Grilled Beef Tenderloin,
   w/Onion Rings. $21.50

Apple BBQ Lamb, New Zealand
   Full Rack $21.95
Chocolate Intemperance, Mousse . . . $ 5.50
Apple Walnut Pie,
   w/Cinnamon Ice Cream . . . . $ 4.95
Open: Lunch Monday-Friday. . 11:30- 2:30
Dinner Sunday-Thursday 5:30-11:00
Friday-Saturday   5:30-midnight

Sylvan's on Lanier

6950 Holiday Road
Lake Lanier Islands, GA 30518
945-8787
Located: Lake Lanier Islands Hilton Resort
Seating: 104
Chef: Tim Williams
Cuisine: American w/Continental Accents
Opened: 1988
Overall Rating: ♥♥♥

Commentary: Watch a breathtaking sunset of Lake Lanier in a in-door garden terrace-style setting. Named after Sylvan Meyer, who brought the idea of making Lake Lanier an resort, this summery, spacious dining room breathes casual comfort. Take all the time with dining, and enjoy tasty samples from a varied menu. Keeping family in mind, the menu offers a great selection of salads with homemade dressings, tasty soups such as gumbo or French onion with sherry, sauteed steaks or grilled salmon. Not forgetting the lighter side for the diet conscious and a children's menu. As always, the Southern friendly staff and Chef Tim, will make dining most pleasing. Timing it right, savor a yummy pastry from the pastry cart as the sun sets. And all you have to think about tomorrow is were to sit for breakfast or lunch enjoying good food and more great views.

Dress Code: Casual.
Appetizers . . . . $ 4.95- 7.95
Entrees. $ 7.25-18.50
Desserts . . . . $ 2.95- 4.95
House Specialties & Menu Samples:
Tortellini in Cream Sauce . . . . $ 6.25
French Onion Soup with Sherry . . . . . $ 3.95
Spinach Salad w/Hot Bacon Dressing $ 5.95

Chicken A La Gorgonzola
   w/White Wine $14.95
Grilled Salmon Fillet w/Hollandaise . $16.95
Green Peppercorn Sea Scallops $17.95
Forester's Steak, Sauteed w/Bacon . . $18.95
Sinister Mud Pie . . . . $ 4.95
Sundae on the Lake, a Feast . . . . $ 3.95
Open: Breakfast Daily 6:30-11:00, buffet &
a la carte
Lunch Daily 11:00- 2:00
Dinner Daily 5:00-10:00

The Grille Room
9000 Holiday Road
Lake Lanier Islands, GA 30518
945-8921 ext.51
Located: Renaissance PineIsle Resort
Seating: 90
Chef: Leslie Peat
Cuisine: Traditional American
Opened: 1975
Overall Rating: ♥♥♥♥

Commentary: A four-star resort that proudly presents a four-heart dining room. Elegant dining in a comfortable country club setting, with an magnificent view of Lake Lanier and pine-forest setting. Emphasis are on fresh seafood and prime beef, prepared with creative culinary skill,"stressing on healthy food", says chef Leslie Peat. Enhance the dining experience with an selection from an extensive wine list, while perusing the menu. Some outstanding favorites are melt-in-your-mouth Scottish smoked salmon and the tasty black angus beef. Fresh fruits are married with most selections in a most pleasing presentation. Only with dessert will the chef look the other way, and amaze the diner with sweet ambrosia. Along with these high standards and a proficient staff with 20/20 vision completes an successful dining venture, that is worth repeating.

Dress is resort to dressy
Appetizers . . . . $ 5.75-11.95
Entrees $13.50-27.50
Desserts . . . . $ 4.25

House Specialties & Menu Samples:
New England Crab & Shrimp
   Cakes w/Fruit Salsa . . . . $ 9.50
Smoked Scottish Salmon
   w/Capers & Onions $11.95
Apple Cider & Onion Soup . . . . $ 5.75
Lemon Fettucini w/Crab &
   Asparagus $15.50
Breast of Chicken w/Raspberry
   Tarragon $14.50
Grilled Tuna Steak
   w/Garlic Mashed Potatoes $19.50
Pork Loin Chop w/Apple
   Braised Red Cabbage $21.00
Black Angus Filet
   w/Bearnaise Sauce $24.50
Chilled White Chocolate
   Creme Brulee . . . . $ 4.25
Dark Chocolate Cake
   w/Raspberries . . . . $ 4.25
Open:
Dinner Monday-Saturday 6:00-10:00
May-Labor Day
Tuesday-Saturday 6:00-10:00
Labor Day-April

The Grille Room/Atrium
2450 Galleria Pkwy.
Atlanta, GA 30339
770-953-4500
Located: Stouffer Renaissance Waverly Hotel
Chef: Michael Swann
Cuisine: Brunch
Opened: 1987
Overall Rating: ♥♥♥♥

Commentary: The best brunch in Atlanta. When entering the beautiful, bright 14 story atrium lobby of the hotel, the fascinating site in front of you will "knock your socks off." A culinary dream unfolds as you stroll past tastefully presented white dressed tables emphasizing a culinary specialty. Complementary champagne flows freely, or visit the 25 foot, design-your-own, "Bloody Mary Bar." Waverly's culinary team, headed by chef Michael, present a wondrous world of ambrosia. Graze from a breakfast station with made to order omelettes and waffles, accompanied by tables laden with fresh fruits, imported cheeses, smoked seafood and just about every salad imaginable; a seafood station serves the seasons catch; the carving station offers succulent meats such as beef tenderloin and Oriental ribs; the game station offers quail and venison; and the dessert station is loaded with palette-pleasing Southern specialties and an assorted ice cream treats. The food, the piano music and even a play center for the young ones make for a terrific Sunday afternoon. center.

Dress Code: Casual to dressy.

Adults $24.95

Seniors $15.95

Jrs. . . . . $ 9.95

Brunch Specialties & Samples:

Eggs Benedict w/Cheese Grits, Bacon
Omelettes w/Peppers,Onions,
   Ham,Bacon,Cheeses
Shrimp and Rice Salad, Argentine
   Asparagus Salad
Peel-and-Eat Shrimp, Steamed
   Black Mussels
Roasted Sea Bass, Seafood
   Mediterranean, Mahi Mahi
Herb-Roasted Rack of Lamb,
   Prime Rib, Salmon en Croute
Beef Tenderloin, Beef Stroganoff,
   Chicken Kiev
Grilled Venison, Fried Alligator,
   Quail w/Raspberry
Penne Pasta w/Sundried Tomato,
   Tortellini w/Alfredo
Market Vegetables, Garlic
   Mashed Potatoes, Rice Pilaf
Bakery Fresh Biscuits, Muffins,
   Rolls and Danish
French Pastries, Key Lime Pie,
   Chocolate Truffle Cake
Selection of Gourmet Ice Cream
   w/Toppings.

Open:

Sunday Brunch 10:30-2:00

Tribeca Cafe

2880 Holcomb Bridge Rd.
Alpharetta, GA 30202
770-640-5345.
Location: Alpharetta
Seating: 160
Owner: Michael and Donna Petrucci
Chef: Michael Hosp
Cuisine: Nouveau American/European .
Opened: 1995
Overall Rating: ♥♥♥

Commentary: An intimate and friendly country-style bistro, recently expanded to offer the finest and most extensive selection of California's wines. Named after a Bohemian area of New York, Tribecca offers a sociable piano and warm bar, complete with fireplace, and, perhaps, the only indooor putting green in cafe dining history. A well-qualified staff will help select from an extensive, reasonably priced winelist and varied menu, with plenty of daily specials. Savor the smoked salmon pizza, shrimp gazpacho, or the delightful ravioli with spinach and baby shrimp, all served on large, colorful plates.

Dress Code: Casual.
Appetizers: . . . . $1.50-$5.95
Entrees: . . . . $4.95-$14.95
Desserts: . . . . $3.75-$4.75
House Specialties and Menu Samples:
Tribeca Bread, w/Fresh Herbs. . . . . . $ 1.50
Baked Brie in Puff Pastry . . . . $ 5.95
Shrimp Gazpacho . . . . $ 4.95
Smoked Salmon Pizza. . . . . $ 6.95
Fresh Basil Pesto Pasta . . . . $ 8.95
Ravioli w/Spinach, Baby Shrimp . . . $11.95
Sole in a Potato Crust $10.95
Veal Nicholas, w/Prosciutto $14.95
Applecake w/Ginger Sauce. . . . . $ 3.75
Days and Hours of Operation:
Tuesday-Friday 11:30-2:30
Tuesday-Saturday 5:00-10:30

Van Gogh's

70 West Crossville Rd.
Roswell, GA 30075
770-993-1156.
Location: Roswell

Seating: 225
Owner/Chefs: Michele and Christopher Sedgwick
Cuisine: American Regional with European Influences
Opened: 1990
Overall Rating: ♥♥♥♥

Commentary: This marvelous restaurant welcomes you with a sophisticated warm atmosphere consisting of a mixture of brick walls, modern art, candlelight and fresh flowers. For intimacy, dining is divided into several rooms, and a friendly lounge with fireplace. Here's the opportunity to have a charming and unforgettable dining experience, without the stuffiness. Enjoy the delicious foods served with warm, fresh bread and caviar butter. Choose from an extensive wine menu and munch from the excellent crabcakes to the sinfull tiramisu. Service is friendly and skillful.

Dress Code: Casual to dressy.
Appetizers: . . . . $6.50-$9.95
Entrees: . . . . $12.95-$21.95
Desserts: . . . . $4.50-$5.50
House Specialties and Menu Samples:
Fresh Lumpmeat Crabcake. . . . . $ 9.95
Antipasto Sampler . . . . $ 9.95
Giant Grilled Portobello
   Mushrooms . . . . $ 9.95
Georgia Goat Cheese Salad . . . . $ 6.95
Spinach and Ricotta Gnocchi $10.95
Black Linguine, Tossed w/Ginger
   and Lemon Tuna Loin $13.95
Jumbo Sea Scallops Sauteed
   w/Salmon. $16.95
Olive Tapenade Crusted Snapper
   w/Shitake Mushrooms. $17.95
Grilled Rare Tuna Loin $16.95
Seared Nine Ounce Filet Mignon. . . . $19.95
Killer Tiramisu . . . . $ 5.50
Homemade Fresh Fruit Cobbler. . . . . $ 5.50
Days and Hours of Operation:
Monday-Saturday . . . . . . 11:30 to midnight
Sunday 5:00-10:00

Barbecue

Down East Bar-B-Que
2289 S. Cobb Dr.
Smyrna, GA 30080
770-434-8887.
Location: Smyrna
Seating: 42
Owner/Chef: Sandra Brown
Cuisine: North Carolina BBQ
Opened: 1994
Overall Rating: ♥♥

Commentary: Two smiling pigs greet patrons at the door, and will keep you smiling, once you taste the authentic North Carolina spice and vinegar juicy pork barbecue. "We name our pigs," says owner, Sandra, who always has one cooking in the back. Recognized as one of the best in the metro Atlanta area, this smokey, slow-cooked delicacy has a faithful following. The no-frills restaurant also serves tangy coleslaw, sweet, tender collard greens, and down-home friendliness. Finger-licking baby-back ribs are served Friday and Saturday's only. Try the thick Brunswick stew, another favorite. Take-out is a mainstay of Down East's business, just remember to phone ahead if you are feeding the neighborhood.

Dress Code: Casual.
Entrees: . . . . $3.50-$11.95

House Specialties and Menu Items:

Brunswick Stew. . . . . $ .89
Collard Greens or Candied Yams . . . . $ .89
Bar-B-Que Pork Sandwich
   w/Coleslaw. . . . . $ 3.50
Bar-B-Que Plate, w/Slaw,
   Bread,1 Side . . . . $ 5.75
Combo Plate, 2 Meats
   w/Bread,2 Sides . . . . $ 7.59
Baby Back Pork Ribs
   w/Bread,2 Sides . . . . $ 8.50
BBQ by the Pound, Chopped Pork . . $11.95
Days and Hours of Operation:
Monday-Thursday 11:00-9:00
Friday and Saturday 11:00-10:00

Chinese Cuisine

House of Chan
2469 Cobb Parkway
Smyrna, GA 30080
770-955-9444.
Location: Smyrna
Seating: 60
Owner: Mr. Chan
Chef: Mrs.King Chan
Cuisine: Eclectic Chinese
Opened: 1982
Overall Rating: ♥♥♥

Commentary: Each diner is greeted by Mr. Chan, a most gracious host, then guided through a bustling dining room with an Oriental setting, the start of a most enjoyable dining experience. Experience

a wonderful varied cuisine of Hunan, Mandarin, and Cantonese home cooking, authentically prepared by head chef Mrs. Chan. Ask for Cindy, an entertaining hostess, who will make sampling a delectable experience. Piquant kula pork, king salt shrimp and a most tender sea bass will please the palate. You will love the genuine feeling that the House of Chan imparts.

Dress Code: Casual.
Appetizers: . . . . $1.55-$6.95
Entrees: . . . . $7.95-$17.25
Desserts:. $3.95
House Specialties and Menu Items:
Fried Dumplings Peking Style . . . . . . $ 5.75
Crab Ragoon (six) . . . . $ 4.75
House Special Soup for Two . . . . $ 6.25
Kula Pork, Chan's Specialty $11.75
General Tao's Chicken. $11.75
Jumbo Spiced Salt Shrimp $14.75
Steamed Fish Catch of the Day . . . . . market
Plum Roast Duck Half $15.00
Banana Fritters for Two . . . . $ 3.95
Days and Hours of Operation:
Monday-Friday. 11:30-2:30
Sunday 12:00-3:00
Monday-Saturday. 5:00-10:00
Sunday 5:00-10:00

Little Szechuan
5091-C Buford Highway
Doraville, GA 30340
770-451-0192.
Location: Northwood Plaza
Seating: 200
Owners: Yu Chang Chung and Sherry Wang
Chef: Yu Chang Chung
Cuisine: Szechuan
Opened: 1990
Overall Rating: ♥♥

Commentary: It's the Szechuan cuisine that has put this resaurant on the map. Hostess Sherry Wang greets everyone as a special guest, and service continues with efficiency and smiles. A generous open dining area with two private adjoining rooms, adorned with Oriental decor, makes a sociable setting. Chef Yu Chang Chung, voted in Taiwan as most talented in Szechuan cooking, will take you on a marvelous journey. The most tender of potstickers, spicy-sweet delectible shrimp egg foo yung, and the fiery shredded pork with garlic and stir-fried snowpeas.

Dress Code: Casual.
Appetizers: . . . . $3.25-$7.95
Entrees:. . . . . $3.25-$16.95
House Specialties and Menu Items:
Potstickers w/Chicken. . . . . $ 4.25
Egg Drop Soup Home Style . . . . $ 4.25
Stir Fried Chicken, Plum Sauce . . . . . $ 7.25
Shrimp Egg Fu Yung . . . . $ 9.95
Shredded Pork w/Garlic Sauce . . . . . . $ 6.95
Sizzling Tofu, w/Szechuan Sauce. . . . $ 6.95
Stir Fried Baby Anchovies . . . . $ 7.95
Eggplant w/Garlic Sauce. . . . . $ 6.95
Shrimp w/Yellow Young Chives . . . $12.95
Days and Hours of Operation:
Wednesday-Monday 11:30-3:00
Wednesday-Monday 5:00-9:30

The Orient at Vinings
4199 Paces Ferry Rd.
Atlanta, GA 30339
770-438-8866.
Location: Vinings Square
Seating: 80
Owners: Bill and Agate Lip

Chef: Bill Lip
Cuisine: New Cantonese
Opened: 1979
Overall Rating: ♥♥♥

Commentary: A delightful Chinese restaurant, voted one of the best in Georgia. Offering dining in a sun-splashed, casual yet elegant room, with a black and blue motif, and the presence of legendary god figurines of good fortune, prosperity and longevity. Chef Bill Lip's innovative kitchen creates such imaginative dishes as shrimp sour soup and fire cracker pork, a spicy treasure. Gracious hostess Agate recognizes each patron in her gentle way. Enjoy the luxury of new Cantonese cooking, with constantly changing specials, and the newly added Sunday brunch.

Dress Code: Casual to jackets.
Appetizers: .... $3.50-$5.95
Entrees: .... $7.95-$19.95
Desserts: .... $3.25-$3.75
House Specialties and Menu Items:
Shrimp Sour Soup w/Fresh
    Jumbo Shrimp .... $ 3.95
Sea Twins, scallop wrapped
    w/ shrimp.................... $ 4.95
Sea Dragon Roll, Wrapped Lobster . $ 5.95
Seafood Salad.................. $ 7.95
Fire Cracker Pork, in
    Szechuan Sauce............... $ 9.95
Rainbow Shrimp, w/Fresh Fruits $13.95
Sea Pearls, Oysters
    w/Ginger Sauce $13.95
The Four Seas, Potato Basket
    w/Seafood $19.95
Tapioca Hong Kong w/Fresh Fruit .. $ 3.25
Chef's Special Dessert .... $ 3.75
Days and Hours of Operation:
Sunday-Thursday 11:30-10:00
Friday 11:30-11:00
Saturday 6:00-11:00
Sunday Brunch............. 11:30-2:30

Continental Cuisine

The Abbey
163 Ponce De Leon Ave.
Atlanta, GA 30308
876-8831.
Location: Midtown
Seating: 300
Owner: Bill Swearinger
Chef: Richard Lindamood
Cuisine: Continental
Opened: 1969
Overall Rating: ♥♥♥♥

Commentary: The Abbey has been an Atlanta fine dining institution for over 26 years. A unique dining experience treasured awaits when you enter this 1915 church, featuring massive stained glass windows, forty-foot vaulted ceilings and costumed monk waiters. Tables are set with fresh flowers and crisp linen, classical music is played, and delectable international specialties are served with splendid presentation. Choose from an award-winning winelist, and enjoy the highly professional service as you savor Georgia quail, Maine lobster or crisp snapper filet. Make this a chic evening to celebrate a special occasion.

Dress Code: Dressy, jacket and tie.
Appetizers: .... $8.00-$13.00
Entrees: .... $19.00-$24.00
Desserts: .... $6.00-$8.00
House Specialties and Menu Items:
Lightly Smoked Salmon with
    Salmon Tartare .... $ 9.00
Jumbo Scallop on Corn and
    Crayfish Chowder .... $ 8.00
Ginger Maine Lobster and
    Artichoke Cassoulet $13.00
Glazed Duck Breast w/Roasted
    Sweet Potatoe $20.00
Roast Rock Game Hen w/Garlic
    Potato Cake.................. $19.00
Moroccan Spiced Salmon Filet
    w/Couscous $19.00

Crisp Snapper Filet on Shrimp
  w/Corn Risotto $21.00
Chocolate Hazelnut Torte. . . . . $ 8.00
Georgia Peach Cream Cheese
  Parfait . . . . $ 7.00
Days and Hours of Operation:
Monday-Sunday . . . . 6:00-10:00p.m.

Brooklyn Cafe

220 Sandy Springs Circle, #101
Atlanta, GA 30328
770-843-8377.
Location: Sandy Springs
Seating: 100
Owners: Stephen Buero and Greg Pyne
Chef: Marty Westenberg
Cuisine: Continental with Italian Accents
Opened: November 1993
Overall Rating: ♥♥♥♥

Commentary: Step into an energy-packed, New York-style neighborhood cafe with a lively open bar, charcoal sketches on the wall, and an outdoor patio. All patrons, from native Atlantans to visiting Alaskans (and even New Yorkers) receive a warm welcome from owners Stephen and Greg. The festive atmosphere and the creative cooking that brings forth a hearty, gourmet quality, cuisine makes this restaurant both a meeting place and a culinary delight. Enjoy a great winelist as you graze on giant portobello mushrooms, award-winning veal chiante, and sip an old-fashioned homemade Brooklyn egg cream.

Dress Code: Casual.
Appetizers: . . . . $3.95-$6.95
Entrees: . . . . $4.25-$15.95
Desserts:. . . . . $1.95-$3.95
House Specialties and Menu Samples:
Eggplant Rollatini with
  Four Cheeses . . . . $ 5.25
Grilled Jumbo Shrimps
  w/Mushroom Risotto. . . . . $ 6.95
Portobello Mushroom Sauteed
  with Garlic. . . . . $ 4.75
Angelhair with Pancetta and
  Shitake Mushroom $12.95
Panfried Salmon with Sauteed
  Spinach $14.95

Atlantic Flounder Piccata with
  Polenta $13.95
Vegetarian Cannelloni and
  Spaghetti Squash . . . . $ 8.95
Veal Saltimbocca with Prosciutto. . . $14.95
Homemade Italian Cannelloni. . . . . . $ 3.95
Brooklyn Chocolate Egg Cream. . . . . $ 1.95
Days and Hours of Operation:
Monday-Saturday 11:30-2:30
Monday-Saturday 5:30-11:00
Sunday. 4:30-9:30

Dimitri's

4651 Woodstock Rd.
Roswell, GA 30075
770-587-2700.
Location: Sandy Plains Village Shopping Center
Seating: 225
Owner: Andrew Fotos
Chef: Cuinn J. Sealy
Cuisine: Mediterranean/Italian
Opened: 1992
Overall Rating: ♥♥♥

Commentary: Step into a spacious, polished, brasserie-type restaurant of casual elegance. Watch culinary creations appear from an open kitchen, tended by one of Atlanta's youngest, and most adventurous chefs. No need to travel to Europe and the Mediterranean. An ever-expanding menu offers homemade pastas, fragrant herbs and exotic vegetables; Enjoy the chicken marsala with rosemary, the grilled salmon with a hint of maple syrup, or the roasted lamb crusted with black pepper. Top off the meal a luscious dessert.

Dress Code: Casual to jackets.
Appetizers: . . . . $5.95-$8.95
Entrees:. . . . . $9.95-$21.95
Desserts: . . . . $2.95-$5.95
House Specialties and Menu Items:
Fried Calamari
  w/Homemade Marinara . . . . $ 6.95
Raviol Stuffed w/Cheese and Crab . . $ 7.95
Cream of Portobella Mushroom. . . . . $ 3.95
Mousaka, Beef and Eggplant . . . . $ 9.95
Salmon Marinated in Maple Syrup. . $16.95

Grilled Pork Tenderloin and
   Apple Crepe................... $17.95
Grilled Filet w/Wild Mushrooms ... $18.95
Roasted Lambchops w/Ratatouille .. $21.95
Daily Varied Desserts: .... $ 2.95
Days and Hours of Operation:
Monday-Friday.............. 11:30-3:30
Sunday-Thursday 5:30-10:00
Friday and Saturday 5:00-11:00

Hal's on Old Ivy
30 Old Ivy Rd.
Atlanta, GA 30342
261-0025
Located: Buckhead
Seating: 115
Owner: Hal Nowak
Chef: Ray Allen
Cuisine: Continental with Creole & Italian
Accents
Opened: 1991
Overall Rating: ♥♥♥

Commentary: Buckhead's home away from
home, Old Ivy is furnished with dark woods
and sophisticated tables. Alongside the dining
area is one of Buckhead's most popular restaurant bars. While perusing the menu, sample
wines by the glass. Try the lobster bisque, gulf
trout with crabmeat, or a char-grilled lamb
chop. End with a New Orleans-style bread
pudding.

Dress Code: Smart casual.
Appetizers................ $ 4.95- 7.95
Entrees .... $ 8.95-21.95
Desserts....................... $ 3.95
House Specialties & Menu Samples:
Shrimp Remoulade, w/Tangy
   Creole Sauce .... $ 6.95
Lobster Bisque, w/Chunks of Lobster $ 6.95
Soft Shell Crabs, w/Meuniere or
   Amandine $15.95
Trout with Crabmeat, Fresh
   Gulf trout.................... $17.95
Snapper Franchaise, Sauteed
   White Wine $16.95
Filet Mignon au Poivre,
   w/Cognac Sauce $20.95
Char-grilled Lamb Chops.......... $21.95

New Orleans Breadpudding
   w/Bourbon .... $ 3.95
Triple Decker Chocolate Cake...... $ 3.95
Open:
Monday-Friday at 4:30
Saturday at..................... 5:00

The Restaurant
181 Peachtree St.
Atlanta, GA 30303
659-0400
Located: Downtown, The Ritz-Carlton
Seating: 80
Chef: Daniel Schaffhauser
Cuisine: Continental with French Accents
Opened: 1984
Overrall Rating: ♥♥♥♥

Commentary: World-class fine dining in a
magnificent setting. Deep green walls hung with
hunt art, French collectibles, and the elegant Ritz
furnishings create an unparalleled dining
aestetic. A fine-tuned staff will help make your
dinner a truly memorable experience. Savor such
superb selections as roasted Maine lobster, black
peppered seared tuna loin or roasted roe deer
loin. Close with a sampling of the freshest of
fruits and darkest of chocolates.

Dress Code: Jackets required.
Appetizers .... $ 9.00-12.00
Entrees.................. $21.00-28.00
Desserts .... $ 5.50- 8.00
House Specialties & Menu Samples:
Seared Sweetwater Prawns,
   w/Coconut Curry $10.50
Lump Crab Meat Spinach
   Cannelloni $10.00
Georgia Sweet Potato Soup
   w/Oysters .... $ 8.50
Roasted Pintelle Farm Guinea
   Hen Breast $22.00
Black Pepper Seared Tuna
   Neck Loin................... $23.00
Roasted Baby Sonoma Lamb
   Rack w/Thai Sauce............. $24.00
Grilled Black Angus Filet
   w/Artichoke $25.00
Roasted Maine Lobster
   w/Black Tagliolini $28.00

Valrhona Dark Chocolate
  Souffle Cake .... $ 6.00
Souffle Grand Marnier Orange
  w/Berries .... $ 8.00
Open:
Monday-Saturday 6:00-10:00

Cuban Cuisine

Mambo
1402 North Highland Ave.
Atlanta, 30306
876-2626.
Location: Virginia-Highlands
Seating: 66
Owners: Lucy Alvarez and Hilton Joseph
Chef: Lucy Alvarez
Cuisine: Progressive Cuban
Opened: September 1990
Overall Rating: ♥♥

Commentary: The lively atmosphere is conta-
gious, the tasty food healthy and the value incredible. Indoors a 9-foot mural of Carmen
Mulata seems to gyrate with the background
Latin music. Friendly service is in keeping with
the beat. Try the "Tapa Adventure" served only
Monday through Thursday, and let your taste-
buds mambo as you try the lime-marinated fish
ceviche, the original arroz negro squid inked
rice, or flaky ropa vieja with a glass of beer or
wine. And don't you dare leave without mother's
recipe of homemade flan.

Dress Code: Casual .
Appetizers: .... $3.95-$5.95
Entrees: .... $6.95-$16.95
Desserts .... $2.95-$4.25
House Specialties and Menu Items:
Chorizos Al Infierno,
  Spanish Sausage .... $ 4.95
Ceviche, Lime-Marinated Fresh Fish. $ 5.95
Calamares Bahia Honda Appetizer .. $ 4.95
Mediterranean Tuscan Bean Salad... $ 4.25
Ropa Vieja, Shredded Sherry
  Spiked Steak .... $ 8.95
Puerco Asado, Roast Pork in
  Garlic/Lime .... $ 8.95

Arroz Negro $14.95
Camarones Enchilados
  Shrimp Dish $13.95
Vanilla Flan Cooled with Syrup..... $ 3.25
Days and Hours of Operation:
Monday-Thursday 5:30-10:30
Friday-Saturday.............. 5:30-11:30
Sunday..................... 5:30-10:00

French Cuisine

Anis Cafe and Bistro
2974 Grandview Ave.
Atlanta, GA 30305
233-9889.
Location: Buckhead
Seating: 85
Owners: JacquesHourtal, Jean-Fre Perfet-
tini and Arnaud Michel
Chef: Jacques Hourtal
Cuisine: French Provence
Opened: 1994
Overall Rating: ♥♥♥

Commentary: Three friends merged their
passion for "a taste of Provence cuisine,"
where life is lived outside and people socialize
at a table with friends. Starting with an extremely modest budget, the partners combined
plenty of hard work and ingenuity with a
blending of their individual skills to transform
a tiny home into a romantic cafe with a charming trellis-lined terrace. Provencal food is simple and healthy, relying on olive oil and herbs.
Savor the authentic flavor of salade nicoise or
poulet au crepes with a glass of French wine.

Dress Code: Casual.
Appetizers: .... $3.95-$6.50
Entrees: .... $6.45-$12.95
Desserts: $4.50
House Specialties and Menu Items:
Salade Nicoise, Fresh
  and Authentic .... $ 5.95
Warm Focaccio Toasts
  w/Mozzarella .... $ .95
Shrimps Sauteed in Olive Oil $11.95

Poulet Au Cepes, w/Imported
Mushrooms . . . . $ 9.25
Cote d'Agneau Corsica,
Grilled Lamb $12.95
Ravioli "alla Nissarada" . . . . $ 6.95
Creme Brulee . . . . $ 4.50
Daily Fresh Desserts. . . . . $ 4.50
Days and Hours of Operation:
Tuesday-Saturday. 11:30-2:30
Tuesday-Thurday and Sunday . . 6:00-10:00
Friday-Saturday 6:00-11:00

Babette's Cafe
471 North Highland Ave.
Atlanta, GA 30306
523-9121.
Location: Virginia Highlands
Seating: 72
Owner/Chef: Marla Adams
Cuisine: French Country
Opened: 1992
Overall Rating: ♥♥♥

Commentary: A charming French country
kitchen cafe offering a inventive French country cuisine. The snug and homey atmosphere
is devolves from ivy over old brick walls,
shuttered windows and strategically placed
period antiques on dark wood floors. Delightful chef/owner Marla teases the palate with
superb steamed mussels in white wine, tender
veal with wild mushrooms and rigatoni laced
with basil and watercress. Try "Babette's
Feast," which is a four-course, prix fixe menu
that offers innovative seasonal specialties,
with wine included.

Dress Code: Casual.
Appetizers: $4.00-6.00
Entrees: $9.50-16.00
Desserts:. $4.00-5.00
House Specialties and Menu Items:
Grilled Corn Chowder . . . . $ 3.75
Artichoke and Olive Ravioli . . . . $ 5.00
Steamed Mussels in White Wine . . . . $ 6.00
Spinach Lasagna w/Three Cheeses . . $ 9.50
Rigatoni in Watercress Sauce. $11.00
Chicken Roasted w/Thyme $11.00
Grilled Salmon w/Wilted Spinach . . . $15.00
Veal Scallopini w/Wild Mushrooms . $15.00

Satiny Espresso Flan . . . . $ 4.50
Linda's Wicked Chocolate Cake. . . . . $ 5.00
Days and Hours of Operation:
Tuesday-Thursday. 6:00-10:00
Friday and Saturday 6:00-11:00
Sunday. 4:00-9:00
Sunday Brunch 11:30-4:00

Nikolai's Roof
255 Courtland St.
Atlanta, GA 30303
659-2000
Located: Downtown in Atlanta Hilton &
Towers
Seating: 80
Chef: Marc Benoit
Cuisine: French Continental w/Russian Spe-
cialties
Opened: 1976
Overall Rating: ♥♥♥♥

Commentary: Throw out any misconception
regarding hotel food, and experience one of
America's finest restaurants. For a special occasion or pre-Fox dinner, revel in the rich
ambiance of cobalt blue, imperial reds, cande-
labra's and enjoy the panoramic view of Atlanta. An effective Cossack tunicked staff will
introduce you to a special marinated Russian
vodka, served ice cold. Definitely relaxed,
prepare to savor superb cuisine from a continuously changing five-course prix fixe dinner, each course served with an appropriate
wine. It's impossible to choose a favorite; all
are outstanding. Manager, Richard Eyer, adds
to the ambiance with his special "opening
day" enthusiasm.

Dress Code: Jackets required.
Four-course prix fixe. $48.00
Five-course prix fixe $60.00
House Specialties & Menu Samples:
Petits Piroshkhis de Boeuf et Volaille,
(Seasoned Beef Tenderloin/Chicken Puff
Pastry)
Papillottes De Chevre Et Tomate Confite,
(Grilled Eggplant Roulades w/Goat
Cheese, Roma Tomato)

Rosace De Saumon Et Truite Fumee,
(Smoked Trout Mousseline w/Scottish
Smoked Salmon)
Filet De Boeuf Aux Senteurs Provencales,
(Beef Tenderloin w/Fresh Vegetables,
Provencale Jus)
Filets Mignons D'Agneau Aux Trois
Oignons Et Jus De Curry, (New Zealand
Lamb Tenderloin w/Onions,Coconut
Milk,Curry)
Medaillons De Chevreuil En Compote
De Figues Et Pleurottes, (Sauteed Venison
Medallions w/Figs,Youkon Gold Potato
Souffle)
Filets De Sole Poches Au Beurre D'Oursins,
(Poached Dover Sole w/Purple Potato,Sea
Urchin Butter Sauce)
Creme Brulee Au Chambord,
(Chambord Liquor and Roasted Pecan Nut
Creme Brulee)
Souffle Du Soir,
Souffle Selection of the Evening.
Open:
Daily Dining. 6:30-9:30

South of France
2345 Cheshire Bridge Rd.
Atlanta, GA 30324
325-6963.
Location: Cheshire Bridge
Seating: 120
Owner: Tonino Spinucci
Chef: Luigi Bosco
Cuisine: Country French
Opened: 1985
Overall Rating: ♥♥

Commentary: A romantic mood is set in a
country French bistro with open beams, harvest implements and a wood-burning fireplace.

Relax and enjoy a wine while perusing the
menu by candlelight.

The French onion soup is delectable, and tasty
piquant tournedos de boeuf and delicious es-
calope de veau are all served in grand portions.
The delicate voice of vocalist/guitarist Berne
entertains patrons, Wednesday through Saturday.

Dress Code: Casual to dressy.
Appetizers: . . . . $5.95-$7.95
Entrees: . . . . $10.95-$24.95
Desserts: . . . . $4.00-$6.00
House Specialties and Menus Samples:
Champignons Farci, Mushrooms . . . . $ 7.95
Pate de Campagne, Liver Pate . . . . . . $ 5.95
Soupe a l'Oignon Gratinee . . . . $ 3.95
Crevettes du Midi, Jumbo Shrimp . . $17.95
Grouper St. Maxime $17.95
Les Tournedo de Boeuf Bordelaise. . $19.95
Carre d'Agneau a la Dijonaise $21.95
Chocolate Mousse . . . . $ 4.00
Strawberries Romanoff . . . . $ 6.00
Days and Hours of Operation:
Monday-Friday 11:30-2:00
Monday-Thursday 6:00-10:00
Friday and Saturday 6:00-11:00

Indian Cuisine

Heera of India
595 Piedmont at North Ave.
Atlanta, GA 30308
876-4408.
Location: Downtown
Seating: 90
Owner: Pinto Ahluwalia
Cuisine: North Indian
Opened 1989
Overall Rating: ♥♥♥

Commentary: A casual and peaceful elegance greets you, as a courteous host seats you
at a romantic candlelighted table. Quiet music
sets the mood to enjoy authentic North Indian
foods made with personal selected spices.
Choices are mild to hot, piquant to pungent.
Try the Indian antipasto and the tandori
cooked meats permeated with exotic spices.
To add more spice to your dinner, come on
Saturday and enjoy the bellydancing.

Dress Code: Casual or jackets.
Appetizers: . . . . $2.50-$5.95
Entrees: . . . . $6.25-$15.50
Desserts: . . . . $2.00-$2.75

House Specialties and Menu Samplers:

Kulcha Naan, Indian Bread
w/Onions,Spices . . . . $ 2.75
Exoctic Assorted Appetizer Plate. . . . $ 5.95
Tandori Chicken, Marinated
and Baked . . . . $ 7.25
Lamb Vindaloo, Diced Lamb in
Spicy Sauce . . . . $ 8.95
Shrimp Masala in Delectable Sauce. . $11.95
Baingan Bharta, Sauteed Eggplant. . . $ 5.95
Special Biryani, Shrimp, Lamb,
Chicken . . . . $ 9.95
Gulab Jamun, Deepfried Dough
in Syrup . . . . $ 2.25
Mango Kulfi, Homemade Mango
Ice Cream. . . . . $ 2.00

Days and Hours of Operation:

Monday-Sunday 11:30-2:00
Monday-Sunday 5:30-10:30

Italian Cuisine

Alfredo's

1989 Chesire Bridge Rd.
Atlanta, GA 30324
876-1380.
Location: Buckhead East
Seating: 50
Owner: Perry Alvarez
Chef: Enco Finetti
Cuisine: Regional Italian
Opened: 1977
Overall Rating: ♥♥♥

Commentary: Welcome to an old-world '50s
style Italian Restaurant, serving homey-style
Italian food for 22 years. A handsome, soft-
lighted, dining room with warm wood panel-
ing, dressed tables and a rest-your-elbows bar
provides a perfect setting for a relaxing evening. Owner, Perry Alvarez, greets first-tim-
ers and regulars with his ever-present good
cheer as he helps them settle into the comfortable booths. Sip a glass of chianti or a barolo
while savoring the raviolini pomodoro, or the
snapper casalinga, or the Linguini pescattore.
Top off the evening with a Sicilian cannoli and
Cognac.

Dress Code: Casual to jackets.
Appetizers: . . . . $4.50-$5.95
Entrees: . . . . $9.95-$17.50
Desserts: . . . . $2.95-$3.95
House Specialties and Menu Items:
Baked Clams Casino . . . . $ 5.95
Minestrone alla Milanese . . . . $ 2.25
Antipasta Misto, Casalinga . . . . $ 5.95
Raviolini Pomodoro w/Goat Cheese $10.95
Penne Salmone, Salmon in Vodka . . $11.95
Snapper Casalinga w/Wine, Capers . $15.95
Linguini Pescattore w/Seafood $14.95
Filet alla Fiorentain, Sauteed. $15.50
Tiramisu. . . . . $ 3.95
Sicilian Cannoli . . . . $ 3.50
Days and Hours of Operation:
Sunday-Thursday 5:00-10:00
Friday and Saturday 5:00-11:00

Basta

659 Peachtree St.
Atlanta, GA 30308
874-8980
Located: Midtown. Georgian Terrace Hotel
Seating: 110
Owner: Jude Hettick
Chef: Alfonso Martinez
Cuisine: Italian
Opened: 1994
Overall Rating: ♥♥♥

Commentary: A relaxed neighborhood atmosphere greets the eclectic pre-Fox crowd
and regulars. Set in a turn-of-the-century
brick-walled basement, this restored circa
1911 grill today delivers a Soho cafe look. A
display of local artist paintings, and slide-on
bar, gives a no-rush feeling. Specialties from
a reliable menu include smoked salmon fettuccine and penne amatriciana with a pleasant
bite of hot peppers and tomatoes. For the pizza
gourmet, ask the chef to surprise you with a
sophisticated combination. There's great exotic beer on tap and validated parking at the
Georgian Terrace Hotel.

Dress Code: Casual.
Appetizers . . . . $ 3.95- 5.95
Entrees . . . . $ 7.95-13.95
Desserts . . . . $ 3.95

House Specialties & Menu Samples:
Caprese Salad, w/Fresh Mozzarella . . $ 5.95
Fried Cheese Ravioli, Spicy . . . . $ 4.25
Eggplant Parmesan, w/Angel Hair . . . $ 7.95
White Pizza, Sundried Tomato,
  Onion,Peppers . . . . $ 8.95
Smoked Salmon Fettucini,
  w/Spinach $10.95
Penne Amatriciana, Proscuitto,
  Hot Peppers . . . . $ 9.95
Southwestern Chicken Pasta,
  w/Tequila $10.95
Linguini Genovese, Garlic,Basil,
  Pinenuts . . . . $ 9.50
Tiramisu, Worth the Calories . . . . $ 3.95
Chocolate Mousse Torte, Rich, Rich . $ 3.95

Open:
Lunch Monday-Friday 11:30-2:30
Dinner Monday-Saturday 5:30-10:00

Bertolini's
3500 Peachtree Rd.
Atlanta, GA 30326
233-2333.
Location: Buckhead at Phipps Plaza
Seating: 154
Owner: Quantum
Chef: Bill Bowls
Cuisine: Italian
Opened: 1993
Overall Rating: ♥♥♥

Commentary: A warm and festive atmosphere awaits at this authentic trattoria, a place to enjoy an evening out or business meeting. Italian music and a colorful decor gives the flavor of a true European experience. Feast on homemade rosemary bread, pasta favorites such as delicate angel hair with basil and garlic, taglionini with lobster or fazzoletto confunghi, all made with imported cheeses and special ingredients, served by a most sophisticated staff. An extensive assortment of wines, coffees and cappuccinos will make this one of the best Italian dining experiences!

Dress Code: Casual to jackets.
Appetizers: . . . . $3.50-$6.95
Entrees: . . . . $8.50-$14.50
Desserts: . . . . $4.95-$6.95

House Specialties and Menu Items:
Calamari Fritti w/Spicy
  Tomato Caper Sauce . . . . $ 5.95
Antipasto Misto, Assorted
  Fresh Antipasti . . . . $ 5.50
Prosciutto e Mozzarella Affumicata . . $ 6.95
Insalata di Pollo con Pasta . . . . $ 8.50
Cappelli d'Angelo al Pomodoro e
  Basilico . . . . $ 9.50
Tagliolini ai Frutti di Mare $13.50
Fazzoletto con Funghi $11.50
Suprema di Pollo alla Romana $13.50
Tiramisu . . . . $ 5.95

Days and Hours of Operation:
Sunday-Thursday 11:30-10:00
Friday and Saturday 11:30-midnight

Dominick's
95 South Peachtree St.
Norcross, GA 30071
770-449-1611.
Location: Historic Norcross
Seating: 280
Owners: Paul Derrico and Rob Pedlow
Chef: Adrian Pincever
Cuisine: Italian
Opened: 1994
Overall Rating: ♥♥

Commentary: An old New York Italian theme, is brought to life in a handsomely renovated warehouse. Old brick walls are hung with vintage family photos, there's a pressed tin ceiling, stained glass windows and old lamp posts; Owners Paul and Rob strive to serve authentic Italian cuisine. Dominick's is a family place, servings are large, easily enough for two people. Try the spinach stuffed mushrooms or the browned veal marsala. The chicken scarapiello with sausage and roasted peppers is also popular as is the reshly baked focaccio. For dessert share a delicious Cannoli or New York Cheesecake.

Dress Code: Casual.
Appetizers: $6.00-13.00
Entrees: $11.00-26.00
Desserts: $3.00
House Specialties and Menu Items:
Stuffed Mushrooms $10.00

Calamari Fritti w/Marinara......... $10.00
Mozzarella en Carrozza .... $ 7.00
Ravioli di Dominick.............. $13.00
Rigatoni w/Eggplant, Mozzarella.... $13.00
Chicken Scarapiello $18.00
Veal Marsala, Lightly Browned..... $18.00
Homemade Cannoli .... $ 3.00

Days and Hours of Operation:
Monday-Friday.............. 11:30-3:00
Monday-Thursday 5:00-10:00
Friday and Saturday 5:00-11:00
Sunday 5:00-9:00

La Grotta
2637 Peachtree Rd.
Atlanta, GA 30305
231-1368.
Location: Buckhead
Seating: 110
Owners: Sergio Favalli and Antonio Abizanda
Chef: Antonio Abizanda
Cuisine: Northern/Regional Italian
Opened: 1978
Overall Rating: ♥♥♥♥

Commentary: For outstanding classic Italian cuisine La Grotta is a must. The elegant clubby atmosphere and charming outdoor patio provide the perfect backdrop for Owner Sergio as he welcomes each patron. Choose from one of the Best Italian wine lists in Atlanta and from such menu favorites as carpaccio with arugola and truffle oil, zesty stuffed ravioli with goat cheese and apples, and delectable swordfish with caramelized onions. It won't take long for you to understand why the regulars are regulars.

Dress Code: Jackets preferred.
Appetizers: .... $6.50-$7.25
Entrees: .... $12.75-$22.95
Desserts:................. $4.50-$4.75
House Specialties and Menu Items:
Cappe Sante Con Scalogno,
  Sea Scallops.................. $ 7.25
Ravioloni con Caprino,
  Stuffed Ravioli $13.25
Farfalle con Salmone Affumicato ... $13.75
Scaloppine di Pesce Spada,
  Swordfish................... $18.75

Capriolo al Madeira, Sauteed
  Venison.................... $19.50
Scaloppine di Vitello alla Grotta.... $18.95
Filetto di Manzo al Gorgonzola $18.95
Zabaglione al Marsala............. $ 4.50
Fresh Pastries.................... $ 4.75
Days and Hours of Operation:
Monday-Saturday 6:00-10:30

La Strada
2930 Johnson Ferry Rd.
Marietta, GA 30062
770-640-7008
and
8550 Roswell Rd.
Dunwoody, GA 30350
552-1300
Seating: 80 and 160 respectively
Owners: Tino Venturi and Eric Hald
Chef: Eric Hald
Cuisine: Italian with Northern and Southern Accents
Opened: 1989
Overall Rating: ♥♥♥

Commentary: Voted as best casual Italian neighborhood restaurant, the setting is casual with a European atmosphere of knick-knacks, ferns and dressed tables. Enjoy trattoria-style dining. Quality foods are served with a variety of tasty daily specials. Be sure to try the famous tender calamalone and the grilled salmon in basil sauce. Choose a robust glass of wine and expect resourceful service.

Dress Code: Casual.
Appetizers:............... $4.75-$5.95
Entrees:................. $8.75-$13.95
Desserts: .... $2.95-$3.50
House Specialties and Menu Items:
Marinated Portobello Mushrooms ... $ 5.75
Blackened Jumbo Shrimp with
  Remoulade .... $ 5.75
Capelli d'Angelo and Fresh Marinara. $ 7.95
Calamalone, Tender Calamari Steaks $12.50
Salmon and Scallops a La Caprese .. $11.25
Gamberoni Ripieni, Shrimp Stuffed
  w/Crab $12.95
Scaloppine di Vitello Marsala $11.95
Tiramisu....................... $ 3.50

Chilled Creme Brule. . . . . $ 3.50

Days and Hours of Operation:

Sunday-Thursday 5:00-10:00

Friday and Saturday 4:30-11:00

Lombardi's

94 Upper Pryor St.,

Atlanta, GA

522-6568

Located: Above Underground Atlanta

Seating: 110

Owner: Alberto Lombardi

Chef: Salvadore

Cuisine: Italian

Opened: 1990

Overall Rating: ♥♥♥♥

Commentary: Dine in the casual elegance of an Italian trattoria. An experienced staff will introduce you to such marvelous favorites as crispy calamari with authentic tomato caper sauce, spicy penne arrabiata and delicious classic lasagna, all served piping hot. An always dependable menu, combined with gracious host Gabriel Paz, will make you a devotee from you first visit. Validated parking.

Dress Code: Casual to business.

Appetizers. . . . . $ 6.00- 7.25

Entrees . . . . $ 8.95-15.95

Desserts. . . . . $ 4.50- 5.00

House Specialties & Menu Samples:

Calamari Fritti, w/Tomato Caper

  or Marinara . . . . $ 6.50

Mozzarella Lombardi, wrapped

  w/ Prosciutto/Basil . . . . $ 5.95

Pollo Affumicato Pizza,

  Smoked Chicken,Cilantro . . . . $ 9.50

Linguine alla Vongole,

  w/Fresh Clams. $12.50

Lasagna Verde Bolognese,

  w/Meat & Bechamel Sauce $11.50

Penne Arrabiata, Spicy Tomato,

  Pancetta, Basil $10.50

Tagliolini al Salmone con Vodka,

  Smoked Salmon. $11.50

Scaloppine di Vitello alla

  Parmigiana, Veal $15.95

Tiramisu, Blends of Espresso

  w/Mocha Mousse . . . . $ 5.00

Cioccolato con Cioccolato,

  Rich Chocolate Cake . . . . $ 5.00

Open:

Monday-Thursday 1:00-10:00

Friday. 11:00-11:00

Saturday. 5:00-11:00

Luna Si

1931 Peachtree Rd.

Atlanta, GA 30309

355-5993.

Location: Buckhead

Seating: 70

Owner: Juan Luna

Chef: Albert Luna

Cuisine: Italian/Mediterranean

Opened: 1993

Overall Rating: ♥♥♥

Commentary: Do you like to write on walls or tables? Go ahead! Canvas banners are suspended from the ceiling, the walls are filled with graffiti, and "padded" chairs give Luna Si a distictive, asylum-like atmosphere. A pleasing menu changes monthly to bring the patrons in-season specialties such as delicious soft-shell crabs, succulent pan-charred veal loin, or robust pappardelle noodle with goat cheese, all presented artisticly on oversized plates.

Dress Code: Casual to jackets.

Appetizers: . . . . $5.00-$6.00

Entrees: . . . . $9.00-$17.00

Desserts: . . . . $3.75-$4.50

House Specialties and Menu Items:

Raw Seasonal Seafood and

  Chili Madness. . . . . $ 6.00

Portobello with Aged Ricotta

  and Lime. $ 6.00

Pappardelle Red Peppers and

  Goat Cheese $10.00

Angel Hair with Shrimp, Garlic,

  Escarole $11.00

Soft Shell Crab in Soy Vinaigrette. . $17.00

Veal Loin Pan-Charred and Shiitake $17.00

Peach Creme Flan . . . . $ 4.50

Flourless Chocolate Cake . . . . $ 4.25

Days and Hours of Operation:

Monday-Saturday 5:30-10:30

Sunday 5:30-10:00

Pasta da Pulcinella

1027 Peachtree St.

Atlanta, GA 30309

892-6195.

Location: Midtown

Seating: 64

Owner/Chef: Roberto Boratto

Cuisine: Italian/American

Opened: August 1994

Overall Rating: ♥♥♥

Commentary: What a delicious find! A fun and hip dining room, in the mode of Greenwich Village, where patrons order from the counter. This little cafe tends to fill quickly with pasta lovers, dressed from shorts to suits. Chef Roberto creates a one-of-a-kind regional pasta menu with unbeatable prices. Served in deep plates, some favorites are homemade spinach Tagliatelle and Tortelli filled with Granny Smith apples and sausage. No wonder this new kid on the block is already widely-acclaimed.

Dress Code: Casual.

Salads: . . . . $2.50-$4.50

Entrees: . . . . $4.95-$6.50

Desserts: $3.95

House Specialties and Menu Items:

Traditional Caesar Salad . . . . $ 4.50

Linquine, Pesto or Roasted Garlic . . . $ 4.95

Tagliatelle Verdi alla Bolognese . . . . $ 5.95

Tortelli ala Menta, Vegetarian . . . . . . $ 6.50

Ravioli Sardi di Melanzane, Eggplant $ 6.50

Tortelli di Mele, Apple and Sausage . $ 6.50

Dessert of the Day . . . . $ 3.95

Days and Hours of Operation:

Monday-Friday 11:30-2:30

Monday-Thursday 5:30-10:00

Friday and Saturday 5:30-11:00

Japanese Cuisine

Kamogawa

3300 Peachtree Rd.

Atlanta, GA 30305

841-0314.

Location: Buckhead, Hotel Nikko

Seating: 120

Owner: Kamogawa Grand Hotels

Chef: Kobi Chiba

Cuisine: Japanese

Opened: 1990

Overall Rating: ♥♥

Commentary: Serene elegance greets you when, gracious host, Ryohei Yokogaki, guides you past an Oriental garden to the dining rooms. Shoes are neatly lined by the tatami rooms, as kimono-clad servers glide noiselessly past the low tables. With a 300-year history in Japan, this restaurant offers authentic Japanese cuisine in individual dining settings. From a six-page menu select favorite specialties such as tasty shabu shabu, sukiyaki, exotic varieties of sushi or an elaborate kaiseki banquet with eight to ten courses.

Dress Code: Casual to jackets.

Appetizers: . . . . $3.50-$6.75

Entrees: . . . . $14.25-$35.00

Desserts: . . . . $3.00-$4.75

House Specialties and Menu Samples:

Zensai Sushi, Appetizer Sushi . . . . . . $ 6.50

Kaki Tosafumi, Poached Oysters . . . . $ 6.75

Moriawase Tempura,Seafood/

   Vegetables $18.75

Shabu Shabu, Cook Own Foods

   at Table $22.50

Sukiyaki, Beef/Noodles/Tofu/

   Vegetables $22.50

Sushi Course, Complete $25.00

Wafu Steak Course, Steak/Sushi/

   Tempura $30.00

Ginger Ice Cream . . . . $ 3.00

Coffee Jelly . . . . $ 3.00

Days and Hours of Operation:

Monday-Saturday 11:30-2:00

Sunday-Thursday 6:00-10:00

Friday and Saturday 6:00-10:30

Ru San's

1529 Piedmont Rd.
Atlanta, GA 30309
875-7042
Located: Midtown, Across Ansley Mall
and Monroe
Seating: 72
Owner: RS.D.P.Inc.
Chef: Ru Nagata
Cuisine: Japanese/Sushi Bar
Opened: January 1993
Overall Rating: ♥♥♥♥

Commentary: A Japanese-style bistro with a large sushi bar and consistently good food draws a huge loyal following to Ru Sans. Watch sushi chefs display their skills amidst Japanese shouts, cajoling with customers, and the filling of large lacquered trays with delicacies. While sipping hot saki at the sushi-bar, fill out your dinner ticket from an extensive sushi menu, (most only $1.00). In addition to the sushi, try the lightly battered tempura, tofu favorites, vegetarian delights, sushi pizza and Ru San's special dinners.

Dress Code: Casual.

Appetizers . . . . $ 3.95-12.45
Sushi Yakitori . . . . $ 1.00- 1.50
Nouveau Entrees $11.95-19.95
Sushi Entrees . . . . $ 3.00-14.50
Japanese Entrees . . . . $ 9.45-14.95
Desserts . . . . $ 2.50- 4.50
House Specialties & Menus Samples:
Suzuki Sushi, Striped Bass . . . . $ 1.00
Hotategai Sushi, Scallop . . . . $ 1.00
Eggplant Sesame Yaki, Panfried . . . . $ 3.50
Ru Maki, Ebi, Kani, Kaiware, Ikura . $ 6.00
Tofu Scallop Kuzuni . . . . $ 7.95
RuSan's Sushi Pizza,
    Assorted Sushi . . . . $ 8.50
Gomoku Ankake BeeFun, Pasta . . . . $ 8.95
Miso Seared Pagoda Salmon Dinner $14.25
Curry Blackened Mekajiki Swordfish $14.25
Udon Bird's Nest Lobster Cake
    w/Lobster Tomato Bataki Sauce . . . $19.45
Tempura Vanilla Ice Cream . . . . $ 4.50
Open:
Lunch Monday-Saturday 10:30- 2:30

Dinner Sunday-Thursday 4:30-10:30
Friday-Saturday 4:30-11:00

Shiki Japanese Restaurant

1492 Pleasant Hill Rd.
Duluth, GA 30136
770-279-0097.
Location: Duluth
Seating: 130
Owner: Hiro Kameayashi
Chef: Yukio Watanabe
Cuisine: Japanese
Opened: 1992
Overall Rating: ♥♥♥♥

Commentary: Voted as one of the top Japanese restaurants in the South, Shiki proudly continues serving an excellent authentic Japanese cuisine. Masterfully managed by Seiko Kusaoka, within the modern three-dimensional dining area are a sushi bar, a teppanyaki room and traditional dining area. Attired in a brocade kimono, gracious headserver Emiko Ishioka glides quietly past patrons with an receptive eye, as sushi Chef Yojiko skillfully creates delicate sushi from glistening-fresh fish. Savor gyoza, a steamed stuffed dumpling, divine eef negima yaki, and the popular Georgia Roll. With dining so authentic, this must be Tokyo.

Dress Code: Casual to jackets.
Appetizers: . . . . $3.00-$15.00
Entrees: . . . . $8.50-$26.00
Desserts: . . . . $1.50-$3.00
House Specialties and Menu Items:
Gyoza, Steamed Stuffed
    Dumpling . . . . $ 4.50
Ebi Age Shinjo,
    Fried Shrimp Ball . . . . $ 5.50
Georgia Roll, Eel, Caviar, Avocado . . $ 6.50
Yawaragani Kara Age, Soft
    Shell Crab . . . . $ 7.00
Beef Negima Yaki, Grilled Beef $15.00
Sashimi , Fillet of Raw Fish $19.00
Filet Mignon Steak,
    Hibachi Grilled $19.50
Shabu-Shabu $20.00
Green Tea Ice Cream . . . . $ 1.50

Ice Cream Tempura,
Fried Ice Cream . . . . $ 3.00
Days and Hours of Operation:
Sunday-Thursday 5:30-10:00
Friday and Saturday 5:30-11:00

Mediterranean Cuisine

Basil's Mediterranean Cafe
2985 Grandview Ave.
Atlanta, GA 30305
233-9755.
Location: Buckhead
Seating: 110
Owners: Sam and Joseph Kahwach
Chef: Sam Kahwach
Cuisine: Mediterranean
Opened: 1989
Overall Rating: ♥♥♥♥

Commentary: Nestled among shops and homesis an oasis in the heart of Buckhead. A large patio shaded by massive elms and colorful umbrellas is perfect for early evening dining; or try the charming lounge-dining area inside, graced with crisp linens and live foliage. Valued by loyal patrons for its health-conscious delicacies. Savor the likes of sauteed shrimp cakes, zesty pasta paella and the ever-popular grilled grouper on cous cous. Joseph's charisma and "mama's" expertise with herbs help round out Basil's continuing success with Atlantans.

Dress Code: Casual to jackets.
Appetizers: . . . . $3.95-$5.50
Entrees: . . . . $8.25-$14.95
Desserts:. . . . . $3.75-$4.50
House Specialties and Menu Items:
Tabouleh, Hummus and Baba
Ghanouge. . . . . $ 4.50
Sauteed Shrimp Cakes . . . . $ 4.50
Fattoush Salad w/Toasted Pita Bread. $ 3.75
Pasta Paella on Saffron Angel Hair . . $12.95
Fettucini with Grilled Chicken. . . . . . $ 8.25
Grilled Grouper on Cous Cous. $13.25
Shrimp, Scallops and Mussels $11.50
Grilled Peppered Pork Tenderloin . . . $12.95

Desserts of the Day . . . . $ 4.50
Days and Hours of Operation:
Monday-Saturday 11:30-2:30
Monday-Saturday 6:00-10:00
Friday and Saturday 6:00-11:00

Cassis
3300 Peachtree Rd.
Atlanta, GA 30305
365-8100
Located: Hotel Nikko Atlanta
Seating: 145
Chef: Don Burchell
Cuisine: Mediterranean
Opened: 1990
Overall Rating: ♥♥

Commentary: Diners are greeted at the foyer by a collection of fine European and Asian art, fresh flowers and the staff's warm welcome. The elegant well-appointed dining room, with hemispheric globes of light, and French-European decor presents a serene setting overlooking Atlanta's award-winning authentic Japanese Garden with its flowing waterfall.

Dress Code: Jackets required.
Appetizers . . . . $ 7.00-12.50
Entrees. $20.00-29.00
Desserts . . . . $ 7.00- 7.75
House Specialties & Menu Samples:
Lentil Soup w/Julienne of
Tasso Ham, Scallions. . . . . $ 5.00
Escargot w/Provencal Herbs on
Crispy Potato Nest . . . . $ 7.50
Crab Cakes w/Charred
Tomato Compote $12.50
Angel Hair w/Lobster and
Artichokes, Cilantro $24.00
Peppercorn Crusted Salmon and
Crab Ravioli $26.00
Loin & Rack of Lamb, Turnip
Potato, Port Wine $29.00
Seared Grouper Fillet
w/Langostino Skordalia Potato . . . $26.00
Grilled Beef Tenderloin,w/Artichoke
& Porcini $28.00
Cassis Chocolate Truffle Gateau. . . . . $ 7.00
Orange Creme Brulee . . . . $ 7.25

Open:
Breakfast Daily. 6:30-10:30
Lunch Monday-Saturday 11:30- 2:30
Dinner Monday-Thursday 6:00-10:30
Friday-Saturday 6:00-11:00
Sunday 6:00-10:00
Sunday Brunch. 11:30-2:30

Mexican/Southwestern Cuisine

Nuevo Laredo Cantina

1495 Chattahoochee Ave.
Atlanta, GA 30318
352-9009.
Location: Midtown/West
Seating: 110
Owner: Chance Evans
Chefs: The Maldonado Sisters
Cuisine: Mexican
Opened: June 1992
Overall Rating: ♥♥♥

Commentary: Drive up to an authentic South-of-the-border Mexican Cantina. Sociable upper and lower dining with colorful wood furniture, old Mexican revolutionary photos and Mexican background music. Voted best Mexican restaurant in 1993 and 1994. Taste the authentic homecooked Mexican, not "gringo", food.

Diners enjoy the homemade flavor of the chicken mole, tender chili relleno and tasty fajitas. Friendly service, easy prices and lots of parking make this cafe a fun place to take friends or family.

Dress Code: Casual.
Appetizers: . . . . $1.95-$5.95
Entrees: . . . . $4.95-$10.95
Desserts:. . . . . $1.50-$1.95
House Specialties and Menu Items:
Chile con Queso, White Melted
   Cheese Dip . . . . $ 2.95
Nuevo Laredo Nachos . . . . $ 5.95
Chicken Mole Puebla Style . . . . $ 8.95
Brisket Barbacoa Barbecued
   Laredo Style . . . . $ 8.95

Chile Relleno, Poblano Pepper . . . . . . $ 7.95
Shrimp Fajitas w/Onions and
   Peppers. $10.95
Mole Vegetable Enchiladas. . . . . $ 7.50
Sopapilla, Mexican Tortilla Dessert . . $ 1.50
Days and Hours of Operation:
Monday-Thursday. 11:30-10:00
Friday-Saturday. 11:30-11:00

Sundown Cafe

2165 Cheshire Bridge Rd.
Atlanta, GA 30324
321-1118.
Location: Cheshire Bridge
Seating: 128
Chef: Eddie Hernandez
Cuisine: Creative Mexican and Southwestern
Opened: October 1991
Overall Rating: ♥♥♥♥

Commentary: Superb frosty margaritas and mouth-watering creative regional specialties pack the house, even amidst the odd thunderstorm. Relax in casual comfort in the colorful dining room or the small umbrellaed porch and enjoy efficient service and effective surroundings. Bring a healthy appetite, for the servings are generous, and the variety of salsas is a treat. Start with a creamy poblano corn chowder and shellfish burritos. Then savor Eddie's ork with ancho mashed potato. Head honcho, Scott, always in good humor, already knows you will return again and again.

Dress Code: Casual.
Appetizers: . . . . $2.95-$4.55
Entrees:. . . . . $7.95-$13.95
Desserts: . . . . $1.99-$2.50
House Specialties and Menu Items:
Shrimp Juan Tons . . . . $ 4.55
Poblano Corn Chowder. . . . . $ 3.25
Southwestern Guacamole Salad . . . . . $ 5.95
Pollo Loco w/Lemon Cream Sauce . . $ 9.95
Eddie's Pork w/Ancho Potatoes $10.95
Shellfish Burritos w/Herb Rice. $12.95
Pescado Sundown, Tilapia Fillet. . . . $11.95
Chocolate Chimichanga . . . . $ 2.50
Nattia, Chilled Rice Pudding. . . . . . . $ 1.99
Days and Hours of Operation:
Monday-Friday 11:00-2:00

Sunday-Thursday 5:30-10:30
Friday and Saturday 5:30-11:00

Seafood

Indigo Coastal Grill
1397 N. Highland Ave.
Atlanta, GA 30306
876-0676.
Location: Virginia-Highland
Seating: 100
Owner: Dan Carson
Chef: Joe Scully
Cuisine: Seafood
Opened: 1986
Overall Rating: ♥♥♥

Commentary: Welcome to a place where "vacation is a state of mind." Old floorboards, brick walls with an array of family photos and fun art, and a happy tropical fish tank are part of the relaxing atmosphere. Enjoy daily seafood specials designed with exotic tastes of the Caribbean, Pacific Rim, Mediterranean and Asia. Everything is fresh, from home-grown salad greens to the key limes directly imported from Mexico. Savor the fresh Maine lobster chowder, and definitely try the award-winning key lime pie. Have fun with the menu, enjoy great wine and energetic service. What a vacation!

Dress Code: Casual funwear.
Appetizers: . . . . $3.95-$6.95
Entrees: . . . . $12.75-$18.95
Desserts: . . . . $3.95-$4.95
House Specialties and Menu Items:
"Hot Shots" Oysters
   (Drizzled w/Tequila) . . . . $ 5.25
Lobster, Corn and Fresno Chowder . . $ 4.35
Minimum Daily Requirement
   Gazpacho . . . . $ 4.50
Grilled Catch Fresh Alaskan
   Halibut $17.95
Jerk Chicken, Grilled Jamaican Style $14.95
Lobster Bouillabaisse $18.95
Catch in a Bag, Gulf Rock Shrimp. . . $16.95
Dan's Mom's Key Lime Pie. . . . . . . $ 4.50

Strawberry/Rhubarb
   Cobbler (Seasonal) . . . . $ 4.95
Days and Hours of Operation:
Monday-Sunday 5:30-11:00
Brunch Saturday-Sunday 9:00-3:00

Steak

Chicago's
2500 Old Alabama Rd., #1
Roswell, GA 30076
770-552-9298.
Location: Village Terrace Shopping Plaza
Seating: 175
Owners: David and Anita Howard
Chef: Eric Andreen
Cuisine: Steaks
Opened: 1995
Overall Rating: ♥♥

Commentary: Tucked behind trees in a small plaza is a comfortable restaurant done up in a Chicago "speakeasy decor", dark and handsome mahogany with piano entertainment in the lounge. A large blackboard shows current specials. Chet Huntley, general manager, greets diners with an easy smile. Try the mushroom soup topped with puff pastry, the sizable full-flavored pork chop with madeira, or the filet au poivre. A fine place to take the family, and Friday and Saturday evenings, you can danc the night away in the lounge.

Dress Code: Casual to jackets.
Appetizers: . . . . $3.95-$6.95
Entrees: . . . . $6.50-$18.95
Desserts: . . . . $3.25-$4.95
House Specialties and Menu Items:
Mushroom Soup w/Sherry,
   Puff Pastry . . . . $ 3.95
Blackened Scallops w/Angel Hair . . . $ 6.95
Roasted Vegetable Platter . . . . $ 7.50
Pork Chop, Roast Loin w/Madeira . . $13.95
Filet of Salmon, Oven Roasted $14.50
Roasted Prime Rib. $12.95
Petite Filet and Crab $15.95
Filet au Poivre, Peppercorn/Cognac . $15.95
Creme Brulee. . . . . $ 3.75

Derby Pie . . . . $ 3.75
Days and Hours of Operation:
Sunday-Thursday 5:00-10:00
Friday and Saturday 5:00-11:00

Thai/Fusion Cuisine

Bangkok
1492A Piedmont Rd.
Atlanta, GA 30309
874-2514
Location: Midtown
Seating: 66
Owner: Chai Vongvichai
Cuisine: Thai
Opened: 1977
Overall Rating: ♥♥♥

Commentary: Known as the first Thai restaurant to open in Georgia, be ready to feast on quality Thai food in a snug, spotless and friendly family atmosphere. There are linen covered tables, and the service is robust. Owner Chai is very attentive and offers an experts' knowledge of the fresh Thai specialties. Be sure to try the much-acclaimed original cheeseroll, and, voted as best dish, the scrumptious Pud Thai. This Asian delight is so popular, it needs a parking lot of its own.

Dress Code: Casual.
Appetizers: . . . . $2.75-$7.95
Entrees: . . . . $5.50-$10.95
Desserts: . . . . $2.00-$2.50
House Specialties and Menus Samples:
Cheese Roll, Delicate Wrapped
   Cream Cheese . . . . $ 2.75
Bangkok Roll, Crispy Spring Roll . . . $ 2.75
Satay, Tender Thai Marinated
   Chicken . . . . $ 5.50
Fowl Play Soup, Chicken and
   Coconut Milk . . . . $ 2.75
Basilia, Fresh Thai Basil
   w/Shrimp/Chicken . . . . $ 8.50
Panang Curry, Traditional Curry
   w/Meats . . . . $ 8.95
Pud Thai, Thai Noodle w/Shrimp
   or Chicken . . . . $ 8.50

Shrimp Ashore, Large Shrimp
   Stir Fried . . . . $ 8.95
Coco Ice, Homemade Coconut
   Ice Cream . . . . $ 2.00
Gold Thread, Thai Egg Custard . . . . . $ 2.50
Days and Hours of Operation:
Monday-Friday 11:30-2:30
Sunday-Thursday 5:00-10:00
Friday and Saturday 5:00-10:30

Royal Orchid
931 Monroe Dr., #106
Atlanta, GA 30308
892-4345.
Location: Midtown Promenade Shopping Center
Seating: 62
Owners: Chino Manacsineda, Supat Kongprasert and Csutima Buyasaranand
Chef: Csutima Buyasaranand
Cuisine: Thai
Opened: 1993
Overall Rating: ♥♥♥

Commentary: Comfortable, spacious and a modern twist give this Thai restaurant a unique look. Sleek black chairs and white linen-covered tables, with a sprinkle of art deco on the walls, sets the mood for healthy and crispy fresh foods. Discover such favorites as delicate basil rolls, and zestful Siam chicken, all pleasantly presented with attentive service.

Dress Code: Casual.
Appetizers: . . . . $1.95-$6.25
Entrees: . . . . $4.95-$7.95
Desserts: $1.25
House Specialties and Menu Samples:
Basil Rolls, Fresh Spring Roll . . . . . . $ 3.25
Satay, Grilled Pork Strip
   w/Peanut Sauce . . . . $ 4.25
Royal Orchid Salad w/Peanut
   Dressing . . . . $ 2.50
Masaman, Thai Curry w/Meats . . . . . . $ 7.95
Siam Chicken, Spicy and
   Lightly Fried . . . . $ 7.75
Royal Spicy Basil Shrimp . . . . $ 6.50
Snap Dragon, Sauteed Veg. w/Meats . $ 5.95
Fried Coconut Ice Cream . . . . $ 3.25

Days and Hours of Operation:

Monday-Thursday 11:30-2:30
Sunday-Thursday 5:30-10:00
Friday-Saturday 5:30-11:00

Surin of Thailand

810 N. Highland Ave.
Atlanta, GA 30306
892-7789.
Location: Virginia-Highlands
Seating: 160
Owner/Chef: Surin Technavapong
Cuisine: Thai
Opened: February 1991
Overall Rating: ♥♥

Commentary: A comfortable open dining room with a 15-foot tin ceiling, circa 1800, Thai banners, wood floors, and burgundy and blue linen table clothes help create a festive atmosphere in which to enjoy Chef Surin's native cuisine. Savor exotic spices while spooning spicy chicken coconut soup, munching tender sate and crispy-sweet three flavor fish. Attentive servers will help you make the right menu decisions.

Dress Code: Casual.
Appetizers: . . . . $3.00-$5.95
Entrees: . . . . $6.95-$14.95
Desserts: $2.00
House Specialties and Menu Items:
Spicy Chicken Coconut Soup. . . . . . $ 5.50
Fresh Basil Rolls . . . . $ 4.00
Satay Beef or Chicken . . . . $ 5.95
Nuer Nam Tok, Spicy Tenderloin . . . $ 5.95
Wings of Angel, Stuffed
 Chicken Wings . . . . $ 6.50
Thai Noodle, Pan-Fried Shrimp . . . . . $ 7.50
Shu She Salmon, Mild Curry Sauce. . $14.95
Three Flavor Fish, Pan-Fried
 Flounder. $14.95
Homemade Mango or Coconut
 Ice Cream. . . . . $ 2.00
Days and Hours of Operation:
Sunday-Thursday 11:30-10:30
Friday-Saturday 11:30-11:00

Taste of Thai

5775 Jimmy Carter Blvd.

Norcross, GA 30071
770-662-8575
Seating: 50
Owner: Tommy Kanjanampa, Chef Tu
Cuisine: Thai
Opened: 1989
Overall Rating: ♥♥♥

Commentary: This little tucked-away gem of a restaurant, opened May 1990. The dining area is comfortable, bright and fresh, withsmall tables with silk flowers, and a welcoming aroma from the kitchen.

Service is very prompt and friendly. Enjoy one of the best authentic Thai foods in town, and sip a delicious Thai coffee or tea.

Dress Code: Casual.
Appetizers: . . . . $3.00-$5.50
Entrees: . . . . $5.95-$8.95
Desserts: . . . . $1.50-$1.75
House Specialties and Menu Samples:
Fresh Spring Rolls. $4.95
T.O.T. Wings (Stuffed Minced
 Pork & Beanthreads) $4.95
Mee Grob (Crispy Sweet Noodle
 w/Pork, Shrimp). $5.50
Nuer Num Tok (Sliced Tender
 Beef Salad) $6.25
Tom Kha (Coconut Soup) $6.25
Pud Kraprao (Meat with Spicy Basil). $6.25
Hot Sea (Variety Seafood in Hot
 Chile Paste). $7.50
Vegetarians Delight. $5.95
Green Tea Ice Cream. $1.75
Sunkaya-Thai Custard. $1.50
Days and Hours of Operation:
Monday-Friday . . 11:00-2:15 and 5:30-9:30
Saturday. 12:00-9:30

Nifty Restaurants Outside the Metro Atlanta Area

Amici

113 South Main St.
Madison, GA 30650
706-342-0000
Located: On the Square in Madison

Seating: 80
Owners: Kevin Newell, Chris Torino, Ethan Anderson
Chef: Kevin Newell
Cuisine: Italian
Opened: 1993
Overall Rating: ♥♥

Commentary: Locals and visitors love this place. A comfy, energetic cafe surrounded by a high tin-ceiling, modern murals and wooden booths and tables. Home-made pasta's and hand-tossed pizza's are served with quality ingredients, combined with a good variety of beer and wines. Owner Kevin Newell pops in-and-out of the kitchen to greet old friends and newcomers alike. A good-humored staff will fill you in on menu favorites like finger-lickin' buffalo wings, light pesto spagatini and the true gourmet pizza. Friday evenings brings live entertainment; come early or it will be standing room only.

Dress Code: Casual
Appetizers. . . . . $ 1.50- 7.50
Entrees . . . . $ 5.00-15.95
Desserts. . . . . $ 2.75- 3.50
House Specialties & Menu Samples:
Buffalo Wings (10)
 w/Blue Cheese, Celery . . . . $ 4.25
King Caesar Salad w/Feta,
 Plum Tomatoes . . . . $ 5.25
Spinach & Cheese Calzone
 w/Marinara . . . . $ 6.25
Pizza Regina w/Pesto,
 Mushrooms, Onions . . . . $ 7.50
Straccetti, Sliced London
 Broil w/Pasta . . . . $ 7.95
Proscuitto Ham & Artichoke
 Hearts w/Pasta. . . . . $ 7.95
Pesto Spagatini w/Herb Sauce,
 Pine Nuts . . . . $ 7.95
Homemade Cannoli . . . . $ 2.75
Assorted Daily Cheesecakes . . . . $ 3.50
Open:
Monday-Thursday 11:30- 9:30
Friday-Saturday 11:30-10:00
Sunday 12:00- 9:00

The Blue Willow Inn
294 N. Cherokee Rd.
Social Circle, GA 30279
770-464-2131
Seating: 268
Owners: Louis and Billie Van Dyke
Chef: Judy Wyman
Cuisine: Southern
Opened: 1991
Overall Rating: ♥♥♥♥

Commentary: Desperate for *"Fried Green Tomatoes"* the legendary Lewis Grizzard dropped in for dinner. The rest is history. After his craving was sated, he quickly spread the word and regular customers now travel an hour or more to enjoy the Blue Willow experience.

First relax in the guest-friendly rockers on the wide porch while you sip sweet tea or lemonade. Then enter the magnificent Greek revival mansion. Blue Willow's food, service and ambiance offer a return to the South's past. Dine in one of four elegantly-appointed dining rooms. The bountiful buffet of authentic Southern dishes offers a choice of meats, fish and poultry, a zillion healthy vegetables and yummy desserts. Owners Billie and Louis live by the credo "every customer is a celebrity." And, before you leave, give the gift shop a visit.

Dress Code: Casual to jackets.
Buffet:. . . . . $8.95-$14.95
House Buffet:
Salad Bar: Large Variety of Salads and Shrimp
Meats: Fish & Poultry: Roast Beef, Salmon, BBQ Ribs, Fried Catfish, Porkchops, Turkey, Meatloaf and Fried Chicken.
Vegetables: Collard Greens, Corn, Pole Beans, Okra, Yams, Green Beans, Fried Green Tomatoes and Hush Puppies.
Desserts: Cookies, Pumpkin Cake, Peach Pie, Chocolate Cake, Carrot Cake and Banana Pudding.
Days and Hours of Operation:
Monday-Saturday 11:00-2:30

Monday-Saturday 5:30-9:00
Sunday 11:00-9:00

Bon Cuisine
113 Broad St.
Pine Mountain, GA 31822
706-663-2019.
Location: Downtown Pine Mountain
Seating: 46
Owner/Chef: Charles Duck
Cuisine: Continental of Seven Cuisines
Opened: 1979
Overall Rating: ♥♥

Commentary: Located on a quiet street, fronted with 288 pots of blooming plants and a "scratch and sniff" herb garden. Inside the decor is old Greenwich Village replete with sculptures, antiques, photos and a magnolia branch chandelier. Huge, locally grown mushrooms are delivered daily by the "mushroom man," and fresh garden herbs are used freely. A seasonal menu features the likes of alligator medallions and catfish epicurean. Every last Monday of the month brings a special "Theme Dinner" with entertainment. Bring your own spirits.

Dress Code: Casual.
Appetizers: . . . . $5.95-$8.95
Entrees: . . . . $15.95-$32.95
Desserts: $3.95
House Specialties and Menu Items:
Broiled Stuffed Mushroom Caps . . . . $ 6.95
Escargots in Mushrooms . . . . $ 7.95
Vidalia Onion Soup . . . . $ 3.95
Catfish Epicurean, Grilled $16.95
Tornados of Beef, Sauteed $19.95
Okefenokee Alligator Saute $19.95
Filet Mignon and Filet of Fish $23.95
Desserts. . . . . $ 3.95
Days and Hours of Operation:
Monday-Saturday from 5:30 onwards.

The Grand Old House
502 S. Broad St.
Thomasville, GA 31799
912-227-0108.
Location: Thomasville, across from historic Paradise Park

Seating: 140
Owner/Chef: Albert Ughetto
Cuisine: Continental with French Accents
Opened: 1992
Overall Rating: ♥♥♥♥

Commentary: Once chef to Jacques Cousteau, chef and owner, Albert Ughetto presents an elegant turn-of-the-century atmosphere with high ceilings, sparkling chandeliers and five handsome antiqued dining rooms. Daily creations such as beef tenderloin or Canadian salmon are consistently outstanding. The downstairs pub presents local jazz and offers light meals.

Dress Code: Casual to dressy.
Appetizers: . . . . $3.00-$6.00
Entrees: . . . . $11.50-$21.50
Desserts: $3.50
House Specialties and Menu Items:
Lobster Bisque. . . . . $ 3.00
Wild Mushroom Ravioli . . . . $ 3.75
Crabcake a L'auvergine . . . . $ 6.00
Grilled Canadian Salmon $16.50
Beef Tenderloin Red Wine Sauce . . . $19.00
Roasted Rack of Lamb Provencale . . $19.50
Steamed Maine Lobster(Stuffed) . . . $21.50
Gateau a l'Orange . . . . $ 3.50
Mousse au Chocolat . . . . $ 3.50
Days and Hours of Operation:
Tuesday-Saturday 11:30-2:30
Monday-Saturday 6:00-9:30

Hug's Country Edition
2230 Eatonton Rd.
Eatonton, GA 31024
706-342-9730
Located: I-20 E. & US.441 at exit 51.
Seating: 100
Owner: Jack Flannigan
Chef: Tony Flannigan
Cuisine: Italian
Opened: 1992
Overall Rating: ♥♥♥

Commentary: Treat yourself after that great golf game or exhausting antique shopping spree, and stop to munch at this charming restaurant. Tucked in a old Piedmont-style home, feel comfortable amidst a pleasant clutter of golf memorabilia, antiques and a wall filled with the signatures of famous guests. Sample the chicken limone or flavorful tortellini blue cheese alfredo with home-baked pesto bread and a glass of wine. Charming host, Jack Flannigan, is usually on hand for storytelling.

Dress Code: Casual.

Appetizers. . . . . $ 3.95- 5.95
Entrees . . . . $ 7.95-13.95
Desserts. . . . . $ 3.50- 3.95

House Specialties & Menu Samples:

Baked Sausage & Peppers . . . . $ 5.95
Fried Ravioli. . . . . $ 3.95
Fettuccini Quattro Formaggi . . . . $ 8.95
Angel Hair Carratierre . . . . $ 7.95
Chicken Limone, Sauteed w/Lemon . $10.95
Tortellini Blue Cheese Alfredo $10.95
Veal Marsala. $12.95
Steak Pizzaiola $13.95
Five-Layer Chocolate Torte. . . . . $ 3.95
Home-made Cannoli . . . . $ 3.50

Open:

Tuesday-Saturday. 4:30-10:00

Seagle's Restaurant

105 Osborne St.
St. Mary's, GA 31558
912-882-3242
Located: Riverview Hotel
Seating: 100
Owner: Jerry and Gaila Brandon
Cuisine: Seafood and American
Opened: 1976
Overall Rating: ♥♥♥

Commentary: Continuing a tradition of fine food and a pleasant atmosphere, this turn-of-the-century restaurant still fills it tables from all around. Sit by a window and overlook the harbor and Cumberland Queen Ferry. No-fuss oil cloth clad tables and southern hospitality transforms guests into friends. Starting the meal with home-made shrimp-dip and crackers you know you're onto a good meal here. Feast on lobster-sweet large white shrimp, or spice it up with blackened rock shrimp, and

don't overlook Gaila's shrimp & sausage gumbo. The key lime and peanut butter pie are also excellent.

Dress Code: Casual.

Appetizers . . . . $ 2.75- 4.50
Entrees. . . . . $ 4.95-13.95
Desserts . . . . $ 2.75- 3.50

House Specialties & Menu Samples:

Blackened Rock Shrimp Cocktail. . . . $ 4.25
Shrimp & Sausage Gumbo . . . . $ 3.50
Aunt Sallie's S.W. Chicken,
  Blackened. . . . . $ 7.95
Fettuccine w/Vegetable Primavera . . . $ 5.95
Scallops Seagle's w/White
  Wine Sauce. $10.95
Crab Cakes w/Lime Sauce $10.95
Acadian Grill, Fish Choice
  w/Bearnaise $12.95
Prime Rib, au Jus w/Salad, Potato . . $10.95
Home-Made Peanut Butter
  Chiffon Pie . . . . $ 2.75
Key Lime Meringue . . . . $ 2.75

Open: Daily 5:00-10:00

Sprayberry's Barbecue

229 Jackson St.
Newnan, GA 30263
770-253-4421.
Location: Newnan
Seating: 170
Owner/Chef: Donald Sprayberry
Cuisine: Barbecue
Opened: 1926
Overall Rating: ♥♥♥♥

Commentary: The aroma of succulent, smoke-laced meats welcomes barbecue lovers from Australia to Europe. A single sitting and you'll know why it was a a 37-year ritual for author, Lewis Grizzard. The restaurant appears to be a railroad depot replete with original tin ceiling. Continueing the family tradition, Donald Sprayberry, attends daily to the smoky, slow-cooked, mouth-watering barbecue delicacies. The Brunswick stew is served with white loaf bread and dessert is a delectible toss-up of either ice-box lemon pie or fried peach pie. And, yes, you can take it with you.

Dress Code: Casual.
Entrees: . . . . $2.95-$10.95
Desserts: . . . . $1.30-$3.25
House Specialties and Menu Items:
Brunswick Stew w/White Bread . . . . $ 2.95
Barbecue Sandwich w/Slaw . . . . $ 3.60
Barbecue Plate . . . . $ 7.50
Slab of Smoky Ribs . . . . $ 7.95
Fried Catfish . . . . $ 7.25
Rib Eye Steak $10.95
Lemon Ice Box Pie . . . . $ 1.95
Fried Apple or Peach Pie . . . . $ 1.95
Days and Hours of Operation:
Monday-Saturday 10:30-9:00
Second Location:
Hwy.34 at I-85, Exit 9, 253-5080.

The Yesterday Cafe

120 Fairplay Rd.
Rutledge, GA 30663
706-557-9337.
Location: Across Town Square
Seating: 100
Owners: Teri and Alan Bragg
Cuisine: Modern Southern
Opened: 1991
Overall Rating: ♥♥♥

Commentary: A renovated turn-of-the-century drug store, redone into a saloon-style cafe. Bare brick walls are filled with photographs reflecting the town's history, high ceiling fans, and tiled floors, with a vintage soda fountain bar that sits by the window. Yesterday's is known for such specialties such as biscuits and gravy, pan-fried catfish, Carribean salad and a wonderful buttermilk pie. Owner Teri Bragg serves complementary peach puffs, and makes everyone feel at home with her Southern hospitality, and her home-cooked meals.

Dress Code: Casual.
Appetizers: . . . . $2.75-$4.95
Entrees: . . . . $8.25-$14.95
Desserts: . . . . $1.25-$3.95
House Specialties and Menu Items:

Good Golly Miss Polly,
   Stuffed Jalapeno . . . . $ 4.50
Southern Sampler, Southern
   Favorites . . . . $ 4.50
Caribbean Chicken Salad . . . . $ 7.50
Catfish Filet in Herb Crust . . . . $ 8.25
Chicken Dijon . . . . $ 8.95
Linquini Alfredo w/Sausage in
   Red Wine . . . . $ 9.50
Shrimp Saute, over Pasta $12.95
Ribeye Steak $14.95
Homemade Buttermilk Pie . . . . $ 2.45
Hot Fudge Sundae . . . . $ 2.95
Days and Hours of Operation:
Monday-Sunday   7:30-11:00 and 11:30-3:00
Thursday-Saturday 5:30-9:30

Other Metro Atlanta Restaurants

(Not Reviewed by our Editors)

Southern Cuisine

Blue Ridge Grill
1261 W. Paces Ferry Rd., Buckhead
233-5030..

The Colonnade
1879 Cheshire Bridge Rd., near Piedmont Rd.
874-5642.

East Village Grille
248 Buckhead Ave., Buckhead
233-3346.

Greenwood's
1087 Green St., Roswell
770-992-5383.

Kudzu Cafe
3215 Peachtree Rd. Buckhead
262-0661.

Magnolia Tea Room
5459 E. Mountain St., Stone Mountain
770-498-6304.

Mecca Fine Foods
843 Capitol Ave., Downtown
577-6018.

Pittypat's Porch
25 International Blvd., Downtown
525-8228.

Stone Mountain Park Inn Dining Room
Hwy.78 East, Stone Mountain Park
469-3311.

Thelma's Kitchen
768 Marietta St., Midtown
688-5855.

Top of the Plaza
First Union Bank, 250 E. Ponce de Leon,
Decatur
377-7371.

Top of the Square
19 N. Park Square, Marietta
770-428-9520

The Vinings Inn
3011 Paces Mill Rd., Vinings
770-438-2282.

American Cuisine

57th Fighter Group
3829 Clairmont Rd., Chamblee
770-457-7757.

Alon's Bakery
659 Peachtree St., Midtown
724-0444.

American Roadhouse
842 N. Highland Ave., Virginia-Highlands
872-2822.

Atkins Park
794 N. Highland Ave., Virginia-Highlands
876-7249.

Beesley's of Buckhead
260 E. Paces Ferry Rd., Buckhead
264-1334.

Buckhead Diner
3073 Piedmont Rd., Buckhead
262-3336.

Cafe at the Ritz Carlton
3434 Peachtree Rd., Buckhead
237-2700.

Cafe Opera
Occidental Grand Hotel, 75 14th St., Midtown
881-9898.

Canoe
4199 Paces Ferry Rd., on the Chattahoochee
770-432-2663.

Chow
1026-1/2 N. Highland Ave., Virginia-Highland
872-0869.

City Grill
50 Hurt Plaza, Downtown
524-2489.

Country Place
1197 Peachtree St., Colony Square
881-0144.

Corner Cafe
3070 Piedmont Rd., Buckhead
240-1978.

Joey D's Oak Room
Perimeter Ctr. W. & Crowne Pt. Pkwy.,
Dunwoody
512-7063.

Landmark Diner
3652 Roswell Rd., Buckhead
816-9090.

Palisades
1829 Peachtree Rd., Buckhead
350-6755.

Peachtree Cafe
268 E. Paces Ferry Rd., Buckhead
233-4402.

The Peasant Restaurant & Bar
3402 Piedmont Rd., Buckhead
231-8740.

Peasant Uptown
3500 Peachtree Rd., Phipps Plaza
261-6341.

The Pleasant Peasant
555 Peachtree St., Downtown
874-3223.

Public House
605 Atlanta St., Roswell
770-992-4646.

R.J.'s Uptown Kitchen and Wine Bar
870 N. Highland Ave., Virginia-Highlands
875-7775.

Sun Dial Restaurant
Peachtree & Int'l Blvd., Westin Peachtree
Plaza
659-1400.

The Tavern at Phipps
3500 Peachtree Rd., Phipps Plaza
814-9640.

Terrace Restaurant & Lounge
285 Int'l. Blvd., GA World Congress Ctr.
223-4539.

Tom Tom
3393 Peachtree Rd., Lenox Square
264-1163.

Waterside Restaurant
One Lakeview Dr., Stone Mountain
879-9900.

Waverly Grill
2450 Galleria Pkwy., Stouffer Waverly Hotel
953-4500.

Barbecue

Aleck's Barbecue
783 Martin Luther King Jr. Dr., Downtown
525-2062.

Dusty's Barbecue
1815 Briarcliff Rd. off LaVista Rd.
320-6264.

Fat Matt's Rib Shack
1811 Piedmont Rd., Midtown
607-1622

Low Country Barbecue
6301 Roswell Rd., Sandy Springs
255-5160.

Old Hickory House Restaurant
2655 Cobb Pkwy., above Cumberland Mall
770-952-2220.

The Rib Ranch
25 Irby Ave., Buckhead
233-7644.

Skeeter's Mesquite Grille
2892 N. Druid Hills Rd., Toco Hills
636-3817.

Slope's Barbecue
10360 Alpharetta St., Alpharetta
518-7000.

Breakfast/Lunch

Bradshaw's Buckhead Feedmill
35-A W. Paces Ferry Rd., Buckhead
233-0134.

Brasserie
2450 Galleria Pkwy., Stouffer Waverly Hotel
953-4500

Cafe At the Omni
100 CNN Center., Omni Hotel Downtown
659-0000.

Chez Ponce
760 Ponce de Leon Ave., Downtown
898-0370.

The Flying Biscuit
1655 McLendon Ave., Midtown
687-8888.

Kafe Kobenhavn
265 Peachtree St., Peachtree Ctr. Downtown
577-1234.

Le Cafe
4736 Best Rd., Atlanta Renaissance Hotel.
College Park
762-7676.

Lox Around the Clock
285 E. Paces Ferry Rd., Buckhead
365-0422.

Silver Skillet Restaurant
200 14th St., off I-75/85 N.
874-1388.

The White House
3172 Peachtree Rd., Buckhead
237-7601.

Chinese Cuisine

Hsu's Gourmet Chinese Restaurant
192 Peachtree Center Ave., Downtown
659-2788.

Hong Kong Harbour Restaurant
2184 Cheshire Bridge Rd., near Piedmont Rd.
325-7630.

Mandarin Garden
6180 McDonough Dr., Norcross
770-246-0406.

Oriental Pearl
5399 New Peachtree Rd., Chamblee
770-986-9866.

Pung Mei
5145 Buford Hwy., Doraville
770-455-0370.

Continental Cuisine.

103 West
103 West Paces Ferry Rd., Buckhead
233-5993.

Anthony's
3109 Piedmont Rd., Buckhead
262-7379.

Bacchanalia
3125 Piedmont Rd., Buckhead/Sandy
Springs
365-0410.

Cafe Liberty
9850 Nesbit Ferry, Roswell
770-992-6344.

Carbo's
3717 Roswell Rd., Buckhead
231-4433.

Chef's Cafe
2115-A Piedmont Rd., Buckhead
872-2284.

The Dining Room
The Ritz Carlton, 3434 Peachtree Rd. Buckhead
237-3434.

Florencia Restaurant
Occidental Grand Hotel, 75 14th St., Midtown
881-9898.

The Hedgerose Heights Inn
490 E. Paces Ferry Rd., Buckhead/Sandy Springs
233-7673.

Janousek's
1475 Holcomb Bridge Rd., Roswell
770-587-2075.

Kurt's
4225 River Green Pkwy., Duluth
770-623-4128.

La Tour Restaurant
3209 Paces Ferry Place, Buckhead
233-8833.

Pano's and Paul's
1232 W. Paces Ferry Rd., Buckhead
261-3662.

Partner's Morningside Cafe
1399 N. Highland Ave., Virginia-Highlands
876-8104.

Polaris
Hyatt Regency Atlanta Downtown
577-1234.

Winfield's
One Galleria Pkwy., Perimeter NW
955-5300.

Ethnic European Cuisine

Bistango
1100 Peachtree St., Downtown
724-0901.

Cafe Tu Tu Tango
220 Pharr Rd., Buckhead
841-6222.

Don Juan's
1927 Piedmont Cir., Midtown
874-4285.

Papa Nick's Greek Restaurant
1799 Briarcliff Rd., Sage Hill Shopping Ctr.
875-9677.

Parthenon Greek Restaurant
6125 Roswell Rd., Sandy Springs Shopping Ctr.
256-1686.

Rathskeller
590 W. Peachtree St., Atlanta Renaissance Hotel
881-6000.

Romanian Restaurant
3081 E. Shadowlawn Dr., Sandy Springs
365-8220.

Segovia
75 14th St., Occidental Grand Hotel, Midtown
881-9898.

French Cuisine

The Bistro
56 E. Andrews Dr., Buckhead
231-5733.

Brasserie Le Coze
Lenox Square, 3393 Peachtree Rd. Buckhead
266-1440.

Cafe Renaissance
7050 Jimmy Carter Blvd., Norcross
770-441-0291.

Ciboulette
1529 Piedmont Rd., Midtown
874-7311.

Claudette's French Restaurant
315 W. Ponce de Leon Ave., Downtown
378-9861.

Resto Des Amis
3060 Peachtree Rd., Buckhead
364-2170.

Toulouse
2293-B Peachtree Rd., Buckhead
351-9533.

Violette
3098 Briarcliff Rd., near Clairmont Rd.
633-3323.

Indian Cuisine

Haveli
2650 Cobb Parkway, Smyrna
770-955-4525.

Himalayas Indian Restaurant
5520 Peachtree Industrial Blvd., Chamblee
458-6557.

Raja Indian Restaurant
2919 Peachtree Rd., Buckhead
237-2661.

Samrat Indian Cuisine
5920 Roswell Rd., Parkside Shopping Ctr.
252-1644.

Sonar Gaon
309 Pharr Rd., Buckhead
261-6013.

Touch of India
962 Peachtree St., Downtown
876-7777.

Italian

Abruzzi Ristorante
2355 Peachtree Rd., Buckhead
261-8186.

Amarone Italian Bistro
519 E. Paces Ferry Rd., Buckhead
816-8550.

Arturo's
5486 Chamblee Dunwoody Rd., Dunwoody
770-396-0335.

Asti Trattoria
3199 Paces Ferry Pl., Buckhead
364-9160.

Bugatti
Omni Hotel, 100 CNN Center, Downtown
818-4450.

Cafe Prego
4279 Roswell Rd., Chastain Sq. Buckhead
252-0032.

Camille's
1186 N. Highland St., Virginia-Highlands
872-7203.

Ippolito's Restaurant
6623 Roswell Rd., Sandy Springs
256-3546.

Mi Spia
4505 Ashford Dunwoody Rd.,
  across from Perimeter Mall
770-393-1333.

Nino's Italian Restaurant
1931 Cheshire Bridge Rd., Midtown
874-6505.

Pricci
500 Pharr Rd., Buckhead
237-2941.

San Gennaro
2196 Cheshire Bridge Rd., near Piedmont Rd.
636-9447.

Veni Vidi Vici
41 14th St., Downtown
875-8424.

Villa Christina
45 Perimeter Summit Pkwy., inside I-285
303-0133.

Japanese

Nakato
1776 Cheshire Bridge Rd., off Piedmont Rd.
873-6582.

Sushi-Huku
6300 Powers Ferry Rd., Sandy Springs
770-956-9559.

Toyota Ya
5082 Buford Hwy., Doraville
892-5133.

Yokohama
6280 Roswell Rd., Sandy Springs
255-4227.

Luncheon Landmarks

Carey's
Marietta. 1021 Cobb Pkwy.
Award-winning burgers, chicken and other delicacies. 422-8042

Chick-fil-A
Downtown. 233 Peachtree St.
Serving from early morning's hot breakfast to evening's tender chicken strips. 577-4194. Various locations; consult your *Yellow Pages.*

Gorin's
Midtown. 1170 Peachtree St.
Known for homemade ice-cream and many delicious sandwich selections and growing. 892-2500. Various locations; consult your *Yellow Pages.*

Houston's
Buckhead. 2166 Peachtree Rd.
A long-time favorite in Atlanta featuring great salads and many varieties of grilled, roasted or barbecued chicken, to name a few. 351-2442. Various locations; consult your *Yellow Pages.*

Mick's
Lenox Square, 3393 Peachtree Rd.
Favorite place getting together, enjoying an American menu of all the favorites. 262-6425. Various locations; consult your *Yellow Pages.*

The Varsity
Midtown. 61 North Ave.
The world's largest drive-in and one of Atlanta's famous landmark for sixty years serving hamburgers, fries and well-known onion rings. 881-1706.

Mexican/Southwestern Cuisine

Azteca Grill
1140 Morrow Industrial Blvd. Morrow
770-968-0908.

Elena's
469 N. Highland Ave., off North Ave.
522-9211.

Georgia Grill
2290 Peachtree St., Buckhead
352-3517.

Jalisco Mexican Restaurant
2337 Peachtree Rd., Buckhead
233-9244.

Las Americas Mexican Taqueria
3652 Shallowford Rd., Doraville
770-458-7962.

Los Loros
1455 Pleasand Hill Rd., Gwinnett
923-7016.

Nava
3060 Peachtree Rd., Buckhead
240-1984.

Middle Eastern/Turkish Cuisine

Nicola's
1602 LaVista Rd., near Cheshire Bridge Rd.
325-2524.

Oasis Cafe
752 Ponce de Leon Ave., Downtown
881-0815.
Turkish Cafe
22 Park Place, Decatur.
525-5235.

Pizza

Azio's
220 Pharr Rd., Buckhead
233-7626.
Fellini's
2809 Peachtree Rd., Buckhead
266-0082.

Mystic Pizza
1136 Crescent Ave., Midtown
873-6307.

Rocky's Brick Oven
1770 Peachtree St., Midtown
876-1111.

Seafood

Atlanta Fish Market
265 Pharr Rd., Buckhead
262-3165.

Chequer's Seafood Grill
236 Perimeter Center Pkwy., Dunwoody
770-391-9383.

Showcase Eatery
5437 Old National Hwy., College Park
669-0504.

Embers Seafood Grille
234 Hilderbrand Dr., Sandy Springs
256-0977.

Jim White's Half Shell
2349 Peachtree Rd., Buckhead
237-9924.

Marra's Seafood Grill
1782 Cheshire Bridge Rd., off Piedmont Rd.
874-7347.

McKinnon's Louisiane Restaurant
3209 Maple Dr., at Peachtree
237-1313.

New Orleans Cafe
7887 Roswell Rd., Sandy Springs
770-396-9665.

Nickiemoto's
246 Buckhead Ave., Buckhead
842-0334.

Ray's on the River
6700 Powers Ferry Rd., North Atlanta
770-955-1187.

Steak

Bone's
3130 Piedmont Rd., Buckhead
237-2663.

Chops
70 W. Paces Ferry Rd., Buckhead
262-2675.

The Cabin
2678 Buford Hwy., off Lenox Rd.
315-7676.

The Coach and Six
1776 Peachtree St., Buckhead
872-6666.

Joey D's Oak Room
1015 Crown Pointe Parkway,
  near Perimeter Mall
770-512-7063.

Pilgreen's
1081 Lee St., southwest Atlanta
758-8990.

Take-Out

Alon's Bakery
1394 N. Highland Ave., Virginia-Highlands
872-6000.

Carey's
1021 Cobb Pkwy., Marietta
770-422-8042.

Kool Korner Grocery
349 14th St., Midtown
892-4424.

Pano's Food Shop
265 Pharr Rd., Buckhead
240-6664.

Thai/Fusion Cuisine

Annie's Thai Castle
3195 Roswell Rd., Roswell
264-9546.

Harry and Sons
820 N. Highland Ave., Virginia-Highlands
873-2009.

Sukhothai
1995 Windy Hill Rd. #K, Smyrna
770-434-9276.

Thai Chilli
2169 Briarcliff Rd. Atlanta
315-6750.

Vegetarian

Cafe Sunflower
5975 Roswell Rd, Sandy Springs
256-1675.

New Creation Cafe
3033 N. Decatur Rd., Decatur
299-2030.

Rainbow Natural Foods
2118 N. Decatur Rd., at Clairmont Rd.
770-633-3538

Fun Facts:

- Kudzu is the plant you see covering trees and ancient structures, brought here for commercial purposes from the Orient in 1876

- The oldest named place in Georgia is the Apalachee River (1528).

- Over one zillion streets and at least one city in the greater Atlanta area have "Peachtree" in their name. This occasionally provokes some confusion, particularly among postal workers and taxi drivers.

- The Varsity on downtown's North Avenue is the world's largest drive-in restaurant.

SECTION IX
Golf Atlanta

Commentary

Strange as it may sound, perhaps no person knows exactly how many golf courses there are in and around Atlanta. This is partly due to the complexity of defining what is and what is not in Atlanta, what is and is not a golf course, whether or not to include inaccessible private courses and the fact that new courses and conversions from private to public and back occur frequently.

If you include the privates and the shorties, there are over 140 courses within a one-hour drive from downtown. From these we have culled our favorites. All categories of courses are included in our picks except the privates, which are, for the most part, inaccessible to most of us.

Selected courses are listed by area, Metro Atlanta, Metro North, Metro South, Metro East, and Beyond Metro. Please read the descriptions to find those courses that best suit your golfing predilections. And please remember that course conditions tend to vary throughout the year. Peak conditions in the Atlanta area usually run from March to October.

Metro Atlanta

Bobby Jones Golf Course
384 Woodward Way
Atlanta, GA 30305
355-1009.

Directions and Course Description:
Take I-75 to Northside Dr., turn north and go 1.2 miles to Woodward Way; turn right and follow to the entrance on the right.

Named after Atlanta's great Bobby Jones, the course opened in 1934. It's close to downtown and offers a varied terrain; hills, tree-lined fairways and a few creeks. One of four courses managed by The American Golf Corporation. Resident memberships are available.

Daily Rates:
Monday-Friday $30.04
Weekends/Holidays. $33.04

From the Tips:
Yardage	6155
Rating	69.0
Slope	119
Par	71

Features/Amenities:
Championship 18-Hole Course
Corporate/Group Outings
Snack Bar
Twilight/Senior/Junior Rates

Cross Creek Country Club
1221 Cross Creek Pkwy.
Atlanta, GA 30327
352-5612.

Directions and Course Description:
Take I-75 to exit 106 (Moores Mill Rd.) and turn right; at the first stop light (W. Wesley) take a left, and then a right on Bohler Rd. Continue one mile, the course is on left.

Located right in Atlanta, beautiful Cross Creek is an excellent par three course. A great place for beginners or to work on the short game. Midday and weekends are busiest; otherwise play is under two hours. Carry a short bag or use a pull cart.

Daily Rates:
Monday-Friday $13
Weekends/Holidays. $17

From the Tips:
Yardage	1922

Rating   50.0
Slope   61
Par   54

Features/Amenities:
Executive 18-Hole Course
Restaurant/Lounge
Pool/Tennis
Membership

North Fulton Golf Course
216 West Wieuca Rd.
Atlanta, GA 30342
255-0723.

Directions and Course Description:
Located conveniently within the Perimeter in Buckhead, off Roswell Rd., adjacent to Chastain Park.

Old-timers will remember when this course opened in 1934. It was designed by H. Chandler Egan, and played host to a Pre-Masters Event back in the 1930s. Time has been kind to the course, still one of the most popular in Atlanta, with rolling hills, bermuda greens, and an overall great layout. Scenic and challenging, consistently good iron play is necessary to score well on the smallish greens. American Golf offers low rates and resident memberships.

Daily Rates:
Monday-Thursday $26.00
Weekend/Holidays $28.00

From the Tips:
Yardage   6570
Rating   71.8
Slope   126
Par   71

Features/Amenities:
Championship 18-Hole Course
PGA Instruction
Corporate/Group Outings
Practice Facilities
Complete Pro Shop
Snack Bar
Twilight/Senior/Junior Specials
Walking Rates

Metro North

Centennial Golf Club
5225 Woodstock Rd.
Acworth, GA 30101
770-975-1000.

Directions and Course Description:
From Atlanta take I-75 N. to exit 120, Hwy.92; take a right and go three miles to first traffic light. Take a right onto Woodstock Rd. and proceed one mile to club entrance on right.

Cobb County resident and winner of three major golf championships, Larry Nelson designed and is owner of Centennial.

Situated on a beautiful rolling, wooded site the course plays over 6,800 yards from the championship tees. Mean Creek meanders through most of the front nine holes, and the back nine play quite a bit longer. Nelson throws every challenge in the game your way; drive strongly, hit good irons, and bring your best putter. This course has maintained a reputation of being among the state's finest, with superior greens, and is a favorite for golfers in the Atlanta area. The clubhouse, reminiscent of an old country inn, provides a warm relaxing atmosphere, and a cool shady porch with comfortable rocking chairs.

Daily Rates:
Monday-Friday $38
Weekends/Holidays. $50

From the Tips:
Yardage   6849
Raing   73.1
Slope   134
Par   72

Features/Amenities:
Championship 18-Hole Course
Expansive Practice Facility
Corporate/Group Outings
Nelson Inn Dining Facility
Complete Pro Shop
PGA Instruction
Bentgrass Greens

The Champions Club at Apalachee
1008 Dacula Rd.
Dacula, GA 30211
770-822-9220.

Directions and Course Description:
Take I-85 N. to Hwy. 316 toward Lawrenceville, for approximately 8 1/2 miles to Cedars Rd. Take a left and go 200 yards to a stop sign; take a right onto Hurricane Shoals Rd. and proceed three miles till it ends. Take a left onto Dacula Rd. and drive 3/4 miles to the club entrance.

Named after the Apalachee River that winds through it, this marvelously scenic course, designed by Steve Melnyk, opened in late 1994. Maturing nicely, the course layout with its rolling hills and heavily wooded areas demands accurate drives. Managed by the Riverside Golf Group, Apalachee is the newest member of the Champion family. This topnotch course will challenge players of all ability levels.

Daily Rates:
Monday-Thursday $37
Friday $40
Weekends/Holidays $45

From the Tips:
Yardage	6620
Rating	71.8
Slope	135
Par	71

Features/Amenities:
Championship 18-Hole Course
Corporate/Group Outings
PGA Instruction
Complete Practice Facilities
Georgian Club House
Full Service Grill
Stocked Golf Shop
Limited Memberships
Twilight/Senior Specials

The Champions Club of Atlanta
15135 Hopewell Rd.
Alpharetta, GA 30201
770-343-9700.

Directions and Course Description:
Alpharetta. From Atlanta take Hwy. 400 N. to exit 7 (Windward Parkway). Continue west to Hwy. 9. Turn left .5 miles to Cogburn Rd., Turn right on Cogburn Rd. and continue four miles to the golf course.

A challenging, yet playable, course designed to take maximum advantage of the 180-acre hilly wooded site. Designed by D. J. DeVictor and Steve Melnyk, president of Riverside Golf Group. The eighth hole is the signature hole, a downhill par 4, regarded the one of the most picturesque and challenging in Georgia. The Champions Club of Atlanta is one of Georgia's premier daily-fee facilities. You'll find the amenities and personal service expected of a private club, at affordable rates.

Rates:
Monday-Thursday $45
Friday $49
Weekend&Holidays $59

From the Tips:
Yardage	6725
Rating	72.9
Slope	131
Par	72

Features/Amenities:
Championship 18-Hole Course
Corporate/Group Outings
PGA Instruction
Professional Club Fitting Systems
Limited Memberships
Complete Golf Shop
Full-Service Grill

Cobblestone Golf Course
4200 Nance Rd.
Acworth, GA 30101
770-917-5151.

Directions and Course Description:
Take I-75 north to exit 116 (Barrett Pkwy.), take a left and follow to US.41. Take a right and follow 5.7 miles to Acworth proceeding to West Rd. Take a right and go 1/2 mile to

Nance Rd., making a right and continue to entrance on left.

Originally named the Boulders and recently renamed Cobblestone, this Ken Dye designed 18-hole championship course, is pure pleasure and Cobb County's first county-owned golf course. The serene and relaxing beauty of Lake Acworth creates a picturesque backdrop for almost every hole. Fairways, for the most part, are generous and the greens are putter-friendly. A daily fee facility that has the look and feel of a fine private golf course.

Daily Rates:
Monday-Thursday'$38
Weekends/Holidays'$35
Discount Card Available

From the Tips:
Yardage   6759
Rating   73.1
Slope   140
Par   71

Features/Amenities:
Championship 18-Hole Course
PGA Instruction
Corporate/Group Outings
Practice Facilities
Clubhouse with Snack Bar
Fully Equiped Golf Shop
Twilight Specials

Eagle Watch Golf Club
3055 Eagle Watch Dr.
Woodstock, GA 30188-2333
770-591-1000.

Directions and Course Description:
From Atlanta take I-75 north to I-575 north to exit 5 (Town Lake Pkwy). Turn left of exit, proceed 2.5 miles and turn right into Towne Lake. Eagle Watch is located 1 1/2 miles on the right.

Designed by Arnold Palmer, Eagle Watch Golf Club is a premier public golf course. Known for its wide fairways and water on twelve holes, the course has matured into one of the state's finest layouts. Recent renovations to the clubhouse include a new lounge

and private dining room. The pro shop was voted one of the top 100 in America by Golf Shop Operations magazine. Affordable annual memberships are now available for the first time to Atlanta area golfers. Owned and managed by Cloverleaf Investments Co.

Daily Rates:
Monday-Friday $45 and $25 after 3:00 p.m.
Weekend $65 and $50 after 12:00 p.m. and $35 after 3:00 p.m.

From the Tips:
Yardage   6896
Rating   72.5
Slope   134
Par   72

Features/Amenities:
Championship 18-Hole Course
Driving Range
Corporate/Group Outings
Complete Golf Shop
PGA Instruction
Open Seven Days a Week
Bentgrass Greens

Fox Creek Golf Club
1501 Windy Hill Rd.
Smyrna, GA 30080
770-435-1000.

Directions and Course Description:
Take I-75 north to exit 110, Windy Hill Rd.; turn left and proceed three miles to entrance on the right.

Fox Creek is a real find. Designed by John LaFoy in 1985, this executive style course has bentgrass greens and is reachable in fifteen minutes from downtown Atlanta. One of the top lighted driving range/practice facilities in the country, make Fox Creek the most frequented practice facility in Georgia. The well-maintained executive course offers golfers of every skill level an opportunity to fine-tune their games.

Daily Rates:
Monday-Thursday $20
Weekends/Holidays $25

From the Tips:

Yardage   4048
Rating   59.1
Slope   104
Par   61

Features/Amenities:

Executive 18-Hole Course
Corporate/Group Outings
Lighted Grass/Mat Range
Putting Green/Chipping Area
Club Fitting Center
Senior/Junior/Ladies Rates
Snack Bar
Memberships

Lake Lanier Islands Hilton Resort Golf Course

7000 Holiday Rd.
Lake Lanier Island, GA 30518
770-945-8787.

Directions: Take I-85 N. to exit 45 which is I-985 towards Gainesville. Take exit 2 and turn left onto Friendship Rd. Follow signs for four miles onto Lake Lanier Islands. Then follow resort signs.

This award winning championship 18-hole course was built in 1989 and designed by Joe Lee. The course lies in a beautiful setting of rolling terrain and spectacular views with 13 holes over the waters of Lake Lanier. The course is well-marked, with bentgrass greens and no parallel fairways. Well-laid-out, including 75 bunkers, the course is an challenge from the championship tees. The 8th and 12th holes are true tests of golfing skills as both water and tricky gusts of wind come into play. Slow play is not tolerated, making an average round about four hours. With all the amenities offered, this is one of the most enjoyable and affordable resort courses in the region.

Daily Rates:

Monday-Thursday $45
Weekends/Holidays $50

From the Tips:

Yardage. 6341
Rating 70.1

Slope 126
Par 72

Features/Amenities:

Championship 18-hole Course
Complete Practice Facility
PGA Instruction
Fully-Stocked Golf Shop
Golf Packages
Grill/Lounge
Lockers/Showers
Resort Amenities
Bentgrass Greens

Renaissance PineIsle Resort Golf Course

9000 Holiday Rd.
Lake Lanier Islands, GA 30518
770-945-8921.

Directions: Take I-85 N. to exit 45, which is I-985 heading towards Gainesville. Take exit 2 and turn left onto Friendship Rd. Then follow the signs for four miles onto Lake Lanier Island. Continue past Water Park and follow signs to the golf club.

Designed in 1974 by Gary Player and Ron Kirby, this mature championship 18-hole course hosted the LPGA's Nestle World Championship from 1985-1989. This spectacular course will tease the golfer with rolling Bermuda fairways, strategically placed bunkers and eight holes skirting Lake Lanier. The signature 5th hole is an example of golf course esthetics, as it closely resembles the famous 18th hole at Pebble Beach. Take out your camera at the 13th hole to capture the scenic display of Lake Lanier and the Blue Ridge Mountains. And to keep things interesting, the 18th hole plays twice over water to a small peninsula green. A well deserved drink is waiting at the Clubhouse.

Daily Rates:

Monday-Thursday. $54
Weekends/Holidays. $59

From The Tips:

Yardage 6527
Rating 71.6

Slope. 132
Par. 72
Features/Amenities:
Championship 18-hole Course
Complete Practice Facilities
Award-Winning Golf Shop
PGA Instruction
Clubhouse Restaurant
Golf Packages
Golf Pavilion
Corporate/Group Outings
Bermuda Fairways
Bentgrass Greens

Sugar Hill Golf Course
6094 Suwanee Dam Rd.
Sugar Hill, GA 30518
770-271-0519.

Directions and Course Description:
Take I-85 north to exit 44, turn left and drive
approximately eight miles; cross Hwy.20 and
continue .6 miles to the entrance on the left.

Since its opening in 1992, the Willard Byrd
designed course, has proven to be one of the
most beautiful and artfully laid out courses in
north Georgia's foothills. The level tee boxes,
tight Bermuda fairways and precision greens
make for a challenging golf experience. The
difficult par three 14th demands a blind shot
over water, and the scenic par four 16th is
played from a spectacular and windy vista.
You'll surely satisfy your golfing sweet tooth
at Sugar Hill.

Daily Rates:
Monday-Friday. $28
Weekends/Holidays $38
Seniors (Tuesday-Thursdy) $20

From the Tips:
Yardage   6423
Rating   70.9
Slope   129
Par   72

Features/Amenities:
Championship 18-Hole Course
PGA Instruction
Corporate/Group Outings

Practice Facility
Clubhouse/Dining Area
Golf Pro Shop
Senior/Junior Rates
Bermuda Fairways
Bentgrass Greens

Stonebridge Golf Club
685 Stonebridge Dr.
Rome, GA 30165
706-236-5046/800-336-5046.

Directions and Course Description:
Take I-75 north, from Atlanta, to exit 128; take
a left onto Hwy.140 and follow for 16 miles
until it deadends; then take a left onto Hwy.27
and go 2.1 miles to Old Summerville Rd.; take
a right and go 1 1/2 miles to club entrance on
the right.

Stonebridge is Rome's first 18-hole championship course. It was opened in October 1994,
and is nestled in the foothills of northwest
Georgia. Despite its newness, Stonebridge has
already attracted the interest of those seeking
top-notch courses. Designed by Arthur Davis,
this course provides a wonderful mix of strategy, scenery and difficulty. A 27-acre lake
adds to the danger of the signature par-five
ninth hole. Nearby Berry College is using the
course as its home links. The course is owned
and managed by the Rome City Commission.

Daily Rates:
Monday-Friday $28
Weekends/Holidays. $34
Discount Cards Available

From the Tips:
Yardage   6816
Rating   72.6
Slope   123
Par   72

Features/Amenities:
Championship Golf Course
Complete Practice Area
PGA Instruction
Corporate/Group Outings
Bermuda Grass Fairways
Bentgrass Greens

Towne Lake Hills Golf Club

1003 Towne Lake Hills East
Woodstock, GA 30188
770-592-9969.

Directions and Course Description:
Take I-75 north to I-575 north to exit 5 (Towne Lake Pkwy.) Take a left and proceed approximately 1 1/2 miles; then bear right. Half a mile further on the right is the course entrance.

Maturing extremely well, this 18-hole championship golf course, designed by Arthur Hills, is a challenge for players of all abilities. Opened in December 1994, the course offers rolling hillsides and wooded landscapes, with well-marked fairways. A newly completed clubhouse features a breathtaking view of the 18th-green.

Daily Rates:

Monday-Friday.................... $39
Weekends/Holidays $49

From the Tips:

Yardage   6757
Rating   72.3
Slope   133
Par   72

Features/Amenities:

Championship 18-Hole Course
PGA Staff and Instruction
Corporate/Group Outings
Open Seven Days a Week
Memberships Available
Practice Facilities
Clubhouse w/Golf Shop
Restaurant
Bentgrass Greens
Bermuda Tees/Fairways

White Columns Golf Club

300 White Columns Dr.
Alpharetta, GA 30201
770-343-9025.

Directions and Course Description:
Take GA 400 north to exit 9 (Haynes Bridge Rd.) and turn left onto Academy St., cross Hwy.9, Academy St. which becomes Milton Ave. and then Mid-Broadwell Rd. Turn right on Mayfield Rd. and then left on Freemanville Rd. In about five minutes you'll reach the club which is on the left.

White Columns opened late 1994 and has already received many rave reviews. A Tom Fazio design, known for its demanding layout (which requires a well-placed tee shot), heavy bunkering and marvelous bentgrass greens. Fuji Development paid handily to bring forth this outstanding golf course. The par threes are exceptional, starting with a 221-yard beauty over wetlands. And the par fives are no holiday, featuring the monsterous ninth with 591 yards and plenty of water. Golfers who seek both challenge and superb playing conditions will love White Columns.

Daily Rates:

Monday-Friday $70
Weekends/Holidays................ $80

From the Tips:

Yardage   7053
Rating   73.6
Slope   137
Par   72

Features/Amenities:

Championship 18-Hole Course

PGA Instruction

Excellent Practice Facilities

Fully Stocked Golf Shop

Club House/Patio

Restaurant/Grill

Corporate/Group Outings

Lockers/Showers

Tournaments

Limited Memberships

Crenshaw Bentgrass Greens

Sodded Bermuda Fairways

1997 Tennis/Pool

Metro South

The Champions Club at RiversEdge

300 North Bridge Dr.
Fayetteville, GA 30214
770-460-1098.

Directions and Course Description:
Take I-75 south to exit 77. Drive 10 miles south on Hwy.19/41. Take a right onto McDonough Rd. and go five miles to County Line Rd. Turn left and proceed 2.5 miles to course entrance on the left.

Ranked as one of the top 25 courses in Georgia, the 18-hole championship course was designed in 1990 by Bobby Weed. The scenic course, located along the banks of the Flint River, features rolling hills and undulating bentgrass greens. Voted "Best New Public Course in 1990", the course is owned and operated by American Golf.

Daily Rates:
Monday-Thursday . . $35 ($20 after 3 p.m.)
Weekend/Holidays . . $45 ($25 after 3 p.m.)

From the Tips:
Yardage	6810
Rating	72.9
Slope	135
Par	71

Features/Amenities:
Championship 18-Hole Course
PGA Instruction
Corporate/Group Outings
Complete Practice Facilities
Affordable Memberships
Open Seven Days a Week
Membership/Twilight Specials
Excellent Bentgrass Greens

Griffin Golf Course

9th Street at Kemp Northern Rd.
Griffin, GA 30223
770-227-3627.

Directions and Course Description:
Take I-75 S. to exit 67 (Hwy.16), and go 10 miles to Griffin. Turn left on 8th St. and right at Graef St. Pass the hospital and turn right into the city park and follow the road to this magnificent city golf course.

Old country charm and a well laid out course will have you returning many times. A truly vintage golf course, opened in 1935, offers a natural rolling terrain, old oak trees and small streams. The third hole, par four, is toughest, requiring an accurate uphill drive to a sideslope flanked by trees. And the green of the 8th hole is strategicly positioned to respond to only the most precise of shots. Finish the day with a picnic underneath one of the mighty oaks.

Daily Rates:
Monday-Friday $24.00
Weekends/Holidays. $27.00
Less $9.00 for walkers.

From the Tips:
Yardage	6790
Rating	71.0
Slope	121
Par	72

Features/Amenities:
Championship 18-Hole Course
PGA Instruction
Corporate/Group Outings
Pro Shop/Snack Bar
Membership
Bermuda Greens

Lake Spivey Golf Club

8255 Club House Way
Jonesboro, GA 30236
770-471-4653.

Directions and Course Description:
Take I-75 S. to exit 75 (SR138/Stockbridge) and take a right. Drive 1/2 mile to Spivey Rd. and take a left; go another 1/2 mile to Lake Spivey Country Club and take a right into the subdivision; then follow signs to golf course.

Lake Spivey's 27-holes were designed by D.J. DeVitor; the Lakeside nine is the most challenging, with greatert distance and water at five holes; the Hillside and Clubside nines are shorter than Lakeside but each requires shot-making skills and keen course management.

Daily Rates:
Monday-Friday. $26
Weekends/Holidays $36
Weekday Walking $16
Weekend Walking $26

From the Tips:
Lake/Hillside
Yardage   6592
Rating   72.3
Slope   133
Par   72

Features/Amenities:
Championship 27-Hole Course
PGA Instruction
Corporate/Group Outings
Complete Practice Facility
Clubhouse/Dining
Stocked Golf Pro Shop
Men/Wmn Showers/Lockers
Pool/Tennis
Tournament/Picnic Pavilion
Memberships
Bentgrass Greens

Lakeside Golf Club
3600 Old Fairburn Rd.
Atlanta, GA 30331
344-3629.

Directions and Course Description:
Conveniently located just eight miles from Hartsfield Airport, take I-285 south to exit 3 (Camp Creek Pkwy.) and drive outside the perimeter to the second stop light. Take a left onto Old Fairburn Rd. and follow 500 yards to the club entrance on the left.

Designed in 1962 as a private club by renowed golf course architect George Cobb, Lakeside has since went public in 1991. Since then *Golf Digest* has consistently ranked it among the top 100 public courses in the country. This mature Cobb design has hosted the Seniors Open qualifying and 1995 Nationwide Championship. The challenge of the course lies in its many doglegs and the fastest greens in the east. The tree-lined fairways, rolling terrain and immaculate bentgrass greens make Lakeside the complete golf experience for players of all levels.

Daily Rates:
Monday-Friday $27
Weekends/Holidays. $33
Special Senior Rates

From the Tips:
Yardage   6522
Rating   71.4
Slope   127
Par   71

Features/Amenities:
Championship 18-Hole Course
PGA Instruction
Natural Grass Driving Range
Full Service Golf Shop
Locker Room Facility
Corporate/Group Outings
Dining/Banquet Facility
Bentgrass Greens
Twilight Rates

The Links Golf Club
340 Hewell Rd.
Jonesboro, GA 30236
770-461-5100.

Directions and Course Description:
Take I-75 south to exit 77 (Tara Blvd.); continue south five miles to Hwy.54 west and take a right; then proceed 4.2 miles to the club entrance on the left.

A challenging course for all levels of players. This Scottish-style course designed by Terry Anton and Jack Gaudion is both challenging and fun. Tight, rolling fairways and undulating greens require good club selection and course management. Get the snorkel out for the water-logged 13th par three. A unique nine-hole course, called "Wee Links," is specially designed for youngsters aged six to sixteen. All together a great course for the entire family.

Daily Rates:

Monday-Friday................... $26

Weekends/Holidays................ $30

From the Tips:

Yardage	6376
Rating	69.4
Slope	118
Par	70

Features/Amenities:

Executive 18-Hole Course

Childrens 9-Hole Course

Corporate/Group Outings

PGA Instruction

Pro Golf Shop

Club House/Dining/Snack Bar

Full Practice Facility

Limited Membership

Orchard Hills Golf Club

600 East Highway 16

Newnan, GA 30263

770-251-5683.

Directions and Course Description:

Take I-85 S. to exit 8, then turn right and go 1/4 mile to Hwy.16 and turn right. Proceed one mile to entrance on the left.

Orchard offers a true 18-hole Scottish links design, with gentle rolling terrain. Previously orchards and farmland, this course was designed by Don Cottle, Jr. and opened in 1990. Wide rolling terrain and occasional tabby ruin add to its Southern charm. Wide open fairways with only a few trees and ponds coming into play give the golfer a fine opportunity to lower that handicap.

Daily Rates:

Monday-Friday................... $36

Weekends/Holidays $42

From the Tips:

Yardage	6997
Rating	72.9
Slope	131
Par	72

Features/Amenities:

Championship 18-Hole Course

PGA Instruction

Corporate/Group Outings

Complete Practice Facilities

Complete Golf Shop

Restaurant/Snack Bar

Twilight Rates

Bentgrass Greens

Sugar Creek Golf & Tennis Club

2706 Bouldercrest Rd.

Atlanta, GA 30316

241-7671.

Directions and Course Description:

Take I-285 east to exit 37 (Bouldercrest Rd.) and turn east; continue .2 miles to Sugar Creek Golf Dr. and turn left to the clubhouse.

Owned and operated by DeKalb County, Sugar Creek, with its small bridges and wildlife, is challenging country course designed in 1977 by Evan Marbut. Its a demanding layout, requiring well-placed tee shots to sharp doglegs; other features are deep rough, a swamp and large well-maintained Bermuda greens that will test your golfing knowledge.

Daily Rates:

Monday-Friday $29

Weekends/Holidays................ $32

From the Tips:

Yardage	6717
Rating	72.0
Slope	127
Par	72

Features/Amenities:

Championship 18-Hole Course

Practice Facilities

PGA Instruction

Corporate/Group Outings

Restaurant/Snack Bar

Golf Shop

Resident/Senior Rates

Annual Pass

Tennis

Whitewater Creek Country Club
1904 Redwine Rd.
Fayetteville, GA 30214
770-461-6545.

Directions and Course Description:
From Atlanta take I-85 south to exit 12, take a left onto Hwy.74 and follow 17 miles to Red Wine Rd. Then turn left and proceed three miles to the club entrance on the right.

Get ready for one of the most challenging courses in the state. An 1986 Arnold Palmer design, Whitewater features large rolling fairways and level tee boxes. The par threes are especially difficult with water coming into play on three of them; a sound strategy is required to score well here including accurate tee shots, proper club selection and a sixth sense for trouble. A true test of a shot-makers skills; a tremendous experience for all golf devotees.

Daily Rates:
Monday-Friday $35
Weekends/Holidays $45

From the Tips:
Yardage	6739
Rating	72.3
Slope	133
Par	71/72

Features/Amenities:
Championship 18-Hole Course
PGA Instruction
Complete Practice Facilities
Corporate/Group Outings
Pro Golf Shop
Restaurant/Grill

Metro East

Hard Labor Creek State Golf Course
P.O. Box 247
Rutledge, GA 30663
706-557-3006.

Directions and Course Description:
Take I-20 east to exit 49, take a left off ramp and follow signs for approximately two miles on Fairplay Rd. to the park.

Beautiful Hard Labor Creek Golf Course has challenged golfers for nearly a quarter century. Designed by James B. McCloud, the course features elevated tees overlooking tight, tree-lined fairways. Hard Labor Creek cuts through the course and creates water hazards in five holes. The fifth hole is one of the most beautiful par threes in the state, with an ancient waterwheel framing the hole, next to a gorgeous waterfall.

Daily Rates:
Monday-Friday $33
Weekends/Holidays. $33
Annual Pass Cards

From the Tips:
Yardage	6444
Rating	71.5
Slope	129
Par	72

Features/Amenities:
Championship 18-Hole Course
Driving Range
Pro Shop/Snack Bar
Small Group Outings
Unlimited Play Weekdays Only
Annual Pass Cards/Senior Rates
Rental Cottages/Campsites
Horse Stables/Swimming

Highland Golf Club
2271 Flat Shoals Rd.
Conyers, GA 30208
770-483-4235.

Directions and Course Description:
Take I-20 east to exit 43 (Salem Rd.), turn right and travel 1/4 mile to the first red light at Flat Shoals Rd. Turn left and travel 1/4 mile to the entrance on the right.

In spring and summer a beautiful array of pear trees and azaleas welcomes golfers amidst a rolling terrain. Built in 1961 and renovated in

1986, the course is in excellent shape and offers quality bentgrass greens and wide Bermuda fairways. Strategically placed bunkers and five lakes which come into play provide a challenge for every level of golfer. The tenth hole par three requires a precise shot to avoid an enormous bunker. At the eleventh, the signature hole, floral distractions prevail. You will enjoy this quality course and its friendly staff. Score well.

Daily Rates:
Monday-Thursday $31.50
Friday $33.60
Weekends/Holidays $42.00

From the Tips:
Yardage   6926
Rating   72.6
Slope   132
Par   72

Features/Amenities:
Championship 18-Hole Course
Corporate/Group Outings
PGA Instruction
Stocked Pro Shop
Complete Practice Facility
Lounge/Snack Bar
Lockers/Showers
Memberships
Bentgrass Greens
Bermuda Fairways, Roughs and Tee's

Mystery Valley Golf Club
6094 Shadowrock Dr.
Lithonia, GA 30058
770-469-6913.

Directions and Course Description:
Take I-20 east to exit 37 (Panola Rd.); then turn north and go 4.2 miles to Stone Mountain/Lithonia Rd.; then turn left and go .7 miles to Shadowrock Dr.; then turn right and go 1.3 miles to the golf course which is on the left.

Mystery Valley is as good as its name. Designed in 1966 by Dick Wilson, the mystery is reading the greens. More challenges come into play as wide pine-lined fairways display strategically placed deep bunkers. The course

plays longer and tougher than the card says, and par threes are far from being easy. Combined with some of the most beautiful scenery, this course is one of the best layouts in the metro Atlanta area.

Daily Rates:
Monday-Friday $28.50
Weekends/Holidays. $31.50
Resident and Senior Rates

From the Tips:
Yardage   6705
Rating   71.5
Slope   124
Par   72

Features/Amenities:
Championship 18-Hole Course
PGA Instruction
Complete Practice Facility
Corporate/Group Outings
Complete Golf Shop
Restaurant
Season/Senior/Junior Pass
Golf Packages

The Oaks Golf Course
11240 Brown Bridge Rd.
Covington, GA 30209
221-0200.

Directions and Course Description:
Take I-20 east to exit 44. Take a right off the ramp and follow for 2.1 miles to the club entrance on the left.

For a friendly round, golfers go to The Oaks. Originally a nine-holer, designed by the famed Bobby Jones in 1938, it was vastly redesigned and renovated in 1990 by architect and owner Dick Schultz. He delivered an authentic, well-maintained course which offers wide fairways and level tee boxes. Mid-handicappers are well-rewarded here, with the exception of the eighth hole, a tricky dogleg right par four, and the ninth hole which is well-guarded by that famous oak tree, the course namesake. Only minutes from downtown Atlanta and a real pleasure to play.

Daily Rates:
Monday-Friday $29
Weekends/Holidays $39

From the Tips:
Yardage   6420
Rating   69.5
Slope   118
Par   70

Features/Amenities:
Championship 18-Hole Course
Complete Practice Facility
PGA Instruction
Well-Stocked Pro Shop
Corporate/Group Outings
Conference Room
Snack Bar
Memberships/Winter Rates

Southerness Golf Club
4871 Flat Bridge Rd.
Stockbridge, GA 30281
770-808-6000.

Directions and Course Description:
Take I-20 east to exit 36 (Wesley Chapel Rd.) and take a right. Go to the first light and take a left at Snapfinger Rd., and proceed seven miles to Alexander Lakes Rd. Take a left and go two miles to the club entrance on the right.

Once a cotton plantation, this course rests in a beautiful lush riverside setting. Designed in 1991 by architect Clyde Johnston, Southerness is one of Atlanta's finest 18-hole courses; it was recently awarded 3-star rating by *Golf Digest*. Well-maintained fairways and a blend of seven grasses and bentgrass greens make this course stand out from others. The par threes are a constant challenge and the greens, once lost, are now back and in full glory.

After the game relax in one of the rockers on the porch, and soak up that Southern feeling.

Daily Rates:
Monday-Friday $37.00
Weekends/Holidays $45.00
Twilight $24.50

From the Tips:
Yardage   6766
Rating   72.2
Slope   127
Par   72

Features/Amenities:
Championship 18-Hole Course
PGA Instruction
Well-Stocked Pro Shop
Complete Practice Facility
Corporate/Group Outings
Restaurant/Lounge
Membership
Senior/Ladies Rates
Twilight Rates
Bentgrass Greens

Stone Mountain Park Golf Courses
P.O. Box 778
Stone Mountain, GA 30086
770-498-5715.

Directions and Course Description:
Take I-285 east to exit 30B (Hwy.78/Stone Mtn. Frwy.) and follow 7.7 miles to the park entrance. Once through the gate take an immediate left onto Stonewall Jackson Dr. and follow 1 1/2 miles to the club entrance on the right.

A fantastic family recreational area, Stone Mountain Park offers golfers two 18-hole golf courses. The old front nine of Stonemont, a 1969 Robert Trent Jones design, features holes that are long and narrow with smallish undulating greens. John LaFoy designed the remaining 27 holes making full-use of the mountainous terrain and strategically placing pot bunkers and large undulating greens. Whereas Stonemont is treacherous, the Lakemont and Woodmont courses offer memorable views of Stone Mountain Lake and a rolling green terrain. The challenging and scenic Stone Mountain courses are regarded as two of the best public courses in the nation.

Daily Rates:
Seven Days a Week $40

From the Tips:
Stonemont
Yardage   6683
Rating   72.6
Slope   133
Par   72

Features/Amenities:
2 Championship 18-Hole Courses
PGA Instruction
Corporate/Group Outings
Fully Stocked Golf Shop
Clubhouse/Restaurant
Dining/Banquet Room
Practice Facilities
Lockers/Showers
Memberships

Harbor Club Golf Course
One Club Drive
Greensboro, GA 30642
706-453-9690.

Directions and Course Description:
Take I-20 to exit 53, and take a right off the ramp onto Hwy.44. Follow for 3 1/2 miles to entrance on left.

The Harbor Club Golf Course opened in 1991 and was named one of the best new courses in America. Designed by award-winning architects Tom Weiskopf and Jay Morris, the course is considered one of their best. Dramatic elevations, bridges over wetlands and spectacular views provide for a true aesthetic experience. Featuring short walks from green to tee boxes and open entrances to the greens, the course also demands a keen strategy, course management and intense shot making. Each hole is named appropriately, such as "On Golden Pond," with water in play, or "Arrowhead," aim straight and narrow. Harbor Club's most famous resident, Mickey Mantle, recently passed away, but, for his many friends here, fond memories of him will endure.

Daily Rates:
Monday-Thursday $52
Weekends/Holidays $62

From the Tips:
Yardage   7014
Rating   73.7
Slope   135
Par   72

Features/Amenities:
Championship 18-Hole Course
PGA Instruction
Complete Practice Facilities
Elegant Dining Room/Lounge/Grill
Full Stocked Pro Shop
Corporate/Group Outings
Tennis/Swimming/Equestrian/Croquet
Golf Packages
Country Club Community
Mickey Mantle Memorabilia Room

Port Armor Golf & Country Club
1 Port Armor Parkway
Greensboro, GA 30642
706-453-4561.

Directions and Course Description:
Take I-20 east to exit 53. Take a right onto Hwy.44 and follow six miles to club entrance on the right.

Located along the banks of beautiful Lake Oconee, Port Armor's Scottish-type championship course was created by Robert Cupp, senior designer for Jack Nicklaus for fifteen years. The course is known for its tough carries, beautiful vistas and dynamic changes from hole-to-hole. It has been hailed by *Golf Magazine* as "one of the best in the world." Each hole has four tee boxes; the greens are overseeded with poa trivialis which provides an excellent putting surface. A second 18-hole course is under way, offering more views of the magnificent lake and natural surroundings. The course is owned and managed by Port Armor Investments.

Daily Rates:
Weekly. $53
Weekends/Holidays. $53
Golf Packages . . . . $90-$130

From the Tips:
Yardage   6926

Rating   74.0
Slope   140
Par   72

Features/Amenities:
Championship 18-Hole Course
PGA Instruction
Corporate/Group Outings
Full Service Resort/Memberships
Full Service Clubhouse/
Lounge/Grill/Diningroom
Full Service Pro-Shop
Steam/Sauna/Exercise Room

Reynolds Plantation Golf Course
100 Linger Longer Rd.
Greensboro, GA 30642
706-467-3159.

Directions and Course Description:
Take I-20 east to exit 53. Take a right onto Hwy.44 and follow signs for approximately 15 miles to the entrance on the left.

Golf Magazine named the Plantation Course one of the best new resort courses in the world when it opened in 1988. Designed by Bob Cupp, the course offers a peaceful beauty and subtle shotmaking. The beautiful, relatively wide fairways, minimal rough and rolling, heavily wooded land have also drawn rave reviews. Number five is the signature hole, a 562-yard par five wonder, offering a wide fairway that meanders through dense forest down to a long green backed by a peaceful cove of Lake Oconee. The beauty and amenities surrounding the Plantation Course complete the enjoyment of any round.

Daily Rates:
Monday-Thursday $75.26 (Public)
Weekends/Holidays $65.76 (Members/Guests)

From the Tips:
Yardage   6656
Rating   71.3
Slope   127
Par   71

Features/Amenities:

Championship 18-Hole Course
PGA Instruction
Corporate/Group Outings
Complete Practice Facilities
Excellent Resort Facilities
Special Golf Packages
Tennis/Swimming/Sailing/Fishing
Fully Stocked Pro Shop
Complete Dining Facility
Grill and Lounge
Bentgrass Greens
Country Club Community

Reynolds Great Waters Course
130 Woodcress Dr.
Lake Oconee, GA 31024
706-485-0235.

Directions and Course Description:
Take I-20 east to exit 53 and take a right on Hwy.44. Follow signs to Reynolds Plantation and continue south on Hwy.44 for 3 1/2 miles to caution light and turn left onto Old Phoenix Rd., Travel for 1 1/2 miles and turn left onto Wards Chapel Rd., continue for 1 1/2 miles to the Great Waters entrance on the left. Once on Reynolds Dr., proceed 1 1/2 miles and turn right onto Plantation Drive.

Panoramic views, expansive greens and the views of Lake Oconee seduce the golfer at the Great Waters Course. Designed by Jack Nicklaus in 1992 (who also has a home here) the course reflects his skill and vision in making the most of the natural beauty and the Great Waters peninsula. One of the most stunning holes is the 11th, a 349-yard par four, playing sharply downhill to a green set on a peninsula in the lake. The 18th, a 540-yard par five bordered by Lake Oconee, makes for a memorable finish.

Daily Rates:
Monday-Thursday $91(Public)
Weekends/Holidays $82 (Member/Guest)

From the Tips:
Yardage   7048
Rating   74.7

Slope   140
Par   72

Features/Amenities:
Championship 18-Hole Course
See also Reynolds Plantation.

Beyond Metro Atlanta

Callaway Gardens Golf Courses
Pine Mountain, GA 31822-2000
800-282-8181

Directions and Course Descriptions:
Take I-85 south to I-185 south and follow
signs 12 miles to resort. Callaway Gardens,
home to some of the nation's top-rated
courses, has a golf course for every game,
from a casual family round to a true test of
skill. Four immaculately groomed courses
surrounded by crystal lakes, wooded shores
and lush landscaping, have been ranked
among the best in the nation by both *Golf
Digest* and *Golf Magazine*. **Mountain View** ,
site of the PGA Tour's Buick Southern Open,
designed by Dick Wilson, is the most challenging with tight, tree-lined fairways. **Lake
View**, Callaway's original 18-hole championship course, designed by J.B. McGovern and
Dick Wilson, provides a wondrous golfing
experience in beautiful surroundings; **Garden
View**, designed by Joe Lee, features a hilly
terrain of beautiful orchards and vineyards
requiring an excellent test of shot-making and
course management; and **Sky View's** nine
holes are perfect for a between-meetings
tester.

Mountain View Daily Rates: $80

From the Tips:
Yardage   7057
Rating   74.1
Slope   138
Par   72

Garden View Daily Rates: $65

From the Tips:
Yardage   6392
Rating   70.7
Slope   115
Par   72

Lake View Daily Rates: $65

From the Tips:
Yardage   6006
Rating   69.4
Slope   115
Par   72

Sky View Daily Rates: $19

From the Tips:
Yardage   2000
Par   31

Features/Amenities:
PGA Instruction
Corporate/Group Outings
Complete Practice Facilities
Special Golf Packages
Two Fully-Stocked Pro Shops
Grill and Lounge
Site of PGA Tour Buick Southern Open
Tennis/Swimming/Boating/Fishing/Beach

The Hampton Club
(about five hours from downtown Atlanta)
100 Tabbystone
St. Simons Island, GA 31522
912-634-0255.

Directions and Course Description:
Hampton Plantation is located on the northern
most tip of St. Simons Island. Take F.J. Torras
Causeway onto St. Simons Island. Follow
signs to Hampton Point, then turn left at the
first light onto Sea Island Rd.; then left at the
next light onto Frederica Rd. At the fork, bear
right on Lawrence Rd. to Hampton Point. Left
at Hampton Point onto Butler Lake Dr.; then
an immediate left through the Hampton Plantation entrance gate onto Rice Mill.

Acclaimed for its spectacular design by renowned golf course architect Joe Lee, and its
glorious marsh and river setting, Hampton
Club was named one of the top resort courses

in the nation by *Golf Magazine*. Hampton's four signature holes 12 through 15, offer a breathtaking challenge. Immaculate greens and wide lush fairways make Hampton Plantation a joy to play and behold.

Daily Rates:
Monday-Friday.................... $78
Weekends/Holidays $78

From the Tips:
Yardage   6465
Rating   71.4
Slope   130
Par   72

Features/Amenities:
Championship 18-Hole Course
PGA Instruction
Complete Practice Facility
Corporate/Group Outings
Fully Equiped Pro Shop
Dining Facility/Lounge
Memberships
Swimming/Tennis/Social Events
Golf Packages
Resort Community

Innsbruck Resort & Golf Club
(about 1 1/2 hours from downtown Atlanta)
Bahn Innsbruck, P.O. Box 1145
Helen, GA 30545
706-878-2100/800-642-2709.

Directions and Course Description:
Take I-85 north to Hwy.985 north to exit 7. Follow signs to Hwy.129 north and continue 25 miles to Cleveland. Take a right on SR75 north in Cleveland and follow for eight miles. The resort is one mile south of Helen.

Just 75 minutes north of Atlanta, this fine hillside course was designed in 1987 by Bill Watts. Innsbruck is a versatile course suited for the average golfer, yet challenging enough for the professional. The par three signature 15th hole features a breathtaking 160-foot drop from tee to green. Keeping with the natural terrain and panoramic views, wild turkeys, deer, springs and carp ponds do come

into play. The 19th hole requires golfers to hit their tee shot from the veranda.

Daily Rates:
Monday-Thursday.................. $35
Weekends/Holidays................ $49

From the Tips:
Yardage   6748
Rating   70.1
Slope   132
Par   72

Features/Amenities:
Championship 18-Hole Course
Complete Practice Facilities
Corporate/Group Outings
Golf Packages/Senior Rates
Open Seven Days a Week
Restaurant/Grill
Bluegrass Fairways
Bentgrass Greens

Jekyll Island Pine Lakes Golf Course
(about five hours from downtown Atlanta)
322 Captain Wylly Rd.
Jekyll Island, GA 31527
912-635-2368.

Directions and Course Description:
From I-95 take exit 6 onto Hwy.17, continue east onto Jekyll Causeway. Continue onto Beachview Dr. and take a left; a few blocks up at Capt. Wylly Rd.; take another left.

Jekyll's 63-holes of championship golf attract golfers from near and far. Each of the four layouts, three 18-hole courses and one 9-hole course, has its own challenge and character. Pine Lakes, a Dick Wilson design, is the longest and tighest layout. Enjoy the tree-lined fairways, offering doglegs left and right, amidst natural beauty and balmy ocean breezes. And keep your eyes open for the occasional deer or sunbathing alligator.

Daily Rates:
Peak Season (March-April 15) $50
Off Season (April 16-February) $39
Twilight rates it the Off Season

From the Tips:

Yardage   6802
Rating   71.9
Slope   130
Par   72

Features/Amenities:

Championship 18-Hole Course
Corporate/Group Outings
PGA Instruction
Fully Equiped Pro Shop
Practice Facilities
Dining/Banquet Facilities
Golfers Heaven Program

Osprey Cove Golf Club

(about five hours from downtown Atlanta)
123 Osprey Dr.
St. Marys, GA 31558
912-882-5575/800-352-5575.

Directions and Course Description:

Located minutes from St. Marys, take I-95 exit 1, and two miles east.

This beautifully maintained course, with immaculate greens and great tee boxes, was designed in 1990 by touring pro Mark McCumber. Host for the past two years of the PGA Tour, the links-style challenge is set among Georgia pines, pristine salt marshes and fantastic natural beauty. Sculptured wide fairways are not too severe a test, but stay clear of the 81 wide, steep bunkers. Large undulating greens add to the fun you will have playing at one of the most picturesque and challenging courses in the Southeast.

Daily Rates:

Tuesday-Friday. $44.52
Weekends/Holidays $49.82

From the Tips:

Yardage   6791
Rating   73.0
Slope   130
Par   72

Features/Amenities:

Championship 18-Hole Course
PGA Instruction

Golf Tips

These golfing tips, if followed religiously, will greatly enhance your Georgia golfing pleasures and assure your place in the golf course owners "Player's Hall of Fame."

1. Never hit (or swing your club) unless you know 100% that the way is clear.

2. Never throw a club or smash it into the turf. Golf is difficult and everyone misses the occasional shot. Play smartly and quietly.

3. Always repair at least two ball marks on greens, rake bunkers and repair your fairway divots.

4. Never retrieve your ball from the cup with anything but your hand.

5. Play fast and pick up at your eighth, ninth or tenth stroke per hole. The higher your handicap, the faster you should play.

6. If you want to play to your best, don't consume alcohol during a round. Less than one player in 10,000 improves with alcohol.

7. Yell "fore" if your struck ball is even remotely approaching any person.

8. Before departing for the course, relax; check your gear and attire; then be sure to arrive an hour before your tee time; stretch, warm up, and practice your short game. Leave work at the office including your cellular.

9. Always keep carts away from greens and bunkers and observe the 90 degree rule where applicable.

10. Treat the course as you would your own fiefdom, leaving it in better shape than you found it.

11. Be alert to sun, lightning, wayward shots and adventurous bets.

12. Before you tee off, read the score card and any info in the golf cart.

SECTION X
Shopping Atlanta

Commentary

(See also Bookstores and
Art Galleries in Section V.)

Atlanta's retail markets are booming. If you can't find it in Atlanta, perhaps it doesn't exist. From the malls and markets to the specialty shops and areas, its all a mecca for the South's serious shoppers. It's all here, from mega-malls such as **Lenox Square**, **Phipps Plaza**, **Perimeter Mall** and the **Galleria** to that nearly extinct species of mercantilism known as the general store.

Rich's is Atlanta's homegrown department store, opened by Morris Rich in 1867. You'll find Rich's still thriving, but its got plenty of competitive company from the likes of **Lord and Taylor**, **Saks Fifth Avenue**, **Nieman-Marcus**, **Macy's** and **Parisian**. But, don't forget to leave plenty of time to shop the neighborhoods and the specialty stores and malls where there's plenty of fun and treasure to be found. View the antiques and experience the rural charm of Chamblee and Roswell, check-out the trendy shops and restaurants of Virginia-Highlands and Little Five Points and experience the excitement of downtown **Atlanta's Underground**, **Peachtree Center** and the futuristically designed **Rio**. In fact, almost everywhere you drive or MARTA you'll be sure to discover friendly shops, splendid neighborhoods and hordes of treasure.

Ancient Prices

Before you venture forth entertain for a moment what it would be like to journey back to the year 1850. Prices sure seemed a lot lower. A pair of suspenders went for $.12, a thimble for $.06, a ladies saddle for $11.00, a toothbrush for $.12. Scissors cost $.30, ink $.10, a dictionary or hymn book $.30, and a shovel for a $1.00. You could get an overcoat and Panama hat for $10.00 and a lb. of nails for a dime. Sugar and coffee went for about $.12 a lb. and a reasonably fit horse went for $35.00. But, before you cry remember this, there really wasn't much variety and, if you could find a job, it took about two days to earn a dollar, or a days labor equalled about 6 1/2 thimbles.

Atlanta's Fine Shopping Malls

Downtown's Underground Atlanta, at Peachtree and Alabama Sts., has been evolving since 1890, long before anyone ever conceived of a shopping mall. It was entirely renovated in 1989 and is now home to a zillion shops and restaurants. The food court has a good mix of ethnic and fast food. The open-air Kenny's Alley is a courtyard of bars and restaurants. Heritage Row is a chronological documentary of Atlanta's history from past to present, and the Olympic Experience honors the 1996 Summer Olympic Games. 523-2311.

The Mall at Downtown's Peachtree Center, located at Peachtree St. and International Blvd., is the retail component of the huge Peachtree Center complex designed by famed Atlanta architect John Portman. The mall is connected by pedestrian bridges to many downtown buildings, including the Marriott Marquis, Hyatt Regency, Westin Peachtree Plaza and the Apparel and Merchandise Marts. Its 75 businesses include restaurants, fast food outlets, shops and salons. 614-5000.

Downtown's Rio Shopping Center, at the corner of Piedmont and North Aves., features a huge geodesic dome which serves to anchor this specialty mall. Shops include Tic-Tac-Toe, which sells men's and women's hats and unique T-shirts; Blue Moon at Rio, which offers original black art and fine home accessories; Crab House Restaurant; and The 3rd Act musical revue dinner theater. 874-6688

Buckhead's Lenox Square, at Peachtree and Lenox Rds., Atlanta's first, opened in 1959, expanded in 1972, 1987, 1993 and 1995 it contains 1.5 million square feet, making it Atlanta's largest. Its 200 stores, attract 14 million visitors a year. Rich's, Macy's and Neiman Marcus are the anchors. 233-6767.

Buckhead's Phipps Plaza, located at 3500 Peachtree Rd., across from Lenox Square, opened in 1969, was fully renovated 1992 and is presently anchored by Lord and Taylor, Saks Fifth Avenue and Parisian. 262-0992.

Marietta's Cumberland Mall, located on Cobb Parkway, at the intersection of I-285 and I-75, was renovated in 1989; its anchors are Rich's, Macy's, Sears, J.C. Penney and an interesting food court. 770-435-2206.

Marietta's Galleria Specialty Mall, at the intersection of I-285 and I-750, includes 32 unique, owner-operated stores, an eight-screen theater, a 108,000-square-foot exhibition hall and the Stouffer Renaissance Waverly Hotel. 770-955-9100.

Atlanta's Special Shopping Areas

Five Points/Downtown

The big Macy's store, 180 Peachtree, 221-7221, opened in 1927; its tall, chandelier-lit main floor recalls the glory days of elegant department store shopping. Underground Atlanta (see listing under malls) offers gifts at nearly every price level, beginning with the always-lively Everything's A Dollar store. At the east end of Underground, the World of Coca-Cola has a shop filled with Coke-theme gifts, 676-5151; there's no admission charge to visit the store.

Downtown's most unusual and fun stores are south of Five Points. The Five Points Flea Market, 82 Peachtree , 681-9439, is a bazaar of designer-look-alike T-shirts, gold-tone jewelry and cheap sunglasses. Scope out the bargains at Kessler's Department Store, 87 Peachtree , 525-8594; pick up that new costume or disguise at Sun Wigs, 69-B Peachtree St. , 522-0510; buy some flashy trinkets at Atlanta Gift and Novelty, 80 Peachtree St., 524-7200; and, for good luck, swing by Rondo, 171 Mitchell St. , 522-4379, and get a "Money-Drawing" or "Law Stay Away" prayer candle. For a few cents extra, the clerk will "dress" it, sprinkling your candle with glitter and a fragrant, dark green oil. And, for a perfectly charming old-fashion downtown lunch, stop into Tasty Town Grill, 67 Forsyth St. 522-8565.

Especially during the day, downtown is relatively safe; but use the same precautions you would in any large city. Watch your belongings, and don't talk to strangers.

Little Five Points

The area around the intersection of Moreland, Euclid and McLendon avenues is Little Five Points. It's rather like Atlanta's answer to New York's East Village; hip, funky and artistic. The district's many old storefront make it a favorite location site for movies and TV: Most memorably, this was where Morgan Freeman drove Jessica Tandy to the store in Driving Miss Daisy. The part of the Piggly-Wiggly was portrayed by Sevananda Natural Foods Community-Owned Grocery, 1111 Euclid, 681-2831. Other fun stores include: Wish, high-style hip-hop wear, 447 Moreland,

880-0402; Throb, shiny club wear and accessories, 1140 Euclid, 522-0355; Boomerang, terrific '50s and '60s-style furniture, 1145 Euclid, 577-8158, and Junkman's Daughter, new and used club wear and novelties, 464 Moreland, 577-3188. Little Five is served by the Inman Park/Reynoldstown MARTA station. From the station walk north on Hurt, then right on Euclid (about six blocks); or take the 48 Lenox bus.

Buckhead

Buckhead retailing is dominated by the huge malls Lenox Square and Phipps Plaza, but there are also plenty of small shops with unusual merchandise. The heart of Buckhead is the intersection of Peachtree and Roswell Rds., but the district covers a big area. A few of the shops in Buckhead include: Axis Twenty, 200 Peachtree Hills Avenue, 261-4022, selling 20th-century classic furniture; Play It Again, 273 Buckhead Avenue, 261-2135, better secondhand women's apparel; Laura Ashley Home Store, 1 West Paces Ferry Rd., 842-0102, home furnishings and fabrics; Beverly Bremer Silver Shop, 3163 Peachtree Rd., 261-4009; Pepperidge Farm Thrift Store, 318 Pharr Rd., 262-7580; and Beverly Hall Furniture Galleries, 2789 Piedmont Rd., 261-7580.

Virginia-Highlands

You'll see plenty of interesting retail and street life in the Virginia-Highlands section. There's a cluster of shops and restaurants on N. Highland Avenue near the intersection of St. Charles Avenue and another half-mile north near the intersection of Virginia Avenue. The last shopping section is at the intersection of N. Highland and Lanier Boulevard, after which the neighborhood is all residential. Some interesting shops: 20th Century Antiques, home furnishings, gifts and accessories from around the world, 1044 N. Highland Avenue, 892-2065; Earth Baby, organic cotton clothing for babies and children, wooden toys and rattles and organic baby food, 776-B N. Highland Avenue, 607-1656; Back to Square One, antiques, handmade crafts by regional artists for the home and garden, 1054 N. Highland Avenue, 815-9970; Bang! and Rapture featuring modern men's and women's apparel, 1039 N. Highland, 873-0444; Maddix Deluxe with flowers and gifts, 1034 N. Highland, 892-9337; Bill Hallman Designs offering hip clothes for men and women, 876-6055; The Common Pond, 1402 N. Highland Avenue, 876-6368, specializing in environmental friendly gifts for people and their pets.

Amsterdam Avenue

Monroe Drive intersects with Amsterdam Avenue about a half-mile north of the corner of Monroe and Virginia. Turn left; at the end of this dead-end street you'll find an eclectic mix of off-price and specialty shops, including Shoemaker's Warehouse, 881-9301; Malepak, 892-8004, with bodybuilder wear; and Let The Music Play, 892-6700, a mecca for nightclub DJs.

Buford Highway

Thanks to a large concentration of apartment complexes, Buford Highway is home to many international Atlantans, especially people from Central and South America and Asia. The stretch of Buford Highway between Shallowford Rd. and the Perimeter has dozens of Asian stores, restaurants and service companies. Little Szechuan is highly recommended for spicy Szechuan cuisine, 5091-C Buford Highway, 451-0192. Korean-influenced Chinese food is the specialty at Pung-Mie, 5145 Buford Highway, 455-0435. In Asian Square Shopping Center, 5150 Buford Highway, the major tenant is 99 Ranch Market, 458-8899, a full-size supermarket packed with amazing Asian products.

Chattahoochee Avenue Warehouse Shopping District

On the west side of town off Howell Mill Rd., bargains abound in the Chattahoochee Avenue warehouse shopping district. Freedman Shoes, 1240 Chattahoochee Avenue, 355-9009, offers discounts on name-brand men's shoes. LoLo, 935-D Chattahoochee Avenue, 352-9355, discounts women's apparel. AJS Shoe Warehouse, 1788 Ellsworth Industrial Boulevard, 355-1760, offers deals on women's shoes, handbags and accessories. K & G Men's Center, 1750-A Ellsworth Industrial Boulevard, 352-3527, discounts men's wear.

Stone Mountain

Eagle's Nest Gifts
In a house built in 1847, this shop offers a variety of unusual gifts and collectibles. You'll find Baldwin brass candle holders, designer baskets of willow and pine and handmade treasure boxes from Vintage Lumber made by Georgia artisans. Eagle's Nest has plenty of hand carved miniatures, leaded glass crystal, antique furnishings, Georgia honey and peach spreads. It's closed on Mondays January through March. Located on 994 Main St., 770-498-9078

Grandma's Stuff
This charming shop, situated in the Eagle's Nest (described previously), is chock-full of affordable country and primitive antiques. The owner chooses each piece personally and in most cases can provide buyers with detailed background information on the store's wide array of accessories and small furniture pieces. Unusual quilts, one-drawer stands and wooden boxes are among the finds here. This shop is closed on Mondays from January through March.

Stones
With an array of semi-precious stones, this store offers several ways to adorn yourself. You can make your own jewelry from loose beads. Choose from the pieces on display, or let the owners do the work on a custom-designed pin or pair of earrings. Repair services and jewelry classes are offered. Located on 955 Main St., 469-5536

Kelly Kaye's
Choose from around 400 handbags and travel cases made of 100-percent leather. The items originate in Mexico and sell in the $20 range. Souvenir T-shirts, other apparel, costume jewelry, sunglasses, umbrellas and more complete the wares. Located on 913-C Main St., 469-0779

Country Manor
Very traditional Southern antiques and decorative pieces abound here. Among them are local folk art pieces, such as bird houses and wood carvings. Gift items include Rowe pottery, hand-carved wooden decoys and Bob Timberlake furniture and accessories. Located on 933 Main St., 498-0628

Maxwell's
Collectibles, gourmet specialties, gift items and greeting cards comprise the unique merchandise in Maxwell's two locations. One popular feature is the very large selection of seasonally oriented decorations. You'll find many items for the garden, such as wind chimes, bird feeders and statuary. For collectors, the store carries a significant selection of Precious Moments, Harbor Light and Department 56. Angel-motif gifts include everything from lapel pins to figurines. A second store is at 1715 Howell Mill Rd., 351-3931. Located on 5367-A E. Mountain St., 879-4797

Special Stores and Places to Shop

Accessories

Antiques From Around The World- Bennett St. and Beyond Midtown's Bennett St.

BJ's Hats & Accessories
Dunwoody. 1213 Dunbrooke Lane.
Treat yourself to an unique shopping experience of exquisite designer merchandise. A wonderful selection of styles, and easy on the pocketbook. 394-3557.

Lalo
Buckhead. 134 E. Andrews Dr.
Imagine, the luxury of beautiful leather Italian and French handbags for only a fraction of the price you would expect. Let's see, one leather briefcase for work, one casual sporty looks, one bejeweled evening clutch for that little evening gown... 233-9675.

Mori Luggage
Buckhead. 2385 Peachtree Rd.
Since 1971 travelers and business people have found more than 40 lines of luggage and 300 business cases from top-quality makers in this specialty store. 231-2146.

Puttin' On The Glitz
Downtown. 233 Peachtree St. #B-33
Unusual fashion jewelry, sterling silver jewelry and accessories. 525-0624.

Stone Mountain Handbags
Stone Mountain Village. 963 Main St.
Made right here in Georgia, gorgeous first quality, leather bags. Owned and operated by the manufacturer, you will delightfully surprised to see a fine selection of handbags, briefcases and accessories. 770-498-1316.

Tic-Tac-Toe
Midtown. Rio Shopping Center. 595 Piedmont Ave.
Hats for every occasion; baseball caps, romantic hats, European-style berets, straw beach hats or safari hats. And hats to make your own occasion. 888-0118.

Out of the Woods
22-B Bennett St.
Experience "art shopping" showcasing artwork from contemporary and ancient cultures, to wear, to use, and to accent the home. Owner Deb Douglas selects the item's artistic merit, cultural or historical significance, accessibility and price. The scope of the gallery includes furniture, sculptures, paintings, jewelry, decorative accessories and unusual gifts from the U.S. and throughout the world. Here the buyer will experience comfortable environment and affordable good art. 351-0446.

Kilim Collection
22 Bennett St.
Treasure the colors of mother nature with a one-of-a-kind kilim flat weave carpet and pillows. Handwoven by nomadic tribes of Turkey, these all wool rugs come in a multitude of sizes and colors. Highly prized for their warmth of color and rich texture, these old world tapestries will make your home a place of luxury and comfort. Old World beauty, you'll be delighted by the prices. 351-1110.

John Overton Oriental Rugs and Antiques
25 Bennett St.
A wealth of luxurious oriental rugs will welcome the most discriminate of shoppers. John Overton's carpet experience specializes in handmade antique rugs from the Orient, Persia and Turkey. Enhance the beauty of your home or office, with the rich luxury of colors and design. Known as a "decorator's source", John will help and steer you to create he right essence. 355-9535.

The Stalls
116 Bennett St.
At the end of Atlanta's favorite Bennett Street

you will find an eclectic display of many stalls displaying American and European antiques, home accessories and decorative arts. From the whimsical antique jewelry and tureens, to the antique period pieces and hand-fashioned linens. Spacious, affordable, friendly service,and a british cafe tucked in between, will make your shopping trip a success. 352-4430.

Bittersweet, Ltd.
45 Bennett St.
Step back into history and surround yourself with English antique treasures large and small in this intimate shop. You discover gate leg tables, oak chests, antique decorative plates, ceramic lids and more. Explore further and a very charming Carol will enlighten this journey as you browse through more finds of sporting antiques for gentlemen, from antique golf paraphernalia to decorative walking canes. 351-6594.

Interiors Market
55 Bennett St.
Featuring 45 plus upscale antiques and decorative arts shops and a bustling cafe. Items include 18th and 19th century American, French and European antiques, rugs, paintings, primitives, imports, architectural and garden statuary. All under one roof; shop Monday through Saturday from 10-5 p.m. 352-0055.

Gallery of Ethnic Folk Art
25 Bennett St.
You can create an exotic and multi-cultural look with the help of owner Veronica Kaplan who will cultivate you on the historical ethics of her unusual folk art. Admire Amazon burden baskets, African gourds, Peruvian santos, electrifying Mexican masks, antique Tai textiles and Kuba cloth, beaded prayer bowls from the Huichol Indians, and a colorful selection of beads from South America to create your own jewelry. 352-2656.

Designer Antiques
25 Bennett St.
This antique shop was first to bring Atlanta antique european pine from England creating one of-a-kind custom made furnishings.The imported old timber is transformed into armoires, chests,tables, chairs, beds and much more. To get a better idea come and admire these pieces, you will see an excellent product at an affordable price to work magic with your existing accessories. 352-0254.

Nottingham Antiques
45 Bennett St.
Direct importers of European antique furniture and reproduction of English furniture made from antique pine wood or new woodswill give you the choice of creating anything from a nightstand to an entertainment center with table and chairs. Enhance your home joining the old with the new created by hand with timeless design. 352-1890.

Jeff Baker Clock Repair
25 Bennett St.
If your antique timepiece has squeaky arms or otherwise needs refurbishing we have found one of the rare craftsman of clock repair right here in Bennett St. His masters touch will re-energize any French, English or other european timepiece.Trust your most treasured antique in his hands and he will ensure you the exact time. 350-8301.

The Nash Collection
25 Bennett St.
For the discriminate collector that wants only the authentic, you can feast your eyes on pure antique prints. Owner Harryet Nash's will show you a selective potpourri cross section of the world with decorative antique Italian, French and Oriental prints. Also decorative handmade colored lithographs from the turn of the century would satisfy even the most critical of connoisseurs. 352-9388.

Bennett St. Gallery
22-F Bennett St.

Brighten your day by visiting this contemporary art gallery, alive with the vibrant colorful paintings of local artists, and the delicacy of hand blown glass hummingbird feeders. A happy and most unpretentious shop that has something for everyone. Make this a fun journey by choosing from quality silver sterling jewelry, unusual glass goblets, dainty perfume decanters, cheerful ceramics and more. Your choices will seem infinite. 352-8775.

Beaman Antiques
25 Bennett St.

Feast your eyes and wander through an well displayed shop of fine English 18th and 19th-century antiques. Observe linen presses and chests of rich mahogany and walnut, gilded framed mirrors, and neo-classical figurines. And if the timing is right, charming British owner, Lynford, will escort you through an ever-changing selection of glazed Georgian secretaries, twin pedestal dining sets and antique lamps. 352-1890.

Allan Arthur Oriental Rugs
25 Bennett St.

For over eight years, owner Allan Arthur, with a vast knowledge of oriental rugs, has made rug buying a enjoyable experience. You will see handmade rugs from every major rug weaving center of the world. Specializing in antique Persian rugs, antique and Deco Chinese, European tapestries and collectable central Asian pieces, all to give your home a reflection of your good taste. 350-9560.

Red River Gallery
22-G Bennett St.

Enter a most unique gallery that highlights contemporary crafts in a different sense. Featuring novel black and white ceramics and abstract paintings by owner Steve, unusual palette and knife Haitian oil paintings, eye-catching brightly colored wooden clocks, and vibrant colors of "woven" watercolors. These are just a few of ongoing production of art pieces that will reward you each time you visit the gallery. 352-5163.

Other Area Antique Outlets

Antiques of Vinings
Vinings. 4200 Paces Ferry Rd.

A wonderful little shop for fine antiques and collectibles including porcelains, Staffordshire, formal and country furniture, jewelry and much more. 434-1228.

Dupre's Antique Market
Marietta. 17 Whitlock Ave.

Forty plus dealers invite you to visit the 10,000-square-foot showroom of antiques, decorative accessories and other nostalgic memorabilia. 770-428-2667.

Red Baron's Antiques
Sandy Springs. 6450 Roswell Rd.

Quoted as "The World's Best Antique Store", 50,000-square-feet of important architectural antiques, decorative arts and collectibles. Auctions thrice yearly. 252-3770.

Roswell Clock & Antique Co.
Roswell. 955 Canton St.

Specializing in antique clock restoration since 1976. Featuring also the unique in antique furniture, paintings, porcelains and accessories. 770-992-5232.

Art Supplies

Binders
Buckhead. 2581 Piedmont Rd.

A fully-stocked store of discount art supplies from vast variety of paints, brushes, canvas and more. 233-5423

DeKalb Art Supply
Decatur. 3892 N. Druid Hills Rd.

Featuring a fine supply of calligraphy materials, clip art and art books, artists paints, brushes, canvas and fine papers. 633-7311.

Dick Blick Art Materials
Roswell. 1117 Alpharetta St.
Featuring commercial and fine art materials from easels, oils, acrylics, watercolors to drafting supplies, transfer letters and sign making supplies. 770-993-0240.

If It's Paper
Dunwoody. 8610 Roswell Rd.
Specializing in paper goods for art, business, catering, household, party and school supplies. 998-9226.

Pearl
Buckhead. 3756 Roswell Rd.
One of the largest art and craft discount centers, with a full line of art and drafting supplies and do-it-yourself framing. 233-9400.

Camera's and Supplies

Camera Bug
Midtown. Sage Hill Shopping Center. 1799 Briarcliff Rd.
For the shutterbug featuring the best in cameras, telescopes, binoculars, repairs, rentals and much more. 873-4513.

Crown Camera
Midtown. 1000 Piedmont Ave.
Personal service in camera equipment, audio visual, darkroom supplies, film developing and professional stockhouse. 873-2102.

Showcase Inc.
Buckhead. 2323 Cheshire Bridge Rd.
Stocks complete line of quality Canon cameras, lenses and accessories, with darkroom supplies and one-hour processing. 325-7676.

Wolf Camera & Video
Midtown. 150 14th St.
One of the nation's largest camera and video retailer, specializing in photo and video equipment and one hour film developing. 892-1707.
Various locations; consult your *Yellow Pages*.

Children's Clothing and Toys

Abbadabba's
Buckhead. 322 E. Paces Ferry Rd.
Sports shoes such as Converse and Teva sandals for kids. 262-3356.

Atlanta Kids Outlet Store
East Buckhead. 747 Miami Circle.
Parents and kids alike will enjoy the fashions and prices at this outlet for Frog Pond, clothing for boys and girls. This store is current with the fashions, unlike some discount stores. Have fun! 233-1353.

Caroline's
Buckhead. 99 W. Paces Ferry Rd.
Walk into a cloud of puffy white crinolines, and dresses of voile, silk and linen. Baby's to preteens will look like angels at christenings, communions or weddings. With names such as Posie's, 0Strasburg and Isabel Garreton, each individual creation is hand-cut, some smocked, in adorable designs and matching socks, bows and shoes. 364-0233.

The Children's and Prep Shop
Buckhead. 2385 Peachtree Rd.
You have a young preppy in the family? You have found the perfect look here from plaid skirts to Oxfords. 365-8496.

Coggins Shoes for Kids
Marietta. 2139 Roswell Rd.
A fully stocked shoe store for kids, from baby shoes to eight and nine-year olds. 770-973-5335.

Earth Baby
Virginia-Highlands. 776-B N. Highland Ave.
Natural and environmentally friendly, for your precious little ones. Organic cotton clothing, bedding, wooden toys, natural diapers and bath products. 607-1656.

Gazoyks
Little Five Points. 912 Austin Ave.
Specializing in educational toys and unusual

gifts such as puzzles, globes, wind-ups, rubber stamps and other gazoyknixs. 688-7735.

The Great Train Store
Alpharetta. 1000 North Point Cir. #1030
For both kids and adults alike ,"The Train Store." A fabulous selection ranging from Thomas the Tank Engine to collector-quality Lehmann Gross & Bahn trains. 770-751-0943.

Hobbit Hall Children's Bookstore
Roswell. 120 Bulloch Ave.
Kids and teens will bury their noses in books from old classics to the newest releases. 770-587-0907.

Kangaroo Pouch
Buckhead. 56 E. Andrews Dr.
Kids are looking for fun and bright colors; mom's look for value; both are here. You'll find complete one-of-a-kind outfits for school, sturdy funwear, or sassy party looks. Definitely the cutest of watercolor vinyl rain wear found anywhere, and top off your shopping trip with accessories and toys. Whether your shopping for babies or preteens, its impossible to leave this shop empty-handed. 231-1616.

Koplin's Kids
Sandy Springs. 6307A Roswell Rd.
Updated contemporary fashions for boys and girls, infant to preteens, with accessories and gift items. 303-7114.

Learningsmith
Buckhead. Phipps Plaza.
Known as an anti-toy store, instead, intelligent and creative toys, mind games, building sets and top-quality software. 364-0084.

Through The Looking Glass
Buckhead. 3802 Roswell Rd.
A wonderful collection of children's clothing and gifts, featuring a large selection of layette and baby gifts. 231-4007.

Spiffy Shoes
Buckhead. 3145 Peachtree Rd.
Fashionable shoes that spell KIDS. Excellent selection of Stride Rite, Shoebedoo, Cole-Haan, Keds and K-Swiss. 365-0746.

Zany Brainy
Sandy Springs. 6285 Roswell Rd.
Kids will forget the TV when they see a zillion educational "toys". Creative kits for infants to young teens. Chemistry sets for the scientist, clay for the artist, building sets for the architect, or software for the computer whiz. 252-3280.

Compact Discs/Cassettes/Records

Best Buy Co. Corp.
North Atlanta. Perimeter Mall.
1201 Hommond Dr.
Wide selection of all types of music on cassette and cd's with competitive prices. 392-0454.

Earwax Records
Midtown. 1052 Peachtree St.
Specializing in hip hop, R&B, reggae, jazz and classics, in records, tapes and cd's 70's to present. 875-5600.

Harrison E. Smith Record Shop Inc.
Downtown. 2472 Martin Luther King Jr. Dr.
Presenting the widest selection of gospel in Atlanta, with rhythm & blues and jazz in cassette and cd's. 696-9947.

Oxford Book Store
Buckhead. 360 Pharr Rd.
Specializing in classical and opera, with some accents on jazz, nostalgia and children's. 262-3333.

Computer Shops

CompUSA
Buckhead. 3400 Wooddale Dr.
Full-service computer store.
814-0880.

Micro Center
Marietta. 1221 Powers Ferry Rd.
Full-service computer store.
770-859-1540.

Day Spa Salons

Methode Jeanne Piaubert PariSpa
Buckhead. Phipps Plaza.
Women in Atlanta can enjoy France's most renowned authority on beauty, skin care and body treatments. 842-0011.

Spa Sydell
Buckhead. 3060 Peachtree Rd.
Make yourself look and feel good all over, with full facial and body treatments, as well as an exclusive line of skin care and body products. 237-2505.

Repose
Dunwoody. 8610 Roswell Rd.
Pamper yourself in a private and restful salon, and allow the experts to enhance skin, body and nails. 587-0480.

Natural Body
Virginia Highlands. 1403 N. Highland Ave.
Both a day-spa with full-service of personal grooming and retail store of natural make-up and products. 876-9642. In Buckhead, 237-7712.

Furriers

Avanti Furs Inc.
Norcross. 6115 Jimmy Carter Blvd.
Largest selection of furs and leathers in the Southeast. Offering also fur cleaning, restyling and storage. 770-446-0141.

Helen Frushtick Furs
Downtown. Atlanta Apparel Mart. at 250 Spring St.
Offering the finest fur apparel in the Southeast, from hats, jackets to full-length. Also a wide selection of leathers and estate jewelry. 659-2257/800-281-1533.

York Furs in Buckhead
Buckhead. 3201 Peachtree Rd.
"A safe place to buy for those who don't know furs," teamed with expertise personal service. 237-6766.

Gardening Supplies

Birdfeeders, Etc.
Dunwoody. 5495 Chamblee-Dunwoody Rd.
Fine feathered friends will seek out your garden when selecting an unusual birdhouse or bird bath. An extensive selection of designs, colors and decorative garden accessories, additional to annuals and perennials. 393-2570.

Boxwoods
Buckhead. 100 E. Andrews.
A small garden cottage beckons "green thumbs" with bright garden paintings, and unique hand-picked plants displayed in colorful ceramics and old urns. Gardener's already seek out Dan Belman's new shop, for his knowledge of plants, garden design, and exotic orchids. Wander outdoors and select from iron architectural pieces, made-to-order trellis', antique garden benches and balustrades or birdhouses, and create your own private conservatory. 233-3400.

Flowers From Holland
Buckhead. Lenox Square.
From Atlanta's freshest flower market savor the beauty of tulips from Holland, wild flowers from South Africa or orchids from Singapore. 233-0081.

Flowers From The Woods
Buckhead. 3209 Paces Ferry Pl.
Fine quality garden flowers designed with the utmost attention to the small details of creating. 848-9663.

Garden South
Lawrenceville. 950 Hwy.20 South.
Nature and garden center featuring plants, books, koi, nature tapes, wind chimes, garden tools and more stuff. 770-963-2406.

Hastings Nature & Garden Center
Buckhead, near Lenox Square. 2350 Cheshire Bridge Rd.
We found them! Aquatic gardens for your backyard, complete with large varies of fish, pumps, and choices of water lilies. Also a full-service nursery, and a musical aviary of feathered friends and bird feeders. We could go on forever. 321-6981.

Landscape Techniques
Alpharetta. 440 Fowler Rd.
Experts on landscape architecture, boulders and rock gardens, natural water features and landscape lighting. 770-751-7041.

Michal Evans
Buckhead. 34 Irby Ave.
Enjoy being seduced by fresh European flowers arranged Flemish style in a combination of urbane sophistication and elegant simplicity, spiced with a dash of casual abandon. The Michal Evans signature is recognized by a clientele that expects the finest of floral designs, displayed as if still growing in a natural environment. Known as one of the top 12 floral designers in the country, you may use the "Evans Signature" to enhance your next soiree or special event. 365-0200.

The Potted Plant
Buckhead. 3165 E. Shadowlawn Ave.
Voted as best in Atlanta, Ryan Gainey presents an original shop specializing in unique plants, decorative garden accessories, and colorful array of one of a kind of urns and cachepots. A true green haven. 233-7800.

Rocky Mountain Patio
Roswell. 5323 Roswell Rd.
Stretch and relax on the veranda or garden on patio furniture to suit any taste. From wrought iron to wicker and redwoods, it will bring a total state of relaxation. 256-0165.

Gift and Specialty Shops

Artlite
Midtown. 1851 Piedmont Rd.The greatest selection in the Southeast of complete and unique fine writing instruments, such as Waterman, Cross, Sheaffer and Mont Blanc. A treasure for executive and writer alike. 875-7271.

Beverly Bremer Silver Shop
Buckhead. 3164 Peachtree Rd.
Smile as you enter the brilliant world of silver. Be greeted by its first lady, Beverly Bremer, a gracious hostess and confessed workaholic. Forced by family hardships to sell her own silver, Beverly started out buying and selling silver at flea markets around town. Today customers and collectors from around the globe seek out the floor-to-ceiling-filled shop with 1,000+ flatware patterns, from the one missing piece to the odd fish fork or trifle tongs. While flatware is the backbone of her business, Beverly has an incredible selection of unusual old-silver goblets, tea and coffee services, carafes, candelabras, ladles, tureens, jewelry and more, each marked with the silver content in ounces. The back room is humming with silver polishers and computers serving a national clientele. Atlanta admires this famous lady who would rather own silver than IBM stock. 261-4009.

Chef
Virginia-Highlands at 1046 N. Highland Ave.
Enjoy the fragrance of 65 specialty coffees from around the world, and discover hard-to-find kitchen gadgets, cook ware and gift items. 875-CHEF.

Christmas House and Christmas Cottage
Stone Mountain Village. 987 Main St.
It's Christmas all-year-round. Gifts, decorations, and fine collectibles. 770-498-9887.

City Art Works
Buckhead. 2140 Peachtree St.
Fine hand-blown glass accessories in the form of stemware, jewelry, perfume bottles and more wonderful creations. 605-0786.

Classic Comics
Buckhead. 1860-A Piedmont Rd.
Reminisce while perusing one of the widest selection of vintage comics up to present. 892-4442.

Crystal Blue
Little Five Points. 1168 Euclid Ave.
Discover unique treasures of wind chimes, crystals, gemstone jewelry, oil, incense, fantasy gifts and books. 522-4605.

The Frabel Gallery
Buckhead. Lenox Square.
Wander about & delight while viewing the objects displayed at the world's largest and best known boron glass sculpture studio. Proprietor/artist Hans-Godo Frabel's glass sculpture are truly world class. His creations include the Magnolia Branch for former President Reagan, the life-size Hand and Crystal Keyboard for Elton John & a crystal torch for 1996 Summer Olympics. You can illuminate a special place in your home with a Frabel creation. 233-8129.

Fragile
Sandy Springs. 175 Mount Vernon Hwy.
The ultimate elegant bridal registry shop, specializing in personal service, one-of-a-kind gifts and art glass. 257-1323.

Giftissimo!
Buckhead. 3137 E. Shadowlawn Ave.
Discover the wonderful charm of France. Unique famous Gault street miniatures, artsy poupees Millet by Cerri'Art, and a fine variety of Limoge boxes to please even the most discriminating taste. 233-4563.

Hibernia
Buckhead. 2140 Peachtree Rd.
Featuring an unique showcase of contemporary handmade goods from The British Isles, from jewelry and tableware to clothing and home accessories. 351-8332.

Juan-N-Only
Buckhead. 2990 Grandview Ave.
Be mesmerized by one-of-a kind brilliantly colored, hand-carved dragons, lizards, pigs and cats to name a few of the art pieces on sale at the gallery. Owner Scott travels deep into Mexico to collect such hand-made treasures as Oaxacan wood carvings, Lacandone Indian clay figures, pottery from the Aquilar sisters, wool rugs from the Teotitlan and much, much more. Tremendous value for the artistically oriented gift giver and home decorator. 233-5826.

Juniper Tree
Marietta. 15 West Park Sq.
Selections galore from nation wide sought after Steiff collectible bears and Rick Cain wildlife sculptures to the fine American art pottery and more fine selection of American and European collectibles. 770-427-3148.

Marina's World of Collectibles
Buckhead. Phipps Plaza.
Collectibles from around the world, offering Lomonosov china, Russian lacquer boxes, icons and nesting dolls, and most unusual jewelry. 264-0111.

Old Time Pottery
Marietta. 2949 Canton Rd.
Selections galore of pottery, bric-a-brac and glassware, with a continuous flow of new inventory. "When it's gone, it's gone." 770-419-9360.

Peridot
Buckhead. 514 E. Paces Ferry Rd.
A wealth of distinctive gift ideas can be found making it impossible to leave empty-handed. A potpourri of jewelry, glassware, bath products and unique baby items and more for that special person. 261-7028.

The Plantation Shop

Buckhead. 96 E. Andrews Dr.

Located in a Victorian-style cottage. Fine gifts of antique silverware, colorful plates, gentleman's picnic baskets are just some of the selection. Not to forget locally made preserves, mustards, relishes and fragrances for well-received gifts. 841-0065.

Pure Indulgences

Buckhead. 3872 Roswell Rd.

An unexpected pleasure awaits the shopper offering skin and body care products, massage and facials service, fashionable sleep wear and gift items. 231-1005.

Taste of Britain

Norcross. 73 S. Peachtree St.

British accents throughout this specialty shop featuring fine china, foods and teas from the British Isles. Gift baskets made to your specifications. 770-242-8585.

Wow, What a Card Shop!

Downtown. Rio Shopping Center. 595 Piedmont Ave.

Now this is a card shop! Decide, it will be tough, from the largest selections of cards and gifts targeted to the "child" in every adult. Also local handmade art collectibles and Afro-centric. 897-5530.

Yanzum

Across the High Museum. 1285 Peachtree St.

Step into a soothing calm, and admire Santo's from Guatemala, oil drum art from Haiti, carved wooden animals from Oaxaca and collector quality African art in the adjoining art gallery. 874-8063.

Gourmet Savories

Alfresco

Atlanta North. Stouffer Renaissance Waverly Hotel, 2450 Galleria Pkwy.

Fabulous 24-hour deli specializing in tender carved meats, cheeses, homemade pizza's and savory desserts. 770-953-4500.

Alon's Bakery

Midtown. 659 Peachtree St.

Out of this world desserts! Atlantan's take sabbatical's from diet's just to taste assorted sinful varieties of cheesecakes,dark real chocolate cakes and ever revolving fruit cakes, tarts, and chunkiest cookies. Served with espresso or cappuccino. 724-0444.

Cafe Intermezzo

Buckhead. 1845 Peachtree Rd.

Also on the top of the best-desserts hit-parade of town with 71 varieties on display. Favorites such as Frutti di Bosco with currents and raspberries, Autumn Flower Chocolate cake and wicked Turtle Cheesecake. This cafe goes all out with its desserts. 355-0411.

Chamberlain's Gourmet Chocolatier

Dunwoody. 5527 Chamblee Dunwoody Rd.

Put your diet on hold, and visit a full-line gourmet chocolatier creating sweet delights at the premises. Freshness guaranteed, enjoy assorted and molded chocolate pieces, 18 varieties of luscious truffles, rich caramels, and the best pralines in the Southeast. Ask Mike for a taste. 394-1112.

The Dessert Place

Buckhead. 279 E. Paces Ferry Rd.

Sweets lovers have taken been pleasure for 15 delicious years sampling cream cheese brownies, wonderful cheesecakes and...see for yourself. 233-2331.

The Easy Way Out

Buckhead. 2449 Peachtree Rd.

Yes, you can savor regional and continental cuisine in your own home. For ten years, owner Jane Long, and her five chefs have prepared delicious menu's for you, the busy but discriminating food lover. A complete take home supper shop with carefully prepared favorites made in limited quantities to ensure freshness. Enjoy a cool gazpacho, flavorful Indonesian wild rice, elegant deviled crab, or curried chicken salad, to mention a few. Complement this menu with a select bottle of wine and sinful chocolate mousse or a pecan pie, and you have truly taken the easy way out. 262-9944.

Heavenly Ham
Buckhead. 3167 Peachtree Rd.
Atlanta's best savory spiral-sliced glazed hams, smoked turkeys, steaks, bacon and gift baskets.

Henri's Bakery
Buckhead. 61 Irby Ave.
Voted year after year as best bakery and deli since 1929.Some of the bakery's delicious signature items are chocolate eclairs, brownies and of course fresh-baked breads. 237-0202.

J. Martinez & Company
Buckhead. 3230-A Peachtree Rd.
Offering discriminating connoisseurs an extensive selection of fresh coffees and spices. Nationally recognized coffee merchant for over a century, the Martinez family offers estate grown coffees such as Sumatran Luak, Jamaica Blue Mountain and Hawaiian Kona, and of course accompanying coffee paraphernalia. 231-5465.

Kitchen Fare
Buckhead. 2385 Peachtree Rd.
Atlanta's premier cooking supply shop offers wonderful paraphernalia in a "kitchen hardware store." You can't boil water? You will, with in-house cooking classes, the right cookbook and Magnalite Professionale cookware. The professional chef, can select from steamers, pasta cookers, shredders, quality knives and European linen tea towels. Any pastry chef can whip up a delight from a multitude of sizes and shapes of bakeware pans, molds and cutters, as the gourmet can choose from premium oils, balsamic vinegars, pasta's and mustards. No matter how small, a corn skewer or large, espresso machine, you'll find it at Kitchen Fare. 233-0289.

Maxwell's Fine Foods Market
Dunwoody. 5488 Chamblee Dunwoody Rd.
Specialty groceries and hard to find gourmet items, together with fine wines and custom catering is what Maxwell's all about. 396-6410.

Pano's Food Shop
Buckhead. 265 Pharr Rd.
One stop should do it taking home freshly prepared seafood, meat, full entrees, desserts, breads and wines.

Strictly Georgia, Inc.
Marietta/East Cobb. 878 Waterford Green.
An intimate shop with Georgia products, tasty preserves, pecan brittle, and Georgia clay products. Gift baskets are available. 770-998-3554.

Swan Coach House
Atlanta History Center. 3130 Slaton Dr.
One of Atlanta's most favorite places, combining a unique tearoom, with an gift shop with Georgian delicacies and art gallery exhibiting fine and contemporary art. 261-0224,

Touch of Georgia
Downtown. 225 Peachtree St.
A perfect shop to enjoy delectable Georgia products for yourself or as a gift. An assortment of peach scents, specialty jams and condiments, decorative wreaths and *Gone with the Wind* memorabilia. Serving Atlanta with five more locations. 577-6681.

Hair Salons

Daweeds of Buckhead
Buckhead. 1935 Peachtree St.
Some of Atlanta's hottest hair designers bring their vast salon experience to the heart of Buckhead. This full-service, upscale, salon delivers precision cuts, hair coloring, perms and corrective relaxers. Their logo is "healthy and shiny hair" matched with skin, nail and massage therapy for total relaxation and comfort. Trust your hair to their creative hands. 355-3440.

Fugi

Buckhead. 3060 Peachtree Rd.

Award-winning salon has created good looks for men and women since 1974, for hair, nails and skin. 231-1774.

Joseph's Salon

Buckhead. 3201 Paces Ferry Pl.

Young at heart and vibrant, owner Joseph Roybal, continues a 19-years of service in the heart of Buckhead. Known as a national expert in hair, skin care, make-up and innovative coloring, woman beat a path to the salon. Experts without being stuffy assure your satisfaction. Co-owner Richie Arpino has a new following of well-knows such as Julia Roberts and Darryl Hannah who know where hair is number one. 231-5092.

Also in Marietta at 625-B Johnson Ferry Rd. 770-973-2471.

Van Michael Salon

Buckhead. 39 W. Paces Ferry Rd. 237-4664.

Philip John Salon

Buckhead. 2282 Peachtree Rd.

Philip John and wife Nina will welcome you to Atlanta's first fresh air full-service salon. Skylights and glass French doors give customers a fresh air salon environment. The styling room is active and upbeat while such services as massage and skin care are conducted with privacy. Their bilingual talented staff are attuned to professional pampering. 351-2289.

Health Food Stores

Life's Essentials Market

Downtown. 1388 Ralph David Abernathy Blvd.

Featuring over 500 herbs and spices, vitamins, organic vegetables and fruits, nuts, grains, diet products and books. 753-2269.

Return To Eden

North Atlanta. 2335 Cheshire Bridge Rd.

A complete vegetarian supermarket with many choices of cheese, yogurt, veggie deli meats, breads, organic fruits and vegetables spices and more. 320-EDEN

Sevanada

Little Five Points. 1111 Euclid Ave.

The oldest and largest natural co-op food store in the Southeast, presenting the most complete selection of natural foods and organic foods in the region. 681-2831.

Home Furnishings

C'est Moi

Marietta. 1100 Johnson Ferry Rd.

Beautiful American and European home accessories, china, glassware, bed and bathroom accessories. 770-977-8468.

Chandler Hagelman Ltd.

Buckhead. 12 Kings Circle.

Pleasant dreams can be bought in a small exquisite linen shop. European bed and table linens, with names such as Puymorin, Vis A Vis, and Oliver Desforges. Each incorporating their trademark with color, unique embroidery and innovative designs. 509-8528.

Charles Willis of Atlanta

Buckhead. 465 E. Paces Ferry Rd.

Choose from over 350 patterns and dish out atmosphere selecting from delicate Limoges, mix and match colorful place settings from Portugal or Italy, or casual looks from an extensive selection. 233-9487.

Garson Goodman

Buckhead. 1244 W. Paces Ferry Rd.

Any table would be thrilled to be set with hand-painted porcelain from Dominique Paramythiotis, fine European linens, and unique gifts collected from travels around the world. 841-9111.

Georgia Lighting

Midtown. 530 Fourteenth St.

For over thirty years customers in Georgia

have enjoyed quality lighting. The brilliance of chandeliers, traditional sconces, sleek modern looks, handsome hand-polished solid brass to Victorian reproductions, light up your life. 875-4754.

The Heirloom
Marietta. 65 Church St.
Handmade iron and brass beds built in the South to last for generations. Choose from an multitude of styles and finishes creating an harmonious and private sanctuary. 770-514-0556.

The Home Store Futon Gallery
Little Five Points. 1154 Euclid Ave.
Futons from A to Z satisfying every taste, featuring solid woods and quality workmanship. Also convertibles, lighting and accessories. 586-9647.

Horizon Pacific Home
Northside area at 1775 Commerce Dr.
Fabulous antiques, custom upholstery, handmade oriental rugs, antique carpets, and a hodgepodge of accessories make Horizon Pacific Home one of the most eclectic home furnishings stores in the entire Southeast. It's 40,000 square feet of home furnishings nirvana. This store is the maker as well as the retailer, which means great prices every day of the year! Located just off I-75 and Northside Drive, near the Chattahoochee shopping district, Horizon Pacific Home is just minutes from downtown Atlanta. Phone for directions. 352-9990.

Intimate Home
Buckhead. Phipps Plaza.
A delightful store of European bed and table linens, French towels and other home accessories. 261-9555.

The Linen Loft
Marietta. Akers Mill Square. 2971 Cobb Pkwy.
The connoisseur of fine linens will appreciate the pure cotton and linen bedding from Europe. With additional boudoir luxury of

goose down comforters and pillows, wool blankets and cozy robes. 770-952-7558.

Progressive Lighting
Roswell. 11580 Alpharetta Hwy.
Brilliance spells chandeliers. Be dazzled by chandeliers of unique alabaster, crystal with gold finish, polished brass, or wrought iron from Spain. Selecting a style from traditional to contemporary to grace any home will be easy at any of the nine showrooms available. 475-9987.

Jewelry

AdaMark Silversmiths Jewelers
Sandy Springs. 6136 Roswell Rd.
Specializing in silver jewelry, antique and estate jewelry, with the expertise of restoration, replating and repairs. 252-1185.

Maier & Berkele
Buckhead. 3225 Peachtree St.
Savor the brilliance of diamonds, the satiny luster of the finest Mikimoto's pearls, the warm radiance of 14-carat and 18-carat gold, and exquisite time pieces such as Rolex, Tissot and Omega. These are some of an captivating selection at Maier & Berkele, Jewelers to the South since 1887. Family owned, Frank Maier Jr. travels the world to bring you the finest quality jewelry. Winners of numerous jewelry design awards, and honored owner of the fabled Faberge Olympic Egg, you will see exceptional works of art, many one-of-kind, treasured for their perfection. The expertly trained staff will guide your selections, a full-service estate department handles appraisals, and Swiss-trained watch specialists assure the precision of your timepiece. 261-4911.

Reed Savage Vintage Jewelry
Buckhead. 110 E. Andrews Dr.
Sought out by the discerning, this tucked-away little shop is a treasure trove of one-of-a-kind vintage jewelry. The largest store in Georgia of it's kind has placed many a smile

on the faces of a shopper looking for a specific diamond ring or sophisticated platinum treasure. Peruse and find exotic Oriental accessories, charismatic rare watches and bejeweled pins. 262-3439.

Richters
Buckhead. 87 W. Paces Ferry Rd.
Known as one of the oldest estate jewelers in the country featuring exquisite 20th century period jewelry with accents on Art Deco. 262-2070.

Tracy Southwest
Buckhead. Phipps Plaza.
If you love the cool sleek looks of silver, you must not miss the unique sterling silver and 14-carat gold jewelry from Native American artist Ray Tracy. Authentic Southwestern jewelry capturing the beauty of the Southwest. 237-5929.

Men's Clothing

Custom House
Marietta. Galleria Specialty Mall.
For a perfect fit, custom-made suits, sports coats, shirts and slacks are hand-made on the premises. And, yes, designer ties also. 770-980-1430.

Dagher
Buckhead. 3210 Roswell Rd.
Men's and Women's Fashions.
Dagher brings to Buckhead the finest in Euro-styled clothing. His fashion statement is simple yet sophisticated. A proffered coffee or glass of wine helps produce a fun and relaxed atmosphere. See for yourself why his customers say, "It's definitely Dagher's." 816-2772.

Formal Atlanta
Buckhead. Lenox Square.
The complete men's formal store from suits, shirts, to cummerbunds, cufflinks and the best place for suspenders. Rental suits also available. 237-8340.

Guffey's
Buckhead. 3340 Peachtree Rd.

Full-service men's store, of traditional clothing and accessories. Including suits from Hickey Freeman and Ikebehar shirts, and shoes from Cole-Haan. 231-0044.
North Atlanta. Galleria Specialty Mall. 1 Galleria Pkwy. 770-955-0500.

International Man
Buckhead. Phipps Plaza.
An Atlanta-based boutique, specializing in fashion design for professional men. 841-0770.

Marco Polo
Buckhead. 3112 Roswell Rd.
One of Atlanta's finest specialty clothiers for the professional man presents Italian suits with style, such as Antonio Baldan and Giane-Franco-Ferrie. Not to be found in the malls; discover fine European tailoring. Have a cappuccino and calculate your next choice of combed cotton shirts in a variety of styles and natural colors, accompanied by quality footwear by A. Testoni. Receive personalized service with husband and wife team, Imad and Inaya, who may even share the names of their favorite restaurants with you. 233-1044.

Muse's
Buckhead. Phipps Plaza
Atlanta's oldest and finest clothier offers casual, career and leisure wear for men and women. 364-6748.

Men's Shoes

Bennie's Shoes
Buckhead. 2581 Piedmont Rd.
Much awarded and family owned since 1909, men's top-quality discount dress shoes such as Allen-Edmonds and Rockport from a vast selection, combined with personal service and complete family shoe repair. 262-1966.

Bill Hallman Shoes
Virginia Highlands. 776 N. Highland Ave.
For the modern man who is looking for the unusual and funky, yet the contemporary boot

or club shoe. Names such as Georgia Boots, Steve Madden, Luichiny and more. 607-1171.

Bob Ellis
Buckhead. Phipps Plaza.
One of Atlanta's best footwear shops from the worlds greatest designers. For any occasion, simple classic black or velvet pump to an eye-popping trendy design, Bob Ellis shoes complete the look. 841-0215.

Friedman's Shoes
Downtown. 209 Mitchell St.
Open since 1929, Atlanta's first men's discount store still specializes in customer service and low prices. Look for Friedman's own label of wingtips and tassels, also Rockport, Docksiders, or Steeple Gate, to name a few. 523-1134.

Newsstands

Borders Book Shop
Another of Atlanta's terrific book emporiums that features a vast array of national, local and international magazines and newspapers. 3655 Roswell Rd. 237-0707.

Oxford Books
Newspapers and magazines of every ilk, national, local and international can be found at this fantastic bookstore.
360 Pharr Rd. 262-3333.

Eastern Newsstand Corp.
Operates more than a half-dozen newsstands throughout the metro Atlanta area. 659-5670.
Lobby locations are:
Downtown. 100 Peachtree St.
Downtown. 133 Peachtree St.
Downtown. 231 Peachtree St.
Buckhead. 3495 Piedmont Rd.
Buckhead. 950 E. Paces Ferry Rd.

Tower Lobby Shops
Call their main office. 804-9151.

U.S. News Inc.
Two Peachtree locations: 1100 and 1201 Peachtree St.

Office Supplies

Office Depot
Buckhead. 2581 Piedmont Rd.
Complete office supply store of furniture, business machines, office products and business service center. Various locations, check yellow pages. 261-4111.

Office Max, Inc.
Buckhead. 3183 Peachtree Rd.
Supplying Atlanta with a fully-stocked store of office supplies. 266-2552.

Sandy Springs Office Supply
Sandy Springs. 6126 Roswell Rd.
Office supplies and discounted furniture, computer supplies, copying, fax, notary, business cards, ribbons, seals etc. 255-6670.

Pharmacies

Eckerds
Zillions of locations. Consult your *Yellow Pages* for the location nearest you.

Sporting Goods

Breyer's Golf
Kennesaw. 440 Ernest W. Barrett Pkwy.
Quality Pro-Line golf equipment and apparel, accessories, custom club fitting, gifts and in-house club repair. 770-590-7990.

The Classic Angler
Buckhead. 35 E. Paces Ferry Rd.
Fish will swim out to you when they see the professional "line" of Thomas & Thomas equipment. One stop is all, for fly-fishing needs from the rods to clothing. 233-5110.

Golf Warehouse
Norcross. I-85 to exit 38,
Indian Trail Access Rd.
A hole-in-one when you visit the 22,000 sq.
ft. showroom. Offering the widest range of
golf shoes, golf bags and 200 different sets of
clubs for a par three price. 770-447-4653.

Identified Flying Objects
Little Five Points. 1164 Euclid Ave.
The ultimate shop for the frisbee expert, also
kite's and boomerangs. 524-4628.

International Golf Discount
Roswell. 10701 Alpharetta Hwy.
True discount prices on quality golf equipment and accessories. All major brands in
stock. 770-640-8111.

Outback Outfitters
Little Five Points. 1125 Euclid Ave.
Without a doubt, Atlanta's best selection of
ATB's accessories and cycling apparel. Com-
plete backpacking gear, outdoor clothing and
rugged footwear.

Peter Glenn of Vermont
North Atlanta. Galleria Specialty Mall.
One Galleria Pkwy.
Specializing in snow skiing equipment, clothing and accessories for the whole family, also
waterski equipment and in-line skates.
770-951-0151.

Pro Golf Discount
Marietta. 1671 Cobb Pkwy.
Great savings on top name products, fully
stocked golf shop, club rentals, club repairs
and swing analyzer. 770-955-9500.

Sports Centre Warehouse
Midtown. 1708 DeFoor Pl.
No matter what you are looking for, it's here.
From hats, shorts, pennants to collectibles
from NFL, NBA, World Series, Olympics and
much more. 355-8788.

Supermarkets

Very competitive. Our favorites are Kroger,
Harris Teeter and Winn-Dixie. Consult your
Yellow Pages for complete listings.

Women's Clothing

... and Baby Makes Three
Buckhead. 56 E. Andrews Dr.
New mom's to be, we've found a store that is
fresh, fun and a must for the vanishing waist.
No frumpy maternity looks here; instead
you'll find a perfect little black dress, a fashionable business suit, and drawstring pants
with a vest or jacket. A most helpful staff will
help you find that perfect accessory or romantic evening wear. 261-4711.

Atlanta Beach
Buckhead. 3145 Peachtree Rd.
Show off your best assets and choose from the
largest selection of swimwear in Atlanta. A
broad selection of one-of-a-kind suits from
high fashion designer styles to the separate
and mix and match two-piece. You will make
a fashion splash. 239-0612.

Barami
North Atlanta. Perimeter Mall at 4400 Ashford-Dunwoody.
Career wear focusing on contemporary looks
with classic accents, in a wide range of styles,
sizes 0-12. 770-399-6500.

Bill Hallman Boutique
Virginia-Highlands. 792 N. Highland Ave.
The cutting edge of fashion makes local designer Bill Hallman much sought after by the
unisex crowd. Bill's designs are marketed
worldwide, and many visitors seek out his
boutique for it's cotton zip jackets, satin baby
doll dresses, vinyl and lurex club wear, and
cool casual tops, at all times keeping you one
step ahead of fast fashion. For casual and fun

looks, or electrifying club wear, this boutique is a must. 876-6055

Bonnie White
Buckhead. 87 W. Paces Ferry Rd.
Since 1978 modern women in Atlanta have enjoyed the most fashionable and wearable clothes presented by vivacious owner Bonnie White. There is Bonnie White Expressions at Phipps Plaza presenting timeless fashions to the sophisticate woman; BW Lifestyles in Perimeter Mall offers a fine selection of the casual look; and the BW Platinum Collection at 87 W. Paces Ferry Rd., is created for discerning women who want attentive personal service. Offering creative fashions from casual, business to formal, and also distinctive gifts, accessories and unique home furnishings from around the world. Create your own personal style while pampered by the staff's high caliber personalized service. 233-7234.

Canyon
Buckhead. Phipps Plaza.
The one classic that never goes out of style, The Jean. Popular labels such as Big Star and Diesel, from slim to shapely, with a true fit. Plus, have a look at the Betsey Johnson dresses. 364-0427.

Celebrity
Buckhead. 99 W. Paces Ferry Rd.
Celebrity presents fashion gowns for special events from charity balls to mother of the bride. Devoted to the total you in every sense, select from influential designers such as Mary McFadden, James Benjamin or Susan Perkins. Each designer creates the elegant and unique with 4-ply silks, satins, brocade and lace. Your wardrobe will shine with added sparkle with the addition of one-of-a-kind simple silk suits, elaborate gold-threaded gowns and splendid embroidered jackets. 237-5565.

Cornelia Powell
Buckhead. 271-B E. Paces Ferry Rd.
For the romantic this small shop is for you. Know for its vintage clothing and accessories.

Treasured antique lace dresses, jewelry, linens and bridal accessories. 365-8511.

Earth Angel
Virginia Highlands. 1196 N. Highland Ave.
Feel like an angel in beautiful creations of sheer fabrics, delicate lace and soft hues of colors. 605-7755.

Impressions
Buckhead. 99 W. Paces Ferry Rd.
Selected as one of the top ten true bridal salons, owner Joan Ellis presents a distinguished, spacious, salon for the woman who appreciates world-class evening gowns; exclusive designs by Vera Wang, and the best in bridal design by Helen Morley. Expect service to the extreme from a knowledgeable staff. 841-6202.

MEAJ
Buckhead. 3112 Roswell Rd.
Look no further for haute couture custom made designs and reproductions. With an strong European background, Atlanta's mother and daughter team Evie Wallace and Jennifer Thomsen bring European one-of-a-kind designs from young promising designers such as Garfield and Marks, and in-house designer Alix G. Michel designs ready-to-wear and evening wear with hand-painted organza and hand-beading. A fashionable statement can also be made with Kate Pendleton's silk scarves, and jewelry designed for nobility by Countess Zoltowska. Create excitement with your wardrobe, for a fraction of the typical price. 261-8833.

Patchington
Roswell. 690 Holcomb Bridge Rd.
Private label fashions for the distinctive and career oriented women. 770-643-9414.

Pink Flamingos
Little Five Points. 1166 Euclid Ave.
Modern clothing for everyone, by designers Betsey Johnson and Urban OutFitters, unusual jewelry and reasonably priced shoes.

Precious Things
Buckhead. 99 W. Paces Ferry Rd.
Romance and beauty and the thrill of discovery await you in this elegant specialty shop. Find a precious collection of affordable satin and silk lingerie, priceless imported linens for bed and table, with designer bed and bath accessories. Choose from samples of spreads, covers and linens customizing to your needs. And brides will find a memorable trousseau selection teamed with a full monogram service for towels, all in a personal and friendly atmosphere. 233-8617.

Rene Rene
Little Five Points. 1142 Euclid Ave.
Nationally known, and voted "Atlanta's Best" by Atlanta Magazine, Atlanta designer Rene Sanning fashions are inspired by the past restored into modern looks. A must see store. 522-RENE.

Rexer-Parkes
Buckhead. 2140 Peachtree Rd.
Atlanta's own New York style shop with an Southern flavor. Many of the fashions are one of a kind, from snappy casuals, business suits to a striking cocktail gown. 351-3080.

Sasha Frisson
Buckhead. 3094 E. Shadowlawn Ave.
An ultra-sophisticated boutique featuring American and international haute couture designer collections from casual to evening attire. 231-0393.

Texanne
Little Five Points. 1145 Euclid Ave.
For the country and western gals, located inside Boomerang, you don't have to be Tanya Tucker to afford handmade designed Western shirts, vests and jewelry to boot! 577-8158.

Tootsies
Buckhead. Phipps Plaza.
Contemporary and career ladies apparel, bridge to designer prices, sizes 2-14, with fine selection of footwear. 842-9990.

Tracy Southwest
Buckhead. Phipps Plaza.
Upscale high-fashion for women and men with an Southwestern flavor, expanding your options with jewelry and accessories. 237-5929.

White Dove
Buckhead. 18 E. Andrews Dr.
Beauty and romance is the keynote here. Find a world of crinkly chiffons, lace and silkiness. From the unusual to the classic, there are suburban soft flowing suits, bodysuits to numerous to mention, and delicate spaghetti strapped dresses and beaded Keds. You will fall in love with the lovely feminine fashions, and the warm welcome of actress/designer Earline Smith. 814-1994.

Women's Shoes

Bob Ellis
Buckhead. Phipps Plaza.
The worlds greatest footwear designs can be found at this fashionable store. 841-0215.

AJS Shoe Warehouse
Midtown. 1788 Ellsworth Industrial Blvd.
One of the best places in Atlanta for shoe bargains. From casual footwear to European designer styles. 355-1760.

Gallery Shoes
Downtown.Peachtree Center at
231 Peachtree St.
Fine selections of quality women's footwear from casual, career into evening wear. 577-7592.

The Glass Slipper
Alpharetta. 312 N. Main St.
Atlanta's only bridal shoe salon and dazzling evening footwear. 770-772-9515.

Antique and Flea Markets

Atlanta Antique Center and Flea Market
Chamblee. 5360 Peachtree Industrial Blvd.;

I-85 N. to exit 23A. Open every weekend with free parking and admission, this 80,000 square-foot market features more than 150 dealers. 770-458-0456.

Atlanta Swap Meet and Flea Market
Chamblee. 3265 Expressway Access Rd. Every Saturday and Sunday of the year the North 85 Twin Drive-In hosts this popular market where bargains abound. The drive-in is two miles inside the Perimeter on the one-way access road between Shallowford and Chamblee-Tucker roads; from Atlanta, exit at Shallowford. Park alongside the access road; admission is free. The market opens at 8:30 a.m. on Saturday and 6 a.m. on Sunday. 770-451-4570 and 233-3889.

Bargainata
Buckhead. 791 Miami Circle. This big sale comes only once a year (around the second week in November) and lasts just five days, but it always causes quite a stir. Bargainata, which marked its 25th year in 1994, is a secondhand clothing sale held by the National council of Jewish Women. The sale starts with designer and other fine apparel, priced low; by the last day, the remaining merchandise is sold off at an additional 50% discount. 262-7199.

Buford Highway Flea Market
Doraville. 5000 Buford Highway. This market features lots of designer-look goods, Atlanta souvenirs and flashy home accessories. It's open Friday, Saturday and Sunday. 770-452-7140.

Cheshire Bridge Rd.
East Buckhead. Cheshire Bridge Rd. between Piedmont and LaVista. Numerous antique dealers are scattered throughout the area, including **A Cherub's Attic**, 2179 Cheshire Bridge Rd., 634-9577; and **Milou's Market**, 1927 Cheshire Bridge Rd., 892-8296.

Gold's Antiques and Auction Gallery
Southwest Atlanta. 1149 Lee St. Gold's presents a variety of antiques Monday through Saturday. It holds an auction at 6 p.m. every Tuesday night. 753-1493.

Great Gatsby's
Chamblee. 5070 Peachtree Industrial Blvd. This 100,000-square-foot "wholesale to the public" market is one of Atlanta's most fun stores. You can spend hours ogling everything from exquisite antiques to kitschy advertising memorabilia to huge architectural fragments. Gatsby's supplies hotels worldwide with unusual furnishings; a guitar that had belonged to John Lennon was sold here at auction. 770-457-1905.

Historic Hawthorne Village Antiques and Gifts
Scottsdale. 3032 N. Decatur Rd., just east of Decatur and inside I-285. This is a sort of mini-mall offering antiques and collectibles. In addition to the main cottage store, seven shops offer their own unusual and interesting goods. The merchandise includes antique prints, framed artwork, furniture, glassware, silver, gifts, jewelry and Civil War memorabilia and books. From-time-to-time, the village delights children by staging a Victorian tea party. 294-4585.

Lamp 'N Things
Marietta at 1205 Johnson Ferry Rd., in the Woodlawn Square Shopping Center, offering thousands of lamp shades, plus lamps, mirrors, art, antiques and other home accessories. The store's personnel will also custom-make shades and lamps for individuals and decorators; also lamp repair services. 770-971-0874.

Pride of Dixie Antique Market
Norcross at the North Atlanta Trade Center. Take I-85 to exit 38; east on Indian Trail; right on Oakbrook Parkway; right on Jeurgens Court. Held monthly on the fourth weekend, hosting some 800 vendors. The $3 admission is good for Friday, Saturday and Sunday; parking is free.

Gwinnett Flea Market
Norcross. Take I-85 N. to Jimmy Carter Boulevard; exit and turn left; the market will be on your right.This big flea market is open

daily, except Monday and Tuesday, from 11 a.m. to 8 p.m. 770-449-8189.

Lakewood Antiques Market

South Atlanta. Take I-75/85 south from downtown; exit at Lakewood Freeway East and follow the signs. 2000 Lakewood Avenue. This popular market is held on the second weekend of each month and features thousands of unusual antiques and collectibles. Parking is free; admission is $3 for adults and free for children. The market is held Friday, Saturday and Sunday, but there's a special early buyers' day on Thursday, when admission is $5. 622-4488.

The Wrecking Bar

Downtown. Little Five Points at 292 Moreland Avenue. The Wrecking Bar sells architectural art and antiques, from hardware and chandeliers to large mantles and statuary. The store occupies an 1895 mansion listed on the "National Register for Historic Places." 525-0468.

Atlanta's Farmers Markets

All of Atlanta's farmer's markets offer tremendous values, huge selections and a memorable market experience. Many persons use these markets to shop for exotic items, others for super values on selected items and still others as value centers to stock up on basic supplies. The chefs of Atlanta's top restaurants make good use of these markets.

Atlanta Municipal Market

Downtown at 209 Edgewood Avenue.
Opened in 1918, the building is a huge structure housing dozens of individual, ethnic vendors. Meat, particularly pig, is the specialty of the house. 659-1665.

Atlanta State Farmers Market

Forest Park. I-75, exit 78, 16 Forest Pkwy. A 146-acre open-air retail and wholesale market, the largest in the Southeast and one of the largest in the world. It's open 24 hours a day every day except Christmas. Thousands of shoppers each day find groceries and household supplies are abundant and vastly reduced. 366-6910.

DeKalb Farmers Market

Decatur. 3000 E. Ponce de Leon Avenue.
A huge international food market which offers an incredible selection of deli, fish, cheese, produce, baked bread and muffins, wine, beer, and plenty more. Employees come from every corner of the globe and wear badges listing the languages they speak. This is real market shopping; be prepared for the rush of the crowd. 377-6400.

Harry's Farmers Market

Alpharetta at 1180 Upper Hembree Rd.
664-6300.
Duluth at 2025 Satellite Parkway.
416-6900.
Marietta at 70 Powers Ferry Rd.
770-578-4400.
An unbelievable array of delicacies from around the world including, deli, fish, produce, cheese, wine, flowers and a bakery.

International Farmer's Market

Chamblee at 5193 Peachtree Industrial Blvd.
Meat, cheese, freshly baked bread, produce, liquor, flowers, coffee and much more in a warehouse setting. 455-1777.

Fun Facts:

- Twelve Oaks Plantation from "Gone With the Wind" was inspired by the Lovejoy Plantation, which is 20 miles south of Atlanta.

- Okefenokee Swamp, located in southeast Georgia, is Georgia's largest, covering some 700 sq. miles or 438,000 acres and one of the nation's largest wildlife preserves.

Good Ol' Gal

LOVE ATLANTA

SECTION XI
Georgia's Green Harvest and Trails

Commentary

Due to varying weather conditions and farm locations, if possible, it is advantageous to call ahead to confirm dates, hours and availability.

Harvest Seasons for Fruits and Veggies

Commodity	Harvest Time Frame
Apples	July 25-November 21
Asparagus	March 15-June 20
Beans	May 15-October 20
Beans	May 10-November 5
Blackberries	June 1-July 30
Blueberries	June 1-August 15
Cabbage	May 15-September 25
Cantaloupes	June 1-August20
Collards	October 1-June 20
Corn-Green	May 15-October 10
Corn-Sweet	May 15-July 1
Cucumbers	May 1-July 20
Eggplant	June 15-October 20
Grapes	June 20-October 1
Lettuce	March 15-May 20
Muscadines	July 1-November 1
Nectarines	May 8-August25
Okra	May 20-October 1
Onions-Dry	May 1-June 25
Onions-Green	January 1-June 1
Onions-Vidalia	April 20-June 10
Peaches	May 8-August25
Peanuts	August 15-November 1
Pears	August 1-November 1
Peas-English	January 15-April 1
Peas-Field	May 15-October 1
Pecans	September 1-December 15
Pepper-Sweet	June 1-September 1
Plums	July 1-August25
Potatoes-Irish	May 15-September 15
Potatoes-Sweet	July 15-November 20
Pumpkins	September 15-November 15
Squash	May 20-October 1
Strawberries	March 1-July 1
Tomatoes	May 25-October 15
Turnips-Bunched	January 1-April 15
Turnips-Greens	October 1-March 15
Watermelons	June 25-September 1

Georgia's Roadside Farmer's Markets

Northwest Region

Apple Barrell/Cantrell's Orchard
Ellijay, six miles east on Hwy.52.
706-273-3767.
August 1-December 1, Monday -Saturday 8-6 p.m. Closed Sunday
Apples, fresh cider, hot apple pies, apple chips, fritters and bread, dried apples, peanuts, mountain honey, sorghum syrup, baskets, jellies, vegetables and pumpkins.

Barr-Five Farms
Alice, take Hwy.515, west to County Rd. 255.
706-692-5719.
June-November 7 a.m. until dark. Pick your own.
All types of vegetables, sweet corn, tomatoes, hot and sweet peppers, squash, English peas, broccoli, cauliflower, cucumbers and melons.

Hillcrest Orchards
Ellijay, nine miles east on Hwy.52.
706-273-3838/706-276-1144.
July-December 23, 9-7 p.m.
Apples, peaches, fresh cider, jams, jellies, pies, doughnuts, honey, sorghum and hot caramel apples; Tours, hayrides and farm animals; also a picnic and play area.

Jones' Farm Fresh Produce
Ellijay, seven miles east on Hwy.52.
706-635-3350.

Sept.-Mid-Nov. Monday -Saturday 8-6 p.m.
Sunday 2-6 p.m.
Fresh vegetables, cabbage, Irish and sweet potatoes, collards, tomatoes, turnip greens and squash.

Mercier Orchards (Apple House)
Blue Ridge, two miles north on Hwy.5.
706-632-3411.
July-December Monday -Saturday 8-6 p.m.
Sunday 12-5 p.m.
Apples, apple cider, jams, jellies, baskets, gifts, doughnuts and apple pies. Peaches in season. Gift packs-shipping available.

Oak Hill Orchards
Ellijay, five miles east on Hwy.52.
706-273-3644.
August-Mid-December 8-7 p.m.
Apples, peaches(in seasons), apple and peach cider, jams, jellies, honey, syrup and apple products.

Panorama Orchards Farm Market
Ellijay, three miles south on Appalachian Hwy.5.
706-276-3813/3849.
July-Jan. 9-6 p.m; pick your own.
Apples, cider, fried pies, apple bread, apple butter, sorghum syrup, honey, jam, jellies, chow chow, pickles, peaches and pumpkins.

R and A Orchards
Ellijay, six miles east on Hwy.52.
706-273-3821.
July 1-December 1, 8-7 p.m.
Apples, peaches(in season), apple products, produce, honey, sorghum syrup and canned goods.

Red Apple Barn (Little Bend Orchard)
Ellijay, 3.5 miles west Hwy.76/Ga.282 on left side of road
Route 6, Box 3470, Ellijay 30540
706-635-5898/7674.
August 15-December 1 Monday -Saturday 9-6 p.m. Sunday 12:30-6:30 p.m.

Sanford's Sunset Orchard
Ellijay, 8.5 miles on Ga.Hwy.282/U.S.76 W.
706-635-5710/276-7905.
September to October; Monday -Saturday 9-6 p.m. Sunday 10-6 p.m.

Apples and apple products, honey, jams, jellies, sorghum syrup, pumpkins, gourds, produce and souvenirs.

Waddell Orchard
Ellijay, five miles east on Hwy.52 next to Wagon Wheel Restaurant.
706-273-3813/276-6003.
Mid-August-November, 8-6 p.m.
Apples and apple products, sorghum syrup, honey and jellies.

Northeast Region

Apple Tree Farms
Baldwin, 1/4 mile south of Duncan Bridge Rd. on Hwy.365.
706-754-3421/4003.
August-Jan. 8-6 p.m.
Apples, cider, jams, jellies, relish, pickles, dried apples and local crafts.

Big Apple Farms
Helen, 3.5 miles west of Ga.365 on Hwy.105 toward Helen
706-754-3421/4003.
August-Jan. 8-6 p.m.
Apples, cider, jams, jellies, relish, pickles and dried apples.

Blueberry Hills Farm
Gainesville, 16 miles north of Gainesville off Hwy.365 at Mt. Zion Rd.
706-776-1204.
July-September, Friday-Saturday 9-6 p.m.; Monday-Thursday by appointment; pick your own.
Blueberries and blueberry products.

Fritchey's Farms
Helen, seven miles south on Hwy.17.
706-754-4851.
April 1-December 15, 9-7 p.m.
Tomatoes, beans, strawberries, corn, pumpkins, squash, okra, peppers, eggplant, peas. Milkshakes, pies, tomato sandwiches, canned goods, jams, jellies and cider.

Jaemor Farm Market
Lula, Hwy.365 near Lula.
All year; Monday-Saturday 7-7 p.m. Sunday 1-6 p.m.
Peaches, apples, cider, vegetables, peanuts, pecans, melons, onions, jams, jellies, fruit

baskets, bedding plants, vegetable transplants, farmhouse furniture, gas and groceries.

Lakeview Orchards
Clarkesville, 3.5 miles north of town on Hwy.441.
706-754-3421/4003.
August-January, 8-6 p.m.
Apples, cider, jams, jellies, pickles, dried apples and crafts.

Mountain City Orchards
Mountain City, Hwy.441 north of town on Cathey Rd. at Rabun Gap.
706-746-2380/5335.
April-November, 9-6 p.m.
Apples, cabbage, tomatoes, cider and local vegetables.

Mr. Earl's Country Market
Clayton, Hwy.441 north of Clayton on the right.
706-746-2380.
May-December, 8-6 p.m.; pick your own.
Vegetables, cabbage, beans, melons, apples, tomatoes. Jams, jellies, candies, flowers and plants.

Price Mountain Orchard
Tiger, five miles west of Tiger on Bridge Creek Rd.
706-782-5592.
August-November, 8-6 p.m.
Red and Golden Delicious apples, Rome, Granny Smith, Ozark gold, Arkansas Black, Red June and Jonathan apples, peaches, nectarines and honey.

Stonewall Creek Farm
Tiger, U.S.441 north from Tallulah Gorge, left on Tiger Rd., thru intersection, 3.8 miles on left.
706-782-2966.
Harvest Months June-November, 9-6 p.m.; pick your own.
Organic apples, peaches, apricots. Natural apple, peach and other food products. Also wildflower seeds, gift baskets, organic vegetables and herbs.

Tiger Mountain Orchard
Tiger, across from south Rabun Elem., three

miles south of Clayton. Second location on Hwy.441 at Tiger Rd.
706-782-3290.
August-October, Monday -Saturday, 8-5 p.m.; Sunday, 1-4 p.m.; pick your own.
Apples, raspberries, grapes, blackberries, peaches(in season only), cider, jams and jellies.

Central Region

Berry Patch Farms
Woodstock, seven miles east of town, eight miles west of Roswell at 786 Arnold Mill Rd.
926-0561.
July and October. October-mid-December, 8 a.m. until dark; pick your own Blueberries, pumpkins and Christmas trees.

C.J. Orchards, Inc.
Rutledge, I-20, exit 49 south to Old Mill Rd. farm on right at 1251 Old Mill Rd.
706-557-2635.
June 15-July 15, 8-9 p.m.
Peaches and blueberries.

Cagle's Milk House
Canton, one miles east of Canton off Hwy.140, or 140 west of Roswell at 362 Stringer Rd.
770-345-5591.
All year; Monday, Tuesday, Thursday and Friday, 9-5:30 p.m.
Whole milk, 2% milk, whole chocolate milk and buttermilk. Farm tours (25 minimum), milking and processing facilities, by appointment. Border collie demonstrations, fishing and dove hunting.

Country Gardens
Newnan, I-85 exit 10, five miles east of I-85 on Hwy.154 to 3861 Lower Fayetteville Rd.
770-251-2673/5437.
All year; Spring 8-7 p.m., Winter 8-5 p.m.
Perennials, annuals, herbs, shrubs, trees, bedding plants, vegetable plants and hanging baskets.

Flintwood Farms
Twenty miles south of Atlanta; I-75 S. exit 77, 10 miles south, then four miles west.
770-461-4643.

April-November, 9-6 p.m.; closed Sunday
Bedding plants, hanging baskets. Farm tours
Saturday at 10 a.m. Monday to Friday by ap-
pointment.

Futral Farms Peach Orchard
Griffin, I-75 S. to exit 67, then 1/4 mile
west, right on Jackson Rd., three miles, than
east eight miles.
770-228-1811.
*Mid-June-August, 8-7 p.m. Pick your own
peaches; call for availability.*

Gardensmith Greenhouse and Nursery
Jefferson, Hwy.11 south one mile past
Hwy.124, right on Jackson Trail, 1.4 miles
left on Hogan's Mill, 1/4 mile on left to 231
Hogan's Mill Rd.
706-367-9094.
Seasonal; call for hours.
Bedding plants, herbs, vegetable plants, topi-
ary and hanging baskets.

Gardner Farms
Locust Grove, one mile north of town on
U.S.23/Ga.4.
770-957-4912.
June-August, 7-7 p.m.
Peaches, blueberries and blackberries.

Harp's Farm Market
Fayetteville, one mile south of courthouse,
left on 92 south for five miles, blue building
on left.
770-461-1821.
*Mid-March-October, Tuesday-Saturday. Oc-
tober to Christmas; pick your own.*
Perennials, native plants, blueberries, raspberries, blackberries and Christmas trees.
Also nature tours, fall hayride and a pumpkin patch; pick your own cotton, candy,
gourmet foods and gift items.

Hess Tree Farm
Monroe, east from town on Church
St.(Hwy.83). Right on Laboon Rd., right to
1574 Vasco Adcock Rd.
770-267-9428/800-9428.
*Wholesale. October-December; choose/cut
your own; Thanksgiving to Christmas.*
Virginia pine, cedar, wreaths, garland,
flocked trees, stand and potted Leyland cypress.

Lindquist Christmas Tree Farm
Senoia, in town Hwy.16/85 go west on
Hwy.16 1.5 miles to Rock House Rd., make
left, 1/2 miles on right.
770-599-6490.
*November 25 to December 24, Monday -Fri-
day, 12-6 p.m. Weekends, 10-6 p.m.*
Cut your own; choose/cut Christmas trees,
Virginia pines, Leyland cypress and cedar.
Fresh-cut Frasier fir. Live Leyland cypress
in ground; also, containers, wreaths and gar-
lands.

Miller's Blueberries
Watkinsville, three miles from town on
Ga.53, turn left on Union Church Rd., 7/10
miles, sign on left.
706-769-6359.
*Mid-June-August, Monday -Saturday 8 a.m.
until dark, Friday, 8-12 p.m.; Sunday, 2
p.m. until dark; pick your own blueberries.*

Open Air Orchards
Villa Rica, 2.5 miles north of Main St. on
Hwy.61.
624-4169.
*Late June-August 11-7 p.m. Tuesday, Thurs-
day and Saturday; pick your own.*
Blueberries, blackberries, organic herbs,
fruits and vegetables.

Pete's Little Idaho Tater Farm
Winder, six miles north of town, 2.5 miles
south of I-85 off Ga.211, 1.5 miles west on
Old Hog Mtn. Rd.
770-867-8096/3662.
*June-December, daily. All year; Saturday 9-
5 p.m. Pick your own.*
New red and white potatoes, green beans,
butter beans, okra, tomatoes, peppers, Georgia product gift baskets and spiral-sliced
ham.

Ridgeway Christmas Farm
Jackson, I-75 S. to exit 66, Hwy,36 toward
Jackson, three miles to High Falls Rd., turn
right, 1/2 miles on right.
770-775-3120/5538.
*November-December, 10 a.m. until dark;
cut your own.*
Choose/cut Christmas trees and stands. Virginia pine, red cedar and Leyland cypress.

Whimsey Haven Farm
Fairburn, 6.8 miles south of I-285 on Old
National Hwy., eight miles south of airport.
770-461-6742.
*June-early July Monday-Friday 8-12, 5-8
p.m., Saturday-Sunday-8 p.m.; pick your
own.*
Blackberries, herbs and dried flowers.

Yule Forest, Inc. (Location 1)
Stockbridge, I-75 exit 75, Hwy.138 east
thru Stockbridge to Millers Mill Rd.; then
two miles east of town.
770-957-3165/954-9356.
December, 10 a.m. until dark. Cut your own.
Christmas trees, wreaths, ornaments, tree
trimmers. Hot cider, cookies.

Yule Forest, Inc. (Location 2)
Stockbridge, three miles south of Hwy.138
on Hwy.155
*June-berries, October-pumpkins, December-
Christmas trees; cut your own.*
Berries, pumpkins, Christmas trees,
wreaths, ornaments, Indian corn, corn stalks
and cotton.

Southern Region

Branch Bros. Farm Market
Chula, I-75 S. to exit 24, Willis Still Rd.,
and Sunsweet exit.
912-382-7509.
All year; 8-8 p.m.; pick your own.
Peanuts, Vidalia onions, peaches, cider, pecans, candies, relishes, crafts, gift baskets,
syrup, jellies, honey. Tours, RV camping
w/hookups, gas, and gourmet items.

Burton Brooks Orchard
Barney, I-75 S. exit 7, nine miles to
crossroads of Hwy.122 and 76 in town.
May-August; 8-8 p.m.; daily; pick your own.
Peaches, blueberries, tomatoes, nectarines,
melons, jams and jellies.

Calhoun Produce, Inc.
Ashburn, I-75 S. to exit 30, then go seven
miles east to 5075 Hawpond Rd.
912-273-1887/6440.
June to October, 8-7 p.m.

Butter beans, colored butter beans, peas,
butter peas, jams, jellies, syrup, peaches, tomatoes and seasonal produce.

Cotton Patch
Richland, two miles north of town on
Hwy.280
912-887-3988/3300.
All year; 8-5:30 p.m.
Pecans, peaches, jams, jellies and snacks.
Also crafts, artwork and quilts.

Crystal Lake Orchards
Whigham, from Hwy.84 in Whigham, south
on Hwy.179 3.5 miles.
912-762-4986.
*March-September, Tuesday-Saturday 9-6
p.m.; Sunday, 12-6 p.m.; pick your own.*
Strawberries, peaches, nectarines, plums,
blackberries, grapes, tomatoes, cut flowers
and grapevine wreaths.

Dickey Farms, Inc.
Roberta, six miles north of town on
Hwy.341.
912-836-4362/800-732-2442.
May-August 10, 8:30-6:30 p.m. daily.
Peaches, nectarines, t-shirts and gift packs.

Ellis Brothers Pecans
Vienna, I-75 S. to exit 36.
912-268-9041.
All year; 8-7 p.m., 7-11 p.m.
Pecans, peanuts, peaches, Vidalia onions in
season. Candies, jams, jellies, relishes, gift
items, honey and syrup.

Farmer Brown's
Elko, I-75 exit 41 to Hwy.26.
912-987-2929.
May-September, 8-7:30 p.m. daily.
Peaches, Elberta peaches(in season). Vidalia
onions and products, peanuts, pecans, watermelons, cantaloupe, honey, gourmet foods,
candies, gift items and cookbooks.

G. West Long Farm
Bainbridge, 2.5 miles east of city limits on
Old Whigham Rd. on the right side; watch
for signs.
912-246-8086/7519.
*June-September; call for hours; closed Sun-
days; pick your own.*

Peas, butter beans, watermelons, sweet potatoes, cantaloupe, tomatoes, snap beans,
squash, okra, Irish potatoes, peppers, cucumbers, sweet and field corn and blackberries.

Garden with Nature
Milledgeville, Hwy.441 north at 19.1 mile
marker go south from town 15 miles on
Hwy.441.
912-946-2526.
All year; Monday -Saturday 7-7 p.m., Sun-
day 1-7 p.m.; pick your own.
Peas, butter beans, snap beans, cowpeas,
sweet corn, squash, sweet potatoes, okra,
watermelon, sugar cane, collards, turnips,
cabbage, mustard, rutabaga, onions and garlic.

Hudson Paulk Farms
Ocilla, two miles north of town, Hwy.129
north market on right.
912-468-5100.
June-August, 8-6 p.m.
Butter beans, butter peas and peas. Specialist in shelling and cleaning butter beans and
peas.

Kearce Farms Country Store
Albany, four miles south of town on U.S.19
S. to 1627 Liberty Expwy.
912-432-6000.
September-April 8:30-5:30 p.m.; May-Au-
gust, 8-7 p.m.
Pecans, peaches, melons, jams, jellies, candies, peanuts, Vidalia onions, gifts, collectors items, novelties and souvenirs.

Lane Packing Co./Just Peachy Gift Shop
Fort Valley, I-75 exit 44, take Hwy.96 west
five miles to Lane Rd. From town take
Hwy.95 east four miles.
912-825-3592/2891/800-277-3224.
May-October, 8-8 p.m. daily.
Peaches, vegetables, jams and jellies. Fresh
fruit bar with homemade peach ice cream;
also peach and blackberry cobbler.

L and M Enterprises, Inc.
Cordele, Seedling Dr.(off Hwy.41) beside
the Farmers Market.
912-273-4548.
All year; 8-5 p.m.
Pecans(shelled and in-shell). Gift boxes.

Lawson Peach Shed
Morven, I-75S. to exit 5, then 12 miles west
to town on Hwy.133.
912-775-2581/2496.
May-July; 8-8 p.m.; pick your own.
Peaches, melons and tomatoes.

Mark's Melon Patch
Sasser, nine miles from Albany on Hwy.82
west, 1 mile east of Sasser.
912-698-4750.
All year. April-October, 9-7 p.m.; Novem-
ber-March 9-6 p.m.
Watermelons, cantaloupe, pumpkins, sweet
corn, peaches, tomatoes, peanuts-boiled,
raw and roasted, jams, jellies, Vidalia onions, blueberries, grapes, peas, gourds and
pecans.

McFarm Fresh Produce
Valdosta, three miles south of town on
Hwy.41, turn left on Newsom Rd.; first
house on right.
912-247-5675.
April-July 7-6:30 p.m. August-March 9-
5:30 p.m.
Vegetables, all types. Nursery plants, all
types. Antiques and crafts. Anytime by appointment.

Merritt Pecan Company
Weston, halfway between Albany and
Columbus on Hwy.520.
912-828-6610.
All year; 7-9 p.m. daily; pick your own.
Peanuts, pecans year-round. Pecan candies,
farm toys, BBQ, jams and jellies. May 15-
September 1, peaches, vegetables, gas and
convenience store.

Miller's Produce
Sandersville, Hwy.15 south of Sandersville
on south Harris St.
912-552-2834/2434..
April-December, 9-6 p.m.; pick your own.
Cabbage, collards, turnips, sweet and Irish
potatoes, tomatoes, squash, peas, okra, peppers, jams, jellies, relish and gourds.

Sasnett Fruits and Nuts
Byron, I-75 S. to exit 45, east on 247 Conn.
to Hwy.41, then north two miles; on left.
912-953-3820/3417.

All year; Monday -Saturday 8-8 p.m. Sunday 1-6 p.m.; pick your own.

Peaches, nectarines, plums, scuppernongs, muscadines, figs, jams, jellies, vegetables and pecans. Pecan cracking and shelling service.

Skipper Farms

Macon, I-75 south of Macon to exit 47, then east to Skipperton Rd., south to Jones Rd., turn left, farm on right. 912-788-2260.

June 1-November 15, Monday -Friday 7:30-7 p.m.; Saturday 7:30-4 p.m.; pick your own.

Picked and shelled butter beans, sweet corn, peaches, blueberries, cantaloupe, watermelons, peppers, Indian corn, peas, sweet potatoes, tomatoes and squash.

Stripling's General Store

Cordele, 12 miles south of I-75, exit 32 on Ga.300 S. Ga./Fla.Pkwy.
912-535-6561/4547.

All year; 7-7 p.m. daily.

Country pork sausage, fresh/smoked in mild, medium, hot. Country-cured meats, fresh pork and beef. Syrup, jellies, pecan candies. Groceries and gas.

Tom Sawyer Farms

Cochran, one mile off Hwy.257, Roddy Community, North Dodge County.
912-934-7584.

June 15-August 1; 7-7 p.m.; daily; pick your own.

Peaches and nectarines; baskets furnished.

Coastal Region

Buffalo Creek Honey Farm

Nahunta, 3.5 miles south Nahunta (301); left on paved road; cross bridge; first dirt road on the left; fifth house on left.
912-462-5068.

All year; call for hours.

Organically produced Georgia honey.

Folsom Farms

Glenville, four miles south of Glenville on U.S.Hwy.301.
912-654-2568/1456.

All year; 7-5 p.m.; pick your own.

Vidalia onions and onion products, pecans, peanuts and vegetables in season. Jams, jellies, relishes, peaches in season and watermelon, cantaloupe.

Gray Mule Pecan Farm

Garfield, 111 south RR St., Garfield.
Hwy.23 between Twin City and Millen.
912-763-3943.

October-March; 8-5 p.m.; pick your own.

Pecans-shelled or in-shell. Shelling service.

Hendrix Farms

Metter, three miles south of Metter on Hwy.129.
912-685-3320/3220.

All year; 8-6 p.m.; pick your own.
Vidalia onions and products, strawberries, watermelons, cantaloupe, sweet corn, tomatoes, relish, pickles, salsa, BBQ sauce, jellies and jams.

Jacob's Produce

Rocky Ford, approximately four miles south of town on Scarboro Hwy.
912-863-7772/682-3104.

April-August; 8-7 p.m.; pick your own.

Strawberries, corn, watermelons, cantaloupe, tomatoes, squash, peas, cane syrup and hanging baskets.

M and T Farms, Inc.

Lyons, three miles east of Lyons on Ga.292. Inside city limits.
912-526-6128.

All year; 8-5 p.m.; pick your own.

Vidalia onions and products, watermelons, pecans.

Mathews Farms

Baxley, four miles southwest of Baxley on County Farm Rd.
912-367-2363.

March-June; 8-5 p.m.; pick your own

Strawberries and Vidalia onions.

Old South Market

Glennville, three miles north of town on U.S.301.
912-654-1647.

All year; 8-8 p.m.; pick your own.

Vidalia onions and products, pecans, corn, tomatoes, peas, half runner beans, snap beans, butter beans, watermelons, squash, jams, jellies, homemade syrup, pecan candies.

Vidalia Onion Factory and Farmers Mkt.
Vidalia, east of town on Hwy.280.
912-526-3466/3575.
All year; Monday-Saturday 9-5 p.m. Closed Sunday.
Vidalia onions and onion products. Fresh hot vidalia onion rings. Produce, souvenirs. Lunch served daily 11-2 p.m.

- Source: Georgia Farm Bureau Marketing Association

Georgia's Peach Orchards and Berry Farms

Georgia Peach Orchards

Most of these orchards are located along highways and roadways. Always make it a point to make a pit stop. A freshly-picked Georgia peach is an unbeatable taste delight.

Central Region

Big Six Farm, Zenith Mill Rd., Fort Valley. 912-825-7504. Open Monday-Saturday 8-6 p.m., June, July and August. From I-75 S. take exit 46 (Byron). Travel south on Hwy.49 approximately eight miles. Turn right onto Hwy.49 Connector W. Turn right at four-way stop onto Hwy.341 North. Travel approximately four miles and turn left at Big Six sign. Big Six Farm is ahead one mile on right.

Evans Farms, Hwy.96 East, Fort Valley. 912-825-2095. Open Monday-Sunday 8-6 p.m., May, June, July and August. From I-75 south take exit 44 (Housers Mill Road). Travel west on Hwy.96 E. to Fort Valley approximately eight miles. Evans Farms is on the left.

Lane Packing Company, Hwy.96 East, Fort Valley. 912-825-2891. Open Monday-Sunday 8-6 p.m., June, July and August. From

I-75 S. take exit 44 (GA.96). Travel west on Hwy.96 approximately five miles. Lane Packing company is on the right.

Taylor Orchards, Hwy.96 West, Reynolds. 912-847-4186. Open Monday-Sunday; 8-6 p.m.; May, June, July and August. From I-75 south take exit 46 (Byron). Travel west on Hwy.49 to Fort Valley. Turn right on Hwy.96 West to Reynolds. Taylor Orchards is west of Reynolds approximately 1/4 mile from city limits. Taylor Orchards is on the right.

Meadows and Porter, Porter Rd., Cochran. 912-934-6419. Open Monday-Sunday; 8-6 p.m.; June, July and August. From I-75 south take exit 43 (Perry). Travel south on Hwy.341 to Hawkinsville approximately 20 miles. Travel east on Hwy.26 approximately 1/4 mile. Travel north on Upper River Road (also known as Porter Road). Meadows and Porter is on the left (10 miles from Hawkinsville).

Miami Valley Fruit Farm, Hwy.41 N. Centerville. 912-953-3703. Open Monday-Saturday 8-7 p.m.; Sunday 10-6 p.m., June, July and August. From I-75 south take exit 45 (Warner Robins/Centerville). Travel east on 247 Connector approximately two miles. Turn left on Hwy.41 approximately one mile. Miami Valley Fruit Farm is on the right.

Dickey Farms, Hwy.341 N. Musella. 912-836-4362. Open Monday-Sunday, 9-6 p.m., June, July and August. Traveling south on I-75 take exit 63 (Forsyth Hwy.42). Travel south on Hwy.42 approximately 18 miles. Turn left on Hwy.341 (Peach Blossom Trail). Dickey Farms is on the left.

Southern Region

Burton Brooks Orchard, Hwy.122, Barney. 912-775-2710. Open Monday-Sunday, 8-8 p.m., May, June, July and August. From I-75 south take exit 7 (Barney). Travel west on Hwy.122 approximately nine miles. Burton Brooks Orchard is on the right.

Hiers Peach Orchard, State Road 133, Morven. 912-775-2027. Open Monday-Sunday, 7-7 p.m., May, June, July and August. From I-75 south take exit 5 (Valdosta/State Road 133). Travel west on State Road 133 approximately 15 miles. Hiers Peach Orchard is on the left.

Lawson Peach Shed, State Road 133, Morven. 912-775-2581. Open Monday-Sunday, 8-6 p.m., May, June and July. From I-75 south take exit 5 (Moultrie Hwy.). Travel west on State Rd.133 approximately 12 miles. Lawson Peach Shed is on the right.

Source: Georgia Peach Commission

Georgia's Pick-Your-Own Berry Farms

Crop dates may change depending on weather conditions.

Call ahead for days, hours and crop availability.

Berry-Picking Tips

- Wear a hat and comfortable shoes to keep feet dry if picking early in the morning dew, and a belt on which to tie bucket.

- Pick early, before the heat of the day sets in.

- Dress children comfortably. They will usually pick for only a short while, then play while parents work.

- Some pick-your-own farms offer tables and shade trees, so pack a picnic with cold drinks to enjoy after all your work.

Atkinson County

Pelz Farm: Frank Pelz, Route 2, Box 202, Pearson. 912-422-3467. Sweet corn, including silver queen; bring containers.

Baldwin County

Robbie Hattaway, 220 West Washington St., Milledgeville. 912-452-9622. Blueberries; through July 25; bring containers.

Pot Luck Nursery, 282 Cox Woodland Rd., Milledgeville. 912-932-5390. Blueberries; through July; containers furnished.

Bibb County

Skipper Farm, 4164 Jones Rd., Macon. 912-788-2260. Corn, butter beans, green beans, tomatoes, peaches, blueberries. Kids can see farm animals, from llamas to chickens; through November; call for availability; containers furnished.

Burke County

Hawkins Peach Orchard, 763 Hwy.23 S., Waynesboro. 706-554-7576. Through August 1. Bring containers.

Mr.and Mrs.James Eshleman, 645 Hwy.24 S., Waynesboro. 706-437-1295. Blueberries; through mid-August; bring containers.

Camden County

Lyde T. Thomas, 11 St. West at Lake Circle Dr. 912-576-5235. Blueberries; through July; by appointment only; containers available.

Carroll County

Pat Dees, 325 Old Four Notch Rd., Whitesburg. 832-8905. Blueberries. through mid-August; bring containers.

Cherokee County

Robin Gassett, 2679 Airport Road. 770-720-6191, 479-3591. Blueberries and apples; pesticide-free; through August; bring containers.

Gus Kirchhof, 199 Trinity lane, Canton. 770-889-2131. Blueberries. Last week in June through last week in August.

Cobb County

Rock Farm: Ed Harris. 4470 Wesley Chapel Rd., Marietta. 770-992-1669 evenings. Blackberries and tomatoes through July. Muscadines in September until frost.

Coweta County

Blueberry Hill Farm, 2270 Smokey Rd., Newnan. 770-251-0843. Blueberries; through early August; containers available.

Bill Spradlin, 461 North Rd., Turin. 770-599-8175. Blueberries; through July; containers furnished.

Don Stambaugh, 757 Fischer Rd., Sharpsburg. 770-251-7161. Blackberries and blueberries; through early August; containers furnished.

George H. Coggin, 1358 Payton Rd., Newnan. White field corn and Silver Queen corn; Ready June 30. 770-253-6091. Containers available.

Fayette County

Harp's Farm Market and Nursery, 1692 Hwy.92 S., Fayetteville. 770-461-1821. Blueberries and plums until early July; containers furnished.

Whimsy Haven Farm, (6.8 miles south of I-285 on Old National Hwy.). 770-461-6742. Blackberries. Through July 10, 8-noon and 5-8 p.m. weekdays; 8-8 p.m. Saturday-Sunday; containers furnished.

Floyd County

James Cordle, 6338 Big Texas Valley Rd., Rome. 706-234-1289. Blueberries. Through August 1; containers furnished.

Steve Coyle, 1057 Radio Springs Rd., Rome. 706-295-7161. Blueberries (organic available). 8-8 p.m.,Thursday-Saturday. Through August 12; containers furnished.

Cordleberry Farm, 6338 Big Texas Valley Rd., Rome. Blueberries; through August 1. 706-234-1289. Tuesdays, Thursdays, Saturdays; containers furnished.

Forsyth County

Bill Callaway, GA.400, north of Cumming. 770-887-4443. Blueberries, beans, sweet corn and more. Appointment only; bring containers.

Fulton County

William Brown, 1055 Jones Rd., Roswell. 770-993-6866. Blueberries; through mid-August; containers furnished.

Gwinnett County

Green Acres Farm, 2839 Lenora Rd., Snellville. 770-979-1336. Blackberries and blueberries; through July 30; bring containers.

J.L. Duncan, 2503 Cammie Wages Rd., Dacula. 770-962-4990. Apples, peaches, blueberries and some vegetables available into August. Will have figs and muscadines in August; containers furnished.

Debra Uhr, 78 Russell Rd., Lawrenceville. 770-962-7310. Organic blueberries. Through Labor Day weekend. Monday-Saturday, 8-noon 6 p.m.; Tuesday-Friday, until dark.

Phyllis Hughes, 1235 Chandler Rd., Lawrenceville. 770-962-5372. Blueberries; July-August; call for appointment.

Habersham County

James T. Shook, Toccoa-Clarkesville Hwy.17, Mount Airy. 706-754-2585. Blueberries and vegetables. July 4 through September; bring containers.

Callie and Ed Sapp, Route 1, Box 1614, Demorest. 706-754-5871. Blueberries. Call for directions; bring containers; picking aprons furnished.

Blueberry Hills Farm, off Hwy.365 at Mount Zion Rd., 16 miles north of Gainesville. 706-1217 or 706-776-1204. Blueberries. Early July through mid-September.

Hall County

Elizabeth Smith, 3803 Gillsville Hwy. 770-531-9617. Blackberries; through late July. In August, figs and scuppernongs; bring containers.

Haralson County

Mitcham's Farm, 52 Ploof Rd., Bremen. 770-646-3583. Blackberries and blueberries; ready July 4. Open daily; bring containers.

Henry County

Gordon's Berry Patch, 490 Dorsey Rd., Hampton. 770-946-3525. Blueberries; through August 15; containers furnished.

Tony Hiers, 388 McCullough Rd., Stockbridge. 770-957-2423. Blueberries; through August 1; containers furnished.

Indian Creek Farm, Cheryl Mailand, 1319 Crumbley Rd., McDonough. 770-957-8524. Blueberries and blackberries; through early August. Saturday 7-5 p.m., Wednesday 7-noon; containers furnished.

M.C. Seabolt, 2323 Le-Guin Mill Rd., Locust Grove. 770-957-3196. Thornless blackberries; through July; containers furnished.

Linne East Widney, farm off Campground Road and GA.42 near McDonough. 770-961-9459. Blueberries; through July 15; call

for directions and availability. Picking on Tuesday and Saturday mornings only; bring containers.

McMurry Farms, Stephen and Cindy McMurry, 43 Danner Dr., Ellenwood. 770-474-7043. Corn, peas, beans, tomatoes, okra, squash, and cucumbers. Call for details.

Thomas Singley, 325 Singley Dr., Locust Grove. 770-957-3786. Corn, peas, okra, watermelon, cantaloupe, butter beans and more; call for availability; containers furnished.

Lamar County

Sunray Farms, 709 Piedmont Rd., Barnesville. 770-358-4536. Blueberries; through August 1, 8 a.m. until 8 p.m. Monday-Wednesday, Friday-Saturday; containers furnished.

Macon County

Cimino Farm, Route 1, Box 154, Reynolds. 912-847-2231. Organic tomatoes, sweet corn, squash, pole beans and more; through fall.; call for availability. 7 a.m. to 7 p.m. Thursday-Saturday; bring containers.

Jones Berry Farm, John Gordon Rd., four miles east of Reynolds. Blueberries. 912-847-3292. Through July; Monday-Saturday, 8 a.m. to 8 p.m.; Sundays, 1-6 p.m.; bring containers.

W. J. Roberts, Route 1, Box 201, Montezuma. 912-472-8315. Blueberries; through July; containers furnished; open daylight hours.

Meriwether County

Dot's Berry Farm, two miles north of Greenville, Alt. U.S.27, exit 8 from I-85. 706-672-4901. Blueberries; through August; containers furnished.

Briar Patch Plantation: Rusty Miller, off Shelton Road in Greenville. 706-672-1111.

Blueberries; ready mid-July; call in advance; bring containers.

Monroe County

Bolingbroke Blueberry Farm, 1170 Estes Rd., Bolingbroke. 912-994-2769. Blueberries. July 5 through August 5. Open 7 a.m. until noon daily; bring containers.

McDuffie County

B & B Blueberry Farm, 583 Plum St., Thomson. 706-595-6979. Blueberries. Through August 1; containers furnished. First light to 10 a.m. and 6 p.m. until dark daily.

Oconee

Miller's Blueberries: James and Nancy Miller, 1371 Union Church Rd., Watkinsville. 706-769-6359. Blueberries; through August; bring containers.

Paulding County

Tanner Farm, 1225 Elsberry Mountain Rd., Dallas. 770-445-3703. Blueberries; call ahead; bring containers.

Rockdale County

Mobley Tree Farm: Bill Mobley, 4351 Bowen Road, Stockbridge (1.5 miles south of Hwy.155 and Hwy.138). 770-929-8341. Blueberries; through July; bring containers.

Spalding County

Bill Ison Farm, 6855 Newnan Hwy., Brooks. 770-599-6970. Blueberries; through July; containers furnished.

Buck Creek Farm, 175 Chappell Mill Rd., Orchard Hill. 770-228-2682 or 228-2514. Blueberries and blackberries; through July. Tuesday, Thursday, Saturday; containers furnished.

Futral Farms Peach Orchard, 5081 Jackson Rd., Griffin. 770-228-1811. Peaches through late August; 7:30 a.m.-8 p.m. daily; containers furnished.

Wilson Organics, 437 Lindsey Rd., Griffin. 770-412-8212. Organic vegetables through October; 9-7 p.m. Monday-Saturday; bring containers.

Upson County

Tyrone B. Casteel, 779 North Delray Rd., Thomaston. 706-648-6171. Blueberries; through late July; containers furnished.

Walton County

Nepenthe Farms, 2259 Liberty Hill Church Rd., Monroe. 770-267-7951. Blueberries; 10-6 p.m.; Wednesday-Sunday.

Lula M. Mikle, 3079 Pebble Brook Dr., Loganville. 770-466-4516. Blueberries; through September; bring containers.

Whitfield County

Floyd Dugger, 3450 Hearicker (off Airport Road), Dalton. 706-226-5971. Thornless blackberries; through July.

Source: The Atlanta Journal-Constitution

A Brief Season-By-Season Guide to Gardening

Winter

Winter Blooms

Daffodils, tulips, pansies, snapdragons, wallflowers, columbine, trillium, roses, flowering apricot, witch hazel and wintersweet.

January

- Develop your yearly garden plan.
- Plant and transplant trees and shrubs.
- Spray dormant oil on fruit trees.
- Fertilize with lime.

February

- Fertilize pansies.
- Prune trees and shrubs
- Prune roses.
- Scalp warm season lawn.
- Move perennials in dry periods.
- Seed cool season annuals.

March

- Plant cool season vegetables.
- Divide perennials.
- Plant trees and shrubs.
- Fertilize fescue lawn.
- Fertilize spring-blooming shrubs, (especially azaleas) after flowering.
- Aerate warm season lawn.
- Feed camellias after flowering.

Spring

Spring Blooms

Daisies, sweet peas, nasturtiums, woodland phlox, foamflower, lilies, azaleas, dogwoods and viburnum.

April

- Plant summer vegetable seeds.
- Prune shrubs after flowering.
- De-thatch lawn.
- Plant summer vegetables and flowering bulbs.

May-June

- Weed annuals, perennials and vegetables.
- Begin deadheading annuals and perennials.
- Plant summer annuals.
- Stake perennials.
- Plant summer vegetables.
- Mulch beds.

Summer

Summer Blooms

Lantana, begonia, plumbago, salvia, butterfly weed, verbena, hibiscus, crape myrtle, golden raintree.

- Prune hydrangeas.
- Pinch chrysanthemums.
- Deadhead annuals and perennials.
- Plant perennial seeds.

Fall

Fall Blooms

Zinnia, marigold, pansies, mums, ornamental grasses, salvia, asters, camellias, tea plant and osmanthas.

September

- Plan garden renovations.
- Plant fall vegetables.
- Plant zinnias, marigolds and snapdragons.

October

- Begin preparing for winter.
- Renovate and shelter.
- Begin planting pansies and bulbs.

November-December

- Clean up the vegetable garden.
- Continue to plant shrubs and trees.
- Plant bulbs, plants and trees.

Planting a Fall Vegetable Garden

Here's a clip-and-save chart to help plan and plant a fall crop. Number of days to maturity is from sowing seed or planting transplants in the garden and will vary with cultivar and growing conditions. Your local garden center can suggest other cultivars. Consult seed packets or transplant tags for recommended spacing and planting depth.

Vegetable Planting Dates/Days to Suggested Cultivars Maturity

Vegetable/Date	Maturity
Beans,bush	
Jul 5-Aug 10	50-60
Eagle,Strike,Greencrop Beans,pole	
Jul 1-Aug 1	65-75
Stringless Blue Lake, Kentucky Wonder	
	191
Beans,lima	
Jul 1-Aug	165-75
Henderson's Bush Fordhook	242
Beets	
Aug 1-Sep 20	55-65
Detroit Dark Red Broccoli	
Aug 1-Sep 1	60-80
Green Comet, Green Duke,	
Premium Crop Cabbage	
Aug 1-Oct 1	65-85
Rio Verde, A&C No.5, Early	
Round Dutch Carrots	
Aug 20-Sep 15	70-80
Chantenay, Scarlet Nantes,	
Orlando Gold Cauliflower	
Jul 15-Aug 15	60-75
Snowball Y Improved, White	
Empress Collards	
Aug 1-Sep 1	55-70
Georgia, Vates, Blue Max Cucumbers	
Jul 15-Aug 15	50-65
Ashley, Marketmore	76,
Carolina pickling Eggplant	
Jul 10-Jul 30	75-90
Black Beauty, Florida Market, Dusky Kale	
Aug 1-Sep 1	50-70
Vates, Dwarf Siberian Lettuce	
Sep 1-Oct 1	60-85

Vegetable/Date	Maturity
Bibb, Buttercrunch, Red Sails Mustard	
Aug 15-Sep 15	40-50
Florida Broadleaf, Southern	
Giant Curled Okra	
Jun 15-Jul 10	55-65
Emerald, Clemson Spineless	80
Onions	
Oct 10-Nov 10	100-120
Grano	502
Grannex	33
Peppers,bell	
Jul 25-Aug 10	65-80
Yolo Wonder L, Cal Wonder,	
Jupiter Radishes	
Sep 1-Oct 15	25-30
Cherry Bell, Scarlet Globe Spinach	
Sep 1-Oct 15	40-45
Melody, Winter Bloomsdale Squash	
Aug 1-Aug 25	40-55
Yellow Crookneck, Dixie,	
summer Seneca Zucchini	
Tomatoes	
Jun 15-Jul 15	70-90
BetterBoy(VFN), Celebrity(VFNT),	
Roma(VF) Turnips	
Aug 10-Sep 15	40-60
Purple Top, Just Right, Seven Top	

—Source: Atlanta Journal-Constitution

Fun Facts:

- While the daffodil signals spring-time, it is the remarkably multifarious daylily that serves as the harbinger of summer.

- Georgia marble from Tate was used in building the Lincoln Memorial.

Mrs. Coretta Scott King & Dr. Martin Luther King, Jr.

LOVE ATLANTA

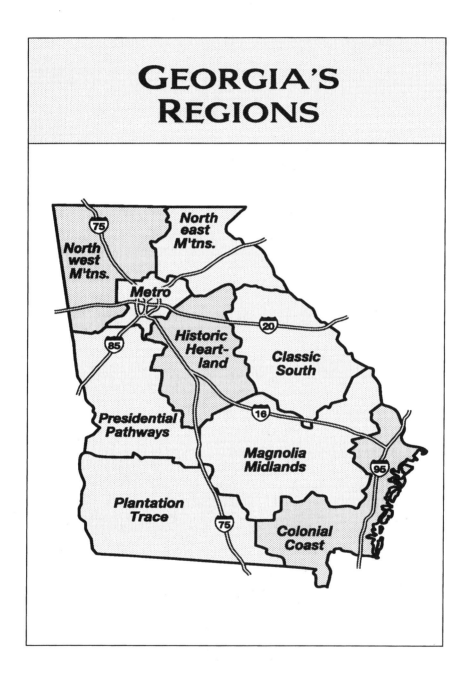

GEORGIA'S REGIONS

Section XII
Traveling Historic Georgia

Commentary

As the largest state east of the Mississippi River, Georgia's natural environment and resources are immensely diverse. From the great **Blue Ridge Mountain** peaks to the resplendent barrier islands and beaches, Georgia offers a spectacular variety of natural and manmade attractions. In its lakes, streams and coastal waters there are over 300 species of fish; 85 species of amphibians; nearly 375 species of birds; and approximately 120 species of mammals.

Starting from Atlanta, we have proceeded first to the coastal area, from **Savannah** to **Brunswick** and sleepy little **St. Mary's**, an area popularly known as **Georgia's Golden Isles**.

Next we venture northward from Atlanta to the areas that are home to the **Lake Lanier Islands**, **Dahlonega** and **Georgia's Northern Mountains**.

Departing mountain country we find ourselves in **Georgia's Historic Heartland**, a place with such historic small towns as **Social Circle**, **Rutledge**, **Madison** and **Newnan**, which will charm you to the marrow.

From the Heartland we continue to the Classic South, home to Augusta and plenty of Civil War history.

From there we visit the **Presidential Pathways** and find the world-famous **Callaway Gardens** in **Pine Mountain, FDR's Little White House** in **Warm Springs**, and the very small town of **Plains**, birthplace and home of the nation's 39th President, **Jimmy Carter**.

After that we're on to **Plantation Trace**, which is home to **Thomasville**, once the South's most sought after vacation spot, and,

also, home to the fabulous **Chehaw Wild Animal Park**.

Our journey ends most pleasingly in the **Magnolia Midlands**, where amongst the zillion acres of farmland you'll find the **Blueberry and Onion Capitals of the World**.

Helpful Traveling Tips

As with travel in and around Atlanta, a good map rapidly becomes the best of friends. And don't forget the great people who are there to help you on your way, the numerous welcome centers, visitors' bureaus and chambers of commerce (see our listings for locations and telephone numbers.) But before setting out, there are some things you should know about the make-up of Georgia's very small towns.

Georgia's Small Towns

- May not have any street corners to hang on but will always have plenty of friendly people to talk to.

- Usually have at least one police officer who takes the 15 mile an hour speed limit very seriously.

- Usually have at least one gas station, but no guarantees that it is open or stocked with petrol.

- Almost always have one main street (lined with historic buildings), one drug store, one welcome center, one mayor, one sheriff, one newspaper, one barbecue, one post office, two antique dealers, one dog catcher, one cemetery (astride the best property), a throng of good ol' boys and a few stray dawgs and cows.

- Are so quiet you can hear the interest accumulate in your savings account.

- Always are a delight to visit and their citizens always mean it when they say "hurry back soon."

- Have main streets that dead-end in both directions, or main street is the only street.

- Have zip codes that start with a minus sign.

- Are too small to attract mosquitos.

- Have fireflies whose wattage exceeds that of Georgia Power.

- Sell six-packs with four cans.

- Have a smiling golden labrador serving as the welcome center.

- Feature evening entertainers are a swarm of crickets.

Georgia's Wonderfully Helpful Visitor's Centers

To assist you on your way stop at any or all of Georgia's ever-helpful visitor centers:

Albany Welcome Center
225 W. Broad Ave.
Albany, GA 31702
912-434-8700

Augusta Welcome Center
32 Eight St. at Riverwalk
Augusta, GA 30901
706-724-4067

Andersonville Welcome Center
114 Church St.
Andersonville, GA 31711
912-924-2558

Athens Welcome Center
280 E. Dougherty St.
Athens, GA 30603
706-353-1820

Atlanta Historical Society
Welcome Center
140 Peachtree St. N.E.
Atlanta, GA 30303
238-0655

Underground Atlanta
Welcome Center
65 Upper Alabama
Atlanta, GA 30303
577-2148

Atlanta Local Welcome Center
Lenox Square Mall
3393 Peachtree Road N.E.
Atlanta, GA 30326
266-1398

Atlanta Local Welcome Center
Peachtree Center
233 Peachtree Street N.E.
Atlanta, GA 30303
521-6688

Atlanta Airport Visitors
Information Center
Atlanta, GA 30320
767-3231

Acworth Welcome Center
Exit 120 off I-75 and State 92
Acworth, GA 30101
770-974-7626

Baxley Welcome Center
501 W. Parker St.
Baxley, GA 31520
912-367-7731

Blue Ridge Visitor Center
Historic Depot, Box 875
Blue Ridge, GA 30513
706-632-5680

Brunswick-Golden Isles
Local Welcome Center
I-95 between Exits 8 & 9
Brunswick, GA 31520
912-264-0202 or
800-933-COAST

Brunswick-Golden Isles
Local Welcome Center
4 Glynn Ave. on US 17
Brunswick, GA 31520
912-264-5337 or
800-933-COAST

Buena Vista Welcome Center
912-649-2842
P.O. Box 427

Conyers Chamber of Commerce
P.O. Box 483
Conyers, GA 30207

Buena Vista, GA 31803

770-483-7049

Chatsworth Welcome Center
Fort. St. Box 327
Chatsworth, GA 30705
706-695-6060

Claxton Welcome Center
4 Duval Street
Claxton, GA 30417
912-739-2281

Clayton Welcome Center
8712 Tara Boulevard
Jonesboro, GA 30237
770-478-6549

Columbus Information Center
I-185 at Williams Road
Columbus, GA 31904
706-649-7455

Calhoun Welcome Center
300 South Wall Street
Calhoun, GA 30701
706-625-3200

Dahlonega Welcome Center
East Main Street
Dahlonega, GA 30533
706-864-3711

Darien Welcome Center
Ft. King George and US 17
Darien, GA 31305
912-437-4192

Douglas County Welcome Center
2145 Slater Mill Road
Douglasville, GA 30133
942-5022

Eagle Tavern Welcome Center
Main St. US 441
Watkinsville, GA 30677
706-769-5197

Eastman-Dodge Welcome Center
407 College Street
Eastman, GA 31023
912-374-4723

Eatonton/Putnam
P.O. Box 4088
706-485-7701
Eatonton, GA 31024

Ellijay
S. Westside Square
706-635-7400
Ellijay, GA 30540

Gainesville Welcome Center
230 E. Butler Pkwy. N.E.
Gainesville, GA 30503
706-536-5209

Garden City Information
I-95
Garden City, GA 31418
912-964-5094

Georgia World Congress Center
285 International Blvd. N.W.
Atlanta, GA 30313
656-0612

Glennville Welcome Center
134 S. Main Street
Glennville, GA 30427
912-654-2000

Gordon County Welcome Center
300 S. Wall Street
Calhoun, GA 30701
706-625-3200

Helen Welcome Center
Chattahoochee Street
Helen, GA 30545
706-878-2521

Kingsland Information Center
I-95
Kingsland, GA 31548
912-729-3253

Martinez Information Center
I-20
Martinez, GA 30917
706-737-1446

Madison Chamber of Commerce
P.O. Box 826
Madison, GA 30650
706-342-4454

Milledgeville Visitors Bureau
200 W. Hancock Street
Milledgeville, GA 31061
912-453-4676

Jekyll Island Welcome Center
901 Jekyll Island Causeway
Jekyll Island, GA 31520
800-841-6586

Lake Park Information
I-75
Lake Park, GA 31636
912-559-5828

Lavonia Information Center
I-85
Lavonia, GA 30553
706-356-4019

Marietta Welcome Center
No. 4 Depot Street
Marietta, GA 30060
770-429-1115

Macon I-75 Welcome Center
I-75
Forsyth, GA 31029
912-745-2668

Macon I-16 Welcome Center
200 Cherry Street
Macon, GA 31208
912-743-3401

Metter Welcome Center
Hwy. 121 at I-16
Metter, GA 30429
912-685-6988

Million Pines Welcome Center
I-16, Exit 17 (UPS)
Soperton, GA 30457
912-529-6263

Peachtree Ctr. Welcome Center
233 Peachtree St. #2000
Atlanta, GA 30043
521-6622

Perry Area Welcome Center
P.O. Box 1619
Perry, GA 31069
912-988-8000

Pine Mountain Welcome Center
101 Broad Street
Pine Mountain, GA 31822
800-441-3502

Plains Information Center
US 280
Plains, GA 31780
912-824-7477

Rabun County Welcome Center
Hwy. 441 North
Clayton, GA 30525
706-782-4812

Reidsville Welcome Center
Hwy. 280
Reidsville, GA 30453
912-557-6323

Rome Welcome Center
401 Civic Center Drive
Rome, GA 30161
800-759-7663

Roswell Visitors Center
617 South Atlanta Street
Roswell, GA 30075
640-3253

St. Mary's Welcome Center
Orange Hall, Osborne Street
St. Mary's, GA 31558
912-882-4000

Savannah Welcome Center
301 Martin Luther King Dr.
Savannah, GA 31499
912-944-0460

St. Simons Island Visitors
St. Simons Causeway
St. Simons, GA 31522
800-525-8678

Sylvania Information Center
US 301
Sylvania, GA 30467
912-829-3331

Thomasville Welcome Center
401 S. Broad Street
Thomasville, GA 31792
912-226-9600

Toccoa Welcome Center
907 East Currahee Street
Toccoa, GA 30571
706-886-2132

Tybee Island Welcome Center
209 Butler Avenue
Tybee Island, GA 31328
912-786-5444

West Point Information Center
I-85
West Point, GA 31833
706-645-3353

Georgia's Local Convention and Visitors Bureau

Metro Atlanta

Atlanta CVB
233 Peachtree St., Suite 2000
Atlanta, GA 30043
521-6600.

Clayton County CVB
P.O. Box 774
8712 Tara Blvd.
Jonesboro, GA 30237
770-478-4800.

Cobb County CVB
P.O. Box COBB
Marietta, GA 30067-0033
770-980-2000.

DeKalb County CVB
750 Commerce Dr., Suite 201
Decatur, GA 30030
378-2525.

Marietta Welcome Center & CVB
#4 Depot St.
Marietta, GA 30060
770-429-1115.

Classic South
Augusta-Richmond County CVB
32 8th St.
Augusta, GA 30901
706-823-6600/800-726-0243.

Thomson-McDuffie Tourism Bureau
111 Railroad St.
Thomson, GA 30824
706-595-5584.

Colonial Coast
Brunswick-Golden Isles CVB
4 Glynn Ave.
Brunswick, GA 31520
912-265-0620.

Jekyll Island CVB
1 Beachview Dr.
Jekyll Island, GA 31527
912-635-3400.

Kingsland CVB
212 N. Lee St., P.O. Box 1928
Kingsland, GA 31548
912-729-5999.

St. Marys CVB
P.O. Box 1291
St. Marys, GA 31558
912-882-6200.

Savannah CVB
222 West Oglethorpe Ave.
Savannah, GA 31401
912-944-0456.

Waycross-Ware County CVB
P.O. Box 137
Waycross, GA 31501
912-283-3742.

Historic Heartland

Athens CVB
P.O. Box 948
Athens, GA 30603
706-546-1805.

Eatonton-Putnam County Chamber of Commerce
P.O. Box 4088
Eatonton, GA 31024
706-485-7701.

Macon-Bibb County CVB
P.O. Box 6345
Macon, GA 31208-6354
912-743-3401.

McDonough-Henry County CVB
P.O. Box 1378
McDonough, GA 30253
770-957-5786.

Milledgeville-Baldwin County CVB
P.O. Box 219
Milledgeville, GA 31061
912-452-4687/800-653-1804.

Perry Area CVB
P.O. Box 1619
Perry, GA 31069
912-988-8000.

Warner Robins CVB
1420 Watson Blvd.
Warner Robins, GA 31093
912-922-8585.

Magnolia Midlands
Statesboro CVB
204 S. Main St., P.O. Box 1516
Statesboro, GA 30458
912-489-1869.

Vidalia Tourism Council
2805 Lyons Hwy.
Vidalia, GA 30474
912-538-8687.

Northeast Georgia Mountains

Alpine Helen/White County CVB
P.O. Box 730
Helen, GA 30545
706-878-2181.

Banks County CVB
P.O. Box 57
Homer, GA 30547
706-677-2108.

Dahlonega-Lumpkin County CC
101 South Park St.
Dahlonega, GA 30533
706-864-3711.

Gainesville-Hall County CVB
230 E.E. Butler Pkwy., P.O. Box 374
770-536-5209.

Rabun County CVB
Hwy.441 North, P.O. Box 761

Clayton, GA 30525
706-782-4812/706-782-5113.

Northwest Georgia Mountains
Carroll County CVB
200 Northside Dr.
Carrollton, GA 30117
800-292-0871.

Cartersville CVB
P.O. Box 200397
Cartersville, GA 30120
770-387-1357.

Dalton-Whitfield County CVB
P.O. Box 2046
Dalton, GA 30722
706-272-7676.

Greater Rome CVB
P.O. Box 5823
Rome, GA 30161
706-295-5576.

Plantation Trace
Albany CVB
P.O. Box 308
Albany, GA 31702
912-434-8700.

Clay County Visitors Bureau
P.O. Box 221
Fort Gaines, GA 31751
912-768-2247.

Destination Thomasville
Tourism Authority
P.O. Box 1540
Thomasville, GA 31799
912-225-5222.

Valdosta/Lowndes County CVB
1703 Norman Dr. Suite F
Valdosta, GA 31061
912-245-0513.

Presidential Pathways

Americus-Sumter County Tourism Office
400 W. Lamar St., P.O. Box 724
Americus, GA 31709
912-924-2646.

Columbus CVB
P.O. Box 2768
Columbus, GA 31902
706-322-1613/800-999-1613.

Coweta County CVB
22 E. Broad St., P.O. Box 1012

Newnan, GA 30264
770-254-2626.
LaGrange-Troup County Tourism Office
P.O. Box 636
LaGrange, GA 30241
706-884-8671.
Pine Mountain Tourism Association
111 Broad St.
Pine Mountain, GA 31822
706-663-4000/800-441-3502.
Warm Springs Area Tourism Association
P.O. Box 261
Warm Springs, GA 31830
800-FDR-1927.

Georgia's Historic Covered Bridges

Georgia's 14 covered bridges reach across the state's modest streams and its historic past. Following is a county-by-county rundown:

Banks County

Lula Bridge, circa 1915, is 34 feet long.
Shortest bridge, restored in 1976 on a private golf course.

Cobb County

Concord Bridge, circa 1872, is 133 feet long.
Between Smyrna and Mableton. Handles almost 9,500 vehicles a day.

Bartow County

Euharlee Creek Bridge, circa 1886, is 116 feet long.
Survived arsonists, thanks to a nearby fire station.

DeKalb County

Stone Mountain Park Bridge, circa 1891, is 151 feet long. Moved from Athens in 1965 where it was popularly known as Effie's Bridge, after a nearby bordello.

Early County

Coheelee Creek Bridge, circa 1883, is 86 feet long. Southernmost covered bridge in the United States, maintained as a county park.

Forsyth County

Pool's Mill Bridge, circa 1900, is 80 feet long.
Shoals provide a beautiful setting in a county park.

Watson Mill Bridge, circa 1885, is 229 feet long. The longest and perhaps prettiest bridge, preserved as a state park. Built by Washington King, son of freed slave and master bridge builder Horace King.

Franklin County

Cromer's Mill Bridge, circa 1906, is 111 feet long.
Closed, unsafe for foot traffic.

Harris County

Callaway Gardens Bridge, circa 1870, is 79 feet long. Built by Horace King, originally in Troup County. Formerly the Neely Bridge, it will be restored.

Meriwether County

Red Oak Creek Bridge, circa 1840s, is 116 feet long. Oldest bridge, built by Horace King.

Oconee County

Elder's Mill Bridge, circa 1897, is 75 feet long.
The mill ruins are picturesque.

Oglethorpe County

Big Clouds Creek Bridge, circa 1905, is 110 feet long. Abandoned and in danger of collapsing.

Upson County

Auchumpkee Creek Bridge, circa 1895, is 120 feet long. Partially destroyed in 1994 flood.

White County

Sautee Bridge, circa 1905, is 37 feet long.
A leaky roof is causing it to deteriorate.

Fun Fact:

- Georgia's major seaports are Savannah and Brunswick.

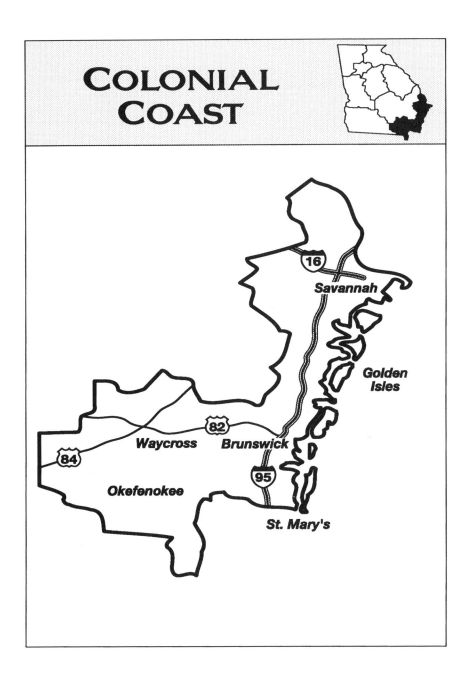

COLONIAL COAST

Savannah

Golden Isles

Waycross   Brunswick

Okefenokee

St. Mary's

Section XIII
Traveling Historic Coastal Georgia

Coastal Georgia and the Golden Isles

Georgia's barrier islands, coastal towns and beaches offer an unbeatable combination: environmentally unique settings, traditional oceanfront pleasures and historic sights. Vast marshlands, winding rivers, ribbon-smooth beaches are awaiting your discovery and enjoyment. An abundance of water sports, golf, hiking, crabbing, antique shopping, or just plain shelling or sunning will insure that you return again and again.

Only four of the barrier islands are accessible by car: **Jekyll**, **Tybee**, **St. Simons** and **Sea Island**. Most of the others **Wassaw**, **Ossabaw**, **St. Catherine's**, **Blackbeard**, **Sapelo**, **Little St. Simons** and **Cumberland Island** are accessible by ferry only.

The barrier islands, teeming with life, are enormously productive and essential to Georgia's multimillion dollar seafood industry. Over the course of 25 years, one acre of marsh can produce a half billion dollars worth of shellfish alone. Wildlife, including alligators, snakes, birds, raccoons, minks and otters, live, breed and feed in these ecosystems. On any causeway near the marshlands and tidal creeks, you may see the graceful great blue herons or snow-white egrets.

Nearly half of the 165,000 acres are protected, with approximately 87,700 acres now developed, a somewhat remarkable ratio compared with other seashore areas. Let's have a closer look.

Savannah

(I-75 S. to Macon; from Macon take I-16 east.)

Commentary

America's foremost example of historic restoration. Savannah's historic city squares and buildings with the live oaks splattered with Spanish moss amaze and delight all. Perhaps the most beautiful city in the nation, and certainly one of the most charming port cities in the world, Savannah is an apt venue for the 1996 Summer Olympic Games.

One of the city's most popular attractions is the **Juliette Gordon Low Girl Scout National Center**. Birthplace of the founder of the Girl Scouts of America, this registered National Landmark was built circa 1820.

Just a tad less famous is **River Street**. Restoration has returned the brick warehouses to their 19th century appearance, and today you will find shops that carry crafts, fine art, antiques, and two sweet-tooth satisfiers in **River Street Sweets** and **Savannah's Candy Kitchen**.

Just two blocks from River Street is City Market, today one of Savannah's foremost architectural restorations. Mixing the past with the present, shops carry everything from antiques to Savannah-made products such as cookies and jellies.

Attractions/Museums

Catch the trolley at the Visitor's Center; it's a good way to see the sights.

Factor's Walk on Bay Street. World cotton prices were decided here.

Old City Market, Jefferson and St.Julian St., 912-232-4903. Once the commercial and social hub. Since the 1700s, the market has survived fires, neglect and threat of demolition. Today past and present are mixed with shops, restaurants and entertainment.

Old Harbor Light and Oglethorpe Bench, near **Factor's Walk**, mark the sight and landing of General Oglethorpe in 1733.

The Savannah River Queen, 9 East River St., 912-232-6404. Ultimate fine dining aboard Savannah's premier dinner/entertainment ship.

Riverfront Plaza, on Old River Street. A contrasting scene of busy tugs on the Savannah River and nine blocks of museums, shops, restaurant, fountains and benches.

Ships of the Sea, 503 East River St., 912-232-1511. Savannah's maritime museum.

Skidaway Marine Science Complex, Skidaway Island Rd., 912-356-2453. An oceanographic center with a 12,000-gallon aquarium, exhibiting coastal archeological finds.

Victorian District. Three neighborhoods of late 19th-century in progress of renovation.

Telfair Academy of Arts, at 121 Barnard St., 912-232-1177. The 1818 Regency-style mansion is the oldest art museum in the South. It houses a fine collection of impressionist paintings, along with 18th and 19th century furniture, silver and decorative arts.

The Savannah History Museum, 303 M.L.K. Jr., Blvd., 912-238-1779. Two hundred and fifty years of Savannah's history is presented in a restored 19th century railroad terminal.

East Shaver Bookstore, 326 Bull St., 912-234-7257. On Madison Square, this building has a dozen rooms with all types of books and maps.

Historic Sites/Homes

Wormsloe Historic Site, 7601 Skidaway Rd., 912-352-2548. A beautiful oak-lined drive-

way brings you up to the ruins of the Noble Jones Home, circa 1739.

Davenport House, 119 Habersham St., 912-233-4501. Built in 1815 by Isaiah Davenport and Savannah's first project for restoration. See the before pictures in the unrestored attic.

Flannery O'Connor Home, 207 East Charlton St., on Lafayette Square, 912-233-6014. The birthplace of one of Georgia's most famous writers.

Juliette Gordon Low Birthplace, 142 Bull St., 912-233-4501. Founder of the Girl Scouts in Savannah in 1912.

King Tisdell Cottage, at 514 East Huntingdon St., 912-234-8000. An 1896 Victorian museum dedicated to African-American heritage.

Parks

Forsyth Park, located at Gaston and Park Avenue. Beautiful fragrant gardens, fountain from 1858, jogging or walking trails, tennis and basketball courts.

Skidaway Island State Park, located six miles southeast of the city on Diamond Causeway, 912-598-2300. Offering trailer and tent sites, fishing, swimming pool and hiking trails.

Ossabaw Island Wildlife Management Area. Public hunting, accessible by boat only. Check with Wildlife Resources Division, 912-651-2221.

Golf

Bacon Park Golf Course, Shorty Cooper Dr., 912-354-2625.

Henderson Golf Club, 1 Henderson Dr., 912-920-4653. An 18-hole course, par 71.

Southbridge Golf Club, 415 Southbridge Blvd., 912-651-5455.

Accommodations

To experience Savannah's Old World charm, stay at an historic inn or bed & breakfast.

Remshart-Brooks House, 106 West Jones St., 912-234-6928. Enjoy Savannah's Southern hospitality and charm in an 1853 town house.

Located in the heart of the historic district, with a three-room terrace garden suite furnished in fitting country antiques.

Offering an open beam sitting room with fireplace, antique game table, TV and sofa bed; a romantic bedroom done in brass and wicker, and a fully equipped kitchen for midnight "raids." The suite opens onto a gorgeous courtyard. And owner Anne Barnett makes sure you will enjoy a continental-plus breakfast in the morning. A private entrance makes this a home away from home.

The Kehoe House, 123 Habersham St., 912-232-1020. A magnificent Victorian mansion with 13 guest rooms.

The Gastonian, 220 East Gaston St., 912-232-2869. Two revitalized 1868 townhouses connected by a graceful garden courtyard, offering 10 guest rooms.

Foley House Inn, 14 West Hull St., 912-232-6622. An elegant 1896 Victorian town house with 20 guest rooms.

Ballastone Inn and Townhouse, 14 East Oglethorpe Ave., 912-236-1484. Rated as one of the most romantic inns, with 24 guest rooms.

St. Julian Street B & B., 501 East St.Julian St., Savannah. Located in the heart of Savannah's Historic District, St.Julian B& B is within walking distance of River Street, City Market and popular restaurants. Two guest rooms, one with a double and other with full-double bed, share a large Victorian bathroom complete with claw-foot tub, shower and old-fashioned water closet. The other guest room has queen-size bed with private bath. All rooms are provided with cable TV and a full continental-style breakfast is served in the dining room. Hosts Bill, Judy or Eric Strong,

will be more than happy to give you sightseeing directions. 912-236-9939.

Dining

Elizabeth on 37th, 105 E. 37th St., Savannah, 912-236-5547. Owner husband and wife team, chef Elizabeth and wine stewart Michael Terry bring exquisite new regional cooking based on old Southern recipes. Served in simple elegance of a turn-of-the-century Southern mansion savor an exotic mushroom ragout or sesame-almond crusted grouper with peanut sauce. Acclaimed by national media, including *Bon Appetit*, the *New York Times*, and the *Atlanta Journal-Constitution*, as the best regional restaurant outside of Atlanta.

Pearl's Elegant Pelican, a local favorite, at 7000 Laroche Ave., 912-352-8221. Fresh seafood served in a casual nautical atmosphere.

Bistro Savannah, 309 West Congress St., 912-233-6266. Louisiana jambalaya and spicy vindaloo chicken.

The Pirate's House, East Broad and Bay St., 912-233-5757. An extensive award-winning menu with scandalous desserts.

The Boar's Head, on River St., 912-232-3196. Savannah's oldest restaurant on River Street serves seafood, poultry, beef, lamb and pastas, combined with live piano music.

City Market Cafe, 224 West St., 912-236-7133. One of the city's finest restaurants offering unusual dishes, fresh soups and delicious desserts.

45 South, 20 East Broad St., 912-233-1881. Fine dining and award winning wine list will make this a special evening. Jackets.

The Old Pink House, 23 Abercorn St., 912-232-4268. Contemporary and colonial Georgia cuisine, with live jazz.

Shrimp Factory, 313 East River St., 912-236-4229. Many ways to enjoy shrimp and seafood. Keylime pie and cheesecake, too.

Bayou Cafe and Blues Bar, 14 North Abercorn Ramp/River Street. The best of two worlds; a Cajun menu and great live entertainment.

Savannah Festivals

February
Annual Georgia Heritage Celebration
Super Museum Sunday
Savannah Irish Festival

March
American Traditions Competition
Savannah on Stage
Kite Festival
Sheep to Shawl
Tara Feis, An Irish Festival
St. Patrick's Day Parade
St. Patrick's Day Celebration on the River
Annual Savannah Tour of Homes and Gardens
Coastal Empire Easter Pageant

April
Seafood Festival
Tour:The Hidden Gardens of Historic Savannah
Tour of Homes at Oatland Island
Siege and Reduction Weekend
Blessing of the Fleet
Sidewalk Arts Festival
Earth Day

May
Candle Lantern Tour of Tybee Island Lighthouse
(May through August)
International Day/First Saturday Festival
Savannah Duck Race
Arts-On-The-River Weekend
Kirkin' O' The Tartans
Annual Scottish Games and Highland Gathering
Environmental Nature Fun Fair
Memorial Day Celebration
The War of Jenkins' Ear at
Wormsloe Historic Site

June
First Saturday Festival
Downtown Saturday Night
Annual Beach Music Festival

July
The Great American Fourth of July
Fireworks On The Beach
Independence Day Celebration
Thunderbolt Seafood Harvest Festival
The Savannah Maritime Festival

August
The Maritime First Saturday Festival
Annual Alee Patrol Kingfish Tournament

September
First Saturday Festival
Savannah Jazz Festival
Open House-
Skidaway Marine Science Complex

October
Oktoberfest On The River
Jewish Food Festival
Savannah Greek Festival

November
First Saturday Festival
Christmas Made In The South

December
Holiday Ice Skating
Christmas Tour of Inns
Holiday Tour of Homes
Christmas On The River

Tybee Island

(I-75 S. to Macon. Then I-16 E. into Savannah. Take the 37th Street exit off I-16, then turn right onto Abercorn Street. Follow Abercorn to Victory Dr. (which turns into Ga.80.) Turn left onto Victory Dr. and continue 15 miles.)

Attractions/Museums

Tybee Lighthouse, located at north end of beach. One of Georgia's first public structure.

Fort Screven, circa 1875, close to the lighthouse. Was used during the Spanish-American wars.

Accommodations

Hunter House, 1701 Butler Ave., 912-786-7515. Built in 1910, a restored beachhouse with its famous second-floor restaurant and lounge. A simple but delicious breakfast can be enjoyed in the dining room, or on one of the porches, while you enjoy the view and ocean breeze.

Ocean Plaza Beach Resort, on 15th St. and Oceanfront, 912-786-7664. Facing the ocean, rooms are modern and clean.

Brunswick

Commentary

Founded in 1771, the shrimp capital of the world has maintained its British street names. At the foot of Gloucester Street in the late afternoon Brunswick's shrimp docks come alive with the catch of the day. The home of Brunswick stew, which is served daily at almost every restaurant, is also the major place of business for many who reside on Georgia's Golden Isles. From Brunswick, St. Simons Island, Jekyll Island and Sea Island are but a few miles away.

Attractions/Museums

Old Town Brunswick. Still retaining British and German street names reflecting historical ties that date back to 1771.

The Courthouse. Located in the center of a square, this impressive building was erected in 1907. Surrounded by moss-draped oaks and Chinese pistachio trees.

Hofwyl-Broadfield Plantation State Historic Site, 5556 U.S.17 N., 912-264-7333. Antebellum rice plantation from 1807-1973 comes to life. Complete with period pieces, film museum and park.

The Piddlers, on M. L. King Jr. Blvd., offers antiques, crystal, linens, vases and collectibles.

Brown's Antiques, on 1526 Norwich, offers oriental rugs, china, silver and collectibles, with an annex across the street that has large estate items.

Lanier Oak. Named after Sidney Lanier, who was inspired under this tree to write some of his finest poetry, such as "Marshes of Glynn."

Mary Miller Doll Museum, at 1523 Glynn Ave., 912-267-7569. Featuring 4000 dolls ranging from pre-Civil War china-heads to Cabbage Patch and Barbies.

Shrimp Docks. Take a stroll on the pier and watch the fleet come in.

Lover's Oak. As legend goes, an Indian lover and his maiden would meet at night underneath the branches of this 900-year-old oak.

Dart-Brown House (circa 1887) at 4 Glynn Ave., with original cypress shingled roof and heart pine floors and home to the Chamber of Commerce, 912-265-0620.

Accommodations

Brunswick Manor, 825 St., 912-265-6889. A stately turn-of-the-century brick home, with the pampering of fresh flowers and sherry, are awaiting guests in this five-room manor.

Rose Manor Guest House and Tea Room, 1108 Richmond St., 912-267-6369. A charming 1890 Victorian bungalow with four guest rooms, surrounded by a wicker-filled wraparound porch.

Major Downing House (circa 1886.) Furnished with antiques and reproductions, carved oak staircase and stained-glass windows, it strikes a pretty picture. Guests enjoy all the modern conveniences with fresh fruit, sherry and comfy terry bathrobes. The inn is at 444, the corner of Prince and Egmont. 912-265-6889.

Dining

Doverspike Station Restaurant, 3365 Cypress Mill Rd., 912-267-0503. Home cooked food, crepes, fettucini, delicious desserts.

The Georgia Pig, I-95/U.S.17 S., 912-264-6664. The best bar-b-que, just ask the locals.

The Oyster Box, 2129 Glynn Ave., 912-264-3698. For the lover of oysters and fresh seafood.

The Captain's Table, Hwy.17 N., 912-265-2549, specializing in coastal seafood at attractive prices.

St. Simons Island

Commentary

British General James Oglethorpe, founder of the Georgia colony, established **Fort Frederica** here in 1736. From here he led his troops to the Bloody Marsh Battle against the Spanish.

Today, **Fort Frederica National Monument** is an archaeological site and park showing some of the still-remaining ruins on a back-river bend, 912-638-3639.

The historic **St. Simons Lighthouse**, first built in 1810 and rebuilt in 1872 after the Confederate Army retreated from Union invaders, is one of the nation's oldest continuously working lighthouses.

Attractions/Museums

Bloody Marsh Battle Site, on Demere Rd., 912-638-9014. Tape recording and monument

describing the 1742 battle site where the British troops defeated the Spanish troops.

Fort Frederica, on Frederica Rd., was built by Georgia's founder, James Edward Oglethorpe. Today it is an archaeological site preserved and maintained by the National Park Service. 912-638-3639.

Lighthouse and Coastal Museum, circa 1872, at 12th St. Stretch your legs and climb the 129 steps to the top of the lighthouse. Cottage contains artifacts. 912-638-4666.

Parks

Neptune Park, south end of the island, 912-638-9014. Has a wealth of fun things to do, miniature golf, picnicking, pier fishing, crabbing, pool and library.

Golf

St. Simons Island Club, 912-638-5130. Offers an 18-hole course with over 80 sand bunkers and fairways lined with towering pines.

Sea Palms Golf and Tennis Resort, 912-638-3351. Enjoy 27 challenging holes of golf on a most memorable course.

Hampton Club, 912-634-0255. One of the most celebrated 18-hole courses in the Southeast. The natural drama and contours of the land make this course unforgettable.

Accommodations

The Island Inn, 301 Main St., 912-638-7805. Enjoy Southern hospitality at this charming inn. Pool and relaxing hot tub. Continental-plus breakfast served in dining area.

The King and Prince Beach Resort, Arnold Rd. and Downing St., 912-638-3631. Enjoy the delights of this resort, elegant dining, reading rooms, tennis, racquet ball, golf and much more.

Shipwatch Oceanfront Condominiums, 520 Ocean Blvd., 800-627-6850. Fully equipped spacious vacation condos.

Dining

Allegro, 24065 Demere Rd., 912-638-7097. Continental, seafood, lamb, beef, veal and pastas.

Dockside Grill, 116 Marina Dr., 912-638-4100. Grilled/Sauteed Seafood, steaks, salads, sandwiches and pasta.

Crabdaddy's Seafood Grill, 1217 Ocean Blvd., 912-634-1120. Mesquite grilled and blackened seafood and steaks, lobster tails, shrimp and crab legs.

J. Mac's Island Restaurant and Jazz Bar, 407 Mallery St., 912-634-0403. Angus steaks, rack of lamb, soft shell crabs, crabcakes and the sounds of jazz.

Little St. Simons Island

Commentary

Accessible only by boat, northernmost of the Golden Isles, this little island is the most secluded. Privately owned, the pristine 10,000-acre island harbors isolated beaches, marshlands, ponds and woodlands. For years it was the family retreat of Philip Berolzheimer, who built the hunting lodge for his family. In 1976 it was converted to an inn with 12 rooms, accepting no more than 24 guests at a time. The guests dine at communal tables and spent their days fishing, crabbing and walking the nature trails. During the summer months the inn rents exclusively to groups that rent the entire island. March, April, May, October and November, it is open to individual guests. 912-638-7472.

Sea Island

Commentary

Reached by a causeway from St. Simons Island, island activity centers around The Cloister, one of the top-rated resort hotels in the world.

Golf

Sea Island Golf Course, 912-638-5118. 36-holes of great golf.

Accommodations

The Cloister, 100 First St., 912-638-3611. A five-star island playground with five miles of beach, championship sports, gardens, historic sights and 10,000-acres of protected forests and serene marshes beside the sea. The sprawling Spanish-style buildings are surrounded by manicured lawns, gardens and live oak trees. Enjoy horseback riding on the beach from the Sea Island Stables, or golf at the Sea Island Golf Club that opens four nine-hole courses just for its guests.

Jekyll Island

Commentary

If you had $125,000 in 1887, Jekyll Island could have been yours; it was sold for that amount to members of the Jekyll Island Club, and from 1886 to 1942, it was the private playground of the rich. Rockefellers, Vanderbilts, Astors and Pulitzers prized Jekyll's seclusion and went there to escape. Some members stayed in the Victorian Club House, while others built "cottages," actually mansion-sized homes.

The Depression took its toll; the Club closed in 1942. But in 1946 the State of Georgia took possession of Jekyll Island and opened its beaches, woodlands and marshes to the entire world. The Club, now a National Historic Landmark, serves the public as a splendid backdrop to Jekyll's miles of uncrowded beaches, nature trails, historic sites, golf and tennis facilities, shops and restaurants.

Attractions/Museums

Fishing Pier, North River Dr. at the Clam Creek Picnic Area, north of the Island. 912-635-3636.

Biking and Jogging Trails, 912-635-2648. Enjoy twenty miles of paved paths through woods, marshes and beach areas.

Faith Chapel. A restored, circa 1904, Gothic structure displaying marvelous stained glass.

Jekyll Island Club Historic District, 912-635-2119. Follow the history from 1886 to 1942, where America's wealthiest families lived.

Jekyll Island Historic Marina, 912-635-2891, offers deep sea fishing and sightseeing charters.

Parks

Summer Waves, on South Riverview Dr., 912-635-2074. An 11-acre water park, complete with wave pool, awesome water slides, children's pool and snackbar.

Water Ski Park, on South Riverview Dr., 912-635-3802. Water skiing without a boat, great for all ages.

Golf

Jekyll Island Golf, 912-635-2368. On Capt. Wylly Rd., take your pick from 63-holes of golf. Oleander, Pine Lakes and Indian Mounds offer 18-hole courses, and Oceanside has a 9-hole course.

Accommodations

Jekyll Island Club Hotel, 371 River Dr., 912-635-2600. Once an exclusive retreat, today the resort has been restored to its original splendor for the visitor to enjoy.

Villas By The Sea Hotel Condominiums, 1175 North Beachview Dr., 800-841-6262. Situated on 17-acres of oak groves along 2,000 feet of beach.

Sapelo Island

Commentary

Settled in the 1500s by Spanish missionaries, Georgia's fourth largest barrier island is reached by ferry from the Hudson Creek Dock. The 30-minute ferry ride through marshy banks which are alive with pelicans, egrets, seagulls and other marsh birds. Experience the natural barrier life, forested uplands, vast expanses of salt marsh and unspoiled beaches. Taking an island tour is the best way of experiencing both the natural and cultural history of Sapelo Island, 912-437-6684.

Blackbeard Island

Attractions

Wilderness, Federal Wildlife Refuge. A national wilderness area of 5,618-acres, only accessible by boat in the daytime. Hiking and fishing is allowed. 912-944-4415.

Darien

Altamaha Waterfowl Wildlife Management Area. A 19,000-acre state-owned public hunting area. On U.S.17 S.

Historic Darien, 912-437-4192. Founded in 1736 by Oglethorpe and his Scottish Highlanders. Stroll the historic squares and see sea captain's homes, shrimping boats and caviar processing.

Fort King George, one-mile northeast of U.S.17, 912-437-4770. A glimpse into the past of the hardships endured at this 18th century reconstructed fort and museum.

Accommodations

Open Gates, on Vernon Square, 912-437-6985. A 118-year-old home with period furniture and family collections, becomes a comfortable bed & breakfast, offering four guest rooms.

Fargo

Attractions

Stephen C. Foster State Park, located 17 miles northeast of Fargo, taking Ga.177, 912-637-5325. The park offers campsites, cottages, museum, store, boating and rentals.

Okefenokee National Wildlife Refuge Entrance, on Hwy.17, off U.S.441, 912-637-5274. One of three entrances into this mysterious wilderness. (See Folkston and Waycross for other entrances.)

Folkston

Attractions/Museums

Okefenokee National Wildlife Refuge Entrance, located off Ga.121/23, 912-496-7836. Another of the three entrances. Walk the 4,000-foot boardwalk and see displays and films of swamp animals at facilities. (See Fargo and Waycross for the other entrances.)

Courthouse, circa 1928, and on the National Register.

Railroad Depot, on Main St., 912-496-2536. Was built in 1903 and today houses railroad artifacts.

Suwanee Canal Recreation Area, This entrance into Okefenokee is on Ga.121/23, 912-496-7156. The refuge also offers boat rentals or tours.

Traders Hill Recreation Park. Located three miles south of Folkston on Ga.121/23, 912-496-3412. Camping by the scenic St. Mary's River, trailer hookups, showers and cooking sheds.

Golf

Folkston Golf Course, 912-496-7155, offers an 18-hole course.

Waycross

(From Brunswick take U.S.82 W., to Waycross.)

Home to the most beautiful, mysterious and foreboding place in Georgia, the **Okefenokee National Wildlife Refuge**. The refuge has three entrances; the north gate, **Okefenokee Swamp Park**, is 13 miles south of Waycross via U.S.1/23 and Hwy.177; the east gate, **Suwanee Canal Recreation Area**, is 11 miles southwest of Folkston off Hwy.23/121; the west gate, **Stephen C. Foster State Park**, is 17 miles northeast of Fargo on Hwy.177.

Bring insect repellant, sunscreen, wear a hat and long sleeves and pantlegs that can be tucked in. This is to protect you not from alligators, but mosquitoes and ticks. The largest danger in the park surprisingly is not the wildlife, although you should use caution where you put your hands and feet, but from lightning caused by electrical storms, very common in the summer. Seek shelter under a thick growth when this happens.

The refuge teems with wildlife from black bears, foxes, deer, bobcats and otters, to alligators, king snakes, water moccasins and snapping turtles.

Much information is available at the entrances. 912-283-0583.

Attractions/Museums

Okefenokee National Wildlife Refuge, 912-285-4260. The northern entrance, one of three, features wildlife shows, restored pioneer homestead and swamp exhibits.

Historic Downtown Waycross. One of Georgia's Main Street towns, it rose in 1872 at the intersections of pioneer trails and stagecoach roads, 912-283-7787.

Obediah's Okefenok, Swamp Rd., 912-287-0090. Restored with great detail an example of a swamper's lifestyle in the 19th-century.

Dixon Memorial Forest Wildlife Management Area, located by U.S.1 S., 912-287-4915. Provides public hunting.

Southern Forest World, at North Augusta Ave., 912-285-4056. An educational center promoting the local logging industry.

Parks

Laura S. Walker State Park, 5653 Laura Walker Rd., 912-287-4900. Pine woods for camping and a 120-acre lake for swimming and boating.

St. Mary's-Cumberland Island National Seashore

Commentary

Founded in 1787, St. Mary's serves as the gateway to **Cumberland Island** and the dividing line between Georgia and Florida. The St. Mary's River offers a splendid canoeing adventure but it is **Cumberland Island** that is one of Georgia's premier treasures. After a 45-minute ferry ride aboard the **Cumberland Queen** (arrive 30 minutes before your reservation time), you'll find wild horses, tranquil beaches and rich waters teaming with fish, ducks, fiddler crabs, logger head turtles, oysters and a great variety of wading birds. In the dense forest you may lay your eyes on deer, raccoons, turkeys, feral hogs and armadillos. There are no stores on Cumberland, so make sure you bring a picnic and sun protection. If you are camping, limited to seven days,

restrooms, cold water showers and drinking water are available.

On the beach each wave brings a treasure of shells, mole crabs and, if he is still there, a lost little baby alligator. When you collect shells make sure you collect only the empty ones; if still occupied by a sea tenant, place it back in the water so that Cumberland will remain a living wonder.

Attractions/Museums

Cumberland Island National Seashore, 912-882-4335. Only accessible by ferry from St. Mary's, daytime only. A beautiful, pristine, natural preserved island, with wild horses, abundance of bird species, wildlife, camping, shelling, swimming and beach bumming.

Crooked River State Park, 912-882-5256, located six miles north of the city. A beautiful coastal setting offers campsites, 11 cabins, boat ramp and swimming.

Braille Trail, 912-882-6200. A walking trail marked in braille showing the 38 historic sites.

The Blue Goose, country collectibles including Yankee Candles, ornaments, Rowe pottery and many unique one-of-a-kind gifts. Minnie, your hostess, will make sure you will find that special something.

McIntosh Sugar Mill Tabby Ruins, 912-882-6200. One of the best preserved tabby structures and oldest industry ruins in Georgia.

Oak Grove Cemetery, 912-882-6200. Settlers and soldiers, some tombstones with French inscriptions, dating back as far as 1801.

Washington Pump, on Osborne St. This pump was one of the original fresh water pumps for the town.

Toonerville Trolley, on Osborne St., was used until 1938. The trolley was made famous by cartoonist Roy Crane in 1935 with the comic strip *"Wash Tubbs and Easy."*

Seabrook Village, 912-884-7008. A new African-American living-history center, shedding the light of this turn-of-the-century community.

Golf

Osprey Cove Golf Course, 912-882-5575. A spectacular,links-style 18-hole course designed by Mark McCumber.

Accommodations

The Goodbread House, on 209 Osborne St., owned by Betty and George Krauss, is an 1870 four-room home, with full length porches both upstairs and down. This carefully restored home exudes warmth and coziness featuring, high ceilings, fireplaces and private baths in each room, including ceiling fans and air conditioning.

Relax on the veranda, or enjoy some good stories with Betty, a perfect Southern hostess. Wine and cheese is served at cocktail hour, and, in the morning, there's a full breakfast in a elegant setting with your newspaper. 912-882-7490.

Spencer House Inn (circa 1872), at 101 East Bryant St., owned by energetic Mike and Mary Neff, with 14 rooms, features a large veranda with rockers. Inside you will find hardwood floors graced with imported carpets, original moldings, fine antique furniture and private baths many with deep clawfoot tubs and pedestal sinks. A tiny elevator is available, and, if it is not too busy, take a look at some of the quaint guest rooms. A full breakfast is served on the veranda. 912-882-1872.

Dining

Seagle's Restaurant, Riverview Hotel at 105 Osborne St. Sit by one of the many windows and enjoy the beautiful view of the ocean and the Cumberland Queen Ferry. Built in 1916, today owned and run by the Mayor of St. Mary's, Jerry Brandon and wife Gaila. A comfortable country-style dining room with oil-cloth clad tables, helps you experience genuine hospitality and "right off the boat" white large shrimp as sweet as lobster, with a tangy keylime pie to satisfy the sweet tooth. 912-882-3242.

**Annual Events and Festivals
in The Golden Isles**

January
St. Simons Island
Island Concert Series
Island Players

February
Jekyll Island
Annual 5K and 10K Island Runs
Sea Island
Weekend for Wildlife Benefit

March
Jekyll Island
Art Associations Festival
St. Simons Island/Sea Island
Tour of Homes
St. Simons Island
Super Dolphin Day Race
Spring Craft Show
Island Players

April
Brunswick
Old Town Tour of Homes
Jekyll Island
Annual Great Easter Egg Hunt
St. Simons Island
Boat Show-Golden Isles Marina
Antiques and Collectibles Show
Easter Sunrise Services
(Jekyll and St. Simons)

May
Brunswick
Blessing of the Shrimp Fleet
(Mother's Day)
Jekyll Island
Memorial Day 5K Run
and Children's One-Mile Run
St. Simons/Jekyll/Brunswick
Tillandsia Festival

June
Brunswick
Kingfish Tournament
Jekyll Island
Outdoor Summer Theater Productions
(through August)
St. Simons Island
Antique and Collectibles Show

July
St. Simons Island
Sunshine Festival, 4th of July
Golden Isles Sport Fishing
Club Tournament
Jekyll Island
Outdoor Theater Productions
Jekyll/St. Simons/Sea Island
4th of July Fireworks

August
Jekyll Island
Beach Music Festival
Mini Triathlon
Outdoor Theater Productions
St. Simons Island
Georgia Sea Island Festival
Antiques and Collectibles Show

September
Jekyll Island
Triathlon
St. Simons Island
Antiques and Collectibles Show

October
Brunswick
Ritz Theater Season Opens
Community Concert Season Opens
Civic Orchestra Season Begins
Jekyll Island
Biathlon
Historic Halloween Haunts
Georgia-Florida Golf Classic
St. Simons Island
Golden Isles Arts and Crafts Festival
Taste of the Golden Isles
Island Players Season Opens
St. Simons by the Sea: An Arts Fest

November
Brunswick/Jekyll/St. Simons Island
Holiday Lights "A Celebration of Community"
(Thanksgiving through January 1)
Jekyll Island
"Golfer's Heaven"

December
Jekyll Island
Bluegrass Festival
Christmas Tour of Homes
St. Simons Island,
Christmas at Frederica
Holiday House Tour
Madrigal Feast

Fun Facts:

- The four to six mile band of salt-marsh that lies behind Georgia's barrier islands compises approximately 400,000 acres.

- Cumberland Island, with some 15,100 acres, is Georgia's largest barrier island and the largest undeveloped island on the Atlantic coast.

- Georgia's Coastal Plain Province encompasses the famous Golden Isles, about 100 miles of shoreline on the Atlantic Ocean. But if all of the barrier islands and bays were included in the measure, Georgia's shoreline would expand to almost 2,500 miles.

- The Georgia coastline consists of over 100 pristine miles with many splendid beaches.

Good Ol' Boy

LOVE ATLANTA

NORTHEAST MOUNTAINS

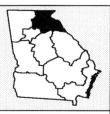

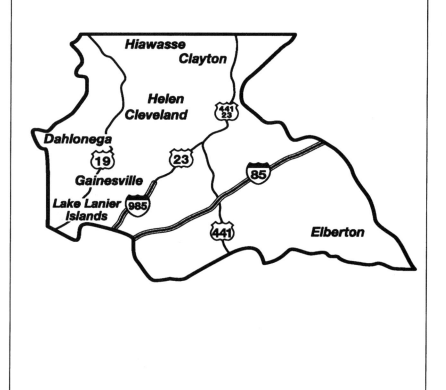

Section XIV
Traveling Georgia's Northeast Mountains

Georgia's Mountain Country

Georgia's northern mountain country (the high country) covers two regions, **"Georgia's Northeast Mountains"** and **"Georgia's Northwest Mountains."** Together, they have ten peaks that exceed 4,000 feet and offer a wonder-laden area of tranquility with thousands of glimmering waterfalls and glittering wildflowers, sparkling lakes and verdant vistas.

Examples of time-honored traditions are found everywhere. You'll find colorful quilts, twig baskets, dulcimers, wooden games and toys, handwoven wall-hangings and plenty of mountain honey and apple butter.

Georgia's Northeast Mountains

Commentary

Only one hour north of Atlanta, discover peaceful places, spectacular sights, and the beautiful freshness of wilderness. Breathtaking waterfalls fall endlessly, towering pines whisper you into contentment, and plenty of wildlife that dares to look back at you with curiosity. Shout with excitement as you tube the **Chattooga River**, tingle with anticipation as you pan for gold in Dahlonega, and lose your earthbound worries as you hike the wondrous **Bartram Trail** or climb **Brasstown Bald**, the highest mountain in Georgia.

Discover the awesome beauty of some of Georgia's finest state parks, world-famous lakes such as **Lake Russell**, **Lake Rabun** and **Lake Burton**, and wonder at the rainbow forming water-

falls such as **Tallulah Falls**, **Toccoa Falls** and spectacular **Anna Ruby Falls**.

Then, find out where the **Cabbage Patch Kids** come from in **Cleveland**, and take the kids to the beach and water park at **Lake Lanier Islands**. You can yodel in **Helen**, a picturesque Bavarian village, or tee it up at the **Innsbruck Golf Course**. To sum it all up, the natural beauty is awesome and unforgettable.

Chattahoochee National Forest

Commentary

Northwest of Helen, the Richard Russell-Brasstown Scenic Highway provides a beautiful mountain drive through the **Chattahoochee National Forest** (which spans both the Northeast and Northwest Mountain areas). Within an hour of Helen is **Brasstown Bald**, the highest point in Georgia at 4,784 feet. After a caution-filled drive on Ga.180, you'll reach a visitors center. There hop on the shuttle bus to the observation deck, or walk the 930-yard trail to the top. The panoramic view encompasses Georgia, Tennessee, North Carolina, South Carolina and Georgia.

Amicalola Falls
Cherokee for tumbling waters.

(Approximately 50 miles due north of Atlanta)
(From Dahlonega take County Rd. 52 W.)

Commentary

With its 729-foot waterfall, **Amicalola Falls State Park** encompasses 1,029 scenic acres. An eight-mile approach trail leads from the falls to Springer Mountain, the southern end of the

2,150-mile Appalachian Trail. There's a 17-site wooded campground with water and electric hookups and the **Amicalola Falls Lodge**, with 57 guest rooms, all overlooking the majestic Blue Ridge Mountains. 706-265-8888.

Blairsville

Attractions/Museums

Blood Mountain Archaeological Area-Chattahoochee National Forest, located at Neel's Gap on Hwy.19 and 129, 706-745-6428. Historic site of the Cherokee and Creek Indian battle.

Brasstown Bald-Chattahoochee National Forest, on Hwy.180, 706-745-6928. Visitors' center perched on Georgia's highest mountain, 4,784 feet.

Cooper's Creek Scenic and Recreation Area-Chattahoochee National Forest, 706-632-3031. Enjoy camping, fishing, hunting and hiking trails in this beautiful area.

Frank Gross Recreation Area-Chattahoochee National Forest, 706-632-3031. Enjoy camping and fishing along the beautiful Rock Creek.

Georgia Mountain Experimenting Station, 2564 Georgia Mountain Experiment Station Rd., 706-745-2655. The station is an agricultural branch of the University of Georgia.

Helton Creek Falls, on Hwy.19 and 129 S., 706-745-5789. Spectacular majestic waterfalls set deep within the hardwood forest.

High Shoals Scenic Area-Chattahoochee National Forest, 706-745-6928. Mountain streams lined with wild flowers, waterfalls and hiking trails.

Lake Nottley, a 4,180-acre lake located off Hwy.19/129, 706-745-5789. Attracting fisherman for its largemouth bass and crappie; also for swimming, camping and picnicking.

Lake Winfield Scott Recreation Area-Chattahoochee National Forest, Hwy.180, 706-754-6221. A recreation area providing a 32-site campground, fishing, swimming, picnic areas and hiking.

Sosebee Cove Scenic Area-Chattahoochee National Forest, Hwy.180, 706-745-6928. A gorgeous terrain of wildflowers and hardwood timber for hiking.

Track Rock Archaeological Area-Chattahoochee National Forest, at Trackrock Gap Rd., 706-745-6928. A large 52-acre area providing a wonder of preserved Indian petroglyphs.

Woody Gap Recreational Area-Chattahoochee National Forest, Hwy.60, 706-864-6173. Enjoy picnicking and hiking along the scenic Yahoola Valley and Appalachian Trail.

Union County Historical Society Museum, 706-745-5493. On the square in the old Union County Court House, exhibiting county history.

Walasi-Yi Center, U.S.129 S. at Neel's Gap, 706-745-6095. This sturdy stone lodge, constructed in 1934, annually sees more than 1,000 hikers pass through. The lodge houses an inn, mountain outfitting store, crafts, books and maps.

Baker's Curio Emporium and Toy Car Museum, 706-745-9509, which provides garage space for more than 5,000 toy cars.

Parks

Vogel State Park, 7485 Vogel Park Rd., 706-745-2628. The oldest and prettiest of state parks in Georgia is tailored around a shaded lake. This full-service park offers cottages, camping, watersports and excellent hiking trails.

Accommodations

7 Creeks Housekeeping Cabins, 5109 Horseshoe Cove Rd., 706-745-4753. (See Hiawassee)

Misty Mountain Inn Cottages, 4376 Misty Mountain Lane, 706-745-4786. Rooms are available in the inn or cottages.

Southern Country Inn, 2592 Collins Lane, 706-379-1603. Eight guest rooms with panoramic view.

Dining

The North Georgia Restaurant, 706-745-5888. On the square, serves home-style breakfasts and lunches.

The Drake House, 706-745-5305. Enjoy a varied menu from pan-fried trout to Greek salad and eggplant parmigiana.

Blair House Restaurant, Hwy.19, five miles north of Blairsville, 706-745-3399. Enjoy a rustic nautical setting while sampling moderately priced seafood.

Chateau Elan
Braselton

(Thirty minutes north of Atlanta. Take I-85 N. to exit 48, and turn left on Ga.211 to entrance. Braselton is five miles further on I-85, exit 49.)

Commentary

Margaret Mitchell wrote that "the blood-red furrows of the north Georgia foothills made the best cotton in the world." But for the creators of **Chateau Elan**, the quartz and mica-rich soil seemed ideal for growing the grapes that would fuel what is now the South's premier winery.

Attractions/Museums

Chateau Elan Winery and Resort. From its beginnings as a winery, Chateau Elan has grown into a world class resort offering a full-service European-style health spa, an 18-hole golf course, tennis courts, a 150-room inn, the Le Clos restaurant (Cafe Elan), an art

gallery, equestrian facilities, free winery tours, and nature trails galore. 800-233-9463.

Chestnut Mountain Winery, Hwy.124 off I-85, exit 48, 867-6914. Set in a 30-acre wooded area, the winery offers free tasting, a wine-cellar tour, rooftop patio and nature trails.

Road Atlanta, 5300 Winder Hwy., 967-6143. Road racing circuit for sports cars, motorbikes and go-karts.

Golf

Chateau Elan Golf Club, 6060 Golf Club Dr., 932-0900. A deluxe 18-hole golf course.

Accommodations

Chateau Elan Winery and Resort, 100 Rue Charlemagne, 932-0900. A luxury resort, winery, health spa and six restaurants.

Dining

Le Clos, at Chateau Elan, 7000 Old Winder Hwy., 932-0900. Gourmet dining.

Brasstown Bald
Hiawassee

Commentary

The Chattahoochee National Forest blankets much of Towns County with Georgia pines and hardwoods. Sections of four national wilderness areas in the county deliver a vast area of peace and seclusion.

Ten to fifteen miles north of Brasstown Bald is **Hiawassee**, a village known for mountain crafts, as Georgia's capital for country music and for its vast rhododendron gardens.

Located in Hiawassee, **Brasstown** is the newest resort in the North Georgia mountains. It is sure to become one of the area's most popular escape destinations. Championship golf, tennis, pools, hot tubs and spa.

Attractions

Lake Chatuge Recreation Area-Chatta-hoochee National Forest, Hwy.288, 706-6928. An angler's favorite, set on a pine-covered peninsula. Camping, boating, fishing and hiking.

Fred Hamilton Rhododendron Garden, Hwy.76 W., 706-896-4966. Over 2,000 rhododendron and azaleas will delight any gardener.

Parks

Towns County Recreation Park, Hwy.76, 706-896-4191. Excellent recreational park with camping, beach with lifeguards, playground, tennis courts, concessions and boat ramp.

Accommodations

Bald Mountain Seven Creeks Housekeeping Cabins offers six well-spaced cabins, each equipped with kitchen, private bath, telephone, TV, washer/dryer and grill. Swim or fish in the stocked, spring-fed lake or nearby trout stream. Over 70 acres of mountainous terrain to hike and farm animals for the kids to pet. Within miles you can golf, pan for gold, river raft or shop for crafts and spend the evenings around a crackling fire. 706-745-4753.

Fieldstone Inn, three miles west of Hiawassee on U.S.76, is listed in the Great Inns of America Directory. Many of its 66 rooms overlook lovely Lake Chatuge. A restaurant, marina, pool and lighted tennis courts complete an inviting package. 800-545-3408; 706-896-2262.

Swan Lake Bed & Breakfast, 2500 Hickorynut Cove, 706-896-1582. Located adjacent to national forest and wilderness; relax at a Cape Cod home, offering two guest rooms.

Grahl's Comfort Zone, River St., 706-896-1358. On the shore of Lake Chatuge, enjoy beautiful scenery, terraced lawn and two light and airy guest rooms.

Birdsall's Mountain Cottages, 2018 Forest Hill Dr., 706-896-2982. Secluded in a beautiful mountain area.

Dining

The Fieldstone Inn, dine casually at the Inn's spacious restaurant overlooking the lake and choose from a varied menu. 800-545-3408; 706-896-2262.

The Georgia Mountain Restaurant, Hwy.76, 706-896-3430. Country cooking popular with the locals.

Black River BBQ, located off Hwy.76 at Hwy.17, 706-896-3142. Grilled trout, chicken or pork are the favorites here.

Deer Lodge, Hwy.75 S., 706-896-2726. As busy as it gets, it is well worth the wait. Hearty entrees served in cozy rooms.

Carnesville

Attractions/Museums

Franklin County Historical Society Museum, Gainesville St., 706-677-4479.

Historic Sites/Homes

Cromer's Mill Covered Bridge, circa 1906, is located eight miles south via 106 E., on County Rd. The 132-foot long town lattice bridge crosses the Nails Creek. 706-384-4659.

Clarksville, Lake Rabun and Lake Burton

(I-85 north to I-985 to New Holland, to U.S.23. Then take U.S.441 north to the Clarkesville, Lake Burton, Lake Rabun area.)

Commentary

Nestled in the beautiful Blue Ridge Mountains of northeast Georgia, Lakes Rabun and Burton offer seas of tranquility. **Lake Rabun** shelters one of the best U.S. Forest Service recreation areas in the Blue Ridge Mountains.

Fishermen seem to favor **Lake Burton**. A mile or so west of the dam at the lake's southern end, signs off Hwy.197 lead drivers down dirt roads to Cherokee Landing. Here you'll find a marina, boat launch, bait store, burger joint and a scattered collection of cabins. The lake's public swimming area, **Timpson Cove Beach**, can be found at the northeastern shore, off Hwy.76 west of Clayton.

The old-time fishing resort of **LaPrade's** off Hwy.197, 706-947-3312, dates back to the town of Burton, which has been submerged under its namesake lake since 1925. Across the road, LaPrade's marina features a boat launch and rentals. A small crafts shop, **One Burton Place**, is nearby.

If all of this natural beauty seems too overwhelming, **Southeastern Expeditions** is there to help you get started. Located on Highway 76, they are Georgia's oldest guide group. Canoe and kayak training are available. 800-868-RAFT.

Clarkesville is a friendly place where progress is measured in quality, not quantity. For example, among the town's admirable B and B's is the **Glen-Ella Springs Inn**, 706-754-7295, with 16 rooms. With much of its original flooring, walls and stone chimneys intact, it has earned a spot on the "National Register of Historic Places." Also listed is the **Burns-Sutton House**, 706-754-5565, with four-poster beds, stained-glass windows and guest-room fireplaces, offering cozy accommodations in a gracious setting of an elegant turn-of-the-century Victorian home. After a refreshing and peaceful night's sleep, enjoy a delicious family style breakfast in the morning and prepare for a stroll through town square.

North of Clarkesville on County Highway 197, you'll find an excellent display of local crafts at **Mark of The Potter**, 706-947-3440. Housed in **Grandpa Watts' Mill**, a 51-year-

old, water-powered corn meal mill, is a 25-year-old shop offering original handmade crafts in wood and metal, and ceramic jewelry, weaving, hand-blown glass and pottery by more than 40 artists. A National Historic Site, visitors can see and feed mountain trout in their natural habitat from the shop's porch over the Soque River.

Attractions/Museums

Downtown Clarkesville, 706-778-4654. Strolling downtown, you will find a score of art galleries, craft and antique shops and restaurants.

Batesville General Store, Hwy.197 and Hwy.255, 706-947-3434. Selling everything a general store should and a cafe in the back for biscuits and burgers.

Parks, Lakes and Recreational Areas

Fern Springs Recreation Area-Chattahoochee National Forest, Dick's Hill Parkway, 706-754-6221. Picnicking and camping at the Springs.

Lake Burton, on Hwy.197 or Hwy.76, 706-754-6036. Sixty-two miles of shoreline. Enjoy boating, camping, or visiting the public beach and marinas.

Lake Burton Trout Hatchery, on Hwy.197 N., 706-947-3112. Trout-filled raceways and fishing pond for children.

Lake Burton Wildlife Management Area, Hwy.197, 535-5700. For the adventurous, discover trails, mountain wilderness, camping, public hunting and fishing.

Lake Russell Recreation Area-Chattahoochee National Forest, located 3.5 miles from Cornelia, 706-754-6221. Operating year-round, the recreation area is set around a 100-acre lake with grassy beach. Perfect for swimming, fishing, camping and boating.

Lake Rabun, Lake Rabun Rd., 706-754-6056. A most popular recreational area since the 1930s. Boating, fishing, camping and beach with a marina.

Lake Seed, right off Lake Rabun Rd.,706-754-6036. Lake Seed is sometimes called, Lake Nacoochee. Unlike Lake Burton, Lake Seed is tight and narrow. It offers primitive camping, boating and fishing.

Lake Tugalo, off Hwy.441 N., 706-754-6036. Boating, fishing and camping are the main attractions at this lake.

Panther Creek Recreation Area-Chattahoochee National Forest, on Old Hwy.441 N., 706-754-6221. Favored with many for cool picnic shelters, hiking trails and a beautiful 80-foot waterfall.

Moccasin Creek State Park, on the shores of Lake Burton, 706-947-3194. Georgia's smallest state park offers 53 campsites, very popular with fishing families.

Rabun Bald Mountain, 706-782-5113. With an elevation of 4,696-feet, follow the Rabun Bald Trail.

Rabun Beach Recreation Area-Chattahoochee National Forest, County Rd., 706-782-3320. In the spring enjoy one of the most beautiful hiking trails amongst flowering rhododendron. Enjoy camping, swimming, boating and fishing.

Historic Sites/Homes

Grace-Calvary Episcopal Church, located two blocks off the square. Built in 1842 by vacationing coastal families escaping the summer heat, this is one of the oldest churches in the state.

Haywood English Home-Big Holly Cabin, three miles west of town, 255-3583. One of the earliest 19th-century pine log homes.

Accommodations

The Barn Inn is another comfortable mountain retreat. Built in the 1920s as a dairy barn, it has been transformed into a comfortable mountain bed & breakfast. After a day of hiking, rafting or golf, settle in by a fire or feel the lake breeze from your deck. Seven spacious luxury rooms. Year-round. 706-782-5094.

The Lake Rabun Hotel, 706-782-4946, has offered guests a high-style rustic retreat since 1922. The stone mountain lodge resembles a classic hunting lodge; a full breakfast is served there.

The Charm House Inn, 108 South Washington St., 706-754-9347. Guests can relax in an elegant 1907 Greek revival mansion with five guest rooms; an inn and restaurant.

Glen-Ella Springs Inn and Conference Center, Bear Gap Rd., 706-754-7295. A rambling country inn, with 14 guest rooms, a pool, gardens and gourmet dining.

LaPrade's on Lake Burton, I-85 N., to US.441 N., onto Hwy.197N. For 70 years, LaPrade's has been serving up its special kind of mountain magic on the scenic shores of Lake Burton. From famous fried chicken and hearty mountain meals to world class fishing, LaPrade's is sure to become one of your favorites. A full-service marina, complete with rental boats, craft and gift shop, and rustic cabins, perfect for a fisherman's getaway, will make you feel right at home. Open April through November. Office, lodging & gift shop, 706-947-3312, marina-dock 706-947-3003, 30 second meal reservation hotline 706-947-3313/800-262-3313.

Dining

Taylor's Trolley, 706-754-5566. Set in a 1907 storefront, daily chalkboard specials vary from mountain trout to prime rib.

LaPrade's Restaurant, 706-947-3312. Located by Lake Burton, enjoy family-style dining with scrumptious homecooking and old-fashioned prices.

Glen-Ella Springs Inn is a gourmet's delight, serving such dishes as smoked tenderloin and artichoke lasagna.

Clayton and Tallulah Falls

(15 miles northeast of Clarkesville on U.S.441.)

Commentary

A historic resort area known for its scenery and mountain climate. The name derives from the Indian word meaning terrible or awesome. Local legend has it that Tallulah Bankhead was named after the falls.

Walk the 500-yard trail along the rim of **Tallulah Gorge**, the only quartzite-walled gorge in the southern Appalachians. Writing in 1819, David Hillhouse described the area as "one of the nation's greatest curiosities." The gorge, the Niagara of the South, is 200 to 1,200 feet deep. The width varies from several hundred feet to a 1/2 mile across and it is two miles long. In 1970 Karl Wallenda crossed the chasm on a two-inch-thick tightwire, and the movie "Deliverance" was filmed here.

Several park pavilions offer information on local flora and fauna, as well as geologic formations. **Terrora Park**, owned by Georgia Power, is a good focal point for your mountain venture. Open year-round, you'll find mountain culture displays plus interactive video exhibits on the falls and the hydroelectric dam that reduced the once mighty river's roar to a relatively calm flow. There is also a white sand beach, playground, tennis courts and a 50-site campground, equipped with electricity and water hookups. Hot showers available in the bathhouse. 706-754-3276.

Attractions

Tallulah Gallery, Old U.S.441, Bypass 15, 706-754-6020.

Parks, Lakes and Recreational Areas

Bartram Trail, 706-782-5113. Naturalist William Bartram, mapped this 57-mile route in 1777.

Coleman River Scenic Area-Chattahoochee National Forest, 706-782-3320. A photographer's delight in this scenic old timber forest, with tumbling streams.

Coleman River Wildlife Management Area, Coleman River Rd., 535-5700. This very rugged terrain offers primitive camping, hunting and fishing.

Ellicott's Rock Wilderness-Chattahoochee National Forest, 706-782-3320. An intersection of three states can be found on Ellicott's Rock Trail—Georgia, North and South Carolina.

Popcorn Overlook-Chattahoochee National Forest, 706-782-3320. Beautiful lookout point.

Southern Nantahala Wilderness-Chattahoochee National Forest, Tallulah River Rd., 706-782-3320. Rugged mountain forest for the serious hiker, involving considerable climbing.

Tallulah Gorge State Park, U.S.Hwy,441, 706-754-3276. A gorgeous park offering camping, swimming, hiking and fishing. Also the oldest natural gorge in the U.S., with a depth of 1,200-feet. Park the car and take one of several trails.

Tallulah Falls Lake, on Hwy.441, 706-754-6036. A gorgeous area, approximately 1,500 feet above sea level. Offers camping, boating, beach and fishing.

Tallulah River Recreation Area-Chattahoochee National Forest, 706-782-3320. For the adventurous, this area offers secluded camping and great trout fishing. Check with information, for some of the river is not suitable for canoeing.

Tate Branch Recreation Area-Chatta-hoochee National Forest, 706-782-3320. A fisherman's delight for trout fishing, camping and hiking.

Tut's Game Preserve, on Hwy.441 S. and Seed Tick Rd., 706-782-6218. Observe deer, peacocks, eagles and Georgia's black bear. Hang gliding facility and a few cabins are available.

Warwoman Dell Recreation Area-Chatta-hoochee National Forest, 706-782-3320. An interpretive trail and pamphlet identify the many flowers and rare ferns common to the region. Picnicking and hiking only.

Warwoman Wildlife Management Area, 535-5700. Primitive camping, hunting and fishing.

Willis Knob Recreation Area of Chatta-hoochee National Forest, Goldmine Rd., 706-782-3320. Rugged mountain scenery, with horse camps and trails.

Wildwater, located 12 miles east of Clayton, 800-451-9972. Variety of river adventures for all ages and levels.

Accommodations

A Small Hotel, 800-786-0624, 706-782-6488, half-mile east of town, on Hwy.76.

English Manor Inns, consists of seven inns sprawled across a heavy seven-acre wooded area. The only inn in Georgia that offers special events such as mystery weekends, written and produced by owner Susan Thornwell. The decor ranges from antique period pieces and elegant wallpaper to country eclectic furniture and fine linens. Each "inn" has from three to seven bedrooms, with its own main room and kitchen facilities. Private baths with each guest room, some with whirlpool tubs. Relax on your own porch in a comfortable rocker or enjoy a hot tub and swimming pool down by the creek. 706-782-5789 or 800-782-5780. Take U.S.23/441 in Clayton, turn east onto U.S.76; the English Manor is one mile further on the right.

Green Shutters Bed & Breakfast Inn, Main St., 706-782-3342. Enjoy the seclusion of the deep woods at this Cape Cod-style home with three guest rooms.

Hang Glider Heaven Cabins provide overnight accommodations. 706-782-6218.

Old Clayton Inn, South Main St., 706-782-7722. Historic lodge inn.

Little Duck Lodge and River Camp, located seven miles south of Clayton on Hwy.441 and Joy Bridge Rd.; look for the windmill. Nature lovers and stressed out city dwellers alike will revitalize in the stunning natural beauty of the mountains. Guests may rent a lodge, covered dock A-frame or two story pavilion with bunks. The lodge, set on the on the Tallulah River also offers camping sites of up to five acres. You can pre-arrange activities such as rafting, trout fishing, canoeing, horseback riding and pontoon boating. For information call Louise or Brent Anthony at 706-782-9936, or write to Box 322, Star Route, Lakemont, GA 30552.

Dining

Clayton Cafe, on Main St. Home-style breakfasts and burgers and basics for dinner.

Green Shutters Restaurant, on Main St., serves three family-style meals a day, Wednesday through Monday. 706-782-3342.

The Stockton House Restaurant, on Warwoman Rd., 706-782-6175. Overlooking a forest enjoy steak, seafood and lunch/dinner buffets.

Cleveland

(Eight miles south of Helen.)

Attractions/Museums

Andrews Cove-Chattahoochee National Forest, along I-75 N., 706-754-6221. This recreational area is located along a beautiful mountain stream in a heavily wooded area. Camping, hiking and fishing.

Babyland General Hospital, the original home of the Cabbage Patch dolls. Collectible soft-sculptured originals are hand-stitched to birth and are patiently waiting to be adopted. In addition to the frequent deliveries of "babies" from the Mother Cabbages, Babyland is full of fun and excitement for children and adults alike. 706-865-2171.

Yonah Mountain, 706-865-5356. Most of Yonah (bear in Cherokee), is in the Chattahoochee National Forest, which provides great mountain climbing.

Gold N' Gem Grubbin' Mine, Town Creek Rd., 706-865-5454. Operating mine offering tours.

North Georgia Candle Factory, Hwy.129 S., 706-865-6131. Watch candles being made and carved. Factory prices.

Downtown Merchants Square, 706-865-5356. Shop at unique crafts and antique shops.

Old White County Courthouse, on the square, 706-865-5356.

Accommodations

Villagio di Montagna, on Hwy.129, 800-367-3822. Luxurious villas in this one-of-a-kind mountain retreat.

The Lodge at Windy Acres, Highway 75, 706-865-6636. Rustic, contemporary lodge, with five guest rooms, offering comfort ato fullfil the needs of guests.

Tyson Homestead, Highway 75, 706-865-6914. Enjoy the tranquil atmosphere in a brick colonial home, which is perched on a wooded hillside; offers five guest rooms.

Parks

Unicoi State Park, just north of Helen, with its 1,000+ acres of highlands and woodlands, threaded by streams, lakes and waterfalls, offers something for the entire family. Walk on 12 miles of trails (guided and unguided) and enjoy the swimming, canoeing and fishing on the 53-acre lake. The handicraft shop in the **Unicoi Lodge** offers a collection of mountain arts, and meals are available in the lodge. Accommodations include camping sites and cottages. 706-878-2824.

Comer

Historic Site

Watson Mill Bridge State Park, Watson Mill Park Rd., 706-783-5349. Circa 1885, this historic covered bridge is 236 feet long.

Commerce

Attractions/Museums

Commerce Historic District. Interesting collection of 19th and 20th century commercial and industrial structures.

New Atlanta Dragway, 500 East Ridgeway Dr., 706-335-2301. Drag racing facilities.

Commerce Factory Stores, 199 Pottery Factory Dr., 706-335-6352.

Tanger Factory Outlet Center, 198 Tanger Dr., 706-335-4537.

Accommodations

The Pittman House, 103 Homer St., 706-335-3823. A spacious 1890 home, with white-columned wrap-around porch, offers four guest rooms with full breakfast.

Cornelia

Attractions

Lake Russell Recreation Area-Chattahoochee National Forest, 706-754-6221. One hundred acre lake offers a grass beach, camping, swimming, fishing and boating.

Lake Russell Wildlife Management Area, 706-535-5700, located next to the recreation area. Primitive camping and horseback trails are available.

World's Largest Apple Monument, at Railroad Depot, 706-784-4654. Located in center of town, this 5,200-pound monument is dedicated to apple growers.

Cumming

Attractions

Lanierland Music Park, 6115 Jot'em Down Rd., 887-7464. Located 12 miles north of Cumming, top country music entertainers perform here May through November.

The Atlanta Steeplechase, Seven Branches Farm, 237-7436. The annual Atlanta Steeplechase is held here.

Historic Site

Pooles Mill Covered Bridge, Pooles Mill Rd., 887-6461. Circa 1906, the 90-foot bridge spans the Settendown Creek, one mile north of Heardville.

Dahlonega
(dah-LON-a-gah)

(90 minutes north on Ga.400.)

Dahlonega is a historic mountain town at the southwestern foot of the Blue Ridge Mountains. Its name is Cherokee for "precious yellow metal."

Learn all about America's first gold rush by visiting the **Gold Museum**, housed in a 150-year-old former courthouse. Looking southwest from the museum, you can see the steeple of **Price Memorial Hall** (part of North Georgia College) covered in Dahlonega gold. If overcome by the gold bug, head for **Consolidated Gold Mines**, which offers tours of an authentic gold mine and opportunities to strike it rich while "gemstone grubbing" and panning for gold. 706-864-8473. You'll see the mine as it was in the 1800s, learn the geology and techniques of the era and maybe find a nugget of your own. You can also pan for gold and gemstones at **Crisson's Gold Mine**, a commercial gold mine where at least 22 strip mines are in operation. 706-864-6363.

Explore the beauty of the north Georgia mountains by way of its spectacular Chestatee and Etowah Rivers. **Appalachian Outfitters** offers canoes, kayaks and tubes. 706-864-7117.

Then try the countryside aboard a horse-drawn restored antique surrey built in 1890. Trips of one to four hours are available. 706-864-1266.

The Smith House serves up large portions of traditional family-style Southern cuisine. The House has a country store and a hotel for overnight guests. In the evenings, you'll hear old favorites rendered on the electric organ. You may catch an impromptu accompanist "playing the spoons" by rapidly tapping the utensils against his knees in flawless rhythm. Browse in such shops as **Mountain Christmas**, a two-story wonderland packed full of unusual ornaments and decorations. 706-864-3566, or 800-852-9577.

Mountain Top Lodge is just outside town. It has 13 guest rooms. 706-864-5257.

Attractions/Museums

Dahlonega Town Square, 706-864-3711. A most inviting scene of 1838 Greek revival courthouse, Victorian storefronts and brick walkways lined with flower barrels.

Appalachian Outfitters, on Hwy.60 S., 706-864-7117. Be adventurous and canoe, kayak or tube the beautiful Chestatee or Etowah River.

Mountain Adventures Cyclery, at Hwy.400 and Hwy.60, 706-864-8525. Ride the beautiful trails of the woodlands on a mountain bike; rentals and guided trail tours available.

Antique Rose Emporium, Cavender Creek Rd., 706-864-5884. Old rose gardens with perennials and herb gardens.

Dahlonega Gold Museum, Public Square, 706-864-2257. The former courthouse, the oldest in north Georgia, was built in 1838, with locally cast bricks that contain gold flecks.

George E. Coleman Sr. Planetarium, on campus of North Georgia College, 706-864-1511.

Cavendar Castle Winery, Wimpy Mill Rd., 706-864-4759. Sitting atop a mountain, this Gothic-style castle and winery exudes old world ambiance.

Consolidated Gold Mines, 125 Consolidated Rd., 706-864-8473. Tour one of the largest mining operations (no longer operating); gold panning is allowed and there's also a souvenir shop.

Crisson Gold Mine, on Wimpy Mill Rd., 706-864-6363. Try your skill at panning for gold and gemstones.

Parks and Recreational Areas

Blackburn Park, Auraria Rd., 706-864-3711. Enjoy such varied activities as archery, swimming, fishing, hiking and panning for gold.

Chestatee Overlook-Chattahoochee National Forest, on Hwy.60 N., 706-864-6173. The overlook offers a scenic view of Blood Mountain Cove.

Chestatee Wildlife Management Area, on Hwy.19 N., 535-5700. Primitive camping, fishing and hunting. The watershed is the famous Waters Creek trophy trout stream.

Desoto Falls Scenic Area-Chattahoochee National Forest, along Hwy.129 and 19 N., 706-864-6173. The scenic area is located in rugged mountainous country. Camping, hiking, fishing and picnicking.

Dockery Lake Recreation Area-Chattahoochee National Forest, 706-864-6173. Surrounded by ridge tops and small valleys, this popular trout fishing spot also offers scenic hiking trails and camping.

Waters Creek Recreation Area-Chattahoochee National Forest, 706-864-6173. Located along a beautiful mountain stream. Enjoy trout fishing, camping and hiking.

Accommodations

Cavendar Castle Winery and Bed & Breakfast, located by U.S.19 and State 60, 706-864-4759. Georgia's only bed & breakfast winery, set in a panoramic mountain setting. Offering six guest rooms and full breakfast served in the wine-tasting room.

Mountain Top Lodge, on Old Ellijay Rd., 706-864-5257. A rustic country inn, with 13 guest rooms, all decorated in country charm with private baths.

Smith House Inn, 202 South Chestatee, 706-864-3566. Operating as an inn since 1922. Visitors can be assured of Southern hospitality and comfort. Offering 16 guest rooms and pool.

Royal Guard Inn, 203 South Park St., 706-864-1713. Restored turn-of-the-century home, featuring a large wraparound front porch and five guest rooms. A full breakfast is served.

Dining

Smith House Inn, known by many for its hearty Southern homecooking, served family style.

Clark's Front Porch Barbecue, 320 Warwick St., 706-864-6677. Hickory-smoked meats served with the traditional side orders.

Nature's Cellar, 706-864-6829. Enjoy a vegetarian cuisine of quiche, hummus and salads.

Caruso's, on Main St., serves Italian cuisine in a casual atmosphere.

Dillard

Attractions

Dillard, 706-283-5651, offers shopping enjoyment with antique mall, craft and specialty shops.

Andy's Trout Farm, Betty's Creek Rd., 706-746-2550. Five miles from town, catch a few trout for dinner. Or, if you like, stay at one of the wooden cabins.

Accommodations

Dillard House, off Hwy.441, 706-746-5348, offers 53 guest rooms in lodges scattered near a swimming pool and tennis courts. Riding stables and petting zoo complete this country retreat.

Chalet Village, located at U.S.441 and U.S.23, 706-746-5321. Deluxe mountain chalets come with fireplace, firewood, TV and some with some jacuzzis.

Elberton

Attractions/Museums

Main Street Elberton, 706-213-0626. A perfect historical setting, a 1890s courthouse and jail, monuments, art and antique shops.

Granite Museum, #1 Granite Plaza, 706-283-2551. Tells the story of this Granite Capital of the World.

Elbert County Wildlife Management Area, located off Hwy.72, 706-595-4211. Public hunting and camping. Inquire first.

Richard B. Russell Dam & Lake, 4144 Russell Dam Rd., 706-283-5121. Guided tours are available.

Historic Site

Georgia Guidestones, located 7.2 miles north of Hwy.77, 706-283-5651. Granite monoliths, sometimes called "America's Stonehenge."

Parks

Bobby Brown State Park, 2509 Bobby Brown State Park Rd., 706-213-2046. Fishing for striped bass is one of the attractions at Clark Hill Lake.

Lake Richard B. Russell State Park, 2650 Russell State Park Rd., 706-213-2045. A recreational park with a beach and boating.

Gainesville

Attractions/Museums

Carousel, 1285 West Washington St., at Lakeshore Mall. Whirl a ride on this Venetian carousel.

Georgia Mountain Museum, 311 Green St., 536-0889. General James Longstreet, model train exhibit and railroad museum.

Lanier Raceway, Hwy.53 E., 967-2131. Concessions, restrooms, playground and tier parking.

Quinlan Arts Center, 514 Green St., 536-2575. Regional and national exhibits, folk art, crafts and sculpture.

Historic Sites/Homes

Green Street Historical District, 536-5209. Walk or drive down historical Green St., which has 19th-century Victorian and neo-classical homes.

Parks

Poultry Park, at Broad and Grove St., 706-536-5209. Poultry Capital of the World statue and gateway to the eastern Blue Ridge Mountains.

Golf

Chicopee Woods, 2515 Atlanta Hwy., 534-7322. A fine 18-hole course for golfers of all skill levels.

Countryland Golf Course, 6560 Mayfield Dr., 523-8737. A tight, hilly 18-hole course.

Accommodations

Dunlap House, 635 Green St., 536-0200. Elegance of the old South is projected with ten luxurious guest rooms and personal touches.

Dining

Rudolph's, 700 Green St., 534-2226. Dine in an English Tudor mansion and savor the fine continental cuisine.

Hartwell

Attractions/Museums

Hart County Wildlife Management Area, on Hwy.77, Alt. E., 535-5700. Primitive camping and public hunting.

Hartwell Lake, located by Hwy.29, 706-376-4788. One of the largest recreational lakes in the Southeast. Offering camping, swimming, boating and fishing.

Hartwell Lake Dam and Powerhouse, U.S.29 N., 706-376-4788. Public tours and recreational areas.

The Historical Society and Museum, 31 East Howell St., 706-376-8590. Circa 1800, Victorian structure containing historical information.

Historic Sites/Homes

Historic Hartwell, 706-376-8590. Historical tour of homes.

Center of the World, located by Hwy.29 S., 706-376-8590. Honoring the Cherokee Indian Assembly with a roadside monument.

Parks

Hart State Park, 330 Hart State Park, 706-376-8756. Cabins and campsites alongside Lake Hartwell.

Helen

(Ga.400, I-75 or I-85 N. For the optimum route from your point of departure, call 800-858-8027.)

Bavarian-style architecture replete with window boxes and rooftop steeples. Numerous gift shops and restaurants strive to offer an authentic Germanic experience. Picnic by the **Stovall Covered Bridge**, in a small park by Chickamauga Creek on Hwy.255. Only 33 feet long, the bridge is one of the shortest anywhere in Georgia. Then visit the **Storyland Petting Zoo** and **Castle of Dolls**, on Hwy.75, four miles south of Helen, which features collectible dolls such as Naber Kids, Wildwood Babies, Naber Babies, Barbie and McGuffy Dolls.

Attractions/Museums

Anna Ruby Falls-Chattahoochee National Forest, Hwy.356, 706-878-3574. Admire the twin falls located high on the slopes of Tray Mountain. Interpretive trail.

Chattahoochee River Recreation Area-Chattahoochee National Forest, located off Hwy.356, 706-754-6221. Camping, fishing and hiking.

Chattahoochee Wildlife Management Area, off U.S.Alt.75, 535-5700. Primitive camping and public hunting.

Dukes Creek Recreation Area-Chattahoochee National Forest, Hwy.348, 706-754-6221. The first bridge south of the Chattahoochee River crosses Duke's Creek. Falls can be viewed from several points on trail.

Russell-Brasstown Scenic Byway, 706-745-6928. Enjoy a breath-taking 38-mile loop drive. Pickup information map.

Creekstone Winery, Edelweiss Dr., 706-878-8466. Featuring award-winning Habersham wines. Wine tasting.

Habersham Vintners. Wineries are in Helen and Baldwin, and produce Southern Harvest, Habersham Estates and Creekstone.

Gold Mines of Helen, on Edelweiss Dr., 706-878-3052. Tour the mine and nature trails, or wile away some time panning for gems and gold.

Museum of the Hills, Main St., 706-878-3140. You can't miss this castle on Main St., learn about the pioneer days of Helen.

Castle of Dolls and Petting Zoo is located four miles south of Helen, 706-865-2939.

Historic Sites/Homes

Sautee-Nacoochee Indian Mound, corner of Hwy.75 and 17, 706-878-2181. Artifacts excavated from this mound date back some 10,000 years.

Golf

Innsbruck Golf Club, 706-878-2100. Beautiful 18-hole mountain course, complete with mountain streams and deep hillsides.

Accommodations

Innsbruck Resort, 800-204-3538. Helen's only full facility resort, offering villas, suites and guest rooms.

Village Inn, 800-844-8466. Unique German style accommodations. Shops and restaurants within walking distance.

The Helendorf River Inn, 33 Munichstrasse, 800-445-2271. Alpine decor, suites with jacuzzis and fireplace.

Tanglewood Cabins, Hwy.356, 706-878-3286. Forty-five cabins, also secluded honeymoon sites.

Unicoi State Park, 706-878-2201. Offering 100 guest rooms and 30 cottages. Restaurant and meeting rooms available.

Georgia Mountain Madness Cabins, 190 Mountain Madness Drive, Helen. Located

four miles north of Helen on Hwy.356, one mile past Unicoi State Park. Bordered by the Chattahoochee and Unicoi State Parks, this rustic cluster of cabins is situated on fifty acres of beautiful private woodlands. The cabins are each set on one-acre lots, and feature full-kitchens, cable TV, VCRs, stereo, queen-size beds and jacuzzis or hot tubs. Relax and renew your romance or go hiking and fishing and experience the magic of the mountains. call gracious host Kay for directions. 770-534-6452.

Dining

Hofbrauhaus Inn, Main St., 706-878-2248. Enjoy fondue, schnitzel or stroganoff, while minstrels play Rhineland favorites.

Mountain Valley Kitchen, on Chattahoochee, 706-878-2508, serves great country cooking.

Unicoi State Park, serves low-cost buffets in a beautiful setting. The dining room serves breakfast, lunch and dinner.

Homer

Attractions/Museums

Wilson Shoals Wildlife Management Area, off Hwy.365. Primitive camping, hiking and public hunting.

Banks County Courthouse, Hwy.441, 706-677-2108. One of the oldest courthouses in Georgia, also houses the Welcome Center.

Jefferson

Attractions/Museums

Crawford W. Long Museum, 28 College St., 706-367-5307. Local history and site of first painless surgery.

Parks

Hurricane Shoals Park, 706-367-6300. Recreational park with playgrounds, swimming pool, amphitheater and historic village.

Lake Sidney Lanier Islands

Located an easy 40 minutes from downtown Atlanta. Take I-85 N. to exit 45; then take I-985 towards Gainesville to exit 2. Turn left onto Friendship Rd. Go approximately one mile and the road will dead end into Buford Hwy. Turn left at S.H.13 and then take an immediate right onto Hwy.347/Holiday Road. Follow signs for 2.5 miles to the gates. Then follow signs to your destination.

Commentary

Lake Lanier was named after the 19th-century poet Sidney Clopton Lanier who was so inspired by the area's beauty he composed his famous "*Song of the Chattahoochee*." This man-made lake was created in 1957 when the valley was intentionally flooded. With a depth of more than 200 feet, the tallest mountain peaks still remain uncovered, thus creating the Lake Lanier Islands.

Surrounded by the foothills of the scenic Blue Ridge Mountains, the 1,200-acre pine forest and 540-miles of shoreline speckled with marina's and beaches, offer outstanding opportunities for a variety of family-oriented sports, including boating, swimming, camping and fishing. Once you arrive and have settled at one of the two resorts, the adventure starts. The lake's **Holiday Marina** is the world's largest floating inland marina and rents such boats as pontoons, fishing and ski boats. Drop your anchor at any small scenic cove or middle of the lake swim in the cool/warm lake or just lay back and savor the beauty. For the sportsmen, the lake offers spotted, striped and big mouth bass, and on land are two deluxe 18-hole golf courses, horseback riding, **Lanier Sailing Academy**, 300-lakeside campsites or the resorts own amenities of tennis, bicycling and exercise rooms. Kids will have a blast at the **Beach and Water Park**, offering a humongous wave pool, kiddies pool, water slides, mini-golf and white sand beach with lounge chairs. The resorts also offer an kids calendar of events, where parents can take a few hours of rest and recreation. In the evening enjoy fine dining and a most breathtaking sunset along with the peaceful sounds of the wildlife creatures settling in.

Attractions

Beach and Water Park, 932-7255. Alright, all of you aquatic, webbed-foot water nuts, here is your paradise. Offering water thrills, splashy spills, and wave riding at the 850,000-gallon wave pool with nine different types of waves. Hop in a bright yellow inner-tube and go for it. Slide down slippery slides named, **Intimidator**, **Triple Threat** or in and out of a dark tunnel called **Typhoon**. Shoot down the **Chattahoochee Rapids**, or speed 25 mph down the **Racing Waters Slide**. For gentle babes there is the **Kiddie Lagoon** with **Wiggle Waves**, colorful fountains and eight foot slides. Paddleboats, canoes and sailboats are free with water park admission. Try 18-hole mini-golf, or just relax in a lounge chair under an umbrella. The **Breakers Gift Shop** offers souvenirs and beach supplies; The **Beachside Cafe** has you cook your own hamburgers or hot dogs; or if you are really hungry try The **Island Grill** and savor hickory-smoked pork barbecue, chicken dinners and sandwiches. The **Wildwaves** refresher helps you cool off with yogurts, daiquiris and cold lemonades. Daily admission is $13.99 for adults, $6.99 for children. (under two free). Lockers and umbrella's for a small fee. (Water Park is not responsible for kids refusing to go home.)

Holiday Marina 932-7255. Has a choice of 24-hr. rentals of houseboats, group boats, pontoon boats, sport and ski boats.

Lanier Sailing Academy, 945-8810. Offering sailing courses and clinics. Also a wide range of sailboat rentals.

Stable and Bicycle Rental, 932-7233. Horseback riding from trail rides to pony rides. Bicycles may be rented by the hour or day.

Golf

Lake Lanier Island Hilton Golf Club, 945-8787. One of the top five new resort golf courses in the U.S. This 18-hole course has all but five holes on the water.

Renaissance PineIsle Resort Golf Course, 945-8921. Featuring a challenging and scenic 18-hole course, the former site of the LPGA's Nestle World Championship.

Dining

Sylvan's on Lanier, located in the Hilton Hotel, 945-8787. Serving breakfast, lunch and delightful continental dining, with such tasty favorites as veal, chicken and beef. Set in a garden terrace atmosphere, with an added bonus of a magical sunset.

The Gazebo, in the Renaissance PineIsle Hotel, 945-8921. Informal all-day dining, with a beautiful lake view. Sunday brunch seasonally.

The Grille Room, in the Renaissance PineIsle Hotel, 945-8921 ext.51. The resorts charming fine dining restaurant with superb seafood and beef entrees, while enjoying the magnificent view of lake Lanier. (**See also our four heart review in the restaurant section, Nifty Restaurants Beyond Metro Atlanta.**)

Accommodations

Lake Lanier Islands Hilton Resort, 7000 Holiday Rd., 945-8787.

When you are ready to get away from it all, watch the sunset over Lake Lanier Islands at this luxury resort, they are waiting for you and family. Opened in 1989 the hotel offers 224 lake and forest-view rooms with 11,000 square feet of meeting space. Guests are greeted with a fast first-rate check-in, and made comfortable in well-appointed guest rooms, all with modern amenities such as remote control color TV, a large selection of video rentals, and quick housekeeping assistance. A large lap-style pool and whirlpool will relax you, as will the a sandwich and drink from the **Emerald Lounge**.

Play golf at the championship 18-hole course, work up a sweat at the health club or on the tennis courts, and of course Lake Lanier will beckon you. The nearby marina has boats to fit most needs; water-ski, fish, swim or picnic to your hearts content. Kids can bicycle, horseback ride or enjoy splashing water thrills at Water Park. And don't forget, Lake Lanier Hilton hosts children's birthday parties. **Sylvan's on Lanier** Restaurant serves a delectable breakfast, ala carte or buffet, lunch and savory dining in a charming garden-style setting. Dynamic manager, Jeff Henderson, is always looking for ways to make guest stays relaxing and fun. Try the yearly summer **Fox Box Regatta & Beach Party**, consisting of cardboard boats crossing the lake, **spring's Fiddlin' and Catfish Festival**, **fall's "Great Pumpkin arts & crafts Festival"**, and mid-November through December's **"Magical Nights of Lights"**, drive gathering after around the campfire at the **Holiday Village**. It's hard to believe, all of this is waiting for you, just a short drive from Atlanta.

The Renaissance PineIsle Resort, 9000 Holiday Rd., 945-8921. Experience the graciousness and impeccable service at the Mobil Four-Star, AAA Four-Diamond PineIsle, and enter another world. Charismatic General Manager Christopher Pollock recently received the Gold Key award, one of the most distinguished awards in the hospitality industry, and is proud of his loyal and genuine friendly staff. The 250-room resort, built in 1975, recently enjoyed an $4 million face-lift, offering large modern decorated guest rooms, with color remote control TV, fluffy robes, in-room safe and refreshment center, complementary morning coffee and newspaper. Some rooms have their own hot-tub on its private patio. The ultimate choice for conventions, offering 25 newly-renovated, equipped meeting rooms, with an white glove service banquet ballroom holding up to 400 people. Enjoy the adventure, playing tennis at one of seven tennis courts, swim at either the heated indoor or outdoor pool, steam a bit in the sauna, sweat a lot in the exercise room, enjoy a leisurely massage. Skim the clear waters on Lake Lanier, water-ski, enjoy horseback riding, picnic at an secluded cove, or pull out the clubs and play a round of challenging golf. Children are kept busy with daily kids programs, "First Mates for ages 4-6, and Kids Krew for 7-12, or thrill them with Waterworld. **The Marina Grill** offers pool side finger foods; **The Clubhouse**, adjacent to golf course serves breakfast and lunch; **The Gazebo**, offers all-day casual dining from salads to light entrees; **The Grille Room** is the resorts specialty dining room, and the **Champions Lounge** entertains with live music and dancing seasonally.

Lavonia

Parks

Clem's Shoal Creek Music Park, 706-356-1092. Enjoyable for the whole family, live entertainment, from gospel to country.

Tugaloo State Park, located six miles north of Lavonia, 706-356-4362. For the whole family, tent and trailer sites, primitive camp-ing, hiking trails, miniature golf, tennis and water skiing.

Mountain City

Museums

Foxfire Museum, on Hwy.441, 706-746-5318. Collections of Appalachian handicrafts, wooden toys and dolls and books of the Foxfire Boys.

Parks

Black Rock Mountain State Park, located three miles north of Clayton, on Hwy.441, 706-746-2141. The 1,502-acre park features ten miles of trails, 17-acre lake for fishing and camping facilities.

Accommodations

The York House, York House Rd., 706-746-2068. Built in 1896 as an original inn, it offers 12 modest but comfortable guest rooms.

Blackberry Patch Bed & Breakfast, Blacks Creek Dr./Route 441, 706-746-5632. Enjoy quiet beautiful rooms.

Rabun Gap

Attractions

Hambidge Center, Betty's Creek Rd., 706-465-5718. The cultural center preserves traditional Appalachian crafts and houses a gallery, studio and cabins.

Historic Site

Sylvan Falls Mill, Taylor Chapel Rd., 706-746-2806. An old gristmill still in operation.

Robertstown

Attractions

Shallow Creek Wildlife Management Area, Hwy.66, 535-5700. Rugged terrain with camping, hiking, fishing and public hunting.

Royston

Attractions

Ty Cobb Memorial, Franklin Springs St., 706-245-7232. Statue and memorabilia of baseball legend, Ty Cobb.

Parks

Victoria Bryant State Park, 1105 Bryant Park Rd., 706-245-6270.

Golf

Victoria Bryant Golf Course, located in State Park. 706-245-6776. Enjoy a short game on a 9-hole course.

Sautee

(Four miles east of Helen at the intersection of Hwys. 17 and 255.)

Commentary

The Sautee area was once the center of the Cherokee Nation. Don't miss **The Old Sautee Store**, corner of Hwy.17 and 225, 706-878-2281. Open since 1873, it is White County's oldest operating store. The store is home to one of the largest collections of old store memorabilia in Georgia, including antique calendars, posters, books and store merchandise. There's also a Scandinavian gift shop featuring hand-carved trolls, crystal, dinnerware, sweaters, jewelry and imported gourmet food items. And in an adjacent sodhouse there's a yule log shop that features international Christmas items.

Attractions/Museums

Gourdcraft Original & Co. Shop and Museum, Duncan Bridge Rd., 706-865-4048. Gourd museum and nature specialty shop.

Sautee-Nacoochee Arts Center, Hwy.255 N., 706-878-3300. History museum and art gallery.

Stovall Covered Bridge (circa 1895), located three miles north of Old Sautee Store on Hwy.255., is but 36.8 feet long, one of the shortest covered bridges in Georgia.

Accommodations

The Stovall House Bed & Breakfast (circa 1837) on Hwy.255 N. in the historic Sautee Valley. This Victorian farmhouse with wraparound porch and five well-appointed guest rooms affords its visitors with a place to relax while enjoying the beautiful valley and mountain views.

Owner Ham Schwartz has received several restoration awards for showing the true beauty of beaded pine walls and ceiling, heart of pine floors, original walnut doors, family antiques and handmade curtains. 706-878-3355.

The Lumsden Homeplace, Guy Palmer Rd., 706-878-2813. Built in 1890 by Mike's great-grandfather, owners Mike and Linda Crittenden are very proud of this award-winning preserved mountain farmhouse. The five guest rooms are furnished with family antiques, iron beds, antique quilts and floral prints. Visitors can enjoy views from both up and downstairs porches, filled with plants, rockers and a swing. For breakfast you can feast on the "chef specialties" served in a sunny breakfast area.

Scarlett's Secret Bed & Breakfast, 1902 Hwy.17, 706-878-1028. Situated in the historic Sautee Valley.

Dining

The Stovall House Bed & Breakfast (circa 1837) on Hwy.255 N. Just three small rooms but plenty of fine Southern and continental cuisine. After dinner, if you're lucky, Sunset, the resident golden retriever, will provide a tour of the farm. Enjoy such dishes as Citrus Trout, Pasta Primavera, Honey-Mustard Chicken and delectable desserts. 706-878-3355.

Sautee Inn, 706-878-2940. Serves buffet lunch and dinner from May through November.

Sky Valley

Attractions

Sky Valley Resort, east of Dillard off Hwy.246, 706-746-5302. Georgia's only ski resort is located in an isolated part of northeastern wilderness. Besides skiing, the resort also offers tennis, hiking, swimming, golf and restaurants.

Golf

Sky Valley Resort, 706-746-5303. A 6452-yard 18-hole course.

Toccoa

Attractions/Museums

Lake Yonah, Yonah Dam Rd., 706-754-6036. Yonah, meaning "big black bear" in Cherokee, covers 325-acres and offers camping, canoeing and fishing.

Currahee Mountain, Hwy.17, 706-886-2132.

Stephens County Museum, 313 South Pond St., 706-886-2132. Interesting local memorabilia, Indian artifacts and railroad museum.

Accommodations

Habersham Manor House, 326 West Doyle St., 706-886-6496. Built in 1906, this Greek revival mansion offers three guest rooms.

Simmons-Bond Inn, 130 West Tugalo Ave., 706-886-8411. This restored 1903 Victorian home is on the National Register of Historic Places. Five guest rooms are available, with a licensed restaurant.

Toccoa Riverside Restaurant & General Store, nestled in the Rich Mountain National Forest is popular with nature seekers and presents casual dining overlooking the scenic Toccoa River. The menu features fresh seafood, vegetables and hand-carved steak and a large outdoor deck with breathtaking views, private dining rooms and seven days a week catering for all occasions. Shop at the authentic country store and gift shop. Call for directions and enjoy the beautiful 1 and 1/2 drive north. 706-632-7891.

Fun Facts:

- States bordering Georgia are Alabama to the west, Florida to the south (with the St. Mary's River at the southeastern corner), North Carolina to the north, South Carolina to the northeast (with the Savannah River forming the northeastern corner) and Tennessee to the northwest. An additional state, euphoria, lies within Georgia's borders.

- Dawsonville's Amicalola Falls, located in the Northern mountains, drops 729 feet, making it Georgia's tallest.

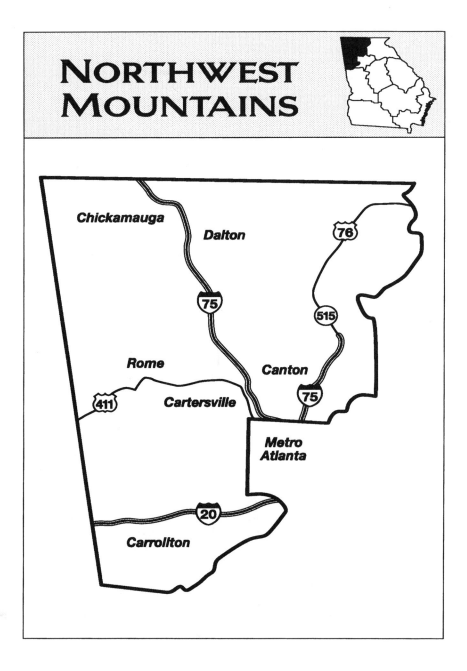

Section XV
Traveling Georgia's Northwest Mountains

Georgia's Northwest Mountains

Commentary

Beautiful natural scenery, wilderness trials and historic sites of a proud heritage starts with but an hours drive north of Atlanta. **Stroll Rome's historic downtown** and see the bronze **Wolf Statue of Romulus and Remus**. Learn about the infamous **"Trail of Tears"** when in 1838 the Cherokees were moved from their lands an made a inhuman 2,000-mile trek. And revitalize at nearby **Cave Springs** pure and medicinal spring waters. North is **Berry College** and the **Martha Berry Museum**, the creation of a remarkable woman that didn't give up.

Reflect back to 1500 A.D. at the **Cartersville Etowah Indian Mounds**, and marvel at **the exquisite Barnsley Gardens in Adairsville**. **Summerville** is the home of artist, Reverend Howard Finster, who's art is displayed in his resplendent **Paradise Garden**. In late summer sample the produce at **Georgia's Apple Capital in Ellijay**, and literally pig-out on mouthwatering barbecue at **Holloway's Pink Pig**.

Collectors and shoppers will find antiques and crafts along each route, and, if you're in need of some new carpeting, **Dalton** is the Carpet Capital of the World. For outdoorspeople, the crystal lake waters of **Lake Allatoona, Carter's Lake** and the spectacle of the Cohutta Wilderness and the **Chattahoochee National Forest** offer immense enjoyment.

Adairsville

Attractions

Barnsley Gardens at Woodlands, 597 Barnsley Gardens Rd. 706-733-7480. Thirty acres of English style gardens, with expert gardening advice at the estate's Garden Shop.

1902 Stock Exchange in Adairsville at 124 Public Square, 706-773-1902. A great antique gallery, that also has a cafe.

Blue Ridge

Attractions, Parks and Recreational Area

Appalachian Trail and Benton Mackaye Trail, 706-632-5680. A wilderness footpath that winds, ascends and descends, through dense hardwood forests, wildflower fields and waterfalls. Much admired by experienced hikers.

Blue Ridge Wildlife Management Area, on Hwy.52, 770-535-5700. Most visitors come to fish and camp. The lake offers muskie, bluegill, walleye and smallmouth bass.

Chattooga Wild and Scenic River-Chattahoochee National Forest, 706-782-3320. World-class guided rafting trips can be made over a variety of rapids.

Cohutta Wilderness Area. With 95 miles of trails, the Cohutta Wilderness is a hiker's dream come true. Call the U.S.Forest Service for wilderness maps. 347-2384.

Lake Blue Ridge, take I-575 from Atlanta to U.S.76, 706-632-2618. A great recreational lake for boating, fishing, swimming and camping.

Nantahala Outdoor Center, Chattooga Ridge Rd., 800-232-7238. World-class whitewater rafting in degrees of difficulty.

Historic Sites/Homes

Merchants Hope Village, 706-632-9000. North of Blue Ridge, beyond Hwy.5, stroll through a replica of a 1700s colonial village. The garden features a British hemlock maze, the only one in the nation.

Parks

Sugarcreek Raceway and Music Park, 706-632-5550. A combination of concerts and stock car racing.

Accommodations

Blue Ridge Mountain Cabins, 706-632-8999.

Bed & Breakfast Hideaway Homes, 706-632-2411.

Dining

Forge Mill Crossing, 706-374-5771, for ribs.

Calhoun

Attractions

Chattahoochee National Forest. Enjoy many beautiful spots for camping, hiking and picnicking. For maps call 706-638-1085.

Calhoun Outlet Center, 455 Belwood Rd., 706-602-1300. Located off I-75, exit 129. Designer outlet shops.

Concerts in the Country, located off I-75, exit 130 & Red Bud Rd., 706-629-0226. Country music entertainment at its best.

Mercer Air Museum, 706-625-3200. Admire aircraft dating back to World War II.

Oakleigh, 335 South Wall St., 706-629-1515. Gordon County Historical Society.

Historic Site

Blue & Gray Trail, 300 South Wall St., 706-629-3406. Sites of the Civil War's dramatic events.

Parks

Salacoa Creek Park, located 10 miles east of Calhoun, 706-629-4390. A recreational lake with camping, boating and the annual bass tournament.

Golf

Fields Ferry Golf Club, 706-625-5666. An 18-hole course with rolling hills and beautiful mountain views.

Accommodations

Stoneleigh, 316 Fain St.,706-629-2093. Two guest rooms, furnished with family antiques and memorabilia.

Jamison Inn, 706-629-8133. Premium rooms with complimentary continental breakfast.

Dining

Shepherd Restaurant, 706-629-8644.

Canton

Attractions/Museums

Ball Ground, off Hwy.5, eight miles north of Canton. Century-old town in the foothills of the Blue Ridge Mountains.

Gazaway Indian Museum, on Hwy.372, three miles off Hwy.20. Interesting collection of Indian artifacts.

Parks

Sweetwater Park, on Hwy.120, by Lake Allatoona. Recreational park with camping facilities, beach, and hiking trails.

Carrollton

Attractions/Museums

The McIntosh Reserve, off Hwy.5 on the Chattahoochee River, 770-830-5879. Family recreational area with ball park, children's fishing pond, picnic areas and camping facilities.

Historical Sites/Homes

Susan B. Hayward Gravesite Monument, 800-292-0871, at Our Lady of Perpetual Care Catholic Church.

The Bonner House, on Maple Street, 770-836-6500. Circa 1845, also serves as a visitors center.

Dining

Maple Street Mansion, 401 Maple St., 770-834-2657. Dine in a century-old Victorian mansion.

The Lazy Donkey Restaurant, 334 Bankhead Hwy., 770-834-8875. Latin and Mexican cuisine.

Accommodations

The Bowdon Inn, 130 W. College Street, Bowden. Located 12 miles west of Carrollton; one hour from Atlanta, this beautifully restored 1877 Queen Anne Victorian-style home offers complete relaxation. There are generous rockers on a wrap-around porch, two guest rooms with private baths and claw-foot tubs, brass and double beds and a decorative fireplace. After a great breakfast visit the on-property gift shop and close by antique shops, clothing outlet, John Tanner State Park, McIntosh Reserve, West Georgia College and enjoy free golf at Bowdon Golf Course. Owner Diane Jackson also hosts wedding receptions and luncheons, and be sure to ask about the inn's "friendly ghost." 770-258-9808.

Cartersville and the Etowah Indian Mounds

(I-75 N., exit at 124, turn left at the end of the ramp and follow the brown signs to Etowah Indian Mounds.)

Attractions/Museums

Etowah Indian Mound Historic Site, 813 Indian Mounds Rd. A well-preserved earthwork center offers a look back to an ancient civilization that thrived here some 400 years ago. 770-387-3747.

Red Top Mountain State Park, off exit 123. A wealth of recreational opportunities, campsites and cottages are spread over the wooded hillsides around 12,000-acre Lake Allatoona. During warm weather, you may sun on a sandy beach, swim and waterski. The rest of the year bring tennis gear, fishing gear, picnic supplies and hiking shoes. The park's new Red Top Mountain Lodge offers 33 modern guest rooms and a quiet cove with full service restaurant. Park information, 770-975-4203; Lodge information, 770-975-4222.

Barnsley Gardens is located 10 miles west of I-75's exit 128, where visitors can stroll through 30 acres of English-style gardens. Created in the 1840s by Englishman Godfrey Barnsley, it features thousands of acres of gardens, cultivated trees, and orchards centered on a 28-room Italianate manor house. Following Barnsley's death in 1873, the estate fell into ruins and weeds. Then in 1988 a Bavarian aristocrat purchased the remaining 1,300 acres and brought Barnsley Gardens to life. Today, visitors can stroll through a wildflower meadow, a hillside with hundreds of flowering rhododendrons, the fernery, and water and bog garden. 770-773-7480.

Air Acres Museum, at Cartersville-Bartow Airport, 770-382-7030.

Bartow History Center, 319 East Cherokee Ave., 770-382-3818. Dedicated to the preservation of the folklore and culture that shaped Bartow County during the past 150 years.

Chieftains Trail, 706-629-3406. A 150-mile trail, exploring the history of native Americans as far back as 1000 B.C.

Etowah Arts Gallery, 11 Wall St., 770-382-8277. Admire local artists works.

Etowah Station, 25 West Main St., 770-606-8696. Handcrafted wooden pictures and desk trophies.

Kingston Confederate Memorial Museum, 13 East Main St., 770-336-5269. Enjoy exploring the town's history.

Noble Hill, 2361 Joe Frank Harris Pkwy., 770-382-3392. North Georgia's first school built for children, today houses the **Black History Museum and Cultural Center.**

William Weinman Mineral Museum, I-75 & U.S.441, exit 126, 770-386-0576. Rockhounds will be in heaven, amidst geodes, arrowheads, petrified woods and gems.

Historic Sites/Homes

Main Street Cartersville, 770-386-6458. One of Georgia's most enjoyable main streets, lined with antique shops and historic sites.

Young Brothers Pharmacy, West Main St., 770-382-4010. The world's first outdoor Coca-Cola sign, painted in 1894.

Cassville Confederate Cemetery, I-75, exit 127, on Cass-White Rd., 770-387-1357. Remains a sad vestige of the dynamic pre-Civil War town that was destroyed by Sherman's torch in 1864.

Cooper's Iron Works, River Rd., 770-387-1357. Once a busy antebellum industrial center, only remnants remain.

Euharlee Covered Bridge, Euharlee Rd., 770-387-1357. One of Georgia's oldest covered bridges, built in 1886, 116 feet in length.

Roselawn, 224 West Cherokee Ave., 770-387-5162. Home of Victorian evangelist Sam Jones, for whom the "Grand Ole Opry" was built.

Parks

Red Top Mountain State Lodge Park, 653 Red Top Mountain Rd., 770-975-0055. A beautiful recreational park alongside Lake Allatoona, with trails, beach and accommodations.

Golf

Royal Oaks Golf Course, 256 Summit Ridge Dr., 770-382-3999.

Accommodations

South Wind Resort, 632 Old Allatoona Rd., 770-917-9282. A beautiful Victorian home built in 1895, features 8 guest rooms.

Red Top Mountain State Lodge Park, take I-75 N. to exit 123, 770-975-0055. Offering 33 guest rooms and 18 cottages.

Dining

Barnsley Gardens, 597 Barnsley Gardens Rd., 770-773-1900. Enjoy new Southern cuisine, in an old plantation setting.

Mac's Steakhouse, Covered Bridge Rd., 770-382-7295. Located in Bartow, the steak is worth the drive.

The Sunset Grill, 28 Wall St., 770-387-1449. Favorite with the locals for seafood and steak.

Cave Spring

(From Rome, 16 miles south on U.S.411.)

In this village of 950 residents and one traffic light, visitors gladly ante up a buck to feel the 56-degree cave temperatures and watch as water flows at the rate of 3-4 million gallons a day. At nearby **Rolate Park** the spring water is bottled and sold commercially. 706-777-8439.

Ironwood Fine Arts Studio Foundry, where Becky David creates bronze sculptures, 706-777-8772, and the **Kudzu Pottery Farm**, 706-777-8789, which sells beautiful dinnerware and pottery, are among the 40+ antique shops.

Parks

Historic Cave Spring and Rolate Park, 706-777-8439.

Accommodations

Hearn Academy Bed & Breakfast, Cedartown St., 706-777-8865. Country style lodge circa 1839, featuring five simple guest rooms.

Cedartown

Attractions/Museums

Historic Driving Tour, information at the Courthouse, 770-749-1652.

Polk County Historical Society Museum and Gardens, off Hwy.27 on College Street, 770-748-3473.

Parks

The Big Spring, on Wissahickon Ave., off Hwy.27. Historical park where Cherokees met for councils, today offers picnicking and wading stream.

Chatsworth

Attractions

Barnes Creek Recreation Area, 401 Old Ellijay Rd., 706-695-6736. Offering scenic picnic areas.

Carter's Dam, U.S.411 & Hwy.136, 706-276-4891.

Cohutta Wilderness, 401 Old Ellijay Rd., 706-695-6736. Before hiking the Cohutta Wilderness, check weather forecasts. Heavy rains can make some trails impassable.

Lake Conasauga, 401 Old Ellijay Rd., 706-695-6736. The highest lake in Georgia, its name is derived from the Cherokee word meaning "grass, or sparkling water." Offering camping, fishing, swimming and hiking.

Horseback Trail Rides, 706-695-9601. Choose from short day rides to overnight camping.

Historic Sites/Homes

Vann House Historic Site, Hwy.82, 225 N., 706-695-2598. Ancestral home, circa 1804, of James Vann, half-Scottish/half-Cherokee leader, who helped establish a mission to educate young Cherokees.

Park

Fort Mountain State Park, three miles east of Chatsworth, on Hwy.52, 706-695-2621. Ancient ruins of the Fort can be viewed. Enjoy camping, cottages, beach, fishing, boating and a 400-foot waterfall.

Accommodations

Cohutta Lodge, five miles east of Chatsworth, 706-695-9601. Quality inn offering comfortable guest rooms.

Key West Inn, 501 GI Maddox Pkwy., 706-517-1155. Inexpensive guest rooms, with restaurants and golf nearby.

Carter's Lake Marina & Resort, 575 Marina Rd., 706-276-4891. Quiet rooms and cabins or houseboats.

Dining

Cohutta Lodge. Offers a 360-degree view from atop Fort Mountain, while enjoying prime rib and seafood buffet. 706-695-9606.

Edna's Restaurant, 706-695-4951, is specially known for its country cooking.

Little Rome, 1201 North 3rd Ave., 706-695-7309. Italian specialties from pizza to lasagna and ravioli.

Dalton

Attractions/Museums

Carpet Capital of the World, over a hundred carpet outlets open to the public.

Creative Arts Guild, 520 West Waugh St., 706-278-0168.

New Georgia Railroad, 706-656-0768. At festival time, ride in an antique locomotive with passenger cars from Atlanta.

Llama Hiking, 1618 Dawnville Rd., 706-259-9310. A unique way of hiking the Chattahoochee National Forest.

Historic Sites/Homes

Crown Gardens and Archives, 715 Chattanooga Ave., 706-278-0217. Circa 1884, the center for local history.

Praters Mill, located off Hwy.2, one mile east of Hwy.71. Historic gristmill, built in 1855 by slaves, today celebrates festivals twice a year.

Park

Dug Gap Battle Park, on West Dug Gap Mountain Rd., 706-278-0217. Still preserved are over 1,000 feet of breastworks built by Civil War soldiers.

Golf

Nobb North Golf Course, 298 Nobb North Dr., 706-694-8505. An 18-hole course, 6,573 yards.

Accommodations

Dalton-Holly Tree House Bed & Breakfast. 706-278-6620. A bed and breakfast in a 1920 Southern home.

Dining

Dalton Depot, 110 Depot St., 706-226-3100. The 150-year-old Depot serves steaks, seafood, pastas and salads.

The Cellar, 706-226-6029, offers fine continental cuisine.

Miller Brother's Rib Shack, 706-278-8510, has smokehouse favorites, also steaks and seafood.

Dawsonville

Attractions/Museums

Amicalola River Rafting Outpost, on Hwy.53 W., 706-265-6892. Have a grand time rafting and tubing on the Amicalola River. Cabins are also available.

Appalachian Trail, 706-265-6278. Georgia has 80 miles of this famous trail, which can be strenuous for some. Test your stamina on a short trail first.

Dawson Forest Wildlife Management Area, on Hwy.318 W. 535-5700. Primitive camping, fishing and hunting. Terrain may be too rough for driving. Inquire about accessibility.

Burt's Pumpkin Farm, on Hwy.52 N., 706-265-3701. This is the place for pumpkins in the fall, and for real fun go on a hayride or Saturday night hoedown.

Dawson County Courthouse, 706-265-6278. Recently restored. Admire the 1858 Greek revival Dawson County Courthouse on the square.

Dawsonville Pool Room, 706-265-2792. Memorabilia on moonshine runners and Bill Elliott. Also, short order meals are served.

Elliott Museum, Hwy.183, 706-265-2718. Famous Bill Elliott's auto racing memorabilia and videos can be viewed.

Accommodations

Amicalola Falls State Park Lodge, 706-265-8888. The four-story lodge offers 57 guest rooms, with the most panoramic view of the Blue Ridge wilderness.

Dining

Amicalola Falls State Park Lodge, serves generous buffets, from roast turkey, baked ham and catfish to salads and desserts. Breakfast and lunch buffets are also served.

Ellijay

(15 miles northwest of Amicalola Falls.)

Commentary

Here at the foothills of the verdant **Appalachian Mountains**, the cool nights and warm days assure Gilmer County's title as Georgia's Apple Capital. The varied crop includes Rome Beauties, Granny Smiths, Yates, Jonathans, Stayman Winesaps, Fujis and Mutsus. Each October brings Ellijay's Apple Festival Arts and Crafts Fair. The town offers one-of-a-kind antique and specialty shops with charming prizes such as apple-head dolls.

Attractions

Appalachian/Beaton Mckay Trail, 5 Westside Square, 706-635-7400. Maps will guide to access points.

Carter's Lake, 706-635-7400. Enjoy camping, swimming, hiking and fishing at the deepest lake east of the Mississippi.

Ellijay's Hillcrest Orchards, open July to December, offer old-fashioned family fun with wagon rides through the orchard, a petting zoo with lambs and piglets, a working cider mill with free samples and plenty more. The farm market overflows with apple peelers, stackers, cookbooks, breads and, yes, pies. 706-273-3838.

Rich Mountain Wildlife Area. Bring maps while hiking scenic trails through the wilderness.

Whitewater Canoeing, 5 Westside Square, 706-635-7400. More activities such as gold panning and horseback riding can be planned here.

Historic Sites/Homes

The Perry House, 10 Broad St., 706-635-5605. Historic home of Miss Ethel Perry.

Golf

Whitepath Golf Course, Whitepath Rd., 706-276-3080.

Accommodations

The Squirrel's Nest Inn, 169 Beaver Lake, 706-276-1690. Bed & breakfast inn.

Elderberry Inn, 75 Dalton St., 706-635-2218. An 1897 Victorian home offers bed & breakfast guest rooms.

Home of Gardener Fatness, 59 River St., 706-276-7473. Beautiful historic home close to town square, offers guest rooms.

Dining

Calico Cupboard Restaurant (on the square), where homecooking is plentiful.

Apple Dumpling Deli at River St. Savor fresh baked bread and cakes, or sandwiches and hamburgers.

White Columns Restaurant, 706-635-7134. Daily buffet with the best fried chicken around.

Sirloin Family Steak House, 706-276-2333. Sometimes serves baked apples with its steaks.

Riverstreet Cafe, 706-635-5500, a local favorite.

Holloway's Pink Pig. "Jimmy and Rosalynn Carter drop by six to eight times a year," says the Pink Pig's proprietor, Bud Holloway. Whole hams are cooked with indirect hickory smoke, Brunswick stew cooks all day. Onion rings and the barbecue sauce are considered outstanding. 706-276-1700.

Fairmount

Museum

Sunrise Planetarium & Science Museum, 1427 Slate Mine Rd., 706-337-2775. Located 17 miles west of Calhoun on Hwy.53, exit 129.

LaFayette

Attractions/Museums

Hidden Creek Recreation Area, 806 East Villanow St., 706-638-1085. A creek that plays hide-and-seek, also offers camping and hiking.

Keown Falls Recreation Area, 706-638-1085. A scenic area with unique rock bluffs and high swampy areas. Twin falls are situated within the 218-acre area.

Pigeon Mountain, 706-375-7702. Pigeon Mountain has many underground caverns and stream channels, including one of the deepest caves in the world. Great hiking and horse trails.

Pocket Recreation Area, 706-638-1085. Pocket Trail is a steep trail climbing Pigeon Mountain. Maps needed for trails and camping.

Ridge and Valley Scenic By-Way, 806 East Villanow St., 706-638-1085. Pick up directions and trail guides at 706 Foster Blvd., 706-638-1085.

Lithia Springs

Attractions

Lithia Springs Water and Bottling Co., Bankhead Hwy., 770-944-3880. Once the site of a restorative resort, it's known today for its natural mineral water.

Parks

Sweetwater Creek State Conservation Park, 770-732-5871. Follow the Factory Ruins Trail and also enjoy camping, fishing and boating.

Lookout Mountain

Attractions/Museums

Battles for Chattanooga Museum, 706-820-2531. A three-dimensional presentation of Chattanooga's Civil War history of 1863.

Rock City Gardens, 1400 Patten Rd., 706-820-2531. Old-style mountain institution, circa 1920, designed as a private walking garden. Stroll across a swinging suspension footbridge and view Fairyland & Mother Goose.

Parks

Lookout Mountain Flight Park and Training Center, 706-398-3541. Learn from certified instructors.

Accommodations

Chanticleer Inn, 1300 Mockingbird Lane, 706-820-2015. Charming stone motel from the 1930s offers sixteen guest rooms.

The Lookout Inn, 706-820-2000. Quiet bed & breakfast located across Covenant College.

Morganton

Attractions

Chattahoochee National Fish Hatchery, located 20 miles south of Morganton, off Hwy.60, 706-838-4723.

Morganton Point, 706-632-8331. The U.S. Forest Service offers tent camping and picnic areas.

Ringgold

Attractions/Museums

Ringgold Depot played an important role in the transporting of Confederate soldiers.

Georgia Winery, Hwy.2, 706-937-2177. Retail outlet and wine tasting, local specialty is peach muscadine.

Historic Sites/Homes

Old Stone Baptist Church, located two miles east of Ringgold, circa 1849.

Whitman-Anderson House. Circa 1850, General Grant's headquarters during the Civil War.

Rome and Berry College

(I-75 N. to exit 125, to U.S.411 W. into town.)

If you'd like to get a little lost in the woods, make a note to visit **Marshall Forest**, on Horseleg Creek Rd., off Hwy.20, four miles west of downtown. This 250-acre preserve is a protected virgin forest, containing a Braille trail and beautiful trail of 300 species of wildflowers and northern red and chestnut oaks mingled with long leaf southern pines. Visit by appointment only. 706-291-0766.

Shoppers may stroll Shorter and Broad Avenues and there find antique collectibles, stained glass, handmade pottery, Victorian jewelry, collectible dolls, porcelains and wildlife carvings.

Attractions/Museums

In 1902 Martha Berry created **Berry College** from a dream; today she is widely honored for her efforts. Under her skilled tutelage Berry evolved from a one-room log cabin to the world's largest campus, occupying 28,000 acres, with many historic buildings. Nearby,

Oak Hill, the Berry family's antebellum mansion, is open to the public. 706-291-1883.

Arrowhead Public Fishing Area, located nine miles north of Rome, off Hwy.156, 706-295-6023.

The Chieftains Museum is Rome's oldest historical landmark. Built as a frontier log cabin in 1794, Chieftains was the home of Major Ridge, the Cherokee leader who signed a treaty that led to the removal of the Cherokee from the area and the tragic "Trail of Tears."

Marshall Forest, Horseleg Creek Rd., 706-291-2121. Georgia's first National Natural Landmark, features primeval woodlands with a Braille Trail.

Oak Hill and the Martha Berry Museum, on Hwy.27 N. & Loop 1, 706-291-1883.

Historic Sites/Homes

Historic Downtown Walking Tour, 706-695-5576. Maps marking many examples of restoration at the welcome center.

Parks

Lock and Dam Park, 181 Lock and Dam Rd., 706-234-5001. Down river on the Coosa River, enjoy a 73-acre area for camping and fishing and the historic 1913 lock.

Golf

Stonebridge Golf Club, 585 Stonebridge Dr., 706-236-5046. The 18-hole course offers a beautiful scenic setting and the most sand bunkers in northern Georgia.

Accommodations

Chandler Arms B & B on Coral Ave., is a 1902 Victorian home serving a full English breakfast and afternoon tea. 800-438-9492.

Claremont House B & B, 906 E. 2nd Ave., Rome. Escape from today's hectic pace into a world of irresistible nostalgic charm of the Victorian era. The Claremont House is rich in unique features such as, the huge antique safe of walnut molding and ornate surface built into the hallway wall. Also the home is known as "the house with the silver urinal." Guest rooms feature opulent woodwork, fireplaces and antiques; and you will feel pampered as you enjoy a full gourmet breakfast in the main dining room, compliments from thoughtful hostess, Patsy Priest. 706-291-0900, 800-254-4797.

Dining

The Partridge Cafe, a local favorite for more than 40 years known for "Mama's Cookin'."

Malone's Grill and Bar located in a restored riverfront warehouse on Second Ave.

Bubba's BBQ, 1 Broad St., 706-291-0618. Great barbecued dishes.

The Landings at Rivers Place, 706-234-5092. Noted for seafood, pastas, ribs and rich desserts.

The Homestead, 706-291-4290. Country-style cooking.

Rossville

Attractions

Lake Winnepausaukah, one mile off U.S.27, 706-866-5681. Family entertainment with roller coaster, paddleboats and more.

Historical Sites/Homes

John Ross House, circa 1797, log cabin of Cherokee nation chief, John Ross.

Summerville

Attractions

Paradise Gardens, located three miles north of Summerville, 100 yards off Hwy.27. Created in the 1940s by visionary folk artist Howard Finster. Unique sculpture grace the grounds and hang from tree branches.

Parks

James H. Floyd State Park, off Hwy.100, south of Summerville, 706-857-5211. Offering a hilly, wooded campground and two lakes for fishing and boating.

Accommodations

Victorian Parlour B & B, located on Lookout Mountain Parkway, Cloudland, a few miles west of Summerville and east of the state line. Gracious host and fashion designer, Jan White welcomes guests to her beautiful Victorian 1927 B & B located in "Georgia's Roof Garden" of the northwest mountains. Choose from four guest rooms, each done in a distinctive potpourri theme of rose, peach, cherry or the more masculine English ivy and awake to the breakfast aroma of fresh-baked breads and muffins, made especially tasty with homemade preserves. Nearby are village shopping, nature trails, golf, fishing and beautiful parks. Guests feel so at home they don't want to leave. 706-862-2870.

Tallapoosa

Attractions/Museums

Jones Taxidermy and Wildlife Museum, 377 Hwy.120 N., 770-574-7480.

West Georgia Museum of Tallapoosa, 21 West Lyon St., 770-574-3125. Museum was created by local residents and depicts the history of Tallapoosa.

Leroy Almon Folk Art Studio, 36 East Mill St., 770-574-5052. Nationally known woodcarver-preacher Leroy Almon.

Goose Chasers Farm, 80 Elizabeth Lane, 770-574-2472. Small farm that offers seasonal flowers and vegetable gardens. You may also stay for lunch.

Golf

Talley Mountain Golf Course, Golf Course Rd., 770-574-3122, offers a 9-hole course.

Trenton-Dade County

Parks

Canyon Creek Fun Park, 1 Wolverine Dr., 706-398-1839. Family entertainment park with mini-golf, go-karts, arcade and batting cages.

Cloudland Canyon State Park, eight miles from Trenton on Hwy.136, 706-657-4050. Large site for tent and trailers, cottages, trails, tennis and swimming.

Villa Rica

Accommodations

Twin Oaks Bed & Breakfast, 9565 East Liberty Rd., 770-459-4374. Home-away-from-home guest cottage, ideal for honeymoon or special occasion.

Ahava Plantation Bed & Breakfast, 2236 South Van Wert Rd., 770-459-2863. Antebellum home with seven guest rooms.

Fun Facts:

- The Ridge and Valley Province and the Cumberland Plateau lie west of the Blue Ridge Mountains. They are home to much of Georgia's textile industry.

- While the number of streets with "Peachtree" in their name continues to grow, so does metro Atlanta's population per sq. mile, from 262 in 1970, to 385 in 1990, to an estimated 471 in the year 2000.

- The U. S. Census Bureau estimates that Cherokee County will grow from a population of 90,204 in 1990 to 130,650 in the year 2000, Clayton County from 182, 052 to 224,134, Cobb County from 447,445 to 607,776, DeKalb County from 545,837 to 625,067, Fayette County from 62,415 to 102,356, Fulton County from 648,951 to 716,710, and Gwinnett County from 352,910 to 531,971.

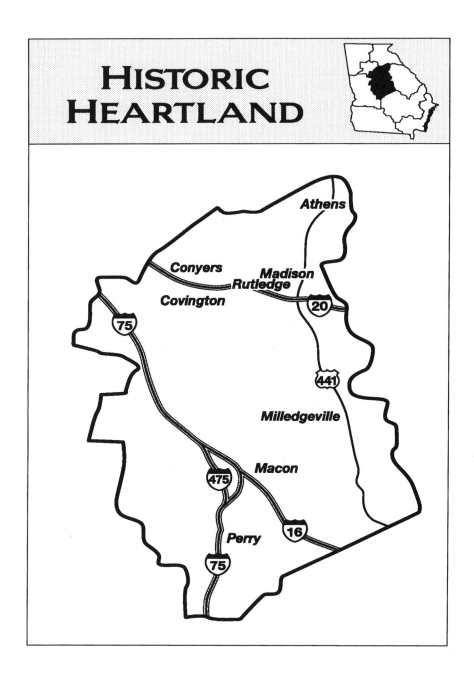

Section XVI
Traveling Georgia's Historic Heartland

Georgia's Historic Heartland

Commentary

Georgia's **Historic Heartland** is a living museum. Just an hour east of Atlanta lies a treasure of 19th-century architecture for all to enjoy. There are classic town squares with true Victorian courthouses such as in **Newton and Madison**. There are numerous Greek revival mansions such as in **Milledgeville**, and historic mainstreets such as in **Social Circle**. And, importantly, the legacy of the native American Indians, as well as the old plantations are preserved in many of the historic sites.

Heartland is known as **the "Region of Regional Trails." The Antebellum Trail** goes for 117 miles showing three decades of architectural beauty of massive columned mansions and magnolia gardens, from **Athens through Madison's beautiful historic district to Macon. The Antiques Trail** is a real treat, offering, as it does, hundreds of antique shops along its route, which **includes the town of Social Circle**, the name says it all, where you may shop at **Balwin Antiques or Turnip's**, and have lunch at the world-famous **Blue Willow Inn**. And a little treasure, the town of **Rutledge** will stop a spinning world. Enjoy **the Peach Blossom Trail** from March to August, pick Georgia's sweet peaches along the way **from Perry to Jonesboro.** Marvelous Macon offers Southern elegance at **the Grand Opera House**, the newly completed **Georgia Music Hall of Fame**, and the annual, most scenic, **Cherry Blossom Festival** with 200,000 trees in light-pink blossoms.

Classic **Athens, offers the University of Georgia**, jazz to blue-grass for music lovers, sculptured gardens at **State Botanical Gardens**, and some mighty fine public golf courses. Surely, you will leave your heart in Georgia's Historic Heartland.

Athens

(I-85 N. to Ga.316 or U.S.78 E. A 75-mile trip.)

Commentary

Founded in 1801, cosmopolitan Athens is the home of the Bulldawgs and the historic center of Georgia's roots in the Old South.

Attractions/Museums

State Botanical Garden of Georgia. A beautiful 293-acre horticultural preserve at 2450 South Milledge Avenue. Georgia's state flower, the **Cherokee Rose**, is among the flowering plants and wishing ponds that grace the sculpted gardens inside and out. Six miles of trails are frequented by small populations of deer, raccoons, squirrels and many different bird species. The garden's tea room serves lunch daily and a gift shop sells small plants and nature-related wares. 706-542-1244.

Butts-Mehre Heritage Hall, at Lumpkin and Pinecrest St., 706-542-9094. An athletic complex that also includes museum that houses athletic awards and memorabilia.

Double Barreled Cannon, City Hall. A cannon from 1863, made to protect from Sherman's Army, failed to fire the two cannon balls simultaneously.

Fire Station Number Two, 489 Prince Ave., 706-353-1801. A 1901 Victorian brick firehouse that today displays an art gallery and is the headquarters of the Athens-Clarke Heritage Foundation.

Georgia Museum of Art, located at University of Georgia, 706-542-3255. Displays 5,000 paintings, drawings and sculptures of 19th and 20th century American artists.

Founders Memorial Garden, 325 South Lumpkin St. Scenic gardens surround an antebellum home, now a Garden Club Center.

Historic Sites/Homes

Morton Theater, at Washington and Hull St., 706-613-3770. The only theater in American that was built, owned and run by African-American businessmen. Today it is a community theater.

State Botanical Garden of Georgia, 2450 South Milledge Ave., 706-542-1244. A beautiful 293-acre showplace, full of sculpted gardens and miles of natural trails.

Taylor-Grady House, 634 Prince Ave., 706-549-8688. An 1840s Greek revival mansion, that was the home of Atlanta Constitution editor, Henry Grady.

Joseph Henry Lumpkin House, circa 1843, at 248 Prince Avenue. The home of Georgia's first Chief Justice of the Supreme Court.

Stephen Upson House, 1022 Prince Avenue. Greek revival home, circa 1847.

Tree that Owns Itself, South Finley Street near Dering, on Athens' only cobblestone street. A professor that enjoyed the shade of this tree deeded the small plot of land to the tree.

University President's House, 570 Prince Avenue. Circa 1850, this home, is surrounded by Corinthian columns.

Golf

Whispering Pines Golf Course, Fourth St., Colbert, 706-788-2720. A scenic 18-hole course.

Dining

The Last Resort, 174-184 Clayton St., 706-549-0810. Pleasant dining with one of the most creative menus in town.

DePalma's Italian Cafe, 401 East Broad St., 706-354-6966. Italian Cuisine in casual atmosphere.

Trumps at the Georgian, 247 East Washington St., 706-546-6388. Elegant dining, serving seafood, veal and lamb.

The Mean Bean, 184 College Ave., for Mexican.

Lu Lu's Normaltown Cafe, 1344 Prince Ave., for home-style Southern cooking.

Chef Wolfgang's European Cuisine on Baxter St.

Accommodations

Hardeman-Hutchens House (circa 1855), 5335 Lexington Rd., 706-353-1855. A delightful antebellum plantation home filled with antiques. The plantation is a working horse and pony farm. Three guest rooms are available.

The Nicholson House, 6295 Jefferson Rd., 706-353-2200. Houses six guest rooms in a historic inn.

Magnolia Terrace, on 277 Hill St., 706-548-3860, offers a spacious guest house built in 1912. The Inn serves breakfast and is furnished with antiques and offers large private baths with clawfoot tubs, showers or jacuzzi.

Conyers

(I-20 E. to the Ga.138 exit, head south
to Ga.212 and follow the signs.)

Commentary

Conyers will host the equestrian events for the
1996 Olympics.

Attractions/Museums

Historic District of Olde Town. Once a train
stopover between Atlanta and Augusta.

Monastery of Our Lady the Holy Spirit,
2625 Hwy.212, 770-483-8705. Founded in
1944 by a group of monks that practice self-
sufficiency. Open to the public for short visits
or extended retreats.

The Georgia International Horse Park,
770-785-6900.

Golf

Highland Golf Club, 2271 Flat Shoals Rd.,
770-483-4235. A well-maintained pleasure.

Fieldstone Golf Club, 2720 Salem Rd.,
770-483-4372. Offering an 18-hole course,
tennis and swimming pool.

Parks

Panola Mountain State Conservation Park,
located at Ga.155 S., 770-389-7801.

Dining

Glenn's Open Pit B-B-Q, Kroger Shopping
Center on Hwy.138, 770-929-0196. A great
local restaurant offering barbecue and
smoked meat meals.

Benjamins, on Green St., 770-860-0071.
World cuisine served in casual elegance.

Michelangelo Restaurant, on Railroad St.,
770-929-0828. Italian cuisine with a formal
atmosphere.

Covington

(I-20 E. to exit 45A.)

Attractions/Museums

National Register District, downtown Covington, 770-787-3868. A gracious city offering
a wealth of antebellum and Victorian homes and
such shops as **In the Heat of the Night**, a
souvenir shop, **Hollywood South Shop**, or **The
Patrick House** for a unique collection of handmade gifts from local artists. Many of the historic
structures may be seen on a self-guided tour.
Local antique dealers specialize in everything
from Victorian and empire furniture to Victorian
silver, jewelry and fine porcelains.

Fox Vineyards Winery, 770-787-5402, one
mile south from I-20 exit 47, a local award-
winning winery offers daily tours, tastings and
sales. Taste Antebellum Rose, Scarlet Fox,
Ambrosia or Muscadew, all made from 100%
Georgia-grown muscadines.

Hollywood South Souvenir Shop, 1160
Monticello St., 770-786-2115. **Covington's**
"In the Heat of the Night" (MGM) souvenir
shop.

Historic Sites/Homes

Newton County Courthouse, downtown. Built
in 1884, this Victorian attraction has been seen
by many on TV's, "In the Heat of the Night."

Golf

The Oaks Golf Course, 1240 Brown Bridge
Rd., 770-786-3801. Beautiful bentgrass greens.

Eatonton/Greensboro

(Twenty miles east from Madison on I-20 E. or 22 miles north on Hwy.441 from Milledgeville.)

Commentary

Incorporated in 1809, Eatonton is filled with tree-lined streets and antebellum architecture. The **Uncle Remus Museum** in Turner Park is the repository of much of the work of Joel Chandler Harris, the creator of the Uncle Remus Tales and of author Alice Walker, who wrote "The Color Purple."

By motoring five miles north of Eatonton, on Hwy.74, you can view **Rock Eagle**, a 6,000 year-old, 102-foot, quartz image crafted from thousands of rocks.

Enjoy the drive around Eatonton as you observe dairy farms, wild meadows and forgotten shacks. **Lake Oconee** and **Lake Sinclair** offer a wealth of recreation with swimming beaches, marinas, bait shops and camping sites.

Attractions/Museums

Lake Oconee, I-20 E. to exit 53, then south on Hwy.441. 706-453-7592. Three hundred miles of beautiful shoreline for camping, fishing and watersports.

City of Greensboro, 706-453-7592, was founded in 1786. A historical city with beautiful homes, claiming five historic districts and seven individual sites.

Uncle Remus Museum, on Hwy.441, in a small park, 706-485-6856. Home of literary legends Alice Walker and Joel Chandler Harris.

Br'er Rabbit Statue. On Courthouse Square.

Greene County Historical Society Museum, Corner of Greene and East St., 706-453-7592. The museum houses artifacts, photographs and manuscripts relating to the history of Greene County.

Iron Horse, 706-453-7592. A impressive 2,000-lb structure, which is now visible in an open field by Hwy.15.

Greensboro Antique Mall and Gallery, with 30 exhibitors housed in circa 1850 warehouse. 706-453-7592,.

Granite Shoals Marina, Walkers Church Rd., 706-453-7639, off Hwy.44, Greensboro. Offers restaurant, lodging, boat ramp, dry dock storage, boat repair, fishing and grocery supplies.

Old Salem Park, located off Ga.44. A 63-acre campsite park with water and electric hook-ups. Hot showers, washer/dryer, play area, beach with lifeguard, dock and boat ramp.

Lawrence Shoals Recreation Area-Ga. Power Co., 125 Wallace Dam Rd., 706-485-5494. RV camping, tenting, picnicking and boat ramp. Beach open June through Labor Day.

Dining

Give yourself a real treat and stop for dinner at **Hugs Country Edition**, 2230 Eatonton Rd., 706-342-9730. In a 150-year-old Piedmont style home, amongst pleasantly cluttered golf memorabilia and famous people's signatures, savor Italian dishes such as Tortellini Alfredo or Chicken Limone, and have a friendly chat with the owner, Jack Flannigan.

Golf

A golfers' mecca offering four major courses and a fifth at **Cuscowila**, a Ben Crenshaw design, presently in the planning stages and should be ready by 1997.

Harbor Club, One Club Dr., 706-453-9690. *"Golfweek"* named this 18-hole course one of "America's Best Golf Courses for 1995."

Port Armor, 1 Port Armor Parkway, 706-453-4561. *Golf Magazine* hailed this beautiful Scottish-type championship 18-hole course as "one of the best in the world.'

Reynolds Plantation Course, 100 Linger Longer Rd., 706-467-3151. This 18-hole course was named one of the Best 10 New Resort Courses in the World by *Golf Magazine.*

Reynolds Great Waters Course, 100 Linger Longer Rd., 706-467-3151. Golfweek named this 18-hole course the second best in Georgia, featuring nine holes of play alongside Lake Oconee.

Accommodations

The Davis House Bed & Breakfast, 106 North Laurel Ave., 706-453-4213. A victorian estate with seven guest rooms.

Early Hill Bed & Breakfast, 1580 Lickskillet Rd., 706-453-7876. Lovely Georgian farmhouse with five guest rooms.

The Crockett House B & B, 671 Madison Rd., Eatonton. Experience the romance of a by-gone era in this stately and gracious circa 1895 Victorian home, which offers Southern hospitality at its finest. Antique-filled guest rooms have private baths and fireplaces. Gourmet breakfasts and elegant candle-lighted dinners are served by reservation. Located only minutes from Lake Oconee and Reynolds Plantation, site of award-winning Jack Nicklaus designed golf course. Call 706-485-2248, and Christa and Peter Crockett will make you feel at home.

Rosewood Bed & Breakfast, 301 North Madison Ave., 706-485-9009. Beautiful 1888 Victorian home with large porch, serving full breakfast.

Forsyth

Attractions/Museums

Confederate Cemetery, located off Hwy.42 S. on Newton Memorial Rd.

Monroe County Museum, on Tift College Dr., 912-994-5070. Housed in a 1899 Victorian Train Depot and operated by the local historical society.

Rum Creek Wildlife Management Area, seven miles east of Forsyth, 912-994-2439. Find a most varied bird population here.

Fort Valley

Attractions/Museums

Peach Capital of the World, 912-825-3733.

Jolly Nut Company, 100 Commercial Dr., 912-825-7733. Historical store with Georgia gourmet gifts.

Massee Lane Gardens and Museum, take I-75 S. to exit 42, 912-967-2358. Blooming camellias November to March, flowering azaleas and dogwood in spring and many other annuals and perennials. Museum houses porcelain sculptures, rare books and an art gallery.

Accommodations

The Evans-Cantrell House, 300 College St., 912-825-0611. Built by "Peach King" A. J. Evans, this Italian Renaissance revival mansion of 1916 offers five cheerful guest rooms.

Indian Springs

Attractions/Parks

Historic Indian Springs Hotel, Hwy.42, 706-775-2493. Built in 1823, by Chief William McIntosh, leader of the lower Creek Nation. An authentic 1800s English garden, with herbs and roses, graces the grounds.

Indian Springs State Park, ten miles east of I-75 take exit 67, off Hwy.42, 706-775-7241. The oldest state park in the nation offers, a historic mansion, native-history museum and medicinal spring water that people want. The 523-acre park also features a lake for swimming and boating, cottages and campsites.

Dauset Trails Nature Center, on Mt.Vernon Rd. off Hwy.42, 706-775-6798. For the nature buff, enjoy over 1,000-acres of hiking trails.

Jackson

Attractions/Museums

Jackson Historic Downtown District, 115 South Mulberry St., 706-775-7535. Enjoy a walk through a past Victorian era.

Butts County Courthouse, on Third St., 706-775-8200. Built in 1898, much of the courtroom and marble floors are still intact.

Jackson Lake, 706-775-4753. Five miles north of Jackson, enjoy boating, swimming and fishing on a 4,700-acre lake.

Parks

High Falls State Park, located 1.8 miles east of I-75 at High Falls Rd., 912-994-5080. The 995-acre park has a lake, swimming pool, miniature golf and 142 wooded campsites with water and electric.

Accommodations

The Carmichael House, 149 McDonough Rd., 706-775-0578. Enjoy a stay in a circa 1897 Queen Anne Victoria home.

Dining

Fresh-Air, at Hwy.23 and 42, south of town, 706-775-3182. Opened in 1940 and one of two favorite barbecue restaurants.

Mathis Brothers Barbecue, on Barnett Bridge Rd., 706-775-6562. A great variety of barbecued turkey, chicken, pork and beef.

Juliette

Attractions/Museums

Jarrell Plantation Historic Site, located eight miles southeast of city, 912-986-5172. Exhibits a working farm from the 1850s.

Juliette Grist Mill, built in 1927, was one of the world's largest grist mills.

Lake Juliette, 912-994-0022. A 3,600-acre recreational lake.

Dining

Whistle Stop Cafe, on McCrackin St., 912-994-3670. Best known for the film version of Fannie Flagg's novel *Fried Green Tomatoes* at the Whistle Stop Cafe. Make sure you sample this specialty.

Macon

(I-75 S. to I-16, about 90 miles.)

Commentary

It's an easy drive to antebellum Macon where white columns and cherry blossoms prevail. A city of wide avenues, lined with white-columned mansions. Best seen in March during the **Cherry Blossom Festival** when the 180,000 cherry trees are in bloom. There are over 2,000 acres of neighborhoods listed n the "National Register of Historic Places." Three walking tours will acquaint you with the bygone days of the South.

Antique buffs will enjoy the **Antique Trail**, linking almost 100 vendors in nine central Georgia locations south from Atlanta, including Macon and nearby communities. Other landmarks include **Wesleyan College**, founded in 1836. Wesleyan was the first college in the world chartered to grant degrees to women.

Attractions/Museums

Historic Downtown Macon offers many unique shops such as, **Curiosities** at 344 Second St., **Popper's Fine Gifts and Antiques** at 1066 Magnolia St., and **Ingleside Village**, on Ingleside Avenue off Riverside Dr.

Ocmulgee Mounds National Monument, 1207 Emery Hwy.912-752-8257. An ancient American Indian civilization. Preserved impressive earthworks of the late Mississippian culture which flourished here on the banks of the Ocmulgee River from A.D. 900 to 1100. The site also shows evidence of much earlier human habitation, dating back as much as 10,000 years.

The Museum of Arts and Sciences and Mark Smith Planetarium, 4182 Forsyth Rd., presents nature trails and a 40-million-year-old fossil skeleton unearthed near Macon. 912-477-3232.

The Palace of the South, at 924 Georgia Avenue. This opulent Italian Renaissance palazzo was finished in 1861. Stained glass windows, exquisite plasterwork, grained woodwork, and some of the country's finest examples of marbleized and trompe l'oeil finishes decorate the rooms of the house, 912-742-8155.

Central City Park, 250 acres southeast of downtown is one of the city's original parks, dating back to the 1820s. Sports fields, picnic spots and concerts are held here. Here the 1929 Luther Williams Stadium is the home field of the Macon Braves, farm team for the Atlanta Braves, 912-745-8943.

Harriet Tubman Historical and Cultural Museum, 340 Walnut St., 912-743-8544. Here, past meets present in the works of local artists. African-American history and culture.

Rose Hill Cemetery, 1091 Dr., 912-751-9119. An outstanding example of 19th century landscape design. The cemetery remains one of the oldest surviving public cemeteries in the U.S.

Southern Antiques and Collectibles Market, on Whittle Rd., 912-994-9882.

Washington Memorial Library, 1180 Washington Ave., 912-744-0800. Busts of famous Macon residents Sidney Lanier and Harry Stillwell Edwards, and an extensive genealogy department.

Sidney's Old South Historic Tours, 200 Cherry St., 912-743-3401. Take a tour with the spirit of Sidney Lanier represented by a costumed tour guide.

Old Cannonball House and Confederate Museum, 856 Mulberry St., 912-477-4799. Built in 1853, this Greek revival Home was the only one in Macon struck by a cannonball in 1864's Union attack.

Historic Sites/Homes

Sidney Lanier Cottage, 935 High St., 912-743-3851. Famous Georgia poet Sidney Clopton Lanier was born in this Victorian cottage in 1842.

Hay House, 934 Georgia Ave., 912-742-8155. A magnificent Italian Renaissance revival mansion that took five years to complete in 1860.

Grant Opera House, 651 Mulberry St., 912-749-6580. Built in 1884, once boasted the largest stage south of the Macon Dixon line. Today, beautifully restored, it remains active with local performances.

Woodruff House, 988 Bond St., 912-744-2715. Built in 1836, this Greek revival mansion overlooks Macon. General Wilson resided here at one time, and President Jefferson Davis and his family were entertained here.

Parks

Lake Tobesofkee Recreation Area, 6600 Moseley Dixon Rd., 912-474-8770. Three parks and 1800 acres of fresh water make Lake Tobesofee a perfect choice for camping, fishing, tennis, skiing and picnicking by beautiful beaches.

High Falls State Park (I-75 S. to exit 65, then two miles on the left.) Its 1000 acres include a lake, swimming pool, nature trails and canoeing, miniature golf and 142 wooded campsites with water and electrical hookups. 912-994-5080.

Golf

Bowden Golf Course, 3111 Millerfield Rd., 912-742-1610.

Accommodations

1842 Inn, 353 College St., Macon. Consider a stay in one of the best-preserved and award-winning antebellum Greek revival, circa 1842, mansions in Georgia. Featuring formal parlors, library and sumptuous guest rooms with fine antiques, Oriental rugs, luxurious towels and linens, king or queen-sized beds; some of the rooms come with jacuzzis. Offering fine European-style services, robes, turndown service with sweets, shoe shines while you sleep and a continental breakfast delivered to your room replete with flowers and the day's newspaper. For evening relaxation, owner Philip Jenkins presents "formal evening hospitality" offering hors d'oeuvres and beverages in the parlor with piano music, even, at times, ticklin' the ivories himself. 912-741-1842, 800-336-1842.

Dining

Len Berg's Restaurant, 240 Post Office Alley, 912-742-9255. Well-worn, comfortable, wooden booths and delicious Southern cuisine. This Macon landmark serves first-class Southern cooking from fried fish and chicken to pork chops, turnip greens, fried okra and hot cobblers.

Beall's 1860 Restaurant and Lounge, on 315 College St., 912-745-3663. Dress is fancy or casual, in an antebellum Greek revival style mansion. Great service and atmosphere, and known for its prime rib and chocolate walnut pie.

Jim Shaw's Restaurant, 3040 Vineville Ave., 912-746-3697. Serving the finest seafood in Macon in a family-friendly atmosphere.

Fresh-Air, Hwy.80 W. at 3076 Riverside Dr., 912-477-7229. The sentimental favorite in finger-lickin' barbecue.

Madison

(I-20 E. to exit 51.)

Commentary

Madison is one of Georgia's loveliest antebellum towns, filled with historic sites and homes, shaded streets and an authentic town square. See century-old storefronts shaded by massive oaks and magnolias and brick sidewalks lined with trim flower boxes.

Attractions

Madison Historic District, 706-342-4454. Over a 100 historic structures.

Madison-Morgan Cultural Center (circa 1895), 434 South Main St., 706-342-4743. Madison's 1895 Classroom Museum that also houses an art gallery.

Morgan County African-American Museum, 156 Academy St., 706-342-9197. Preserving African-American heritage and awareness of the contributions made to the South.

Heritage Hall, an 1825 Greek revival mansion, is but one of the stately structures giving Madison its grand aura.

African-American Museum on Academy St., whose mission is preserving African-American heritage and promoting awareness of the contributions made to the culture of the South. 706-342-9191.

Step Back In Time, a shop offering oak, walnut and mahogany furniture from the 1800s; also depression glass, lamps, vintage linens, pottery and lots of angel items, all displayed by owners Carolyn and Charles Autry, 706-342-3311.

Old Madison Antiques, Madison's oldest antique business, owned by Chris Argo, has a large selection of American furniture dating from the 1840s to the 1940s; comic books, coins and currency and depression glass. We even found old menu's from Jack Dempsey's New York restaurant.

Historic Sites/Homes

Cornelius Vason House (circa 1800s), 549 Old Post Rd., 706-342-4454. Circa mid-1800s.

Baldwin Pharmacy, 137 South Main St., 706-342-1715. On the square since the late 1800s, you may have seen this drugstore in films and commercials. You can still sit at the lunch counter and order a hand-dipped ice-cream cone.

Accommodations

Madison is proud of its fine bed & breakfasts. It's a real treat choosing amongst the impressively restored homes, all within walking distance of the town's historic square.

The Brady Inn, at 250 North Second St., is a charming 1800s Inn, with two Victorian cottages joined by a breezeway. They're encircled by porches with comfortable rockers and even an antique carousel wooden horse. Visitors will enjoy lots of hospitality from owners Lynn and Chris Rasch, who are well-known in town for preserving and restoring a number of homes in Madison. Named after its original owner Sarah Brady, with the Brady family insignia in glass above the front entrance, the inn has high-ceilinged rooms and suites, stained glass, intricate moldings, pine floors, antiques and working fireplaces. The central-hall is well stocked with books, magazines and vintage photos of the Brady family. Each guest room is decorated with antiques and has double or queen-size beds. Every guest is welcomed with a tour of the home and freshly

baked goodies. Also, in the evening the kitchen is open to guests for midnight snacks. A full Southern breakfast is served with the day's newspaper, all making your stay here the best ever! 706-342-4400.

Burnett Place B & B, 317 Old Post Rd., Madison. Leonard and Ruth Wallace's meticulously restored and handsomely furnished, circa 1830, Federal House is located in the center of Madison, the town Sherman found "to beautiful to burn." Indeed, had Leonard and Ruth been in business in 1864, the South would have won the war. Leonard explains, "If the Union's forces had had the opportunity to experience our gracious hospitality, magnificent breakfast and singular philosophies, they would have cast down their swords and put on coats of gray." 706-342-4034.

The Boat House Non-Smokers' Bed & Breakfast, 383 Porter St., 706-342-3061. Built in 1850 by a sea captain, this authentically restored house offers four guest rooms with gorgeous antiques.

Dining

Ye Olde Colonial Restaurant, on the square, is housed in the 1800s Morgan County Bank building, complete with a vault, in which you can dine. The main dining room has flocked red wallpaper, pressed tin ceiling and high arched windows providing a lovely view. For 36 years the restaurant has served genuine Dixie cooking, with such popular dishes as luscious shreds of smoky-flavored pig, crisp and steamy cornbread sticks and custard-rich squash casserole, favorite family recipes; now tended by son and owner, James Cunningham.

For a light lunch of homemade soup or tea and delicious sandwiches stop by the **Heritage Tea Room**, where soft music makes for a relaxing atmosphere.

Or step back into time at the old fashioned soda fountain and grill at **Madison Drug Co.** on Main St. Enjoy homemade salads, traditional grilled favorites such as burgers and fish filets. And don't forget the famous chili cheese slaw dogs, all of course ending with a hand-dipped ice-cream cone or milkshake.

For the hungry visitor and local alike, **Amici's Italian Cafe** is numero uno. Very casual dining, outside or in, featuring Pesto Spagatini, hand-tossed pizza and buffalo wings.

Mansfield

Attractions

Preaching Rock Wildlife Center, 770-784-3060. Primitive camping sites, hunting grounds and 20 fishing ponds.

McDonough

Attractions/Museums

Historic Courthouse Square, 800-436-7926. Built in 1897 and situated on the town's beautiful square.

Old Post Office, 34 Covington St. Built in 1940, featuring a mural displaying the cotton history of the South.

Peachtree Flea Market, located at I-75 and Jonesboro Rd., 770-914-2269. Choose from hundreds of vendors of a wide variety of goods.

Simpler Tymes Antiques Market, 54 Covington St., 770-957-7908. One of the largest single-day antiques markets in Georgia, held on the last Saturday of each month.

Tamingo Farms Equestrian Center, 108 Peach Dr., 770-957-7433. Specializing in teaching the Olympic equestrian sports of hunters, jumpers and dressage.

Golf

Green Valley Golf Club, 434 Hwy.155, 770-957-2800.

Cottonfields Golf Club, 400 Industrial Blvd., 770-914-1442.

Milledgeville

Commentary

Founded in 1803, Milledgeville was Georgia's capital for 60 years. Today the small town of 15,000 boasts more than 20 architectural landmarks, and more than a dozen listings in the "National Historic Register."

Old State Capitol set on the original Statehouse Square is now part of the Georgia Military College campus. Built in 1807, the turreted Gothic three-story structure houses the school's offices and small museum.

The Old Governor's Mansion, built in 1835, has been restored.

Enjoy a perfect two-hour motorized trolley tour conducted by Milledgeville Trolley Tour, which covers many major landmarks.

Two blocks from the **Governor's Mansion** is the **Milledgeville Memory Hill Cemetery** with "slavery-time" graves marked by small linked chains, each chain representing who was born, lived or died as a slave.

Milledgeville is visitor friendly and presents culture and recreation that will have you coming back for more. Being one of the "Main Street Cities," there is an abundance of shopping and dining from rustic fundamentals to Victorian elegance.

Attractions/Museums

Baldwin Forest Public Fishing Area, 912-435-4200. Located five miles south of Milledgeville on Hwy.441. This excellent fishing lake offers bream, channel catfish and large-mouth bass.

Lake Sinclair, 912-452-4687. A 15,000-acre lake that offers camping, full-service RV hookups, condo rentals, restaurants, marinas and boat rentals.

Lockerly Arboretum, on Hwy.441, south of Milledgeville, 912-452-2112. Here find 50 acres of nature trails and ponds.

Museum and Archives of Georgia Education, 131 South Clark St. The museum, circa 1900, displays memorabilia and photo's.

Old Governor's Mansion, 120 South Clark St., 912-453-4545. This elegant peach colored circa 1838 mansion was home to ten of Georgia's governors.

Old State Capitol Building, 201 East Greene St., 800-653-1804. Built in 1807, this Gothic building is one of the oldest public buildings in the nation in that style.

Trolley Tours, 912-452-4687. The town's tourist office at 200 West Hancock St., sponsors trolley tours and also self-guided walking and driving maps.

Historic Sites/Homes

Stetson-Sanford House, West Hancock St. A circa 1812 beauty that received nationwide acclaim for architectural design.

Parks

Walter B. Williams Park, on Ga.22, 912-452-2721. Offers a variety of recreation with an Olympic size pool, eight tennis courts, four baseball fields, picnic shelters, a golf course and gymnasium.

Dining

Chobys, 3090 Highway 441 N., for crispy fried catfish and other fresh seafood.

Hook's Bar-B-Q, 10 miles east of the city at 713 Sandersville Rd./Hwy.24. On Fridays and Saturdays only, attend an actual barbecue where you can help yourself to pit-cooked pig.

Golf

Little Fishing Creek Golf Course, this 18-hole course is located in the Walter B. Williams Park.

Accommodations

Mara's Tara Bed & Breakfast, 330 West Greene St., 912-453-2732. Three guest rooms.

Monroe

Historic Sites/Homes

Davis Edwards House, circa 1845.

Kilgore's Mill Covered Bridge, north of Monroe on Walton-Barrow county line. The 100-foot bridge was built in 1892 and spans the Apalachee River.

McDaniel/Walker Homes. Both homes belonged to former Georgia governors.

Selman-Pollack-Williams Home, circa 1832, on McDaniel St.

Monticello

Attractions

Forsyth Street Historic District, Hwy.83 S., 706-468-8994. The local Chamber of Commerce distributes walk-tour maps of the town's dogwood lined trees with antebellum and Victorian homes.

Rutledge

(I-20 E. to exit 49.)

Attractions/Museums

Downtown Rutledge. Stroll this circa 1871 community. Visit the quality shops, featuring crafts, antiques, furniture, a nifty cafe and a 75-year old hardware store.

Barn Raising, on Fairplay Rd. Select from custom-made 18th and 19th-century Georgia Piedmont-style pine furniture, designed by master craftsman Paul Jones. "Buttermilk-based paint gives their pieces a unique look," he explains. It's applied by hand, then sanded off, then it goes through a three-step oiling process, which gives the pieces an antique appearance. Paul's wife, Pam Jones, is an award-winning quilter. Pam had no formal instruction in quilting but has sewn under her grandmother's tutelage since she was a little girl. She was the youngest artist featured in the art exhibit "Patterns: A Celebration of Georgia's Quilting" that toured the state's art museums.

Rutledge Antique Walk. As you enter the store, owner Beverly Moreau doesn't want you to get lost, so just follow the "yellow brick road" and it will lead you through a 10,000 square foot shop full of rare collectibles. You will find early handmade American furniture, arrowhead artifacts, old lace collars and early electrics. A pump organ from 1860 and Victorian armoire are also up for adoption, and for the serious lamp collector, have a look at the great variety of kerosene and whale oil lamps. At this point you know it is impossible to leave empty-handed. 706-557-9840.

Furlong Farms, 706-342-7044, for trail rides and cowboy cookouts.

Parks

Hard Labor Creek State Park, 706-557-2863. Everything for the whole family. From cottages and camping, to golf, fishing, beach, horseback riding and boating.

Golf

Hard Labor Creek Golf Course, 706-557-3006. Two miles north of Rutledge enjoy a beautiful, state-owned 18-hole course with tight, tree-lined fairways.

Dining

The Yesterday Cafe, tended by gracious hostess Teri Bragg, featuring modern country cooking. Located in a redone turn-of-the-century drugstore, brick walls are filled with regional photographs that date back to the Civil War, and tiled floors. This cafe is known for its "peach puffs," Caribbean chicken salad and trendy pastas, with a must-try delicious buttermilk pie. 706-557-9337.

Social Circle

(I-20 E. to exit 47.)

Commentary

Picture a group of men, sitting around the well at the crossroads, enjoying their usual drink. A stranger walks up and asks to join the circle. He, being a stranger, was greatly surprised at such hospitality and said; **"This is surely a 'social circle.'"** From that day on, the town's name was "Social Circle."

Attractions/Museums

National Historic District. Stroll past more than fifty homes built before the 1900s and some Victorian shops.

Baldwin Antiques, on Cherokee Rd. Proprietor Nancy Baldwin, a friendly hostess, will invite you into her "social circle" amidst antiques in her store. Hanging from the wall is a sign that states the owner's philosophy: "If we don't have it, you don't need it." The old building gives the shop an "antique" feeling, as you browse amongst fine porcelain, antique jewelry, primitive wash-stands, glassware and many odd and unusual collectibles. Aside from antiques, the store also offers potpourri, gifts and crafts. We made a real find with two gold-laced antique dinner plates, for a bargain price.

Turnipseed's, on Cherokee Rd., named for the owner's grandmother, Susie Turnipseed. Not only can you find a sprinkling of crafts, antiques, heart pine furniture and country clothing, but the back is a factory outlet for designer decorator fabrics and silk-screen hand-printed wallpaper.

Town Well. The legend of naming Social Circle, symbolizing the friendliness of the people.

Dining

The Blue Willow Inn, 294 North Cherokee Rd., as discovered and made famous by a very favorable review by the legendary Lewis Grizzard.

Housed in a magnificent Greek revival mansion owned by Billie and Louis Van Dyke. They serve a mouth-watering, all-you-can-eat Southern buffet. If you have to wait a moment before being seated, relax on one of the veranda's oversized rockers, as the attentive staff serves sweet tea and lemonade. With a choice of four elegantly appointed dining rooms, you have the feeling of dining in the antebellum South as it was in its glorious past. Laid out in chafing dishes in the high-ceilinged dining room, the feast features four meats, to-die-for fried chicken (on stage every day), an array of ten or so vegetables (classics like real mashed potatoes, black-eyed peas, fried okra, turnip greens and nationally acclaimed fried green tomatoes from Lewis' mama's recipe).

The Inn is open daily for lunch and dinner, and guests are encouraged to visit the **Blue Willow Inn Gift Shop** located pool-side, which features the work of local artisans.

The Inn's soon to be published cookbook is appropriately entitled *"Fried Green Tomatoes."* 770-464-2131.

Stockbridge

Panola Mountain State Conservation Park, 770-474-2914. Located 18 miles southeast of Atlanta on Hwy.155. A huge granite outcropping resembling Stone Mountain, yet remains undeveloped. Here visitors can enjoy a variety of hiking trails through this protected, fragile habitat.

Warner Robins

Attractions/Museums

Georgia Aviation Hall of Fame, 912-926-6870. Warner Robins is the home of Robins Air Force Base. The Hall of Fame honors the impressive history of military and civilian aviators.

Museum of Aviation, Hwy.247 and Russell Pkwy., 912-926-6870. The museum displays military memorabilia and presents audio-visual shows on aviation history.

Watkinsville

Attractions/Museums

Eagle Tavern Welcome Center, U.S.441, 706-769-5197. Located downtown, once was a Georgia stage stop and tavern, still displays some 18th-century furnishings and artifacts.

Happy Valley Pottery, 1210 Carson Graves Rd., 706-769-5922. Local artisans show their artistic wares.

Haygood House Antiques, 25 South Main St., 706-769-8129. Once owned by Green Haygood, founder of Emory University, the circa 1827 home today is an antiques store.

Historic Sites/Homes

Elder Mill Covered Bridge, circa 1800. On Hwy.15 at Rose Creek. Still being used by the public, this is one of the last wooden bridges.

Parks

Herman C. Michael Park, Hwy.53 and Elder Rd., 706-769-3965. A park for the sports-minded, offering lighted ball fields, jogging and nature trails, tennis courts, basketball and a weight room.

Golf

Lane Creek Golf Course, 2360 Cole Springs Rd., 706-769-6699. A great 7000-yard 18-hole championship course.

Fun Fact:

- Georgia is known by many a nick-name, including: the Empire State of the South, Cracker State, Goober State, Peach State and Buzzard State, but nothing official as yet.

Fun Facts:

- Georgia has 45 state parks, 10 national parks and 14 state historic sites.

- North to south Georgia's longest measure is about 315 miles, east to west about 250 miles.

- But, if you travel the gorgeous country roads you can fill a lifetime.

- Georgia's African-American population of over 1 million is fifth in the nation.

- In 200 years, from 1790 to 1990, Georgia's population grew from 82,548 to 6,478,216.

- In 1990 about 40% of Georgia's farming income came from chicken broilers and peanuts, 28.7% and 11.3% respectively.

- Nearly 700,000 veterans reside in Georgia.

Fun Facts:

- The 1993 population of Georgia was 6,917,000, the 11th largest in the nation, with more than 60% living in urban centers.

- As of 1982 there were 1,269 governments in Georgia: 1 state, 158 county, 533 municipal, 187 school district and 390 special district in all.

- Atlanta is rated among America's top three cities in the area of charitable giving.

- According to the Sports Marketing Group, the Atlanta Braves are the most popular team in major league baseball.

- Since 1929, per capita yearly income in Georgia has grown from $342 to over $19,000.

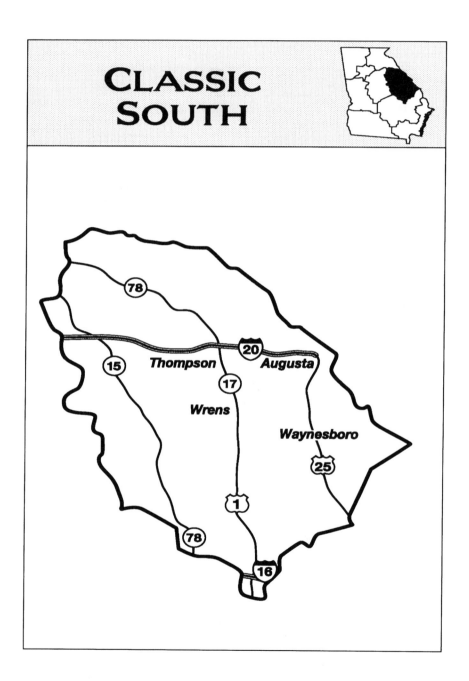

CLASSIC SOUTH

Section XVII
Traveling Georgia's Classic South

Classic South

Commentary

The Classic South reflects the charm and splendor of a bygone era, a time when the rolling hills were a sea of cotton and stately, white-columned, antebellum mansions criss-crossed the land. Today central Georgia retains a number of historic old homes, while the sea of cotton is now wondrous gardens, recreational land and lush-green golf courses.

Augusta, home of the prestigious **Masters Golf Tournament,** is the regions oldest and largest city, with the popular **Riverwalk** (museums, marina, restaurants, and shops) serving as the city's center. **The Savannah River,** that ripples through Augusta, still dominates its surroundings. Having survived the Civil War with little damage, some historical sites, such as the Ezekiel Harris House, date back to colonial times.

Another town of the Classic South, **Washington,** though smaller than Augusta, is also quite historic. Once the temporary Capital of Georgia, it was settled by English and French. The famous **Battle of Kettle Creek** in 1779, was a highly significant turning point in the freeing of Georgia from foreign rule. The Robert Toombs House, circa 1794, home of Confederate Brigadier General and Secretary of State for the Confederacy, still operates as a general store.

Appling

Attractions/Museums

Columbia County Courthouse, circa 1812, at 1956 Appling Harlem Rd., 706-541-1254. The oldest active courthouse in the State.

Heggie Rock, at Old Louisville Rd., 706-873-6946, is one of Georgia's 12 natural landmarks. Eleven of 19 endemic plants that live on granite outcroppings can be observed here.

Parks

Mistletoe State Park, 3723 Mistletoe Rd., 706-541-0321. Located 12 miles north of I-20, exit 60; ten cottages, 107 tent and trailer sites, camping, picnic shelters, hiking trails, beach, lake, fishing and boat ramps.

Wildwood Park, 706-541-0586, is a 975-acre park on Lake Thurmond. Camp sites have electrical and water hook-ups. The park has two large picnic shelters, trails and a beach. Weekend admission is $2.00 a car.

Augusta

(I-20 E. to exit 65, taking State Rd. 28 S. to downtown Augusta.)

Commentary

Founded in 1736 on the banks of the **Savannah River** as an Indian trading post by Georgia's founder, General James Edward Oglethorpe. George Washington, during a visit to Augusta in 1791, was shown the site on which the Old Government House was to be built. A ginkgo tree was planted where Washington stood. Today the tree is the largest ginkgo in the state, 86 feet tall and 13 feet in circumference.

The **Riverwalk** promenade is the city's central attraction, replete with landscaped parks, historic markers and the historic **Cotton Exchange Building**.

For the sports-minded, downtown's **Riverfront Marina** at Prep Phillips Dr. centralizes water recreation on the Savannah River, the focal point of frequent river races. For a more rustic recreation, northwest of town around the **Savannah Lock and Dam**, paddlers put in for leisurely river trips, and wanderers take in the historic mills and canal. The local outfitter **American Wilderness Outfitters, Ltd.**, rents kayaks, canoes, and will organize paddling trips from Augusta down river to Savannah, 706-860-0278.

Flea markets and antique stores abound at the **Augusta-Richmond County Museum**, a Romanesque building, circa 1802, that serves as Augusta's municipal "attic." 706-722-8454.

The Gertrude Herbert Institute of Art is an architecturally outstanding early 19th-century residence that showcases regional and southeastern contemporary art. 706-722-5495.

A favorite spot downtown is the **Word of Mouth Cafe** on Broad St. Enjoy local jazz in a speakeasy setting.

Attractions/Museums

Augusta-Richmond County Museum, 540 Telfair St., 706-722-8454. Telfair Street was the fashionable address of the 19th-century.

Morris Museum of Art, 1 Tenth Street at Riverwalk, 706-724-7501. This museum features a unique collection of Southern art. Large gallery displays of Civil War art and still life.

Riverwalk Augusta, #15 at Eight St., 706-821-1754. A beautiful esplanade along the Savannah River, for shopping, dining, museums and entertainment.

Clark's Hill Lake, 22 miles north of the city, 7,000-acre lake for fishing and picnicking.

Historic Sites/Homes

Augusta College, 2500 Walton Way, 706-737-1444. Built in 1816, today the college campus features a concert hall, gallery and classroom building.

Old Medical College, 598 Telfair St., 706-721-7238. Circa 1835. It was the first medical school in Georgia, and one of the first in America.

Cotton Exchange Welcome Center and Museum, 32 Eighth Street at Riverwalk, 706-724-4067. Circa 1886; was once the center of Augusta's cotton market.

Building Sacred Heart Cultural Center, corner of Greene and 13th St., 706-826-4700. Great example of late Romanesque revival architecture.

Appleby House, 2260 Walton Way. Circa 1830; today hosts summer garden concerts and library.

Ezekiel Harris Home, 1840 Broad St., 706-724-0436. Built in 1797, this home is furnished with impressive Southern furniture.

Lucy Laney House, 1116 Phillips St., 706-724-3576. A house museum of one of Georgia's famous educators, Lucy Laney, who was born into slavery.

Meadow Garden, 1320 Independence Dr., 706-724-4174. Eighteenth-century home of George Walton, a signer of the Declaration of Independence.

Gertrude Herbert Institute of Art, 506 Telfair St., 706-722-5495. A center for art classes and exhibitions.

Woodrow Wilson Boyhood Home, 419 7th St., 706-724-0436.

Parks

Krystal River Water Park, 799 Industrial Park Dr., 706-855-0061. The park is open May through September, and offers water slides, white sandy beach, amusement rides and free video games.

Golf

There are three courses accessible to the public; **Augusta Golf Club**, 706-733-9177; **Forest Hills Golf Course**, 706-733-0001; and **Goshen Plantation Country Club**, 706-793-1168.

Accommodations

Partridge Inn, at 2110 Walton Way, circa 1890, features 105 comfortable suites with modern furnishings, a pool and two restaurants. 800-476-6888.

The Clarion Telfair Inn, 800-241-2407, has transformed a block of turn-of-the-century Victorian homes into an historic inn complex with a pool. Rooms are furnished in period detail. Continental dinners are served Tuesday through Saturday.

Oglethorpe Inn, 836 Greene St., 706-724-9774. Eighteen-room inn with full breakfast.

Dining

French Market Grille, 425 Highland Ave., 706-737-4865. Voted best restaurant and best desert in Augusta. Cajun cuisine in a casual atmosphere.

Michael's Restaurant and Piano Bar, 2860 Washington Rd., 706-733-2860. Fresh seafood, steaks, poultry, deserts and live music.

S & S Cafeteria, 1616 Walton Way, 706-736-2972. Southern style home recipe cooking.

Villa Europa, 3044 Deans Bridge Rd., 706-798-6211. Italian, German and American cuisine.

Crawfordville

Attractions/Museums

Alexander H. Stephens Home and Confederate Museum, I-20 to exit 55, to Park St., 706-456-2221. The antebellum home of the vice-president of the Confederacy. Civil War museum and park with nature trails, fishing, camping and picnicking.

Lincolnton

Attractions/Museums

Amity Recreation Park, on Ga.47, 706-722-3770. A hidden treasure of a park that offers boat ramp, beach, restrooms, picnic area and playground.

Clarks Hill Lake, Route 1, 706-722-3770. The lake offers nine campgrounds, four marinas, three parks and five recreation areas.

Elijah Clark State Park, seven miles northeast of Lincolnton off U.S.378, 706-359-3458. Sites for 165 tents and trailers, 20 cottages, beach, picnic areas, boat ramps, fishing, water skiing and museum.

Historic Homes

Blanchard-Lamar House, on Washington St., circa 1823, 706-359-1737. One of 200 sites registered in the "National Register of Historic Places and Buildings."

Lincoln County Historical Park and May House, 147 Lumber St., 706-359-4697. Beautifully restored home of town's doctor.

Price's Store, 5021 Double Branches Rd., 706-359-4401. One of the few rural general stores still operating in Georgia.

Dining

Lakeside Bar-B-Que House, Hwy.47, Clarks Hill Lake, 706-359-7429. Southern all-you-can-eat BBQ.

Louisville

Attractions/Museums

Old Market House. On Board St., built in 1758, at one time the intersection of two major Native American trading routes.

The Old Cemetery, on Ga.24 E., grave sites of Revolutionary War soldiers and also a U.S.Congressman.

Sandersville

Attractions/Museums

Driving Tour of Sandersville, 119 Jones St., 912-552-3288. Tour historic Sandersville.

Washington County Museum, 129 Jones St., 912-552-6965. Open Tuesday and Thursday 2-5 p.m.

Sparta

Attractions/Museums

Georgia Power's Lake Sinclair, 800-693-1304. The lake offers a 75-mile shoreline with fishing, boating, camping and swimming.

Hancock County Courthouse, Broad St., 706-444-5746. Victorian architecture in a once important cultural trading center.

The LaFayette Hotel, Broad Street, circa 1840, known as the Drummers Home, served as a refugee haven during the Civil War.

Historic Sites/Homes

Rock Mill Plantation, federal style, circa 1820.

Glen Mary Plantation, a Greek revival cottage, circa 1848.

Shoulderbone Plantation, circa 1848.

All are private homes listed in the "National Register" and not open to the public.

Thomson

Attractions/Museums

Bartram Trail/Historic Wrightsboro, located one mile north of I-20, exit 59, 706-595-5584. Brochures available at the Visitors Bureau depict the famous trail and Historic Wrightboro District with cemetery dating back to the Quaker period.

Thomson Downtown Historic District, is two miles south of I-20, exit 59. The Thomson Depot on Main Street has maps and information regarding the town's heritage.

Clarks Hill Lake Wildlife Management Area, 706-595-4222. A public hunting area of 15,000-acres. Restricted camping areas.

McDuffie Public Fishing Area. Proceed on Hwy.278 to Ellington Airline Rd., turn right on Fish Hatchery Rd., 706-595-1619.

Historic Sites/Homes

"Women of the Sixties" Monument, located at Thomson Depot in the park. A fine art sculpture honoring the women who supported the South during the Civil War.

The Rock House, circa 1785, on Rock House Rd., 706-595-5584. The 18th-century stone dwelling was built by an ancestor of former President Jimmy Carter. It is the oldest intact home in Georgia.

Hickory Hill, was the home of Senator Tom Watson, recognized as the father of Rural Free Delivery; today this is a private home.

Accommodations

1810 West Inn, at 254 North Seymour Dr., 706-595-3156. A historic Piedmont Plains farmhouse from 1810, surrounded by lavish lawns and gardens. Eight guest rooms, serving Continental-plus breakfast.

Four Chimneys Bed & Breakfast, at 2316 Wire Rd., 706-597-0220. An imposing 1820s farmhouse with massive chimneys. Four guest rooms, and an ample Continental breakfast.

Twin City

Attractions/Museums

George L. Smith State Park, located 3 1/2 miles southeast of Twin City off Ga.23, 912-763-2759. Home of the Old Mill Pond.

Union Point

Attractions/Museums

City of Union Point. Railroad junction from 1834, showing fine Victorian architecture. Some character landmarks are nominated for the "National Registry."

Jefferson Hall, on U.S.278. A beautifully constructed building from the 1830s, not open for tours.

Union Point, Chipman Union, a 105-year old hosiery mill, located downtown. Still in use today. 706-486-2112.

Warrenton

Attractions

Ogeechee Wildlife Management Area. A 24,000-acre public hunting area. Take Ga.16 SW. to Jewel and follow signs.

Washington

Attractions/Museums

Callaway Plantation, from U.S.78 W. to Lexington Rd., 706-678-7060. Historical pe-

riods of time are shown through furnishings and manuscripts.

Washington Historical Museum, at 308 East Robert Toombs Ave., 706-678-2105. A beautiful antebellum home, circa 1835, displaying Indian artifacts and Confederate gun collection.

Kettle Creek Battlefield, on Ga.44, eight miles southwest of Washington, 706-678-2013. Historical battle of Feb.14, 1779.

Robert Toombs House State Historic Site, at 216 East Robert Toombs Ave., 706-678-2226. Home of Confederate General Robert Toombs. Circa 1797.

Mary Willis Library, 204 East Liberty St., 706-678-7736. The State's first free public library, Victorian style, circa 1888.

Accommodations

Holly Ridge Country Inn, 221 Sandtown Rd., 706-285-2594. The Inn has 10 guest rooms and consists of two homes, formal and informal, with fitting ambiance. State preference.

Waynesboro

Attractions/Museums

Historic Waynesboro, located by U.S.25, 706-554-4889. Step back into time with turn-of-the-century homes and courthouse circa 1856.

Accommodations

Georgia's Guest Bed & Breakfast, 640 East Seventh St., 706-554-4863. A stately two-story Georgian-style home built in 1926, offering three guest rooms, decorated in period antiques and eclectic newer pieces.

Fun Facts:

- Macon Georgia decrees it unlawful for a man to place his arm around a woman without a legal reason.

- Georgia's Dahlonega (Cherokee for precious yellow metal), experienced the nation's first gold rush.

- Georgia marble from Tate was used in building the Lincoln Memorial.

- Georgia is the leading producer of kaolin and in addition to its famous marble produces granite, iron and bauxite.

- Since 1940 the productivity of Georgia's farmers has risen about 700%. One farmer now produces what it took seven farmers to produce back then.

- By land mass, Georgia ranks 21st among the 50 states and has approximately 575 cities, towns and villages.

Fun Facts:

- In 1939 Atlanta became the sixth district headquarters of the Federal Reserve Bank.

- The U.S. Dept. of Agriculture lists Georgia as having 1.4 million cows, 8.8 million chickens, 24 million acres of forests and 12 million acres of farm land.

- The U.S. Dept. of Agriculture lists Georgia as having 1.4 million cows, 8.8 million chickens, 24 million acres of forests and 12 million acres of farm land.

- The azaleas, dogwoods and the golden daffodil herald the onset of springtime in Atlanta.

- Georgia ranks fifth in the nation in defense expenditures, about $80 billion annually.

- Daily per capita water consumption in Georgia is about 187 gallons.

Rosalynn Carter

Jimmy Carter

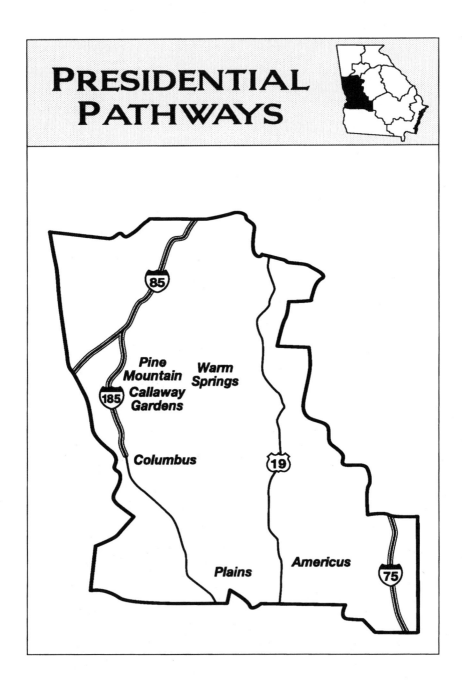

PRESIDENTIAL PATHWAYS

85

Pine Mountain **Warm Springs**

185 **Callaway Gardens**

Columbus

19

Americus

Plains 75

LOVE ATLANTA

Section XVIII
Traveling Georgia's Presidential Pathways

Presidential Pathways

Commentary

This region honors two of America's greatest Presidents, **Franklin Delano Roosevelt** and **Jimmy Carter**. **Plains**, just a little slip of a town, still attract visitors hoping to get a glimpse of the very popular Jimmy Carter. The **Plains Depot** displays Carter memorabilia and **Plains Bed & Breakfast** a former Carter family home. The Anderson Trail, with historic Civil War sites lies along this lower region, with the infamous **Civil War Prison Camp at Andersonville**. The big city is, **Americus**, with its grand **Windsor Hotel**, an elegant 53-room 1892 built structure.

Next door to Plains is **Lumpkin**, with its living history village called **Westville**, the departure point for **Providence Canyon, Georgia's Little Grand Canyon**, an outstanding natural wonder with bands of red, orange and yellow.

Callaway Gardens in **Pine Mountain** is a world-class attraction, a natural setting for 2,500-acres of spectacular gardens, a butterfly conservatory, recreational areas for hiking, biking, swimming and a golfers paradise with 63 holes of championship golf.

Nearby, **Pine Mountain Wild Animal Park** has nearly 300 species of wild animals that roam freely in a 500-acre park. Close by is the **FDR State Park**, at the foot of the **Appalachian Mountains**, with a 23-mile spectacular hiking trail. Nearby visit the **Little White House** at **Warm Springs** and walk through a simple house Roosevelt loved so much.

The **Chattahoochee Legacy**, is told at the **Columbus Museum of Fine Arts** in Columbus, and the **W. C. Bradley Art Collection**, housed in a restored cotton warehouse is truly splendid.

Another little treasure of the **Pathways** is historic **Newnan**, home of the late humorist, **Lewis Grizzard**. The whole square district is listed on the "National Register of Historic Places," and there's fabulous antique shopping at **Three Crowns Antiques**, and finger-lickin' eatin' at **Sprayberry's Restaurant**. Come and enjoy history and a sweep of natural wonders with ageless hospitality.

Americus

Attractions

Main Street Americus, 101 West Lamar, 912-924-4421. View Victorian, antebellum and Greek revival structures.

Historic Sites/Homes

Lindbergh Memorial, located off Hwy.49. Commemorating the visit of Charles A. Lindbergh.

Windsor Hotel, circa 1892, at 104 Windsor Dr. This elegant 53-room Victorian hotel has recently re-opened after restoration, showing off its oak woodwork, crystal chandeliers and antique furnishings.

Golf

Brickyard Plantation Golf Club, 1619 U.S.280 E. 912-874-1234. Semi-private 27-hole course; challenging for any golfer.

Accommodations

The Morris Manor, 425 Timberlane Dr., 912-924-4884. Georgian colonial-style home, amidst pecan and fruit trees, offers five guest rooms.

Guerry House,1833/Springhill Plantation, 723 McGarrah St., 912-924-1009. Circa 1837, Louisiana raised-cottage with wrap-around veranda, offers five guest rooms.

Windsor Hotel. 104 Windsor Dr. The century-old Windsor Hotel is Americus's pride and joy, and, after an extensive and expensive restoration, it's back with elegance. (See, also, Historic Sites/Homes, above.) 912-924-1555.

Merriwood Inn, 912-924-4992. Located five miles from town, it offers three guest rooms in a farmhouse setting.

Dining

Windsor Hotel; should be on your list for fine dining.

Bartow's Variety, 912-924-2461. Well known for its delicious catfish.

Sheppard's House Barbecue, 912-924-8756. A definite for barbecue specialties.

The Dixie Bakery and Diner, 912-928-0952. Homecooking in a casual setting.

Andersonville

Attractions/Museums

Confederate Village and Museum, 114 Church St., 912-924-2558. In 1864 45,000 captured federal soldiers arrived here by train, the largest Confederate military prison. Several war museums, antique shops and restaurant are also on the grounds.

Drummer Boy Civil War Museum, 109 Church St., 912-924-2558. Authentic artifacts, dairies and documents can be viewed.

Easterlin Country Store, 107 Church St., 912-924-0340. Country store with lots of good stuff a country store should have.

Accommodations

A Place Away Cottage B & B
110 Oglethorpe St., Andersonville. There is "A Place Away" just waiting for you, a place where time has slowed and Southern hospitality is abundant. This small, rustic, turn-of-the-century house features heart-pine ceilings, stenciled floors and two guest rooms with private bath, fireplace, TV, refrigerator, all furnished with charming country antiques. Sit by the fire or rock on the porch; there is no hurry here. As Peggy says, "The rates are old-fashioned, the beds are comfortable, the breakfast is hearty and hospitality Southern." 912-924-2558, 912-924-1044.

Buena Vista

(From Columbus take I-185 S. to exit 1 S., then Hwy.280 S. to Hwy.26 E. and go 15 miles to Buena Vista.)

Commentary

If Mike Moon has anything to say about it, the town of 1,500 will continue to transform itself into a replica of Nashville. Moon, who owns 75% of downtown, opened the **National Country Music Museum** across from the courthouse. It exhibits suits worn by the Statler Brothers, a '54 Caddy once owned by Jerry Lee Lewis, Johnny Cash's complete bedroom suite, and the first dollar bill Presley made, amongst others.

Attractions/Museums

Elvis Presley Collection Museum, on 4th Ave., 800-337-6072/912-649-2259, which includes the "King's" 1967 Lincoln Continental, videotapes of Elvis movies, a $2 million collection of Elvis jewelry, suits and other memorabilia.

Pasaquan, 912-649-9444. Artist Eddie Owens Martin transformed his farmhouse and four-acre land parcel into a folk-art environment. Bright colors, outdoor sculptures and pagodas; you will not want to miss.

Hidden Canyon Raceway, Pineville Rd., 800-531-0677.

The Silver Moon Music Barn, on Hwy.41 S., 800-531-0677.

Silver Moon Stampede Arena, located two miles south of Hwy.41.

12 Lakes Scrambles, Hwy.41 N., 800-531-0677. Georgia's newest hare scramble track.

Accommodations

McGraw House, 229 Broad St., 912-649-7307. Situated in a quiet neighborhood, four guest rooms decorated in period antiques.

The 1880 Morgan Towne House, 2 Church St., 912-649-3663. "Sunday dinner" is served everyday at this Victorian home that has three guest rooms.

The 1885 Yesteryear Inn, 229 Broad St., 912-649-7307. An 1866 farmhouse, surrounded by a pecan grove, offers four guest rooms.

Callaway Gardens at Pine Mountain

(I-85 S. to exit 5; then I-185 S. to exit 14; then Hwy. 27 S. for ten miles.)

Commentary

Some come for the azaleas, some come for the butterflies; a place "prettier than anything since the Garden of Eden," is **Callaway Gardens**, a private park and four-star resort set on 12,000 acres of lushly landscaped Southern woodlands.

In July of 1930, Cason J. Callaway first laid eyes on Pine Mountain Valley at a family picnic. He saw worn-out cotton fields in what was once a fertile valley, with occasional spots of colored blossoms. His wife Virginia, having a knowledge of wildflowers, researched and determined the blossoms to be a rare Prunifolia Azalea.

Cason, a man of large ideas, and Virginia Callaway, purchased the land so that they could propagate the Prunifolia Azalea and other native flora, and build a garden.

Then, after 22 years of struggle to bring their labor of love to fruition, in 1952 the Callaways opened Callaway Gardens to the public.

Today, the Gardens attract over 750,000 visitors yearly. Callaway's outstanding exhibits include the **Day Butterfly Center**, a 7,000-square-foot modern glass atrium filled with tropical plants and thousands of free-flying butterflies; the 20,000-square-foot horticultural center, one of the most advanced garden greenhouse complexes in the world; and **Mr. Cason's Vegetable Garden**, producing more than 400 varieties of vegetables, fruits and herbs.

In addition to the spectacular exhibits, there are numerous walking trails and roadways that showcase the world's largest display of hollies, and more than 700 varieties of azaleas and endless varieties of wildflowers. You may swim and sunbathe at a mile-long sandy beach, or cruise the lake in a rental canoe or paddleboat. Hike or bike a seven-mile trail, golf at three courses, tennis on 17 courts, shoot skeet, horseback ride and enjoy a plethora of other fine activities.

It is easy to spend a whole day; some people stay for the whole week. The **Callaway Gardens Inn**, 800-282-8181, offers a modern 350-room hotel with two restaurants and a pool. Townhouses and detached cottages are also available.

South of the main entrance, **Callaway's Country Kitchen** restaurant on Hwy.27 at Hwy.190, serves Southern breakfasts and lunches with a view. The adjacent **Country Store** sells handmade crafts and wonderful preserves, delicious condiments and other mouthwatering specialties.

Special events are continuous at Callaway Gardens, but the **PGA Tour's Buick Challenge** attracts the largest crowds.

Attractions/Museums/Parks

Pine Mountain Wild Animal Park on U.S.27., at 1300 Oak Grove Rd., 706-663-8744, 800-367-2751. A four mile safari ride reveals exotic animals from six continents, including zebras, deer, camels and buffalo that roam and graze freely. Imagine the excitement of seeing, feeding and petting wild animals. Visit the farm area, Old McDonalds Farm, and the nearby alligator pit. Animals are more active in the early morning and late afternoon hours. If you are going to be in the area in the evening, sign up for a hayride. During the rides attendants will shine spotlights on the animals. Dinner is prepared on the outdoor grills and the evening winds up with storytelling.

Chipley Historical Center, McDougald Ave., 706-663-4044. Historical artifacts and photos of pioneering Pine Mountain.

Pine Mountain Trail. For the energetic hiker, 23 miles of beautiful hiking trails. Starting at Callaway Country Store, maps are avaiable at FDR State Park Office.

Roosevelt Riding Stables, FDR State Park, 706-628-4533. Guided horseback trail rides.

Wind Whisper Lodge & Museum, 706-663-8144.

Franklin D. Roosevelt State Park, 2970 Hwy.190 E., 706-663-4858. Including a Liberty Bell shaped pool, the 10,000-acre park also offers lake fishing, riding stables and camping facilities.

Golf

Callaway Mountain View Golf Course, Hwy.27, 706-663-2281. Tight, tree-lined fairways make this particular 18-hole course one of the most challenging.

Callaway Lake View Golf Course, Callaway's original 18-hole course, offering beautiful surroundings along the lake and landscaping of azaleas, dogwoods and seasonal flowers.

Callaway Gardens View Course, offers a picturesque 18-hole course, along beautiful orchards and vineyards. Take care with the hilly terrains and occasional water hazards.

Accommodations

Callaway Gardens Resorts, 800-282-8181. Choose to stay at the 350-room inn, 155 two-bedroom "Country Cottages," or "Mountain Creek Villas" offering 49 two-three-and four-bedroom units.

White Columns Inn on Hwy.27 in Pine Mountain, 706-663-2312.

The Storms House, Harris St., 706-663-9100. In the heart of Pine Mountain an imposing Victorian 1890s home offers four guest rooms.

Fireside Inn, Hwy.27 S., 706-663-4141. Friendly country inn, one mile from Callaway.

Pine Mountain Campground, 8804 Hamilton Rd., Hwy.27, 706-668-4329. Fully equipped campground with laundry and TV lounge.

Dining

Callaway Gardens offers: **The Plantation Room** famous for its generous buffets for breakfast, lunch and dinner; **The Georgia Room**, which invites guests to enjoy the ultimate of fine dining; **The Gardens Restaurant** is known for its delicious steaks and seafood; **The Veranda** features Italian cuisine in a casual atmosphere; **The Flower Mill** features sandwiches, salads and pizzas; **The Country Kitchen** serves breakfast and lunch peppered with such specialties as speckled heart grits and homemade biscuits.

Bon Cuisine, at 113 Chipley Square, 706-663-2019. Georgia's best kept secret, casual dining amongst sculptures, antiques, duck and flamingo paraphanelia. Savor giant local-grown mushrooms, alligator medallions, grilled catfish or filet mignon. Served with genuine local hospitality.

The Oak Tree Victorian Restaurant, serves elegant dinners to local reidents and the Callaway crowd in an 1871 yellow two-story Victorian structure.

McGuire's, Hwy.27 N., 706-663-2640. Serves a delicious Southern buffet or menu items.

Moe's and Joe's Sportman's Grill, Hwy.354, Chipley Village, 706-663-8064. Casual dining with a large outdoor deck, serving American fare from burgers to steaks.

Columbus

(I-85 S. to LaGrange, then I-185.)

Commentary

Home of the Columbus druggist who invented Coca-Cola, Columbus is now aspiring to be the softball capital of the world and will host the 1996 Olympics Fast Pitch Softball competition.

Attractions/Museums

National Historic District in "uptown" Columbus. Much of the city's historical architecture is showcased in a revitalized 28-block area. Many of the homes on these brick-paved, wide avenues were relocated here to preserve them. The homes range from primitive 1800s log cabin to the posh 1870 two-story Victorian townhouse. One of the most intriguing is The Folly, an uncommon, double-octagonal design. The grandest structure in Columbus seemed doomed until determined citizens took action. The Springer Opera House, built in 1871 and host to such stars as Lillie Langtry, Ethel Barrymore and Ruth Gordon, now shines resplendent and restored, with year-round entertainment for the whole family. In 1971, then-

Governor Jimmy Carter declared the Springer as the State Theatre of Georgia; it has been a National Historic Landmark since 1975.

Confederate Naval Museum, with salvaged remains of two Confederate gunboats, recognized as the only museum if its kind in the world. The Infantry Museum houses two centuries of proud military history memorabilia, in what is considered the finest military museum in the nation.

Columbus Museum, the second largest in Georgia, with its fine arts and historical displays of a 1860 urban slave house, a 1900 one-room school and a 1925 shotgun house, provides something for every interest and with a nice twist. Adm: Free.

Columbus Iron Works, built in 1853, operated into the early 1970s, was responsible for transforming Columbus from a frontier town into one of the South's leading industrial centers; today the building is a bustling convention and trade center.

Columbus Georgia Convention and Trade Center, 801 Front Ave., 706-327-4522. Carved out of a 19th-century foundry for cannons, today sports a 77,000-square footage meeting place for conventions, trade shows and major events.

Historic Columbus Foundation, 700 Broadway, 706-323-7979. Housed in an 1870 villa, information on tours and guides can be found here.

Columbus Historic Riverfront Industrial District. Walk along the Chattahoochee River.

Columbus Riverwalk. Starting at Bay Ave., a scenic view will unfold of falls, red brick, iron work and historic old mills at river's edge.

Columbus Black Heritage, 706-322-1713. Self-guided tour showing the development of Columbus' African American community.

South 106 Lunch Box & Collectible Museum, 1236 Broadway, 706-596-5100. Lunch boxes dating back to the 1900s and Columbus memorabilia.

W. C. Bradley Co. Museum, 1017 Front Avenue. View art from local and national artists, housed in an original cotton warehouse.

Patterson Planetarium, 2900 Woodruff Farm Rd., 706-569-2549.

Springer Opera House, 103 10th St., 706-327-3688. Circa 1871, once the stage to many of history's finest stage performers, today hosts musicals, dramatic performances and children shows.

Historic Sites

Linwood Cemetery, 3131 Manchester Expressway, 706-596-1555.

Log Cabin, 708 Half Broadway, 706-322-0756. Dating back to the 1800s, log cabin and farm house also serve as a museum.

The Pemberton House, 11 7th St., 706-322-0765. Home of John Smith Pemberton, circa 1855, originator of the Coca-Cola formula.

Walker-Peters-Langdon House, 716 Broadway, 706-322-0756. Circa 1828 federal cottage style home.

Rankin House, 1440 2nd Ave., 706-324-6396. Lovely Victorian home built in 1850 for James Rankin.

Parks

Golden Park, 100 Fourth St., 706-571-8866. Site for the Olympic Women's Fast Pitch Softball competition in 1996.

Golf

Maple Ridge, 4700 Maple Ridge Trace, 706-569-0966.

Accommodations

The Rothschild-Pound House (circa 1870) at 201 7th St. Proprietors Mamie and Gary Pound offer seven guest rooms with high ceilings, period antiques, fireplaces and beautiful hardwood floors. Fresh flowers, original art and crisp linen, are standard at this Columbus landmark. Enjoy wine and cheese in the evening and a delicious breakfast in the dining room or wrap-around porch. Only two blocks from the Olympic Softball Complex, guests will truly enjoy the spirit of Southern hospitality. 706-322-4075, 800-585-4075.

Dining

Bludau's Goetchius House, 405 Broadway, 706-324-4863. Dress up and dine at a historic antebellum home, sampling swordfish, lobster or chateaubriand.

Country's on Broad, 1329 Broadway, 706-596-8910. Set in a 1930s bus depot, the lively restaurant has a wide menu selection.

B. Merrell's, 2603 Manchester, 706-324-5464. Casual dining, with ribs, salads, and chicken .

Country's Barbecue, 3137 Mercury Dr., 706-563-7604. Barbecue and country cooking, with live music on weekends.

Ezell's Catfish Cabin, 4001 Warm Springs Rd., 706-568-1149, for all-you-can-eat catfish and other seafood selections.

Deorio's, Cross Country Plaza, 706-563-5887. Full Italian menu and voted best pizza in Columbus.

Golf

Bull Creek Course, listed among the top 25 courses by *Golf Digest*.

Cordele

Attractions

Main Street Cordele, 912-273-3102.

Cordele Walking Tour, 501 North 7th St., 912-273-3102. Maps are available.

Lake Blackshear, located at Hwy.280, off Hwy.300, nine miles west of Cordele, 912-273-3811. Cordele's greatest recreational attraction. Enjoy beaches, campgrounds and boat launches.

Parks

Georgia Veterans Memorial State Park, located nine miles west of I-75, exit 33, 912-276-2371. The 1,322-acre park offers swimming, boating, fishing, a pool and 18-hole golf course. View a military museum with weaponry and military artifacts.

Golf

Georgia Veterans Golf Course, 2315 Hwy.280 W., 912-276-2377. Enjoy this 18-hole course located within the park.

Dining

Daphne Lodge Restaurant, Hwy.180 W., 912-273-2596. This restaurant was recommended by "Southern Living" for its good food.

Griffin

Attractions

Main Street Griffin, 770-228-5356.

Cherokee Rose Shooting Resort, 895 Baptist Camp Rd., 770-228-2529. For the whole family, championship sporting clay course.

Double Cabins Plantation, 3335 Jackson Rd., 770-227-6611. A Greek revival mansion, circa 1842, featuring some original artifacts. The plantation also offers bed & breakfast.

Accommodations

Double Cabins Plantation, take I-75 S. exit 69, GA 155 to 3335 Jackson Rd., Griffin. Built in 1842, and listed on the "National Register,"

this plantation home is fully-furnished with period antiques and serves as an exquisite example of Antebellum architecture. The grounds surrounding the columned home are filled with distinctive Southern flowers and shrubs. Pick fresh seasonal fruit and flowers from the nursery; then take a stroll through the woods and feed the horses while enjoying the company of the colorful peacocks. Be sure to ask owner Sinclair Hollberg about the plantation's historic past. 770-227-6611, 770-227-2214.LaGrange

Attractions/Museums

Downtown LaGrange Walking Tour, 224 Main St., 706-884-8671.

Chattahoochee Trace, 136 Main St., 706-845-8440.

LaFayette Fountain, on LaFayette Square, 706-884-8671. Honoring the French Marquis after whom LaGrange was named.

Lamar Dodd Art Center, on Forrest Ave., 706-882-2911. Houses a collection of works by Georgia artist, Lamar Dodd.

Troup County Archives, 136 Main St., 706-884-1828. Historical and local archives.

Historic Home

Bellevue, 204 Ben Hill St., 706-884-1832. Built by U.S.Senator, Ben Hill, shows a stately Greek revival mansion with Ionic columns.

Golf

The Fields at Rosemont Hills Golf Club, 257 South Smith Rd., 706-845-7425.

Dining

In Clover, 706-882-0883. A restaurant within an 1892 Queen Anne Victorian home, presenting haute cuisine at its finest.

Newnan/Palmetto

(I-85 S. for 40 miles.)

Commentary

Established in 1828, Newnan is **"the City of Homes"** because of its outstanding examples of period and contemporary architecture. The historic downtown district is nestled in the midst of quiet tree-lined neighborhoods, and the Victorian commercial court square surrounds a neo-Greek revival style courthouse listed in the "National Register of Historic Places." Park your car and take a stroll around the pleasant city of 12,000.

Attractions

Main Street Newnan, 770-254-3703. Spared from the ravages of the Civil War, this lovely Southern town boasts a nine-block commercial district and Courthouse, both listed on the National Register of Historic Places.

Three Crowns Antiques Ltd., 733 Bullsboro Dr., 770-253-4815. For the antique hound, this is the place. A 25,000-square-foot mall, exhibiting furniture and accessories from 18th century to the 1950s. From the most unusual of silver, rare books, oil lamps and clocks, to fine ceramics, gateleg tables and lamp posts. Visit regularly for selection changes daily.

Scott's Book Store, 28 South Court Square, 770-253-2960. This friendly full service book store is owned and operated by Earlene Scott. She and her staff are always eager to help their customers.

Male Academy Museum, at 30 Temple Ave., is a restored 1883 schoolhouse that was Newnan's first private boys' school. The museum features permanent exhibits such as a typical classroom from the 1800s and furniture from the same in the Zeke Smith Room. Civil War memorabilia and Indian history, period clothing and local records are also covered. 770-251-0207.

Coweta County Courthouse, circa 1904, sits in town square, showing a copper dome and rich interiors.

Manget-Brannon Alliance for the Arts, First Avenue and 24 Long Place, 770-251-0276. Incorporating a rotating art gallery, theatrical events and workshops.

Catalpa Plantation, 2295 Old Poplar Rd., 800-697-1835. Restored 1835 plantation home features period gardens and herb shop with decorative herbal arrangements.

Oak Grove Plantation & Gardens, 4537 North Hwy.29, 463-3010. This, circa 1835, plantation home, has been featured in several magazines for its beauty.

Windemere Plantation in nearby Palmetto. The manor house is Greek revival antebellum style designed in a modified Z-shape. House tours are available by appointment only, 706-463-0940.

Golf

Orchard Hills Golf Club, 600 East Hwy.16, 770-251-5683. Enjoy this 18-hole golf course with a Scottish links flavor and Southern hospitality.

Accommodations

The Parrott-Camp-Soucy House at 155 Greenville St., is a Victorian delight. It was built by one of the area's first settlers but was enlarged and remodeled in 1885 to its present Stick-Eastlake/French Mansard style. It has been honored with numerous awards and is now an elegant B & B.

Southern Comfort Inn, 66 LaGrange St., 770-254-9622. A stately Greek revival mansion, entertaining guests with stained glass windows, clawfoot tubs and breakfast buffet.

Old Garden Inn, a Greek revival B & B made of brick with seven huge 26-foot white pillars on the tiled porch. Rocking chairs, cozy rooms and a delicious breakfast.

Dining

Sprayberry's Barbecue, 229 Jackson St., 770-253-4421. Since 1926 faithful customers from around the world come to Sprayberry's for its uncontested hickory-smoked barbecued pork or beef, and, one-of-a-kind Brunswick Stew. Not to forget the famous fried peach pie, and, to die-for Icebox lemon pie. Don't leave without bringing home a few jars of this delectable BBQ sauce. There is a new second location at Hwy.34 at I-85, exit 9, 770-253-5080.

Gus's Jackson Street Grill, 21 Jackson St., 770-253-5694. A cozy cafe that serves home-cooking for breakfast, lunch and dinner.

Grandpa's Country Buffet, 299 Bullsboro Dr., 770-254-8800. Family owned and operated, serving a full lunch and dinner buffet.

Perry

(The "Crossroads of Georgia," Perry is two hours south of Atlanta on I-75, and 20-minutes south from Macon.)

Commentary

Once an old stagecoach stop, Perry is full of historic sites and some of Georgia's best antique and collectible shops.

Attractions/Museums

Downtown Perry. Stroll through Old Williamsburg Village for specialty shops and downtown's brick sidewalks lined with flowers. Enjoy its specialty shops and peaceful atmosphere. The dogwood is the city's official tree. It blooms profusely during spring, as do the azaleas.

The Georgia National Fairgrounds and Agricenter is home of the Georgia National Fair. Take I-75 S., then U.S.41 to exit 42. The beautifully landscaped 628 acre center is a year-round facility designed for livestock and horse shows, circuses, concerts, trade shows, fairs and sporting events. The largest is the state-sponsored, nine-day, Georgia National Fair, exhibiting antiques, fine arts, food and flowers; featuring livestock, horse shows and a midway with games, rides and nightly fireworks. 912-987-2774.

Cranshaw's One Horse Farm and Day Lily Gardens This wonderful garden on Sandefur Rd., six miles north of Perry, on Hwy.41., is famous for the zillions of varieties of lilies it has nurtured. May-June. 912-987-3268.

Peach Orchards. The orchards along U.S.41 N. offer roadside stands and invite visitors to pick their own peaches. Mid-May through Mid-August.

Perry Antiques and Collectibles Mall, 351 Gen. C. Hodges Blvd., 912-987-4001. Perry's largest selection of antiques from over 35 dealers. Open seven days a week.

Massee Lane Gardens, just west of Perry you'll find the home of the American Camellia Society with seven acres of colorful camellias in bloom from November through March.

Accommodations

New Perry Hotel-Motel and Restaurant, 800 Main St. Built in 1870, it has retained its charm. Southern meals featuring corn relishes and squash lorraine are served nightly.

Plains

Commentary

Founded in 1940 as the Plains of Dura, Plains is the birthplace and home of **Jimmy and Rosalynn Carter**, our nation's first couple.

Plains today is a small strip of shops, surrounded by peanut fields and country roads. Rosalynn and Jimmy Carter still live in a brick house surrounded by a iron fence. The 1888 train depot that Carter used as his presidential campaign headquarters, today houses Carter campaign memorabilia and serves as the visitor center for the 77-acre historic district, 912-824-3413. Visitors hope to get a glimpse of this man who was president, either at church or while he jogs.

When Jimmy Carter isn't building houses for Habitat for Humanity, or off negotiating peace in a distant corner of the world, or working at the Carter Presidential Center, he returns to Plains for rest and inspiration.

Jimmy Carter National Historic Site, 912-824-3413.

Accommodations

The Plains B & B Inn, 100 West Church St., Plains. Once a boardinghouse where Lillian Carter lived, you will feel right at home at this carefully renovated and gracious Victorian inn. Ideally located in the heart of town, across from the Carter Welcome Center, you may watch an unhurried world go by from the wicker-rocker filled porch. Guest rooms all have private baths, central heat and air, and are furnished with antiques. A full Southern breakfast is served in the formal dining room, and charming hostess Grace Jackson will direct you to nearby attractions. 912-824-7252.

The Windsor Hotel, between Americus and Plains, 800-252-7466. An elegant 53-room brick hotel built in 1892.

The Victorian Hotel recently reopened after an extensive $5-million restoration. Turn-of-the-century decor and furnishings are combined with modern amenities.

Thomaston

Attractions/Museums

Historic Courthouse, located downtown, 706-647-8311. Stroll by the historic courthouse, fine antique shops and, circa 1920s art theater.

Flint River Outdoor Center, 706-647-2633. Book excursions here for rafting, tubing or canoeing on the Flint River.

Historic Home

Pettigrew-White-Stamps House, Andrews Dr., circa 1834, exhibits period furnishings and Thomaston artifacts.

Parks

Sprewell Bluff, Old Alabama Rd., eight miles west of Hwy.74. River Park with many beautiful hiking trails along the Flint River.

Accommodations

Whitfield Inn, 327 West Main St., 706-647-2482. Popular with travelers, this graceful 1883 Victorian home offers five guest rooms with full breakfast.

Woodall House, 324 West Main St., 706-647-7044. Turn-of-the-century home with columns and rockers on front porch, offers four guest rooms.

Vienna

Attractions/Museum

Victorian Vienna, 912-268-4554. Stroll this small historic district laced with widow's walks, stained glass, columns and specialty shops.

Walter F. George Law Office & Museum, 912-268-4554. Law office of U.S. Senator Walter F. George, houses personal memorabilia.

Ellis Brothers Pecans, I-75, exit 36, 912-268-9041. Pecan processing plant and outlet.

Warm Springs

(80 miles south on I-85 to Alternate 27.)

Commentary

The peaceful place where Franklin Delano Roosevelt built the **Little White House**, 706-655-5870. In the home and adjacent museum, you'll find a sense of history in a naturally beautiful environment. Serene and slow-paced, the setting moves visitors with its low-keyed spirit of tribute.

President Roosevelt had heard of the restorative powers attributed to the natural springs and began visiting Warm Springs in 1924, finding solace not only in the water but in the countryside's whispering pines and wooded ravines. Nearby are FDR's two classic roadsters.

The nearby village of Warm Springs is filled with interesting boutiques, restaurants and accommodations.

Dining

Main St.'s Victorian Tea Room was formerly a general store.

Bulloch House, circa 1892, on Spring St., sits on a hilltop surrounded by bird houses. Described as "country with class," the restaurant offers home-cooked Southern food with hospitality to match.

Accommodations

The Warm Springs Hotel, circa 1907, offers 14 guest rooms. It's on Ga.27-Alternate 41, the main thoroughfare of Warm Springs, also called Broad St. 800-366-7616. Revived by owners Geraldine and Lee Thompson into a charming B & B, the Warm Springs Hotel's history includes the glory days when FDR's visits created much excitement. The style of bygone days remains alongside the welcome addition of modern conveniences such as individual heating/cooling units.

The rooms feature furniture owned by Mrs. Roosevelt, which the owners call "Eleanor" furniture. One room has an iron bed that is over 100 years old, others "clawfoot" tubs.

The Mountain Top Inn (atop Pine Mountain) is surrounded by the 14,000-acre **Roosevelt State Park.** It is conveniently located midway between Warm Springs and **Callaway Gardens**, just a 5-minute drive to either.

To reach Mountain Top Inn from Warm Springs, turn right on Ga.85. Go up the mountain on this road to Ga.190. The inn is at the seven-mile marker.

Three styles of lodging are offered: (1) House-size log cabins feature rock fireplaces, double-size Jacuzzi tubs, fully-equipped kitchens, gas grills on the porch and all the comforts of home. These cabins, which have from one to seven bedrooms, usually are booked at least four to six weeks in advance; (2) Rustic 1970s-style Alpine chalets, popular for reunions and retreats. (3) An inn consisting of four buildings with five rooms in each. Each room is decorated in a nationality theme, so you can choose to wake up in Paris, Tokyo or some other exotic locale. Added in April 1994 is the 90-seat Log Wedding Chapel, with its bell tower, cathedral ceiling, oak pews, slate backdrop and nearby conference center for receptions.

Inn Scarlet's Footsteps B & B, 40 Old Flat Shoals Rd., Concord. A white-columned, stately antebellum plantation, welcomes every visitor to an elegant era that is truly *Gone With The Wind*. The 8,000 square foot mansion is decorated entirely with one of the nation's largest private collections of "GWTW" memorabilia. The museum on the grounds will have you dreaming of an 18" waist. Enjoy the Old South with catered luncheons, afternoon teas and evening BBQ's and elegant Southern dancing. Located 20 minutes north from Warm Springs and 45 minutes south from Atlanta. 800-886-7355, 706-495-9012.

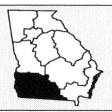

PLANTATION TRACE

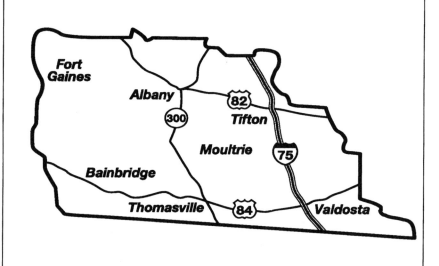

Section XIX
Traveling Georgia's Plantation Trace

Plantation Trace

Commentary

Travelers are rediscovering the charm and vitality in the heart of southwest Georgia plantation country. **Thomasville** was known as the elite retreat for wealthy Northerners escaping the cold. Elegant mansions were built, with well-tended lawns and gardens. Today visitors may rediscover that era by visiting the hunting plantations such as **Pebble Hill Plantation**, and viewing the roses at the glorious **Thomasville Rose Garden**. Afterwards, spend a romantic night or two at the **Victorian Bed & Breakfast Evans House** and visit the historical sites that line brick-covered streets. **Lake Seminole Park**, just a few miles southwest of Thomasville, is a fisherman's dream come true; the pine-covered hills are dotted with excellent fishing lakes. **Kolomoki Mounds State Park and Museum** in **Blakely** tell a story of Indian culture from 5000 B.C.

Albany is the center of the state's pecan and peanut production. It is also famous for the **Chehaw Wild Animal Park** and **Radium Springs** where you can swim in Georgia's largest natural water springs.

In the towns of **Tifton** and **Valdosta** respectively, you may see a 19th-century living-history village, the **Agrirama**, and the rich history of the naval and cotton industries. Throughout **Plantation Trace** there are also plenty of splendid Victorian homes and the region takes pride in its historic Southern hospitality which is its way of life.

Albany

Attractions/Museums

Albany Museum of Art, 311 Meadowlark Dr., 912-439-8400. Best known for its African art collection.

Tronateeska Heritage Museum of History and Science, 100 Roosevelt Ave., 912-432-6955. Indian artifacts, antique automobiles and carriages.

Wetherbee Planetarium, 100 Roosevelt Ave., 912-432-6955. Situated in an old railway office, the planetarium also houses a train museum.

Quail Hunting is offered by a variety of plantations, 912-434-8700.

Radium Springs and Casino, 2511 Radium Springs Rd., 912-889-0244. Swim in one of Georgia's largest natural springs and see a turn-of-the-century Victorian lodge that was once a gambling casino.

Historic Sites/Homes

Albany Civil Rights Movement Memorial, corner of Jackson Street and Highland Avenue. Commemorates Albany's role in the civil rights movement.

Astronauts' Monument, 1822 Palmyra Rd. A tribute to astronauts who lost their lives on NASA flights.

Parks

Chehaw Park, Philema Rd., 912-430-5275. A 700-acre forested recreational park that offers camping, nature trails and play areas.

Chehaw Wild Animal Park. Wild animals roam in a 293-acre natural setting. Small petting zoo for children and concession stand.

Hilsman Park & Hugh Mills Stadium, located between Third and Tift Avenue at Van Buren. Sports and recreational activities.

Golf

American Legion Public Golf Course, 107 Philomena Rd., 912-432-6016.

Dining

David Brothers Suburban, 912-432-1120. Prime rib is the local favorite.

Yesterday's Ole Time Saloon & Restaurant, 912-883-5506. Try one of the savory salads or broiled lobster tails and seafood crepes.

Gargano's East, 912-435-7545. Presenting the best from Italy.

Bainbridge

Attractions

Lake Seminole, Hwy.97, southwest of Bainbridge, 912-662-2001. One of the best bass fishing spots in the nation. Day camping and boating.

Parks

Earl May Boat Basin Park, West Shotwell St. Family recreational park with camping, boat docks and marina, fishing, tennis, playground and picnic sites.

Willis Park, located downtown, is a park from yesteryear.

Historic Homes

McKenzie-Reynolds House. An antebellum home located in the riverside Earl May Park, also houses the Welcome Center.

Accommodations

The White House B & B, 320 S. Washington St., Bainbridge. Situated in the historical district of beautiful Bainbridge, business and leisure travelers enjoy the ambience of a bygone era in modern comfort. Shaded by a huge live oak, the restored antebellum Georgian-style home, circa 1840, stands fronted by the original iron fence. There are three spacious bedrooms furnished with family antiques; other amenities include central heating and air conditioning, a gallery library, a sitting room, an in-ground swimming pool, TV, phone and ample parking. This non-smoking and alcohol free home welcomes children 10 years and over. Call gracious hosts John and Mary Patterson at 912-248-1703.

Wingate's Lunker Lodge, 912-246-0658, is a local fish camp, offering an 18-bed men's dormitory called the "Stag Hangout."

Dining

Marketplace Restaurant, located in the Charter House Motel, 912-246-8550, serves steak, seafood or country buffet.

Blakely

Attractions

Lake George Andrews, Chattahoochee River, 912-723-3741. Boat ramps and picnic sites.

Historic Sites/Homes

Coheelee Creek Covered Bridge, located nine miles south of Blakely, on Old River Rd. Circa 1883; 96 feet long.

Confederate Flag Pole, on Courthouse Square, 912-723-3741. Circa 1861, the last remaining wooden Confederate flagpole.

Peanut Monument, on Courthouse Square, 912-723-3741. Saluting the local peanut growers.

Parks

Kolomoki Mounds State Historic Park, 912-723-5296. Historical mounds built in the 12th and 13th century can be found here. The park also offers fishing, boating, swimming and miniature golf.

Accommodations

Layside Bed & Breakfast, 611 River St., 912-723-8932. Turn-of-the-century Victorian home offers two guest rooms.

Cairo

Attractions/Museums

Roddenbery Library, at 320 North Broad St., presents historical exhibits.

Georgia Pines Plantation, Hwy.111, 912-226-1305, quail hunting.

Dogwood Hunting Preserve, for quail hunting call 912-872-3508.

M & M Ice Co., 309 2nd Ave., 912-377-3422. Watch blocks of ice being made at this old-fashioned plant.

Parks

Davis Park, behind Roddenbery Library, spread a picnic or swim in the pool.

Golf

Cairo Country Club, 912-377-4506.

Colquitt

Attractions

Mayhaw Jelly Capital, 912-758-2400. This is where the famous "Mayhaw Jelly' is made.

Pine Hill Plantation, 912-758-6602. Quail hunting.

Historic Site

Tribute to the American Indian, 912-758-2400. A 23-foot carving of the head of an Indian brave by Peter Toth who has carved one such monument for each state as a tribute to American natives.

Parks

Spring Creek Recreation Park, located off Hwy.27. Scenic trails and wildflowers.

Accommodations

Country Inn Bed & Breakfast, 912-758-5417. Quiet country charm for its guests.

Tarrer Inn, 155 South Cuthbert St., 912-758-2888. Southern hospitality and cuisine.

Dawson

Attractions

Historic District, 912-995-2011. See Victorian Dawson.

Tallawahee Plantation, 912-2265.

Historic Site/Homes

Terrell County Courthouse, circa 1892.

Donalsonville

Attractions

Lake Seminole, 912-662-2001. An anglers' delight, located 18 miles south of Donalsonville.

Parks

Seminole State Park, located south of town on Hwy.39. Camping and cottages, boat ramp and dock, beach and fishing.

Fort Gaines

Attractions/Museums

Frontier Village, off Hwy.39 south of town, 912-768-2984. A replica of the fort, log cabins and grist mills, historical facts from 1836.

Walter F. George Lock and Dam, 912-768-2516 for tours.

Historic Sites/Homes

Dill House, on Washington St., circa 1827.

Outpost Replica, three blocks left on Commerce St., 912-768-2934. Reconstructed fort, 1816-1830.

Parks

Cotton Hill Park, located six miles north of town, 912-768-3061. Offers camp sites, laundry, boat ramp, hiking trails and restrooms.

George T. Bagby State Park, 912-768-2571. The 300-acre park offers marina, boat rentals, lodge, swimming pool, tennis courts and beach for swimming.

Accommodations/Dining

George T. Bagby State Park and Lodge, providing 30 guest rooms; diners can also enjoy family dining buffet style.

Moultrie

Attractions/Museums

Colquitt County Arts Center, 401 Seventh Avenue, 912-985-1922.

Colquitt County Historical Museum, South Main St., 912-985-2131. History of Mountrie-Colquitt County.

The Ellen Payne Odom Genealogy Library, 204 5th St., 912-985-6540.

Main Street Moultrie, 912-985-1974.

Moultrie Olympic Quality Diving Facility, targeted as a site for pre-Olympic training, it also entertains national and international meets.

Old Railway Depot, on Lower Meigs Rd.

State Farmers' Market, Hwy.33, 912-985-3602.

Historic Sites/Homes

Elephant Monument, Pleasant Grove, Hwy.37 E. Marble statue marks the grave of Moultrie native who owned a circus.

Greenfield Church Site, Tallokas Rd., 912-985-2131. Used during the Civil War as hospital and recruiting center.

Southern Magnolia, Courthouse Square, 912-985-2131. Historical 85-year-old site.

Parks

Bert Harsh Park, 5th St., 912-985-6540.

Golf

Sunset Country Club, Hwy.319 S., 912-890-5555.

Accommodations

Country Inn, 912-758-5417. A newly opened bed & breakfast.

The Moultrie Inn, 1708 First Ave., 912-890-2401.

Dining

Bull's Restaurant, 912-985-2202, popular for its Friday night seafood buffet.

The Barbecue Pit, 912-985-5315, for some good barbecue flavor.

Thomasville

(I-85 S. to LaGrange, I-185 to Columbus; then U.S.82/State 520 to Albany; and then U.S.19 S. to Thomasville.)

Commentary

Chartered in 1831, Georgia's **City of Roses** offers a fascinating array of architecture. During the late 1800s Thomasville was the winter vacation destination of first choice for the rich and famous. Presidents, royalty, famous businessmen and actors either visited or owned seasonal homes here. Some enjoyed the therapeutic piney air, others the balsam breeze or long-blooming roses. Whatever the reason, the "hotel era" was in full flower with many elegant winter homes appearing on the rural landscape. With this kind of influence and money came exceptional cultural events.

In the early 1900s the rich and famous discovered Florida and Thomasville's "Golden Age" ended. Today, the Thomasville Entertainment Foundation is a matriarch of classical events. The **Thomas County Historical Society**, 912-226-7664, displays hotel-era memorabilia such as period ball gowns, an 1893 private bowling alley and 1850s pioneer log home.

Some interesting sights are on North Dawson St. You'll find a mustard-yellow outlandish Victorian mansion, now maintained as a museum. Five miles southwest of Thomasville is **Pebble Hill Plantation**, a twenty-eight-room Georgian and Greek revival home, with gardens, stables and kennels. Inside the home are original John James Audubon bird prints and extensive collections of silver, crystal and antiques. 912-226-2344.

Attractions/Museums

Main Street Thomasville, 912-225-3920. Stroll over brick-paved streets, laid around

1907, and see period lampposts, Victorian homes and storefronts.

The Big Oak (circa 1680), at the corner of Monroe and Crawford St., is Thomasville's most beloved landmark. It stands 75 feet high with a limb-spread of 162 feet. The 18-acre Paradise Park on Broad Street retains the look of wild woods, with a stream flowing through its forest of pine, dogwood and crepe myrtle.

Thomas County Historical Society Museum, 725 North Dawson, 912-226-7664. Rebuilt in 1923, the wrought iron fence and 1893 single-lane bowling alley are the only original pieces left from the hotel era of the late 1800s. The museum has many wonderful treasures from that era.

Thomasville Cultural Center, 600 East Washington St., 912-226-0588. Circa 1915, first public school built in Thomasville with tax money, today houses art library, galleries and gift shop.

Thomas County Courthouse, North Broad St., circa 1858. A classical revival/Victorian Renaissance revival building.

All Saints Episcopal Church, 443 South Hansell, 912-228-9242. The oldest original standing church in Thomasville, was originally a Catholic church before it was moved to its current location.

Birdsong Nature Center, 912-377-4408. Enjoy the beauty of birds, butterflies and flower-lined nature trails.

Pebble Hill Plantation, five miles south of town, 912-226-2344. Gracious and rich with the South's tradition, Pebble Hill Plantation, circa 1820s, established by founder of Thomas County, Thomas Jefferson Johnson. Antiques, silver, paintings, vintage prints, animal sculptures and vintage cars are some of a large collection to be viewed.

State Farmers Market, 1842 Smith Ave., 912-225-3919. Second largest fresh produce market in the southeast, with regional delicacies as Mayhaw jelly and Vidalia onions.

Quail Hunting, 912-225-3919. Thomasville is well known for this sport and also duck, deer and dove hunting.

Historical Sites/Homes

Hardy Bryan House, 312 Broad St., 912-226-6016. The oldest, circa 1833, classic revival two-story house in town. Today is headquarters for Thomasville Landmarks, Inc.

Lapham-Patterson House, 626 North Dawson St., 912-225-4004. One of the first winter cottages built, circa 1885, by wealthy shoe manufacturer, Charles W. Lapham. A home built ahead of its time, with hot and cold running water and gas lighting.

Thomas Drug Store, 108 South Broad St., circa 1869. Operating since 1869 as drugstore, some of the famous clientele are Presidents William McKinley and Dwight D. Eisenhower.

Parks

Paradise Park, South Broad St., 912-225-5222. A 26-acre natural park, located in the heart of town, used to be called "Yankee Paradise" for the vacationing Northerners who frequented the park.

Golf

Country Oaks Golf Course, State Rd. 122 (Pavo Rd.), 912-225-4333. Enjoy the 18-hole course, surrounded by beautiful wooded areas and lakes.

Accommodations

Evans House Bed & Breakfast, 725 South Hansell St., 912-226-1343. Directly across from Paradise Park, an exquisitely restored 1898 Victorian house is operated by perfect hostess and host, Lee and John Puskar. Four sumptuous guest rooms, expertly furnished in antique English burl and black-iron beds, with

crisp linens, vintage prints, armoires, private baths with clawfoot tub and thick, fluffy towels. In the evening feel pampered with brandy and home-made cookies. And for breakfast savor a gourmet breakfast in a country kitchen. You will agree, the minute upon entering this sunny home, that guests are treated very special here.

1884 Paxton House, 445 Remington Ave., 912-226-5197. Charming Victorian, elegantly restored six-guest-room home, combined with Southern hospitality.

Susina Plantation Inn, take US 319. south of Thomasville and turn right onto Meridian Rd. The plantation is located but a few miles further on the right. Susina Plantation Inn, circa 1841, is one of few remaining in Georgia of true Southern antebellum elegance. Set on 115 acres of magnificent lawns and woodlands which are often frequented by quail, deer and ducks, you will experience a tranquil timelessness. Eight charming guest rooms with private baths, feature high ceilings, polished woodwork, decorative fireplaces and antiques. Accommodations include a gourmet five-course dinner with wine and full-breakfast prepared by energetic chef/owner Anne-Marie Walker. Also available for use is a lighted tennis court, swimming pool, croquet court, fishing pond and conference rooms. Perfect for wedding receptions, business meetings and luncheon groups. 912-377-9644.

Serendipity Cottage, 339 East Jefferson St., 912-226-8111. Lovingly restored, circa 1906 home offering two guest rooms with full breakfast.

Quail Country Bed & Breakfast, 1104 Old Monticello Rd., 912-226-7218. Gracious and affordable accommodations.

Deer Creek Bed & Breakfast, 1304 Old Monticello St., 912-226-7294. Located adjacent to the woods, creates a quiet setting for the two guest rooms.

Dining

The Grand Old House, 502 South Broad St., 912-227-0108. Dine in classic style, amongst high ceilings, chandeliers and authentic antiquity. Savor delicacies such as; Chilled Gazpacho, Crabcake a l'aubergine, or Grilled Swordfish, plus a delectable dessert tray.

George and Louie's, 217 Remington Ave., 912-226-1218. Family-style seafood platters, hamburgers and fried green tomatoes.

Fallin's Real Pit Bar-B-Que, 2250 East Pinetree Blvd., 912-226-1218. Specializing in this local favorite with chicken, pork or beef.

Homecoming Restaurant, on Albany Rd., 912-226-1143. Log cabin in the woods serving the best fried catfish, seafood, steak and chicken.

Miamore, 229 East Jefferson St., 912-226-0074. Fine Italian food served in a beautiful Victorian house.

Paradise Place, 222 Gordan Ave., 912-227-0885. Located in historic downtown, savor the best Southern fried chicken.

Tifton

Attractions/Museums

Main Street Tifton, 912-382-6231.

Georgia Agrirama Living History Museum, I-75, exit 20, 912-386-3344. Travel back in time to the 19th century and share daily activities of the community, farmhouse, grist mill and fields.

Paradise Public Fishing Area, of U.S.82, eight miles east of Tifton, 912-533-4792.

Parks

Crystal Lake Water Park, located off Hwy.32, 912-831-4655. Offers fun for the family, with sandy lake shores, water slides and boating.

Fulwood Park, at Tift and 8th, is a perfect place to picnic under shady pines.

Accommodations

Myon Bed & Breakfast, 128 First St., 912-382-0959. The Old Myon Hotel, renovated, now offers three guest rooms furnished with simple antiques.

Hummingbird's Perch B & B. Located in Chula, but better known as five miles north of Tifton. From Atlanta take I-75 S. to exit 23 E., and go one mile to the first paved road and turn right. Enjoy bird watching, butterflies, fishing and a beautiful sunset while strolling about the seven-acre fish-stocked lake; Hummingbird's tranquility will refresh your spirit and sooth your mind. The Cape Cod-style home offers modern country living at its best with a touch of elegance; it is the perfect place to relax after a hard week's work. You will love every peaceful minute as hostess Francis Wilson proceeds to pamper you. 912-382-5431.

Dining

Sonny's Real Pit BBQ, 912-386-2626. Enjoy the great taste of this specialty.

Big Jim's, located in Enigma, 912-533-4145. Go where the locals eat and enjoy great Southern meals.

Valdosta

Attractions/Museums

Valdosta Main St., 912-333-1877. Capture the city's charm, centered around the 1905 courthouse square, when touring historical downtown.

Lowndes County Historical Society Museum, 305 West Central Ave., 912-247-4780. Exhibits of Naval and cotton industries and local historical displays.

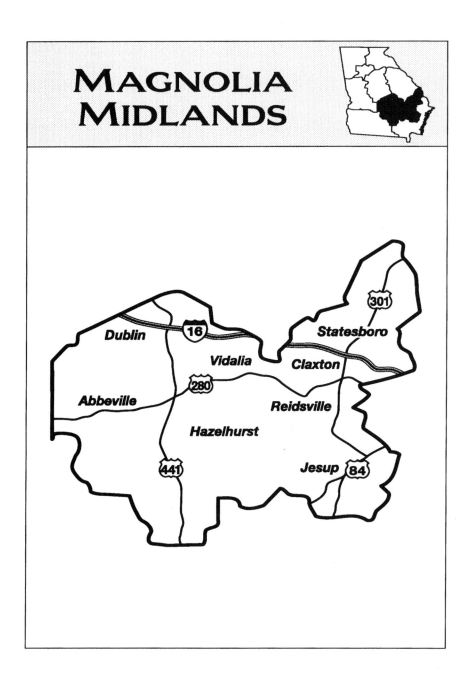

Section XX
Traveling Georgia's Magnolia Midlands

The Magnolia Midlands of Georgia

Commentary

The Midlands are rich and fertile, with shimmering lakes and streams. This region has the highest percentage of farms, and leads the nation in acres of planted trees. **Blueberry farms** provide several million pounds a year, and most familiar of all is the sweet **Vidalia Onion**. Come to Vidalia the weekend after Mother's Day and participate in the **Vidalia Onion Festival**. The town of **Claxton**, known as **the "fruitcake capital of the world"** produces a quality fruitcake at the rate of 85,000 pounds a day. **Hawkinsville** yields pecans and kiwi fruits and **Eastman has delicious Stuckey's Candy.**

The Magnolia Midlands is also known for great fishing at **Ocmulgee River and Hazlehurst's Altamaha River** for the largest largemouth bass. You may see harness racing in **Hawkinsville, the "Harness Horse Training Capital of the South"**, and colorful **Dublin**, Southern flavor with dash of Irish. The Midlands offer wide pine-studded spaces to get away from it all, and has numerous small towns and back roads which offer treasures for the adventurous.

Alma

Blueberry Capital of the World. Located south of Baxley on Hwy.1, Alma produces more than six million pounds of blueberries each year.

Baxley

Attractions

Edwin I. Hatch Nuclear Plant Visitor Center, 912-367-3668. Located 14 miles north of Baxley on U.S.1.

Appling County Courthouse, circa 1907.

Altamaha River-Falling Rocks Park, 912-367-2949. Located 14 miles north of Baxley, also offers campground.

Chauncey

Attractions

Jay Bird Springs, 912-374-4723. Located 12 miles south of Eastman, on Hwy.341 S.

Dexter

Attractions

Malone's Lake, from I-16, Hwy.257, take exit 13, 912-875-3100.

Douglas

Attractions/Museums

Historic Downtown, Main St., 912-384-5978. Architecture, shopping and scenic streets.

Heritage Art Walk, 912-383-0277. Featuring local history, points of interest and art displayed in the halls of the Courthouse.

South Georgia College, 912-383-4213. Oldest coed facility in the University of Georgia system.

Quail Ridge Hunting Preserve, 912-384-0025.

Historic Sites/Homes

Historic Residential District, on Gaskin Avenue. 912-383-0277.

Lott's Grist Mill, on Hwy.158 S., 912-384-6858. A working grist mill with hands-on activities.

Martin Center, 912-384-1389. Circa 1940 movie theater, today a cultural center.

Parks

General Coffee State Park. Located six miles east of Douglas on Hwy.32, 912-384-7082. Find a choice of pioneer camping or tent and trailer sites with water and electric. Nature trails, picnic areas, swimming pool and fishing.

Dublin

Attractions/Museums

Dublins-Laurens Museum, on Bellevue and Academy Aves., 912-272-9242. Displays of native artifacts, vintage clothing and local history exhibits.

Oconee River. Located north of Dublin on Hwy.319, a most popular place to picnic and take in the beauty of the river.

Historic Sites/Homes

Chappell's Mill, 13 miles north of Dublin on U.S.441., 912-272-5128. You can still watch the operation of this old dry-mill process, circa 1811.

Fish Trap Cut. Along Route 19, this 100-yard piece of Oconee River is believed to be an aboriginal fishing hole dating back to 1000 B.C.

Parks

Stubbs Park, 912-272-1620. Enjoy tennis and basketball courts, picnic areas and playgrounds.

Golf

Riverview Park Golf Course. Take I-16, exit 15, Hwy.19 and Glenwood Rd., 912-275-4064. Enjoy a good game at this 18-hole course.

Accommodations

VIP Bed & Breakfast, 501 North Dr., 912-275-3739. A 1910 restored bungalow features an exquisitely furnished suite.

Dining

Ma Hawkin's Cafe, 124 West Jackson St., 272-0941. A family cafe in operation since 1931, serving savory Southern specialties.

Eastman

Attractions

Eastman Discount and Flea Mart, 1107 Herman Ave., 912-374-7868.

Dodge County Public Fishing Area. Call 912-374-0651 for directions.

Fitzgerald

Attractions/Museums

Blue-Gray Museum, on Old Depot and Johnston St., 912-423-5375. The museum houses Civil War memorabilia from both sides and local history exhibits.

Fitzgerald-Ben Hill County Arts Council, 121 South Main St., 912-423-5767. Featuring fine arts.

Main Street Fitzgerald, 119 South Main St., 912-423-3116. Wander through brick streets, shopping, and visit the newspaper office of 1895.

Historic Sites/Homes

Grand Theatre, 117 South Main St. Movie house from the 1930s, used for performing arts.

Parks

Paulk Park, Perry House Rd., 912-423-9357. Offering athletic fields and camping, the park also has a lake for fishing and boating.

Glennville

Attractions

Big Hammock Natural Area, nine miles west of Glennville, Hwy.144. The most expansive and rare example of a strange sand ridge, or dune, formed millions of years ago around an ancient sea.

Phillips Natural Area, ten miles southeast of Glennville off Hwy.121. This 800-acre forest is a national landmark and contains rare botanicals.

Accommodations

The Glennville Inn, 812 Main St., 912-654-3407. For a comfortable night's rest.

Hawkinsville

Attractions/Museums

Hawkinsville Harness Horse Training Facility, U.S.129, 912-892-9463. Known as the Harness Capital of Georgia.

Hawkinsville Antique Mall, 226 North Lumpkin St., 912-783-3607. For the antique hounds.

Butler Brown Gallery, Hwy.26, 912-892-9323. Displaying local artist Butler Brown's works.

Double Q Farms, 1475 Hwy.26, 912-892-3794. The largest producer of kiwi fruit in Georgia, both fresh and jams.

Gooseneck Farms, five miles south on Abbeville Hwy., 912-783-1063. Delicious pecan candy and other pecan products.

Historic Sites/Homes

Opera House, on Broad and Lumpkin St., 912-783-1717. Circa 1907, plays, concerts and local events are still featured here.

"Katie," built in 1883, one of the oldest remaining steam pumping engines for firefighting, is displayed in the Opera House.

Parks

Ocmulgee River, located south of Hawkinsville, offers hunting, fishing, camping and water sports.

Golf

Town Creek Golf Course, 912-783-0128. Stretch your legs and play a few holes of golf on this 9-hole course.

Accommodations

The Black Swan Inn, 411 Progress Ave., 912-783-4466. This gracious Southern 1905 antebellum mansion offers six traditionally furnished guest rooms.

Trotters Inn, 111 North Warren St., 912-783-2914. Restaurant next door.

Hazelhurst

Attractions/Museums

Altamaha River. Parts of the Altamaha River remain nearly as wild now as during the colonial days. Popular for largemouth bass fishing, landings for boating and waterskiing can also be found.

Outback Gun and Bow Range, Kirkland Still Rd., 912-375-0765. Practice with bows, shotguns, rifles and skeet shooting.

Parks

Bullard Creek Wildlife Management Area. A 16,000-acre, public hunting area, with designated camp sites. Check with station, on the south bank of the Altamaha River.

Accommodations

The Village Inn, 312 Coffee St., 912-375-4527. Providing guests with 74 rooms and plenty of Southern food.

Jacksonville

Attractions

Horse Creek Wildlife Management Area. Along Hwy.117, east and west of Jacksonville.

Jesup

Altamaha River, with main entrance on U.S.301 N. The main star of Jesup, offering great fishing, swimming and water sports.

I.T.T. Rayonier, three miles north of Jesup, on Hwy.301. Tour the largest chemical cellulose-producing pulp mill in the world.

Lake Lindsay Grace, located 10 miles west of Jesup, Hwy.99.

Historic Sites/Homes

Wayne County Courthouse, on Brunswick St. The clock at the court house has chimed since 1903.

The Carter House, 311 South Wayne St.

"Little" Red Caboose, located downtown on Broad St.

Accommodations

The Trowell House, 256 East Cherry St., 912-530-6611. Built in 1902, this Queen Anne Victorian house won an award for Excellence in Preservation.

McRae

Attractions/Museums

Liberty Square. Displayed downtown are a Liberty Bell and a replica of the Statue of Liberty, one twelfth its original size.

Muskhogean Wildlife Management Area. Located eight miles west of Jacksonville on Hwy.117., offering 19,000-acres of hardwoods alongside the Ocmulgee River.

Parks

Little Ocmulgee State Park, Hwy.441, two miles north of McRae, 912-868-7474. Providing 58 tent and trailer sites, cottages, 265-acre lake, tennis courts and golf course.

Golf

Wallace Adams Golf Course, 912-868-7474. Part of Little Ocmulgee State Park.

Accommodations

Little Ocmulgee Lodge, Little Ocmulgee State Park. Thirty guest rooms.

Dining

Fairway Restaurant at Little Ocmulgee Lodge. Dining is a la carte or buffet.

Ocilla

Parks

Crystal Lake Water Park, located eleven miles west of Ocilla, Hwy.32.

Jefferson-Davis Memorial Park, is eight miles west of Ocilla, Hwy.32.

Reidsville

Attractions

Ohoopee River Plantation, on Hwy.56 N., 912-557-6464. The adventurous may try canoe floating. Also offers camping, fishing and RV hookups. Inquire about hunting.

Parks

Gordonia-Altamaha State Park, on Hwy.280 at city limits, 912-557-6444. A 280-acre family park, providing tent and trailer sites, swimming, fishing, miniature golf and paddle boats.

Golf

Brazell's Creek Golf Course, located within Gordonia-Altamaha State Park.

Accommodations

Alexander Hotel, Hwy.280, Brazell St., 912-557-6323.

Statesboro

Attractions/Museums

The Boro Bungalow, 204 Main St., 800-LOVE-301. Statesboro's Welcome Center is housed in a 19th-century building.

Georgia Southern University Museum, 912-681-5444. Displaying dinosaur skeletons and exhibits ranging from arts to folk life.

Herty Nature Trail, on Georgia Southern Campus, 912-681-5444. Herty Memorial Pine Forest named after Dr. Charles Herty.

Magnolia Garden, 912-681-5876. Also located at GSU campus, absorb the beauty of rare and native plants at a turn-of-the-century farm.

Historic Sites/Homes

Statesboro, one of Georgia's "Main Street Cities" dedicated to preserving downtown districts.

Main St., 20 South Main St., 912-764-7227. Stroll and enjoy

The Beaver House, 121 South Main St., on the National Register.

Savannah Avenue Historic District. Gardens and homes from the early 1900s have been preserved and are still functioning today as a community.

Statesboro Primitive Baptist Church, 4 South Zetterower Avenue. Tour the largest Primitive Baptist Church in the world.

Golf

Meadow Lakes Golf Club, off Hwy.67., 912-839-3191.

Southern Links, 912-839-3191, a popular 18-hole course.

Accommodations

Statesboro Inn, 106 South Main St., 912-489-8628. Built in 1905, this elegantly restored inn is listed on the National Register.

Alfred's Trellis Garden Inn, 107 South Main St., 912-489-8781. One mile from Georgia Southern University.

Dining

Statesboro Inn, 106 South Main St. The restaurant takes pride in a European chef who specializes in Italian and French dishes.

Beaver House Restaurant, 121 South Main St., 912-764-2821. Great Southern meals are served boardinghouse style.

Vandy's Barbecue, 22 West Vine St., 912-764-2444. Delicious barbecued pork, beef and chicken.

Vidalia and Claxton

(Vidalia, the onion capital of the world, is located between Macon and Savannah, off I-16 onto 297 S.)

Commentary

Unique soil and a mild climate produce Georgia's famous sweet-tasting onion, mild enough to eat as an apple. You can buy them by the sackful at roadside stands.

On Hwy.301 south of I-16 is the **Fruitcake Capital of the World**, Claxton. In 1910, Savino Tos, a young Italian immigrant, opened a little bakery, not knowing that one day a fruit-laden pastry from an old family recipe would become world-known. Now owned by the Parker family, Claxton becomes the sweetest smelling town between September and December as the bakery produces 90,000 pounds of cake a day. 912-739-2281.

Attractions/Museums

The Altama Museum of Art and History, 611 Jackson St., 912-537-1911. Admire a permanent collection of porcelain and traveling art.

Franklinia Playhouse Inc., 205 Main St., 912-537-9347. Local Broadway plays are presented here quarterly by a local group.

Ladson Genealogical Library, 119 Church St., 912-537-8186. Containing one of the largest genealogical research collections in the southeastern United States.

Ohoopee Regional Council for the Arts, 117 Southeast Main St.,912-537-8459. Continuous arts exhibits.

The Onion Run Trail. Enjoy the trail either walking or biking; maps are available at local hotels.

Savannah Luggage Outlet Shop, Hwy.297, 912-537-3016. One of the finest brands of luggage, known as Tumi Luggage, is available here.

Claxton Fruitcake Co., 203 West Main St., 912-739-3441. The world famous fruitcake capital of the world, producing more than six million pounds of delicious cakes.

Wilbanks Apiaries, Hwy.280 W., 912-739-4820. A major beekeeping facility.

Historic Sites/Homes

Leader-Rosansky House, 403 Church St., a folk Victorian style home.

Brazell House, at the corner of Jackson and 6th St., view a restored 1911 home, now an art gallery.

Evans County Courthouse, West Main St., 912-739-1141. Circa 1923; showing an early 20th-century neo-classical design.

Golf

Foxfire Golf Club, located Hwy.130 S. on Forest Lake Dr., 912-538-8670. A new challenging 18-hole course with driving range and clubhouse.

Parks

Canoochee River. Public fishing area located 10 miles east of Claxton, offering swimming, camping, fishing and boating.

Evans County Public Fishing Area, Hwy.280 E., 912-685-6424. Located eight miles east of Claxton. Three lakes, with boat and bank fishing, ramps, piers, picnic tables and restrooms.

Accommodations

The Robert Toombs Inn, 101 South State St., Lyons (five miles east of Vidalia), 912-526-4489. Turn-of-the-century charm is captured in this inn that offers twelve guest rooms and restaurant.

Dining

Mrs. Rogers Restaurant, Hwy.301 S. and Duval St., 912-739-2413. The best home country cooking.

Index

Accommodations 33
Acting Schools 92
Adairsville 265
Additional Reading 12
Aerobics 111
Airlines 25
Airport 25
Albany 313
Alma 323
American Adventures 59
Americus 301
Amicalola Falls 245
Amsterdam Avenue 187
Ancient Prices 185
Andersonville 302
Ansley Park 30
Antiques 189, 205
Apartment Leasing 32
APEX Museum 59
Appalachian Trail . . 265, 270, 271
Appling 293
Archery 111
Art
  Centers 80
  Galleries 80
  Schools 92
  Supplies 191
Ashford-Dunwoody 31
Athens 277
Atlanta-Fulton County Library . 60
Atlanta,
  Attack 116
  Ballet 60
  Botanical Garden 59
  Braves 116
  Celebrity Walk 60
  College of Art Gallery 60
  Convention and Visitors
    Bureau 9
  Diet 125
  Falcons 116
  Fire Ants 116
  Hawks 116
  History Center 60
  International Museum 60
  Knights 116
  Motor Speedway 60
  Opera 60
  Outreach 98
  Restaurants 129
  State Farmers Market . . 60, 207
  Symphony 60
  Thunder 116
Atlanta's Nifty Fifty
  Restaurants 128
Attractions 5, 59
Augusta 293
Automobile
  Insurance 24
  Repairs 23
Babyland General Hospital . . 253
Backpacking
  (see Hiking)
Badminton 111
Bainbridge 314
Baked Goods 197
Banking 26
Barnsley Gardens 267
Baseball 111
Basketball 111
Baxley 323
Beach and Water
  Parks . . 65, 238, 259, 295, 319
Bed & Breakfasts
  (see Accommodations 35
  and Sections XIII to XX)
Berry,
  College 273
  Farms 216, 217
Berry Picking Tips 217
Bicycling 111
Big Shanty Museum 60
Billiards 112
Bird Watching 112
Blackbeard Island 238

Blairsville 246
Blakely 314
Blue Ridge 265
Blue Willow Inn 289
Bookstores 83
Boxing 112
Bowling 112
Braselton 247
Brasstown Bald 247
Breakfast 161
Brookhaven 31
Brunswick 235
Buckhead 30, 187
Buena Vista 302
Buford Highway 187
Bulldogs 116
Bulloch Hall 60
Bungee Jumping 112
Cairo 315
Calhoun 266
Callanwolde Fine Arts Center . . 60
Callaway Gardens 303
Camping 112
Canoeing 112
Canton 266
Carnesville 248
Carrollton 267
Carter Presidential Center
  Library and Museum 60
Cartersville 267
Cavendar Castle Winery 255
Cave Springs 268
Caving 112
Cedartown 269
Centennial Olympic Park . 38, 61
Center for Puppetry Arts 61
Chateau Elan 247
Chatsworth 269
Chattahoochee
  National Forest 245
  Outdoor Center 61
  Nature Center 61
Chauncey 323
Chehaw Wild Animal Park . . 314
Cinemas 98
Clarksville 248
Classic South 293
Claxton 328
Clayton 251
Clayton State College 88
Cleveland 252
CNN Center and Studio Tour . . 61
Coastal Georgia and
  the Golden Isles 231
Coca-Cola Olympic City . . . 38
Coffeehouses 99
Colleges 87
Collegiate Sports 116
Colquitt 315
Columbus 305
Columbus Museum 305
Comedy Clubs 99
Comer 253
Commerce 253
Concert 80
Consulates 94
Conyers 279
Cooking Schools 92
Cordele 306
Cornelia 253
Corporate Atlanta 41
Counties 26
Covered Bridges 229
Covington 279
Crawford W. Long Museum . . 62
Crawfordville 295
Creekstone Winery 257
Cricket 112
Croquet 112
Crystal Lake Water Park 319
Cumberland Island 240
Cumming 254
Cyclorama 62
Dahlonega 254
Dalton 270

Dance Schools 93
Darien 238
Day Spa Salons 194
Dawson 315
Dawsonville 270
Decatur 31
DeKalb County Historical
  Society Museum 62
Dexter 323
Dillard 256
Discovery Zone 62
Dixieland Fun Park 62
Donalsonville 315
Douglas 323
Downtown Atlanta 29, 186
Driving Tips 23
Druid Hills 31
Dublin 324
Eastman 324
Eatonton 280
Elberton 256
Ellijay 271
Elvis Presley
  Collection Museum 302
Emergency Numbers 1
Emory University 31, 50
Employers 45
Entertainment
  (read on)
Equestrian 112
Ethnic Cultural Associations . . 95
Etowah Indian Mounds 267
Events 66
Fairmount 272
Fairs 66
Fargo 239
Federal Reserve Bank
  Monetary Museum 62
Fencing 112
Fernbank
  Forest 62
  Natural History Museum . . . 62
  Science Center 62
Festivals
  Metro Atlanta 66
  Golden Isles 241, 242
  Savannah 234
  (see also Sections XIII-XX)
Field Hockey 112
Fishing 112
Fitzgerald 324
Flea Markets 205
Flying 113
Folkston 239
Football 113
Forsyth 281
Fort Frederica 236
Fort Gaines 316
Fort Valley 281
Fox Theater 62
Franklin D. Roosevelt
  State Park 304
Frisbee 113
Frontier Village 316
Furniture 189, 199
Gainesville 256
Game and Fish Offices 119
Gertrude Herbert Institute
  of Art 294
Georgia Agrirama 319
Georgia
  Dome 63
  Mileages 20
  National Fairgrounds 307
  State Capitol Building 63
  Governor's Mansion 63
  State University 89
  Tech University 30
  World Congress Center 63
Georgia's,
  Favorite Sons and Daughters . . 4
  Historic Heartland 277
  Mountain Country 245
  Northeast Mountains 245
  Northwest Mountains 265

Seafood 125
State Parks 120
Top 100 Corporations 44
Glennville 325
Gliding 113
Golden Isles 231
Golf,
  Courses 167
  Tips 184
Grant Opera House 283
Grant Park 29
Greensboro 280
Griffin 307
Guide to Gardening 220
Gwinnett History Museum . . . 63
Gymnastics 113
Hair Salons 198
Hammonds House 63
Hang Gliding 113
Hartsfield Airport 25
Hartwell 257
Harvest Seasons 209
Headquarter Organizations . . . 41
Health Care
  General Hospitals 103
  Health Insurance 107
  HMO's 107
  Home Remedies 101
  Hospices 106
  Plastic Surgery 106
  Summer Weather Cautions . 2, 102
  Walk-In Clinics 103
Health Food 199
Helen 257
Herndon Home 63
Hiawassee 247
High Museum of Art 63
Highway System 22
Hiking 113
Historic
  Heartland 277
  Sites 123
Hofwyl-Broadfield Plantation . 235
Home Leasing 32
Homer 258
Horse and Carriage 26
Horseback Riding 113
Hot Air Ballooning 113
How To,
  Buy Auto Insurance 24
  Cook a Husband 127
  Obtain Driver's License 24
  Register Auto 24
Ice Sports 113
Indian Springs 281
In-line Skating 113
Interstate Highway System . . . 22
Inman Park 29
Innsbruck Resort 258
Jackson 282
Jacksonville 326
Jefferson 258
Jekyll Island 237
Jesup 326
Jetskiing 113
Jewelry 200
Jimmy Carter National
  Historic Site 309
Jogging 113
Johnny Mercer Exhibit 63
Juliette 282
Kayaking 114
Kennesaw State College 89
Kidstuff 66
Krystal River Water Park 295
Lacrosse 114
LaFayette 272
Lake Lanier Islands . . . 63, 259
Lakes,
  Burton 248
  Lanier 63, 259
  Oconee 280
  Rabun 248
Lavonia 261
Libraries 83

Limo's 26
Lincolnton 295
Lithia Springs 272
Little Five Points . . . 29, 30, 186
Little St. Simons 237
Little White House 310
Lookout Mountain 272
Louisville 296
Lunch 164
Macon 282
Madison 284
Magazines 11
Magnolia Midlands 323
Major Attractions Beyond
Metro Atlanta
Amicalola Falls 245
Appalachian Trail . 265,270, 271
Babyland General Hospital . 253
Barnsley Gardens 267
Beach and Water Park . . . 259
Berry College 273
Blue Willow Inn 289
Brasstown-Bald 246
Callaway Gardens 303
Cavendar Castle Winery . . 255
Cave Springs 268
Chehaw Wild Animal Park . 314
Columbus Museum 305
Creekstone Winery 257
Crystal Lake Water Park . . 319
Elvis Presley
Collection Museum 302
Etowah Indian Mounds . . . 267
Fort Frederica 236
Franklin D. Roosevelt
State Park 304
Frontier Village 316
Georgia Agrirama 319
Gertrude Herbert
Institute of Art 294
Grant Opera House 283
Hofwyl-Broadfield Plantation 235
Hollywood South
Souvenir Shop 279
Jimmy Carter National
Historic Site 309
Krystal River Water Park . . 295
Lake Lanier Islands . . . 63, 259
Little White House 310
Massee Lane Gardens
and Museum 281
Okefenokee,
National Wildlife Refuge . 239
Old Sautee Store 262
Old State Capitol Building . 287
Paradise Gardens 274
Pine Mountain Wild
Animal Park 304
Red Top Mountain State Park 267
Rock House 296
Rocky City Gardens 272
Sky Valley Ski Resort . . . 263
State Botanical Garden . . . 277
Sugarcreek Raceway
and Music Park 266
Summer Waves Park 238
Tallulah Falls 251
Tallulah Gorge State Park . 251
Thomas Drug Store 318
Thomasville Cultural Center 317
Whistle Stop Cafe 282
Windsor Hotel 301, 302
Mansfield 286
Malls, Shopping 185
Cumberland 186
Galleria 186
Lenox Square 186
Peachtree Center 185
Phipps Plaza 186
Rio 186
Underground Atlanta . . 65, 185
Maps
Buckhead 18
Classic South 292
Coastal Georgia 230
Downtown Atlanta 17
Georgia 224
Historic Heartland 276
Magnolia Midlands 322

MARTA 15
Metro Atlanta 16
Midtown Atlanta 30
Northeast Mountains 244
Northwest Mountains 264
Olympic Ring 36
Plantation Trace 312
Presidential Pathways 301
Shopping Areas 185, 186
Marietta 31
MARTA 24
Martial Arts 114
Martin Luther King, Jr.
Birth Home 64
Center for Non-Violent
Social Change 64
Margaret Mitchell House . . . 64
Massee Lane Gardens and
Museum 281
Mass Transportation
(see MARTA)
Men's,
Clothing 201
Shoes 201
Metro Atlanta,
Churches 6
Notables 5
McDonough 286
McRae 326
Media 11
Metro Counties 27
Michael C. Carlos Museum . . 64
Midtown Atlanta 30
Mileages 20
Milestone Dates in the
History of Atlanta 3
Milledgeville 286
Miniature Golf 114
Monroe 287
Monticello 287
Morganton 272
Motor Racing 114
Moultrie 316
Mountain City 261
Music at the Clubs 98
Acoustic 99
Blues/Jazz 98
Classical 99
Country 99
Piano Bars 99
Rock/Pop 99
Variety 99
National Fairgrounds 307
Native Terms 19
Nature Trails 117
Neighborhoods 29
Newnan 307
Newspapers 10, 202
Nifty Fifty Restaurants 128
Northeast Mountains 245
Northwqest Mountains 265
Oakland Cemetery 64
Ocilla 326
Oconee National Forest . . . 280
Okefenokee.
National Wildlife Refuge . 239
Old Sautee Store 262
Old State Capitol Building . . 287
Olympics,
Sports Venues 37
Paralympics 38
Centennial Park 38
Olympic City 38, 61
Transportation 39
Housing 39
Traffic 39
Palmetto 307
Paradise Gardens 274
Parks,
Centennial Olympic 38
Chastain 32
Grant 32
Inman 29
Piedmont 32
Stone Mountain 65
Peach Orchards 216
Perry 307
Piedmont Park 32
Pine Mountain 303

Pine Mountain
Wild Animal Park 304
Plains 308
Plantation Trace 313
Pool 112
Presidential Pathways 301
Private Secondary Schools . . 91
Pro Sports Teams 116
Quail Hunting 114
Rabun Gap 261
Racquetball 114
Rafting 114
Red Top Mountain State Park . 267
Reidsville 327
Rental Cars 26
Resorts,
Callaway Gardens Resort . 303
Lake Lanier Islands
Hilton Resort 260
Renaissance PineIsle Resort 260
Restaurants 128
Restaurants Take-out 166
Rhodes Hall 64
Ringgold 273
Roadside Farmer's Markets . 209
Road to Tara Museum 64
Robertstown 262
Rock City Gardens 272
Rock Climbing 114
Rock House 296
Roller Skating 114
Rome 273
Rossville 274
Roswell 31
Rowing 114
Royston 262
Rugby 114
Running 114
Rutledge 288
Sailing 114
Sandersville 296
Sapelo Island 238
Sautee 262
Savannah 231
SciTrek-Science and
Technology Museum 64
Scuba Diving 115
Sea Island 237
Shopping 185
Accessories 189
Antiques 189
Art Galleries 80
Art Supplies 191
Bakeries 197
Bookstores 83
Cameras 192
Compact Discs 193
Children's Stuff 192
Computers 194
Furriers 194
Garden Supplies 194
Gift/Specialties Shops . . . 195
Gourmet Foods 197
Health Food 199
Hair Salons 198
Home Furnishings 199
Jewelry 200
Malls 185
Men's Stuff 201
Office Supplies 202
Shoes 201, 205
Sporting Goods 202
Supermarkets 203
Toys 192
Women's Stuff 203
Six Flags Over Georgia 64
Skateboarding 115
Skeet and Trap Shooting . . . 115
Skydiving 115
Sky Valley Ski Resort 263
Snow Skiing 115
Soccer 115
Social Circle 288
Southeastern Railway Museum . 65
Sparta 296
Special Shopping Areas . . . 186
Amsterdam Avenue 187
Bennett Street 189
Buckhead 187

Buford Highway 187
Chattahochee Avenue 188
Five Points/Downtown . . . 186
Little Five Points . . . 30, 186
Stone Mountain 188
Virginia-Highlands . . 30, 187
Spectator Sports 116
Sports 111
St. Mary's 240
St. Simons Island 236
State Botanical Garden
of Georgia 277
State Historic Sites 123
State Parks 120
State Stuff 9
Stately Oaks 65
Statesboro 327
Statistics 9
Stockbridge 289
Stone Mountain 65
Sugarcreek Raceway and
Music Park 266
Summer Camps 93
Summerville 274
Summer Waves Park 238
Supermarkets 203
Sweet Auburn 29
Swimming Pools 115
(see also Beaches and Theme parks)
Table Tennis 115
Tallapoosa 274
Tallulah Falls 251
Tallulah Gorge State Park . . 251
Taxi's 26
Team Handball 115
Tennis 115
Theaters 94
Thomas Drugstore 318
Thomaston 309
Thomasville 317
Thomasville Cultural Center . 317
Thomson 296
Tifton 319
Toccoa 263
Trains and Buses 26
Transportation 6
Travel Schools 93
Traveling Historic Georgia . . 225
Trenton-Dade County 275
Twin City 297
Tybee Island 235
Underground Atlanta . . 65, 185
Union Point 297
Universities 87
Useful Numbers 1
Valdosta 319
Vidalia 328
Vienna 310
Villa Rica 275
Vinings 32
Virginia-Highlands . . . 30, 187
Visitors Centers 226, 227
Volleyball 115
Walking 115
Warm Springs 310
Warner Robins 289
Warrenton 297
Washington 297
Water Parks 65, 238, 259
Water Polo 116
Waterskiing 116
Watkinsville 289
Waycross 239
Waynesboro 297
Weather 2
Welcome South Visitors Center 65
What Others Say About Atlanta . 6
White Water Park 65
Whistle Stop Cafe 282
Wild Animal Parks 304, 314
Wildlife Trails 117
Windsor Hotel 301, 302
Wine Sampler 127
Woodruff Arts Center 65
World of Coca-Cola 65
Women's Clothing 203
Wren's Nest 65
Yellow River Game Ranch . . 66
ZooAtlanta 66

YOUR INPUT MEANS A LOT TO US

Your input is much appreciated and will help us stay on top of things. Please list new and/or favorite festivals/events, accommodations, attractions, restaurants, schools, sporting facitities, shops, salons, markets, small towns, neighborhoods, parks, trails, or just about anything else you think will be of general interest to residents and visitors. Forward these to Uxor Press Editors, 541 Tenth Ave., NW #161, Atlanta, GA 30318.

Festivals/ Events:_____

_____

Accommodations: _____

_____

Attractions: _____

_____

Restaurants: _____

_____

Schools: _____

_____

Sporting Facilities: _____

_____

Shops: _____

_____

Salons: _____

_____

Markets:_____

_____

Small Towns:_____

_____

Neighborhoods: _____

_____

Parks:_____

_____

Trails: _____

_____

Other:_____

_____